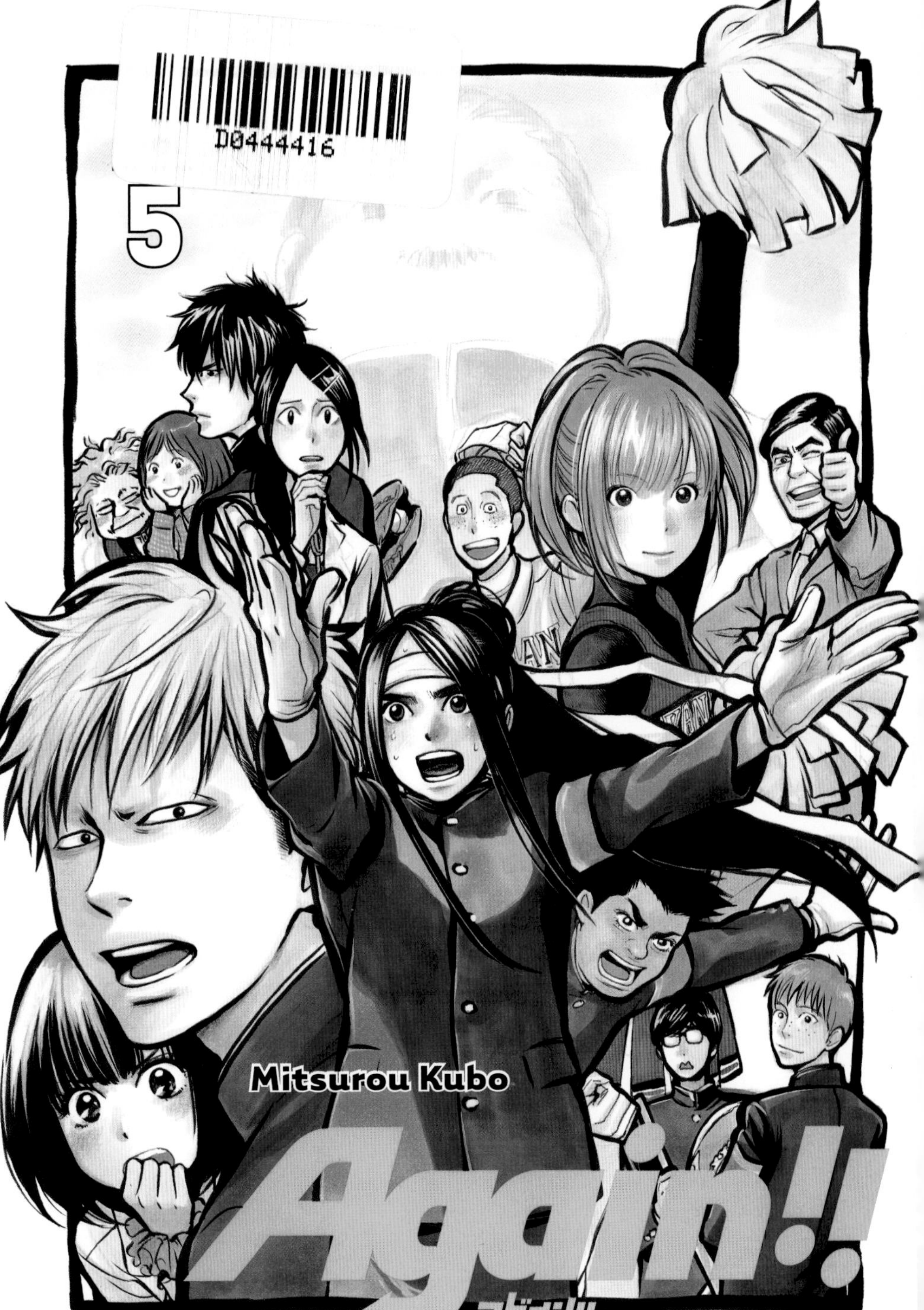
5
Mitsurou Kubo
Again!!
アゲイン!!

contents

# 42. MISUNDERSTANDING × MISUNDERSTANDING

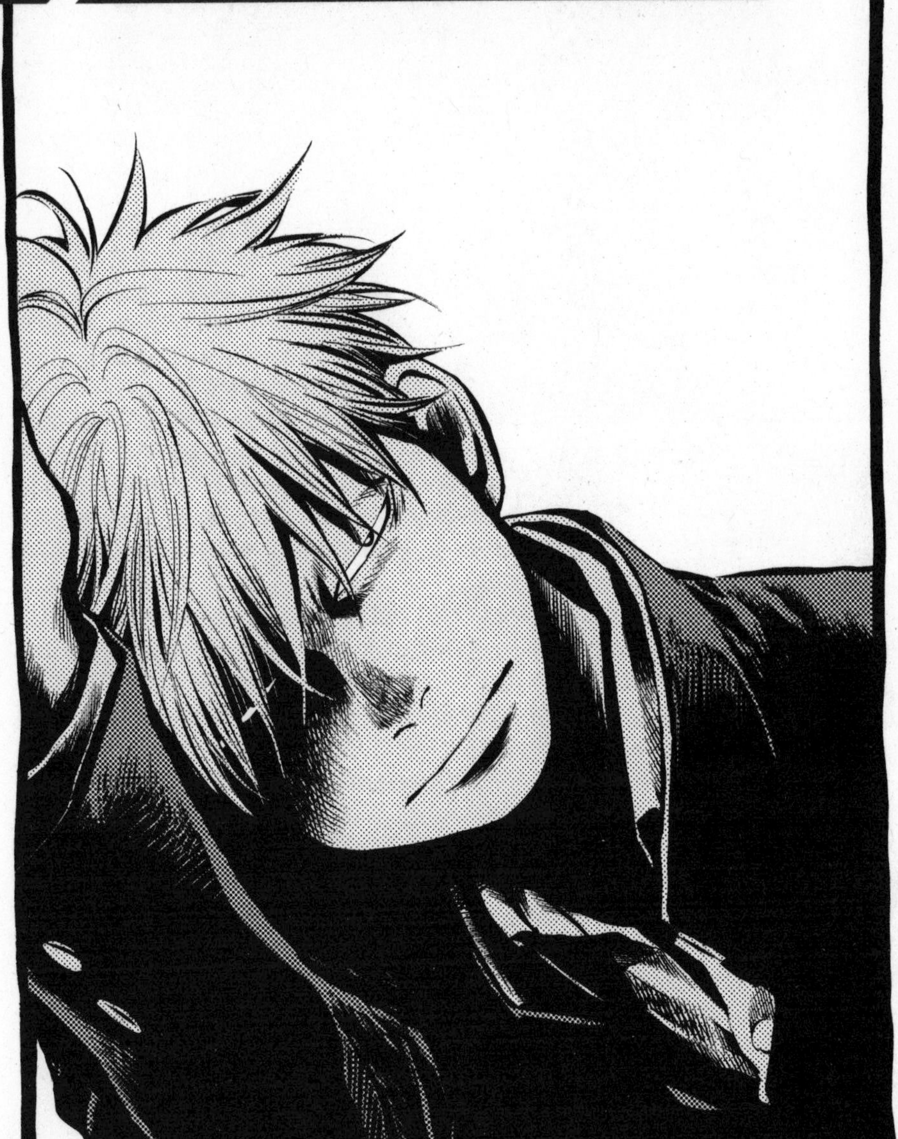

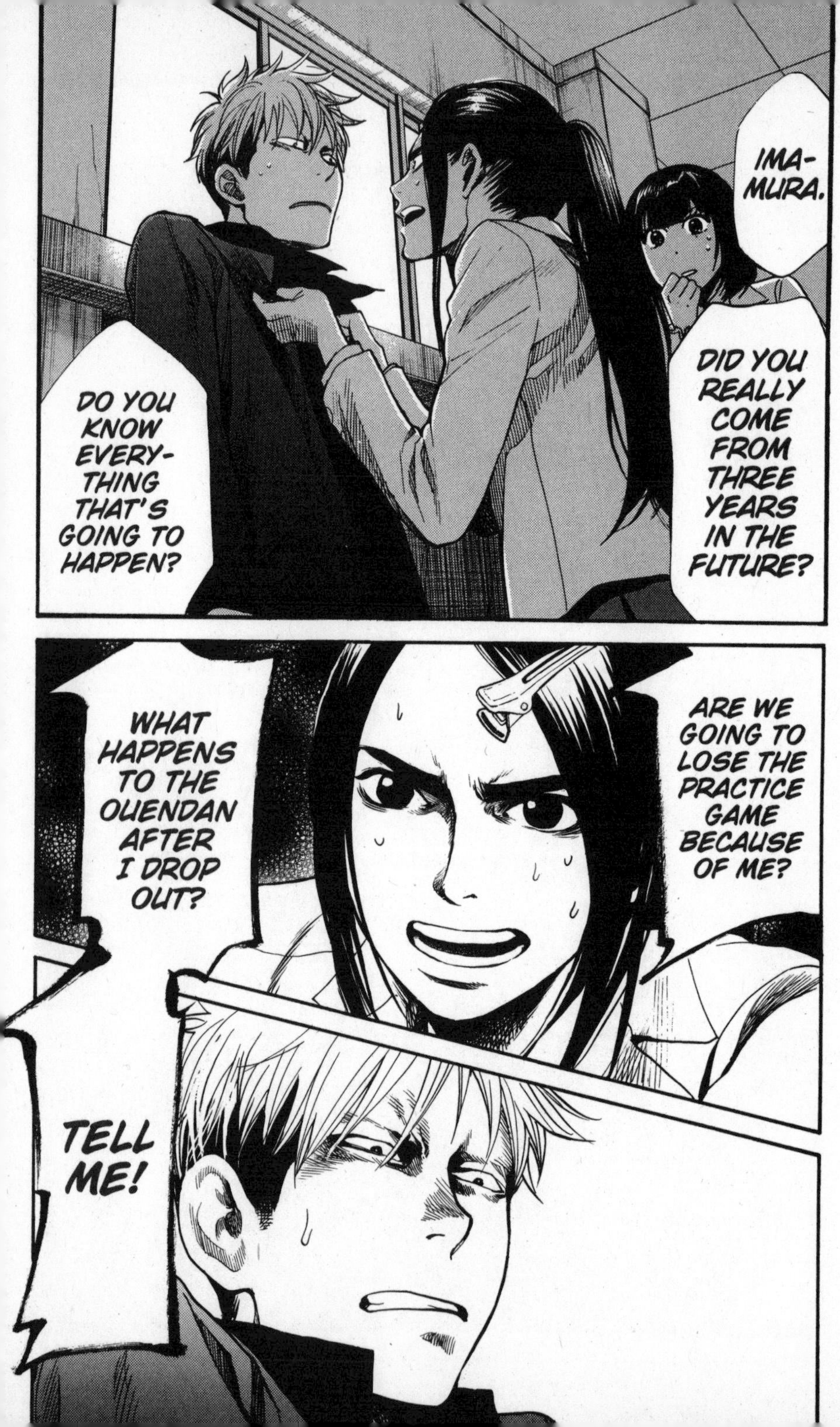
IMA-MURA.
DID YOU REALLY COME FROM THREE YEARS IN THE FUTURE?
DO YOU KNOW EVERYTHING THAT'S GOING TO HAPPEN?
ARE WE GOING TO LOSE THE PRACTICE GAME BECAUSE OF ME?
WHAT HAPPENS TO THE OUENDAN AFTER I DROP OUT?
TELL ME!

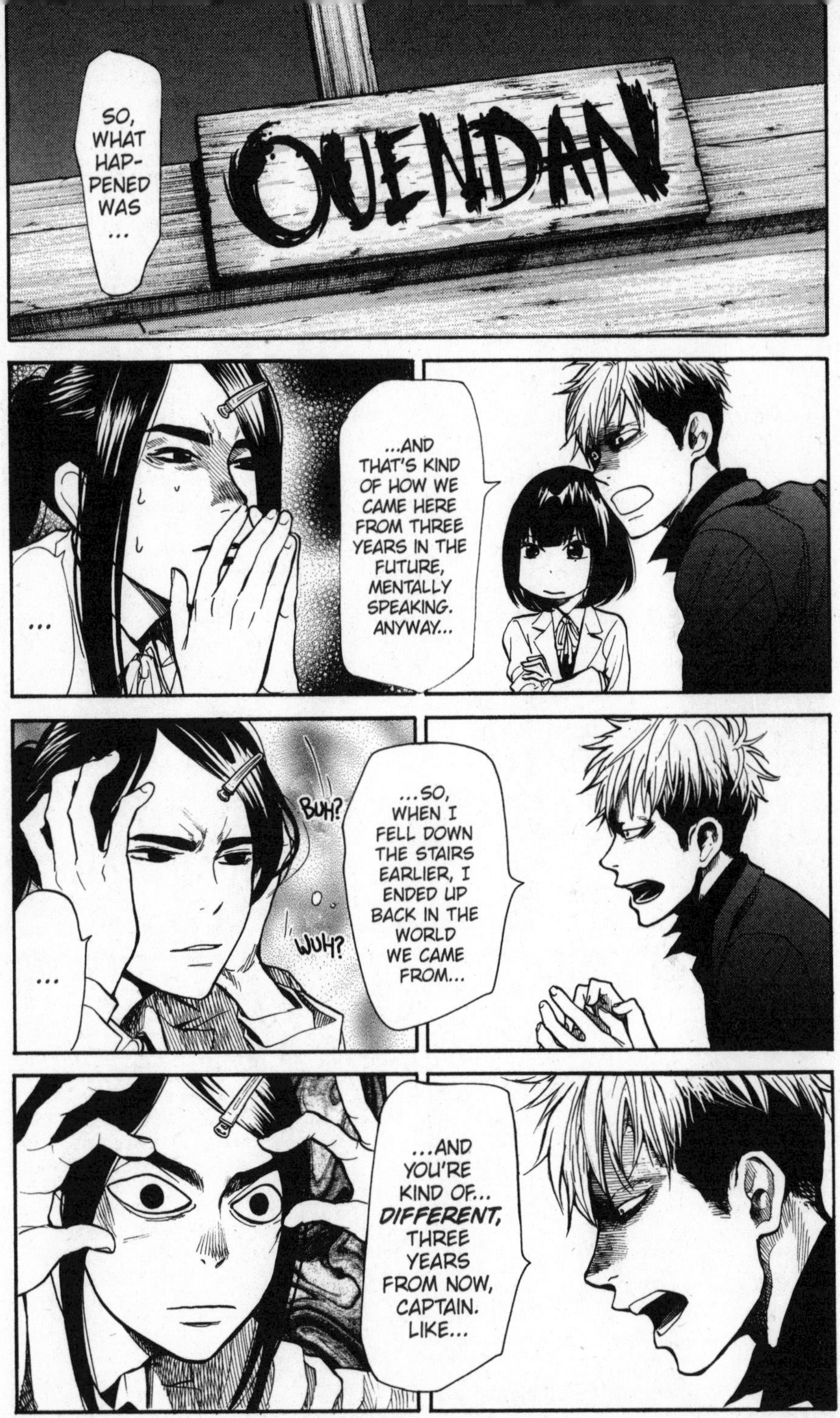
OUENDAN
SO, WHAT HAPPENED WAS ...
...AND THAT'S KIND OF HOW WE CAME HERE FROM THREE YEARS IN THE FUTURE, MENTALLY SPEAKING. ANYWAY...
...
...SO, WHEN I FELL DOWN THE STAIRS EARLIER, I ENDED UP BACK IN THE WORLD WE CAME FROM...
BUH?
WUH?
...
...AND YOU'RE KIND OF... ***DIFFERENT,*** THREE YEARS FROM NOW, CAPTAIN. LIKE...

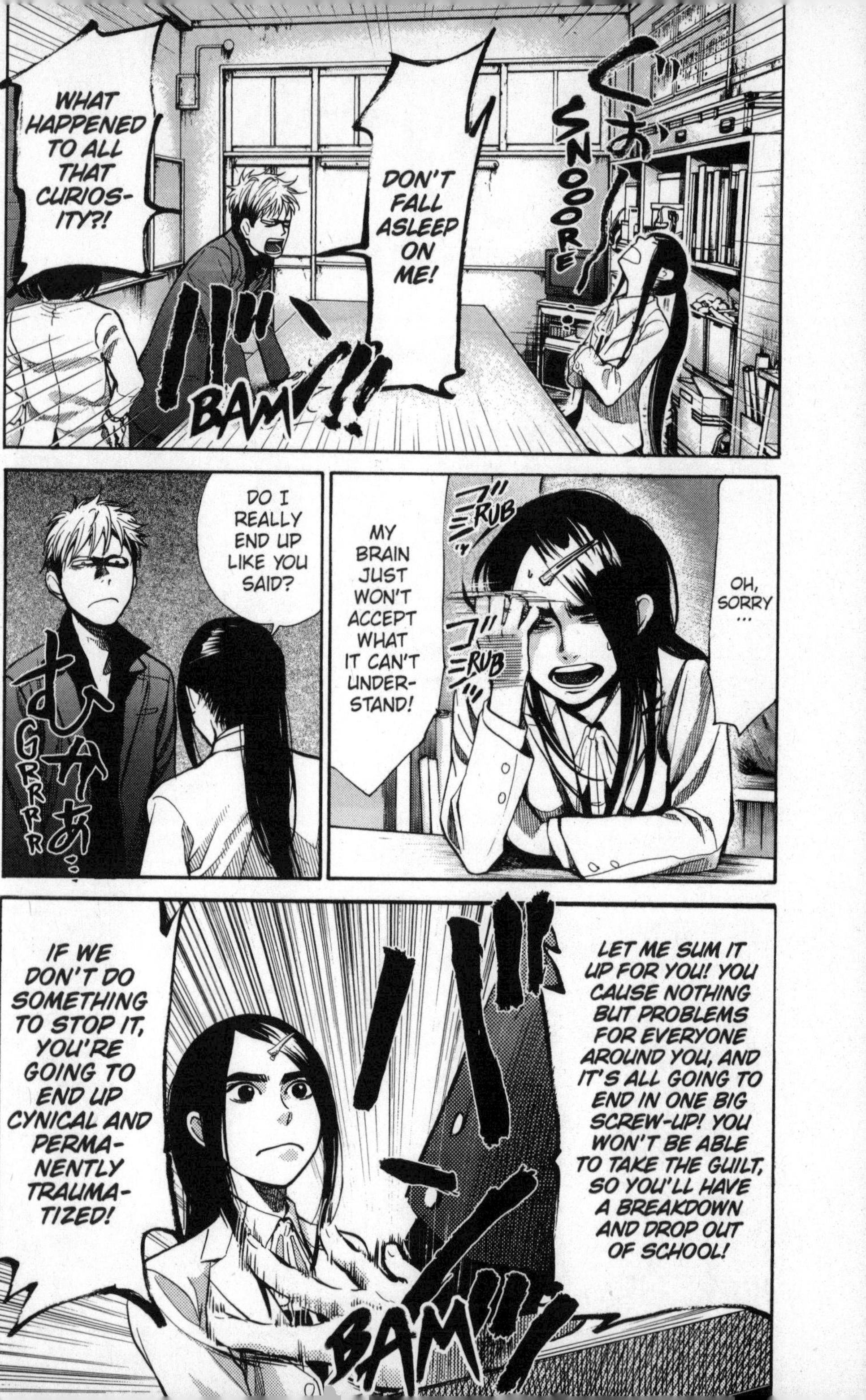
SNOOORE
DON'T FALL ASLEEP ON ME!
WHAT HAPPENED TO ALL THAT CURIOS-ITY?!
BAM!!
OH, SORRY...
RUB
RUB
MY BRAIN JUST WON'T ACCEPT WHAT IT CAN'T UNDER-STAND!
DO I REALLY END UP LIKE YOU SAID?
GRRRR
LET ME SUM IT UP FOR YOU! YOU CAUSE NOTHING BUT PROBLEMS FOR EVERYONE AROUND YOU, AND IT'S ALL GOING TO END IN ONE BIG SCREW-UP! YOU WON'T BE ABLE TO TAKE THE GUILT, SO YOU'LL HAVE A BREAKDOWN AND DROP OUT OF SCHOOL!
IF WE DON'T DO SOMETHING TO STOP IT, YOU'RE GOING TO END UP CYNICAL AND PERMA-NENTLY TRAUMA-TIZED!
BAM!!

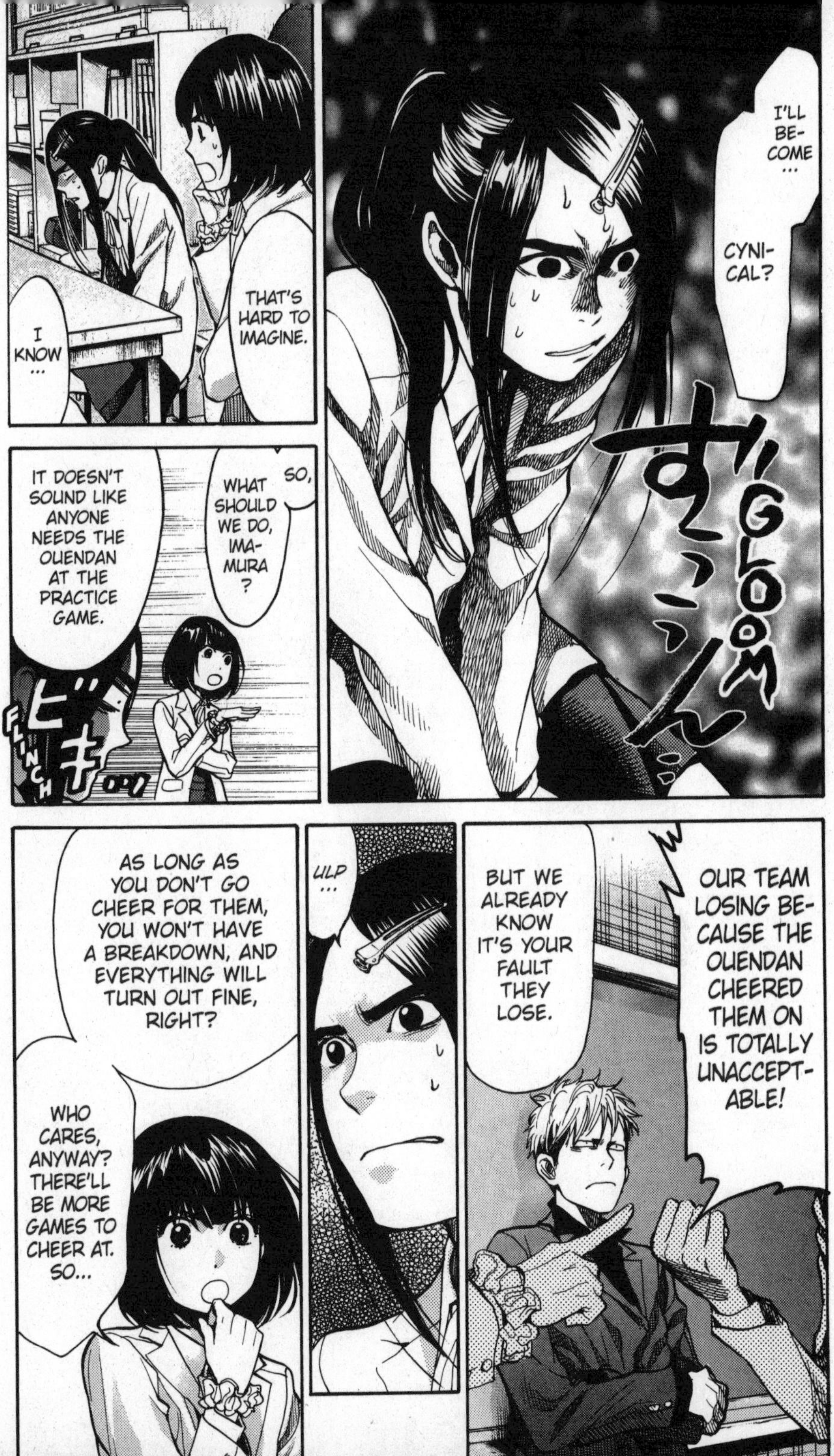
I'LL BE-COME ...
CYNI-CAL?
GLOOM
THAT'S HARD TO IMAGINE.
I KNOW ...
SO, WHAT SHOULD WE DO, IMA-MURA ?
IT DOESN'T SOUND LIKE ANYONE NEEDS THE OUENDAN AT THE PRACTICE GAME.
FLINCH
OUR TEAM LOSING BE-CAUSE THE OUENDAN CHEERED THEM ON IS TOTALLY UNACCEPT-ABLE!
BUT WE ALREADY KNOW IT'S YOUR FAULT THEY LOSE.
ULP ...
AS LONG AS YOU DON'T GO CHEER FOR THEM, YOU WON'T HAVE A BREAKDOWN, AND EVERYTHING WILL TURN OUT FINE, RIGHT?
WHO CARES, ANYWAY? THERE'LL BE MORE GAMES TO CHEER AT. SO...

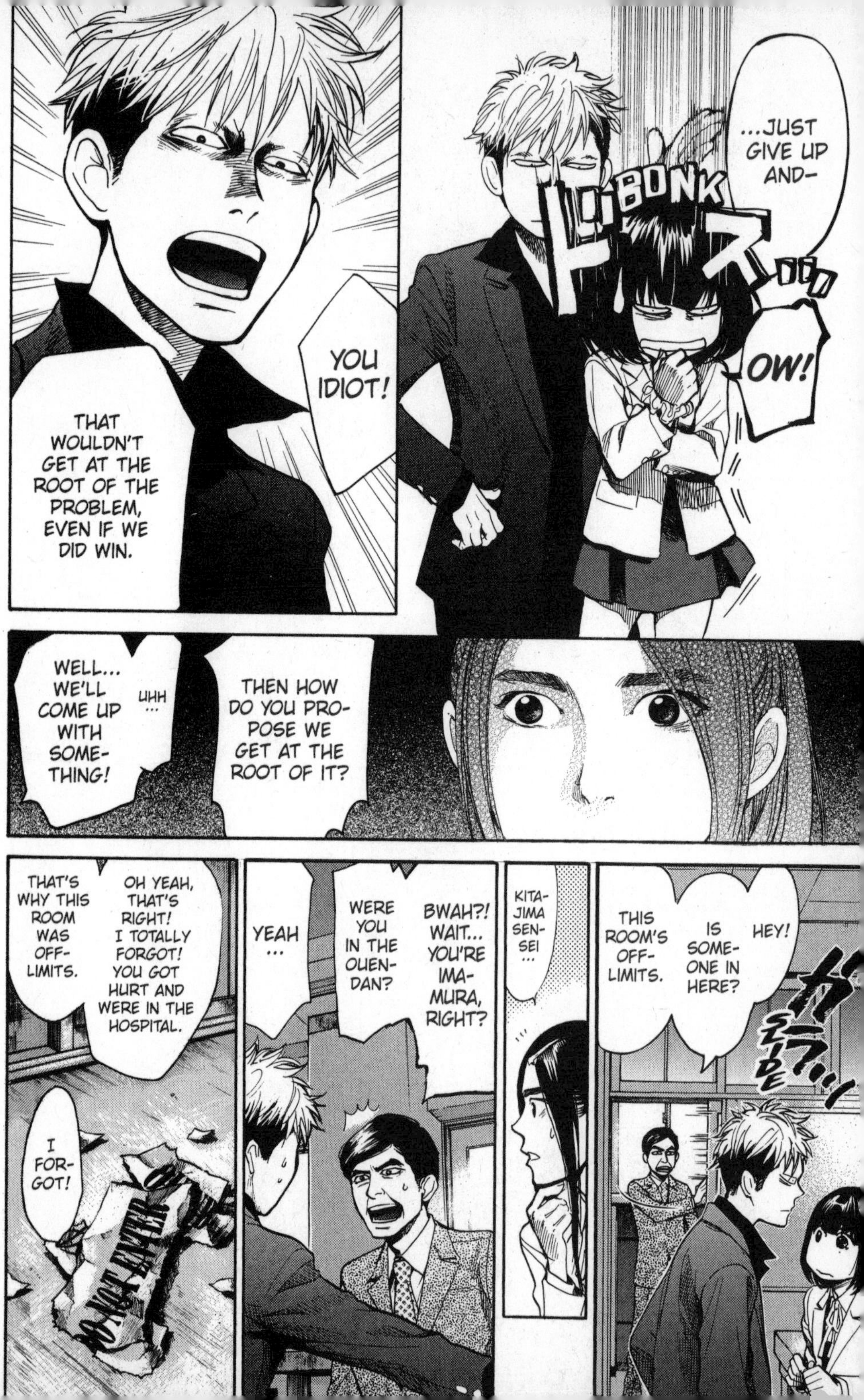
...JUST GIVE UP AND-
BONK
OW!
YOU IDIOT!
THAT WOULDN'T GET AT THE ROOT OF THE PROBLEM, EVEN IF WE DID WIN.
THEN HOW DO YOU PROPOSE WE GET AT THE ROOT OF IT?
UHH...
WELL... WE'LL COME UP WITH SOMETHING!
HEY!
IS SOMEONE IN HERE?
THIS ROOM'S OFF-LIMITS.
SLIDE
KITAJIMA SENSEI...
BWAH?! WAIT... YOU'RE IMAMURA, RIGHT?
WERE YOU IN THE OUENDAN?
YEAH...
OH YEAH, THAT'S RIGHT! I TOTALLY FORGOT! YOU GOT HURT AND WERE IN THE HOSPITAL.
THAT'S WHY THIS ROOM WAS OFF-LIMITS.
I FORGOT!
DO NOT ENTER

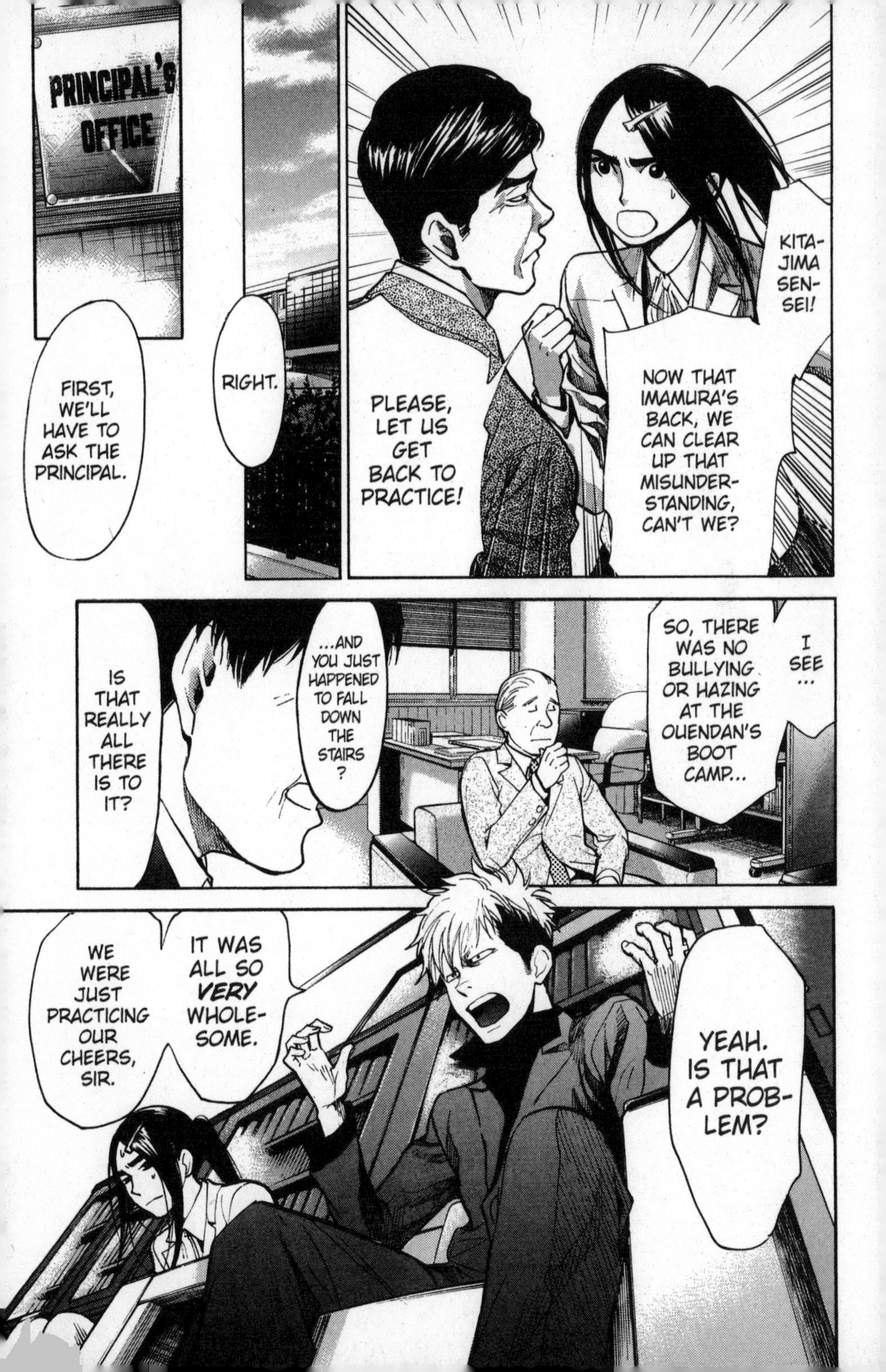
KITA-JIMA SEN-SEI!
NOW THAT IMAMURA'S BACK, WE CAN CLEAR UP THAT MISUNDER-STANDING, CAN'T WE?
PLEASE, LET US GET BACK TO PRACTICE!
RIGHT.
PRINCIPAL'S OFFICE
FIRST, WE'LL HAVE TO ASK THE PRINCIPAL.
I SEE...
SO, THERE WAS NO BULLYING OR HAZING AT THE OUENDAN'S BOOT CAMP...
...AND YOU JUST HAPPENED TO FALL DOWN THE STAIRS?
IS THAT REALLY ALL THERE IS TO IT?
YEAH. IS THAT A PROB-LEM?
IT WAS ALL SO *VERY* WHOLE-SOME.
WE WERE JUST PRACTICING OUR CHEERS, SIR.

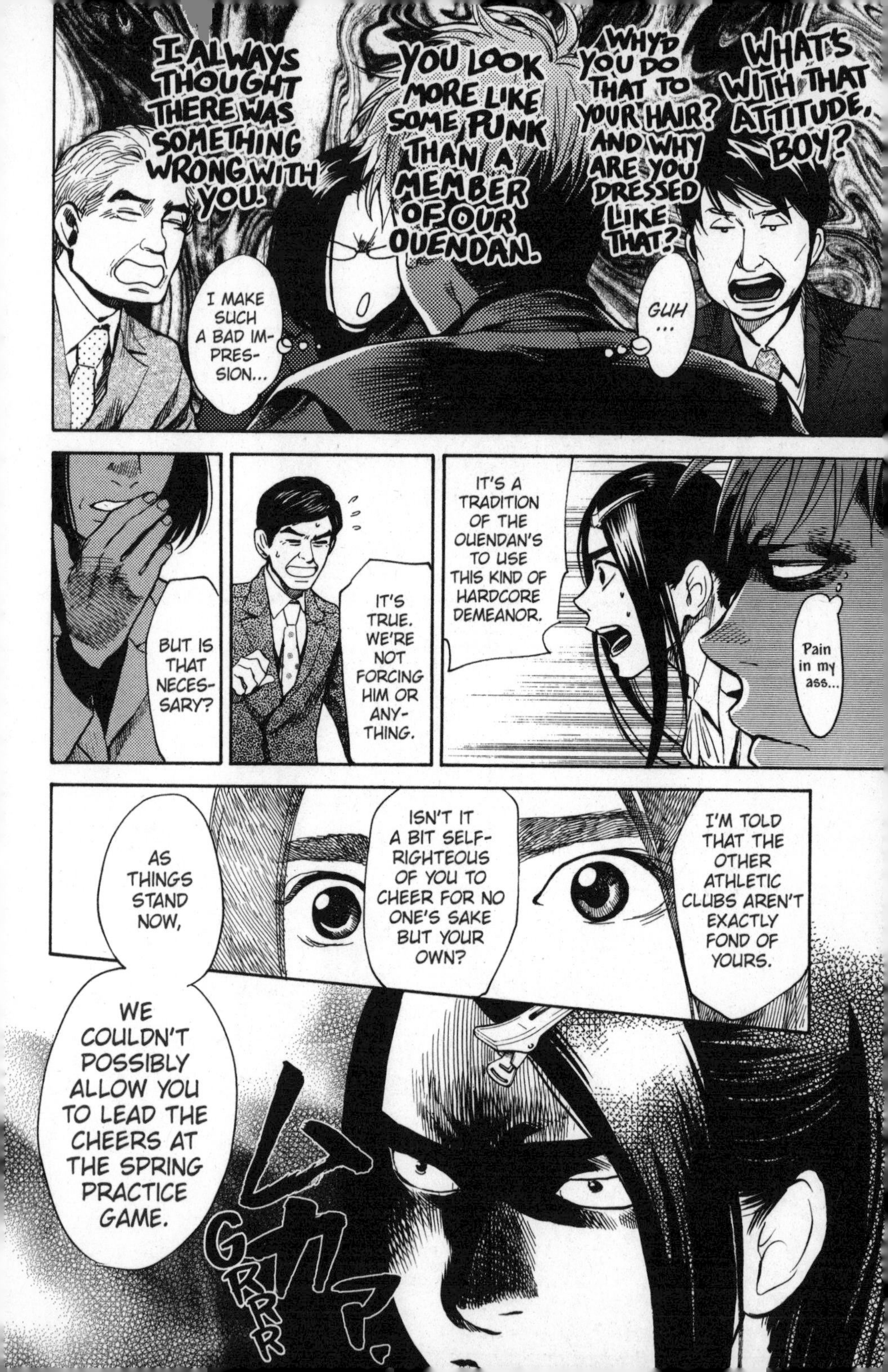
WHAT'S WITH THAT ATTITUDE, BOY?
WHY'D YOU DO THAT TO YOUR HAIR? AND WHY ARE YOU DRESSED LIKE THAT?
GUH...
YOU LOOK MORE LIKE SOME PUNK THAN A MEMBER OF OUR OUENDAN.
I MAKE SUCH A BAD IMPRESSION...
I ALWAYS THOUGHT THERE WAS SOMETHING WRONG WITH YOU.
Pain in my ass...
IT'S A TRADITION OF THE OUENDAN'S TO USE THIS KIND OF HARDCORE DEMEANOR.
IT'S TRUE. WE'RE NOT FORCING HIM OR ANYTHING.
BUT IS THAT NECESSARY?
I'M TOLD THAT THE OTHER ATHLETIC CLUBS AREN'T EXACTLY FOND OF YOURS.
ISN'T IT A BIT SELF-RIGHTEOUS OF YOU TO CHEER FOR NO ONE'S SAKE BUT YOUR OWN?
AS THINGS STAND NOW,
WE COULDN'T POSSIBLY ALLOW YOU TO LEAD THE CHEERS AT THE SPRING PRACTICE GAME.
GRRR

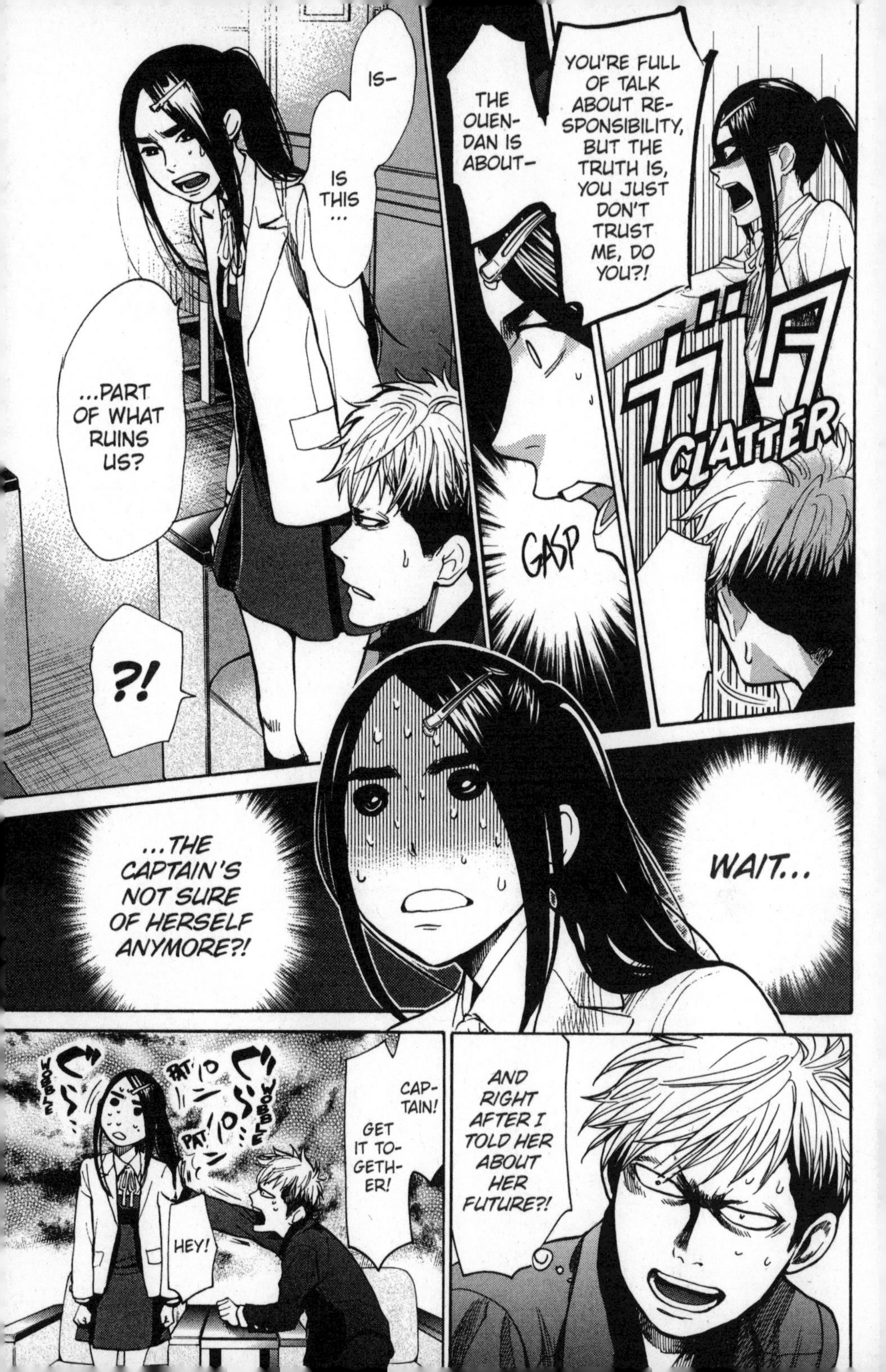
YOU'RE FULL OF TALK ABOUT RESPONSIBILITY, BUT THE TRUTH IS, YOU JUST DON'T TRUST ME, DO YOU?!
ガタ
CLATTER
THE OUENDAN IS ABOUT-
GASP
IS-
IS THIS...
...PART OF WHAT RUINS US?
?!
WAIT...
...THE CAPTAIN'S NOT SURE OF HERSELF ANYMORE?!
AND RIGHT AFTER I TOLD HER ABOUT HER FUTURE?!
CAPTAIN! GET IT TOGETHER!
WOBBLE
PAT
PAT
WOBBLE
HEY!

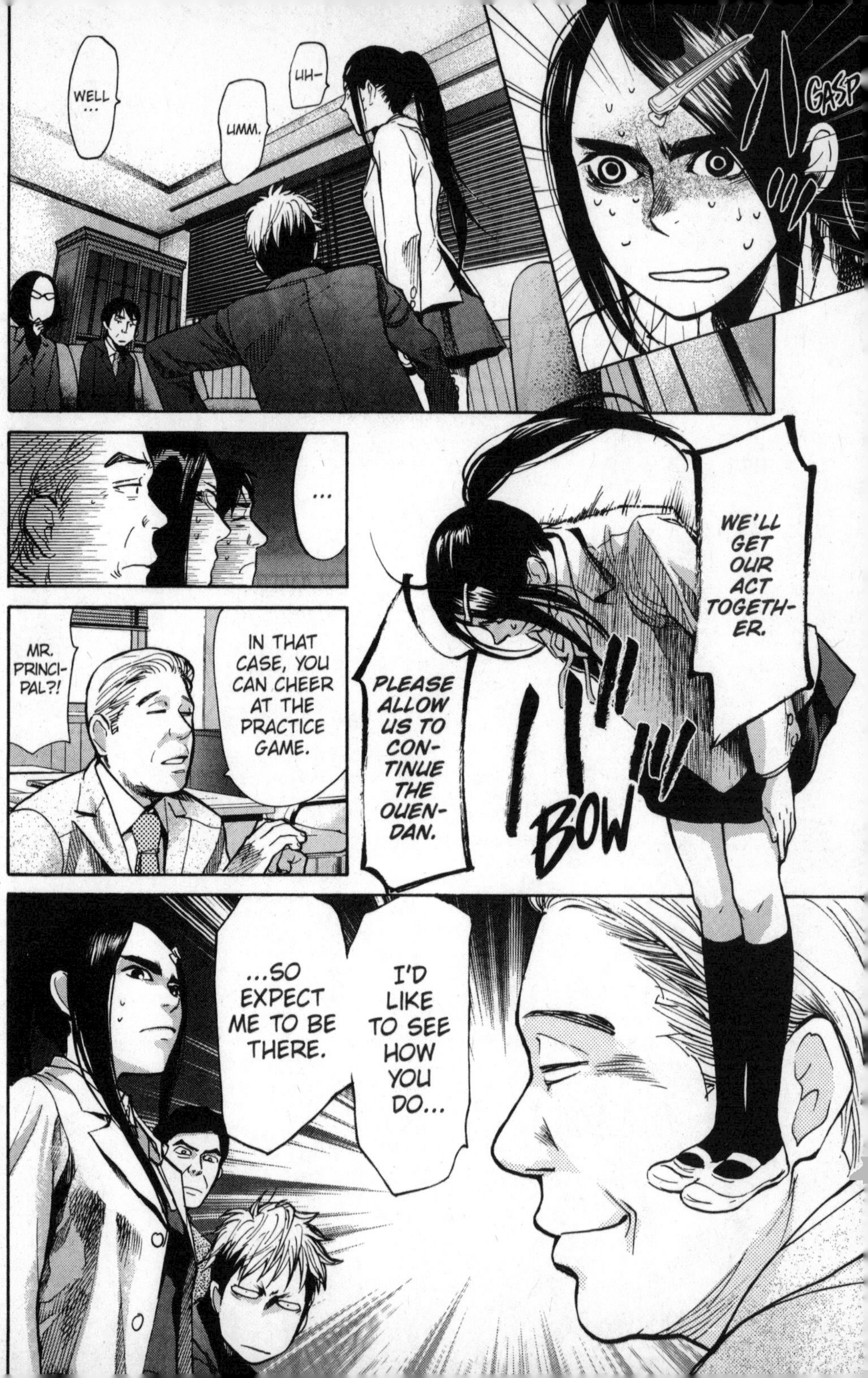
GASP
UH-
UMM.
WELL...
WE'LL GET OUR ACT TOGETHER.
PLEASE ALLOW US TO CONTINUE THE OUENDAN.
BOW
...
IN THAT CASE, YOU CAN CHEER AT THE PRACTICE GAME.
MR. PRINCIPAL?!
I'D LIKE TO SEE HOW YOU DO...
...SO EXPECT ME TO BE THERE.

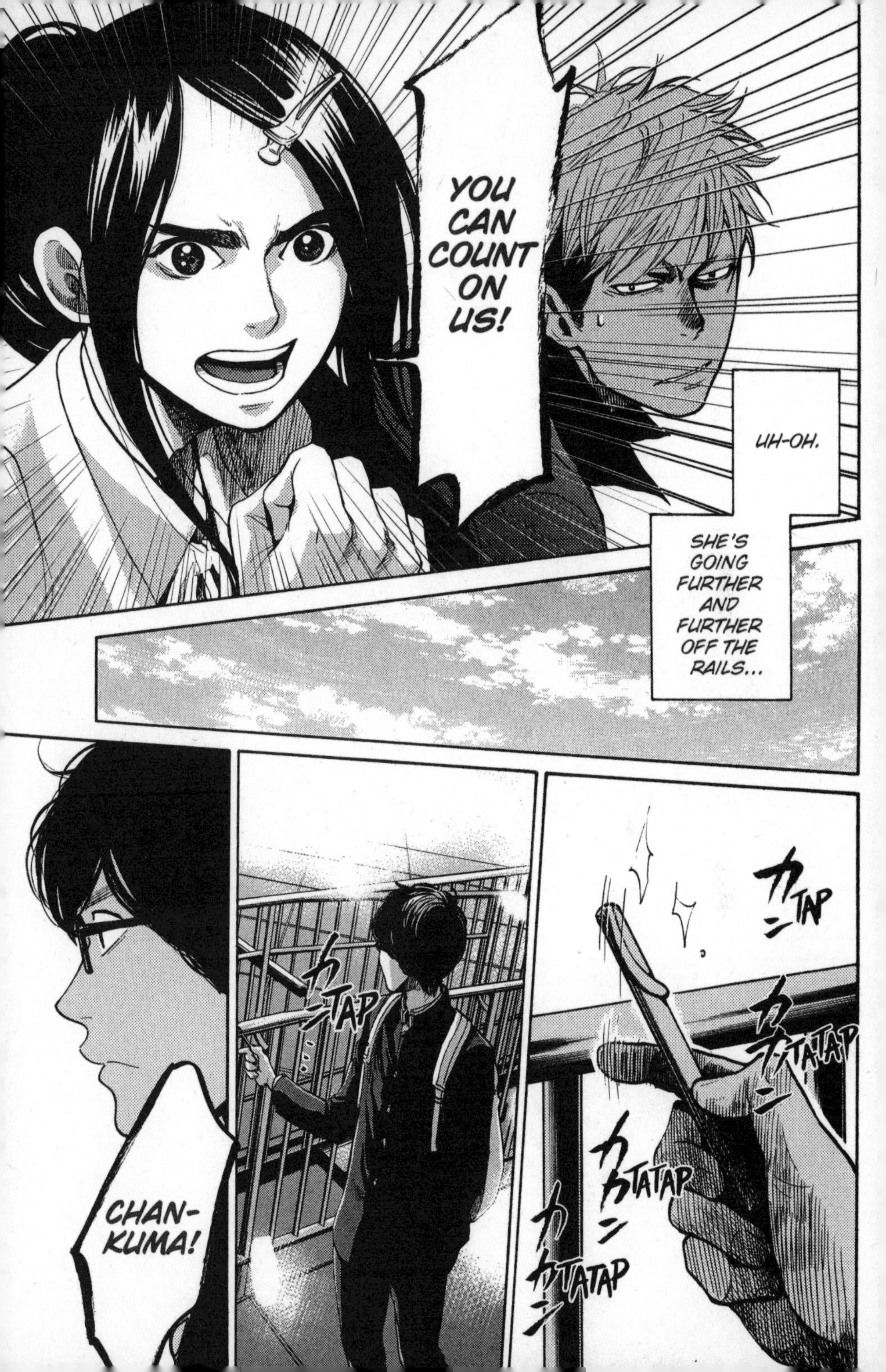
YOU CAN COUNT ON US!
UH-OH.
SHE'S GOING FURTHER AND FURTHER OFF THE RAILS...
カン TAP
カカーン TATAP
カカン TATAP
カカン TATAP
カン TAP
CHAN-KUMA!

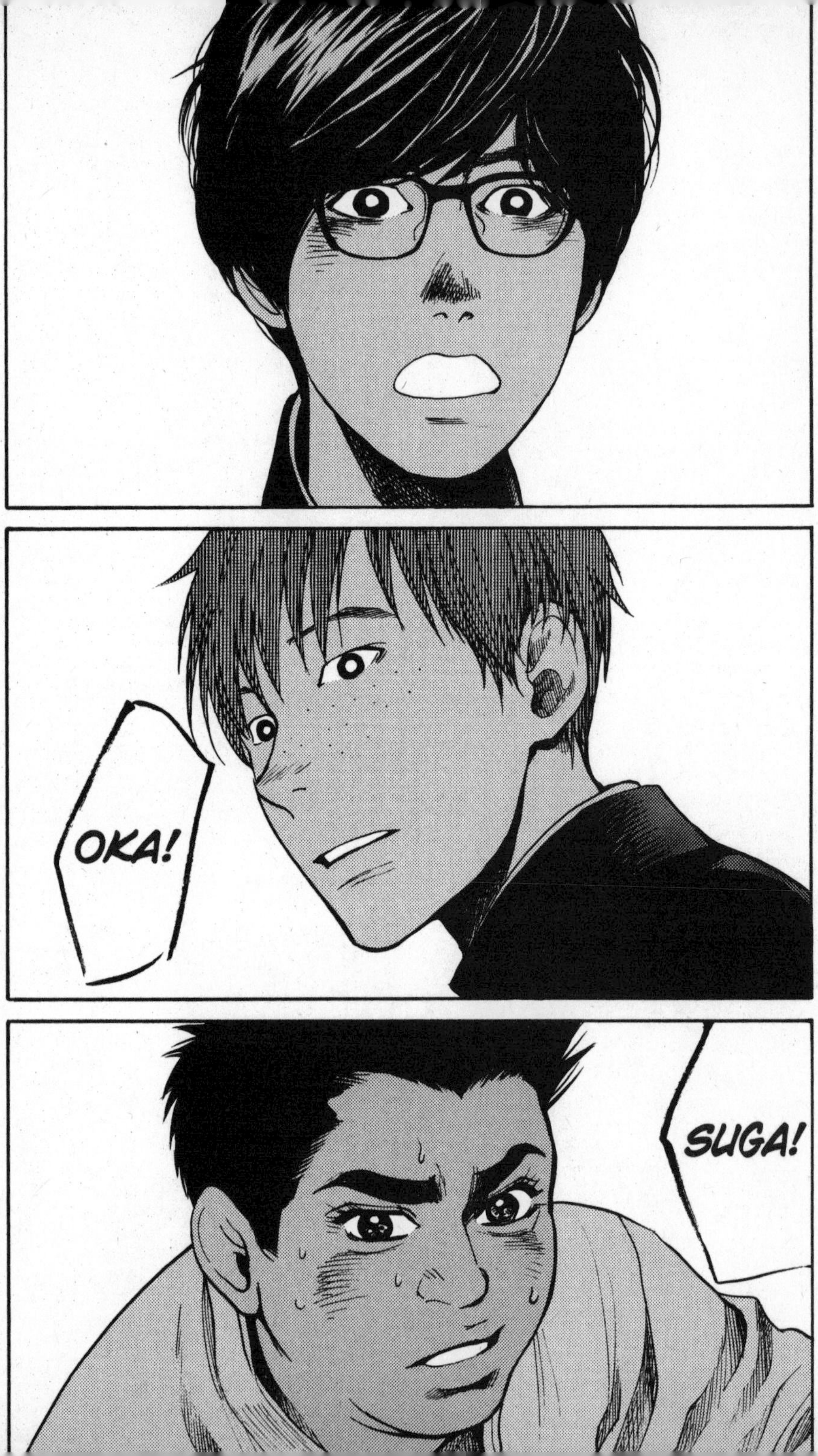
OKA!
SUGA!

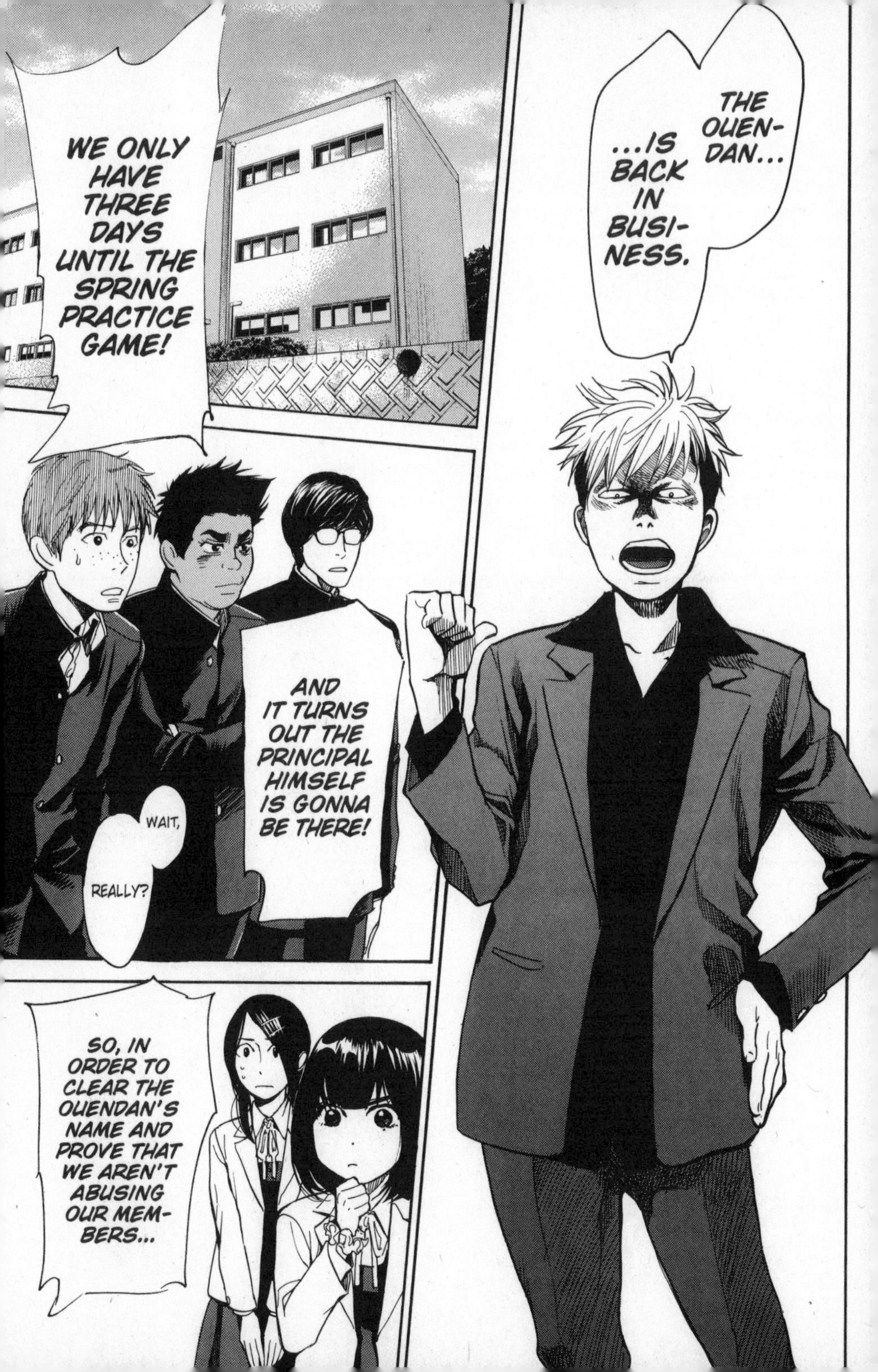
WE ONLY HAVE THREE DAYS UNTIL THE SPRING PRACTICE GAME!
AND IT TURNS OUT THE PRINCIPAL HIMSELF IS GONNA BE THERE!
WAIT, REALLY?
SO, IN ORDER TO CLEAR THE OUENDAN'S NAME AND PROVE THAT WE AREN'T ABUSING OUR MEM-BERS...
THE OUEN-DAN...
...IS BACK IN BUSI-NESS.

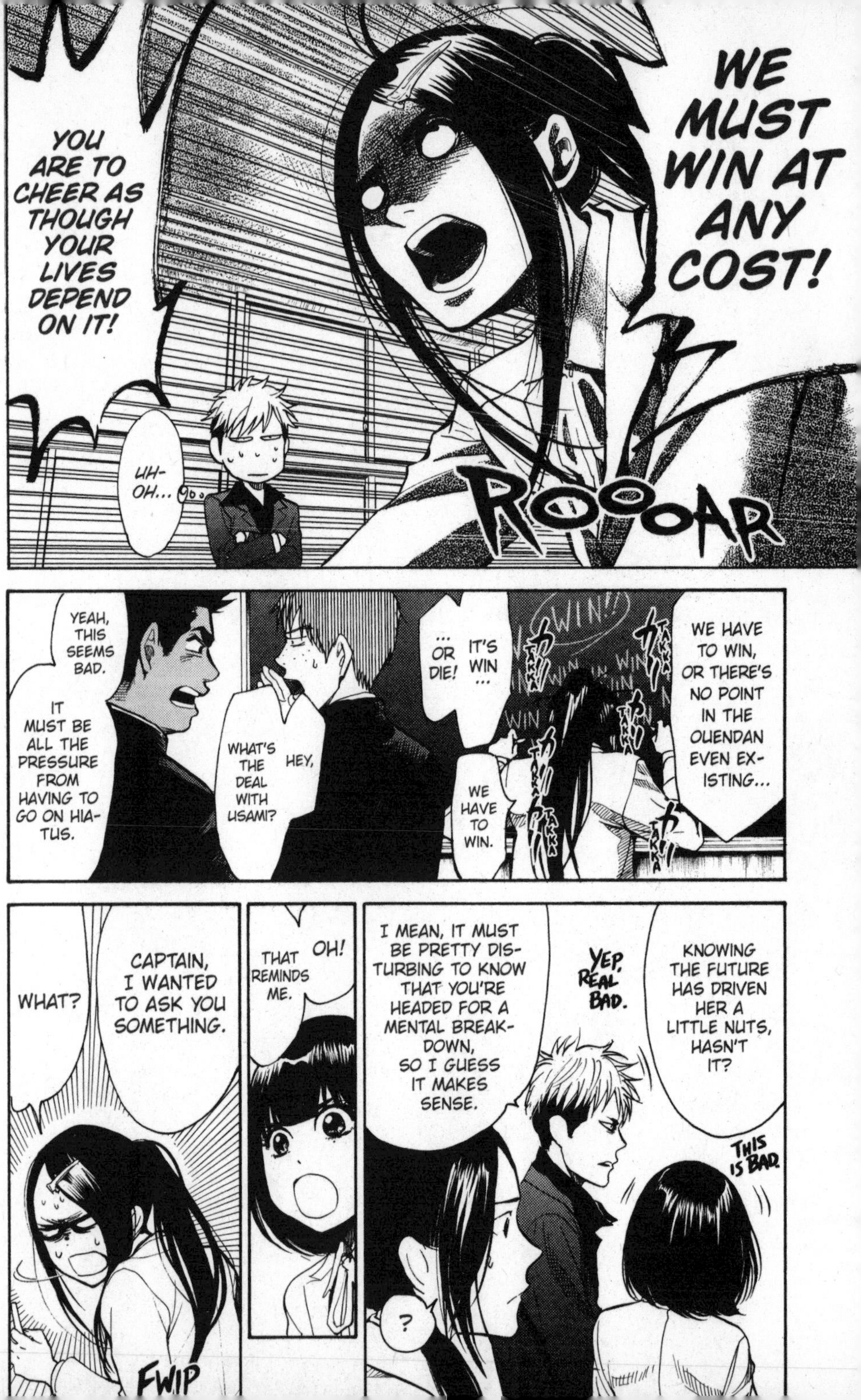
WE MUST WIN AT ANY COST!
YOU ARE TO CHEER AS THOUGH YOUR LIVES DEPEND ON IT!
ROOOAR
UH-OH...
WE HAVE TO WIN, OR THERE'S NO POINT IN THE OUENDAN EVEN EXISTING...
WIN!!
TAKA
WE HAVE TO WIN.
IT'S WIN ... OR DIE!
HEY, WHAT'S THE DEAL WITH USAMI?
YEAH, THIS SEEMS BAD.
IT MUST BE ALL THE PRESSURE FROM HAVING TO GO ON HIATUS.
KNOWING THE FUTURE HAS DRIVEN HER A LITTLE NUTS, HASN'T IT?
THIS IS BAD.
YEP, REAL BAD.
I MEAN, IT MUST BE PRETTY DISTURBING TO KNOW THAT YOU'RE HEADED FOR A MENTAL BREAKDOWN, SO I GUESS IT MAKES SENSE.
?
OH! THAT REMINDS ME.
CAPTAIN, I WANTED TO ASK YOU SOMETHING.
WHAT?
FWIP

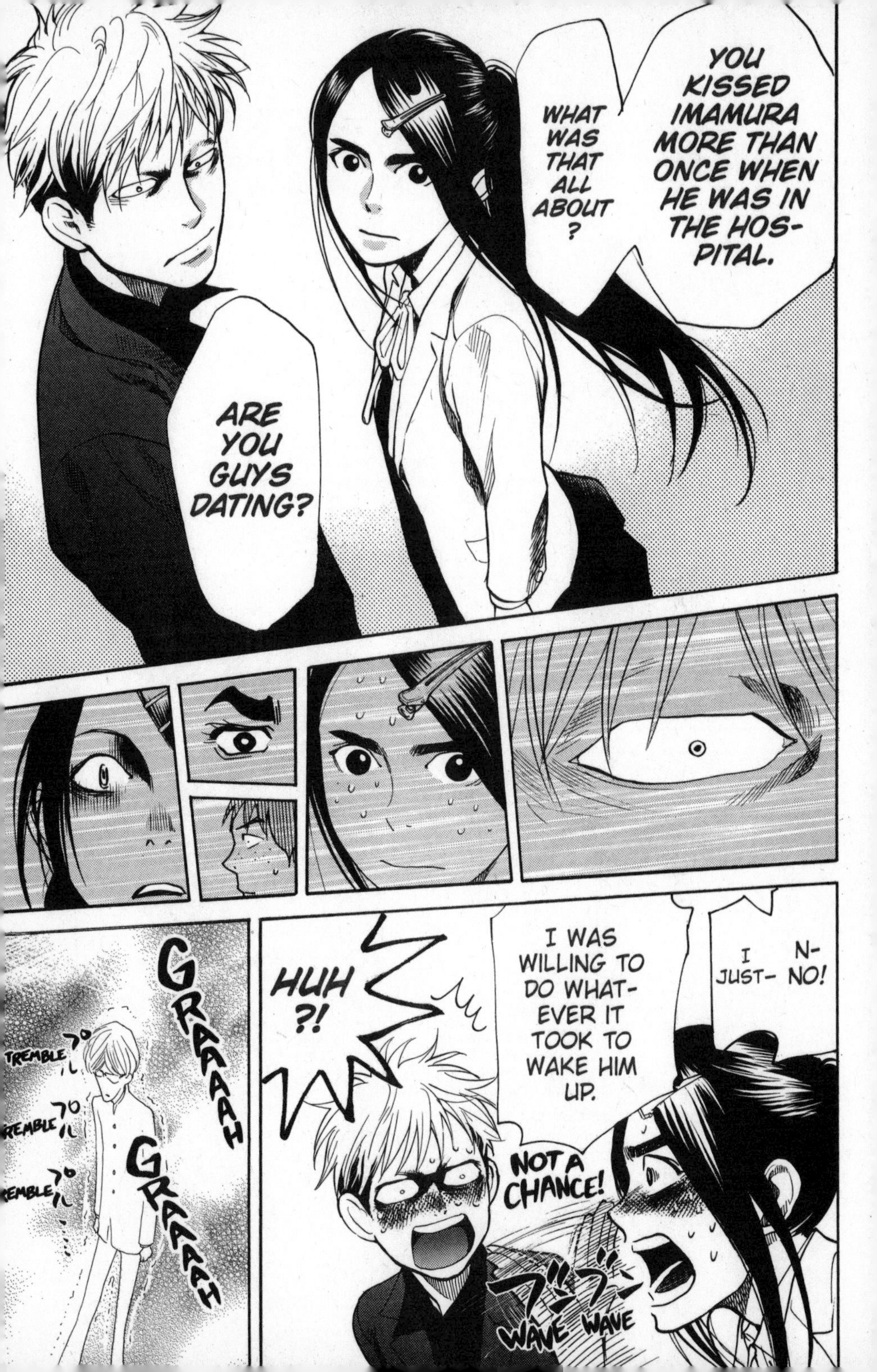
YOU KISSED IMAMURA MORE THAN ONCE WHEN HE WAS IN THE HOS-PITAL.
WHAT WAS THAT ALL ABOUT?
ARE YOU GUYS DATING?
N-NO!
I JUST-
I WAS WILLING TO DO WHAT-EVER IT TOOK TO WAKE HIM UP.
HUH?!
NOT A CHANCE!
WAVE WAVE
GRAAAAAH
GRAAAAH
TREMBLE
TREMBLE
TREMBLE

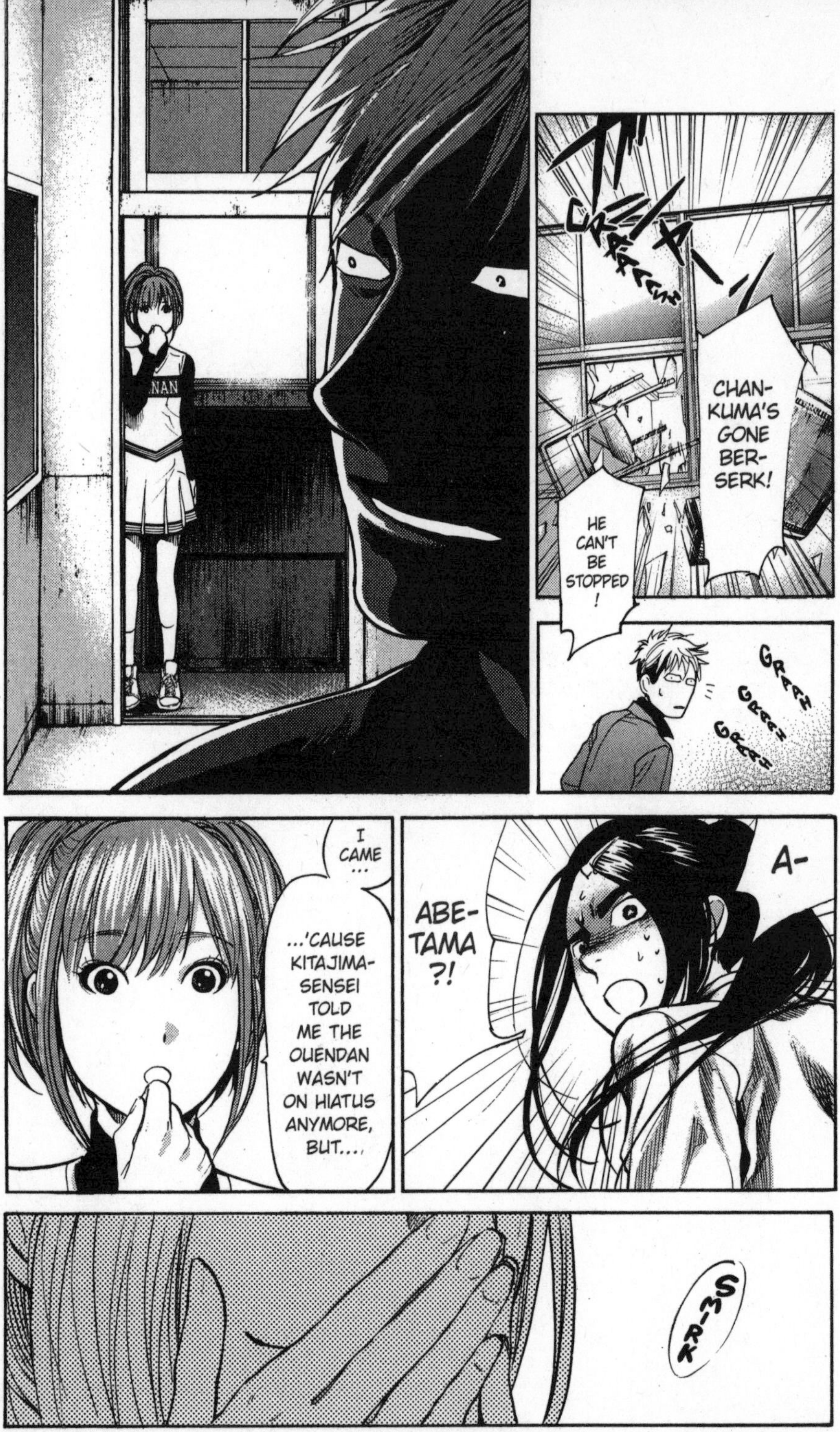
CHAN-KUMA'S GONE BER-SERK!
HE CAN'T BE STOPPED!
GRAAH
GRAAH
GRAAH
A-
ABE-TAMA?!
I CAME...
...'CAUSE KITAJIMA-SENSEI TOLD ME THE OUENDAN WASN'T ON HIATUS ANYMORE, BUT....
SMIRK

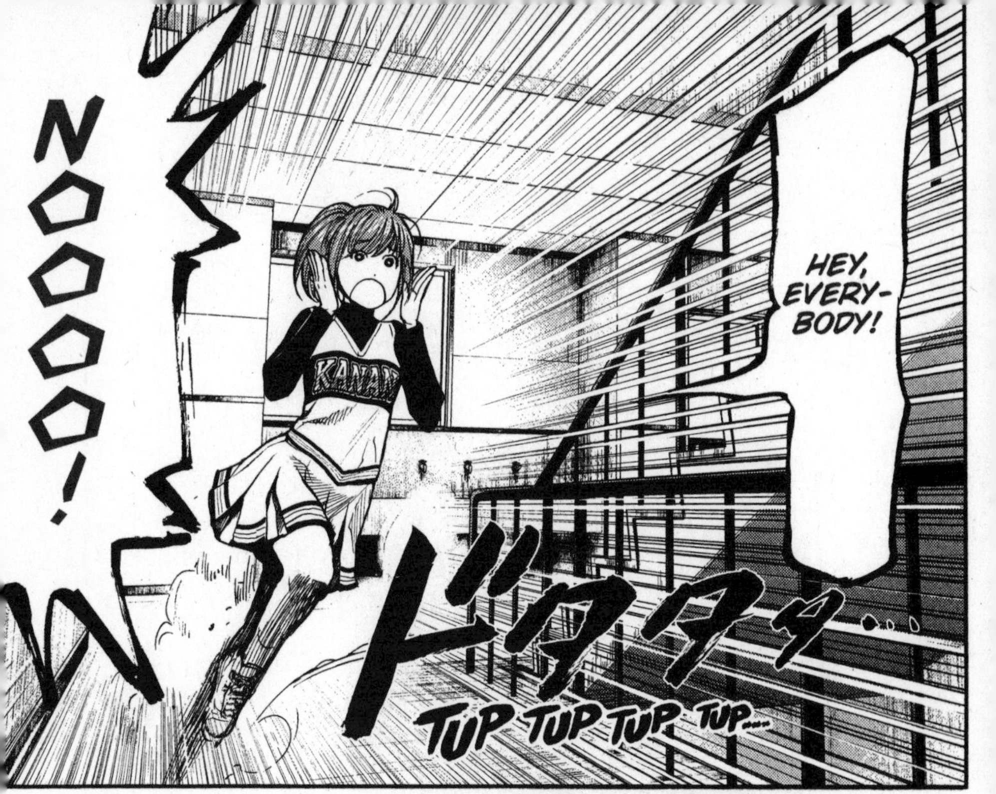
HEY, EVERY-BODY!
ドタタタ…
TUP TUP TUP TUP...
NOOOO!
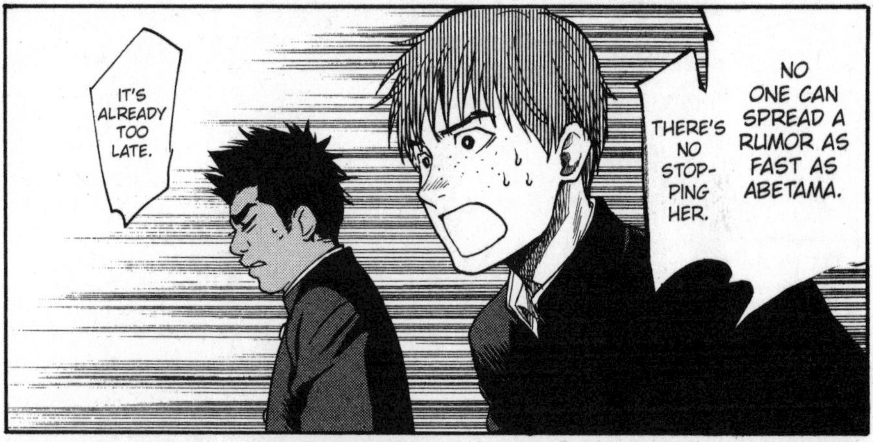
NO ONE CAN SPREAD A RUMOR AS FAST AS ABETAMA.
THERE'S NO STOP-PING HER.
IT'S ALREADY TOO LATE.
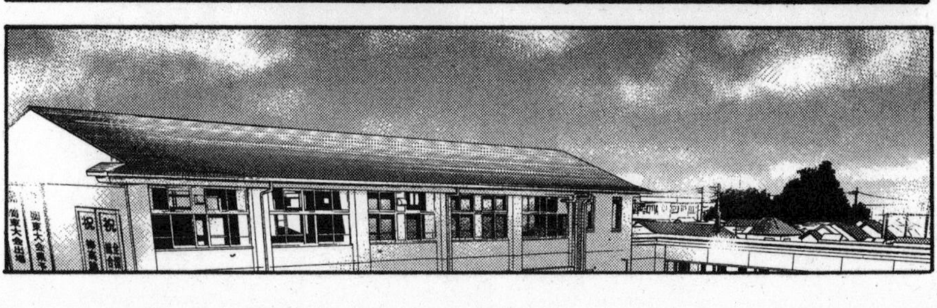

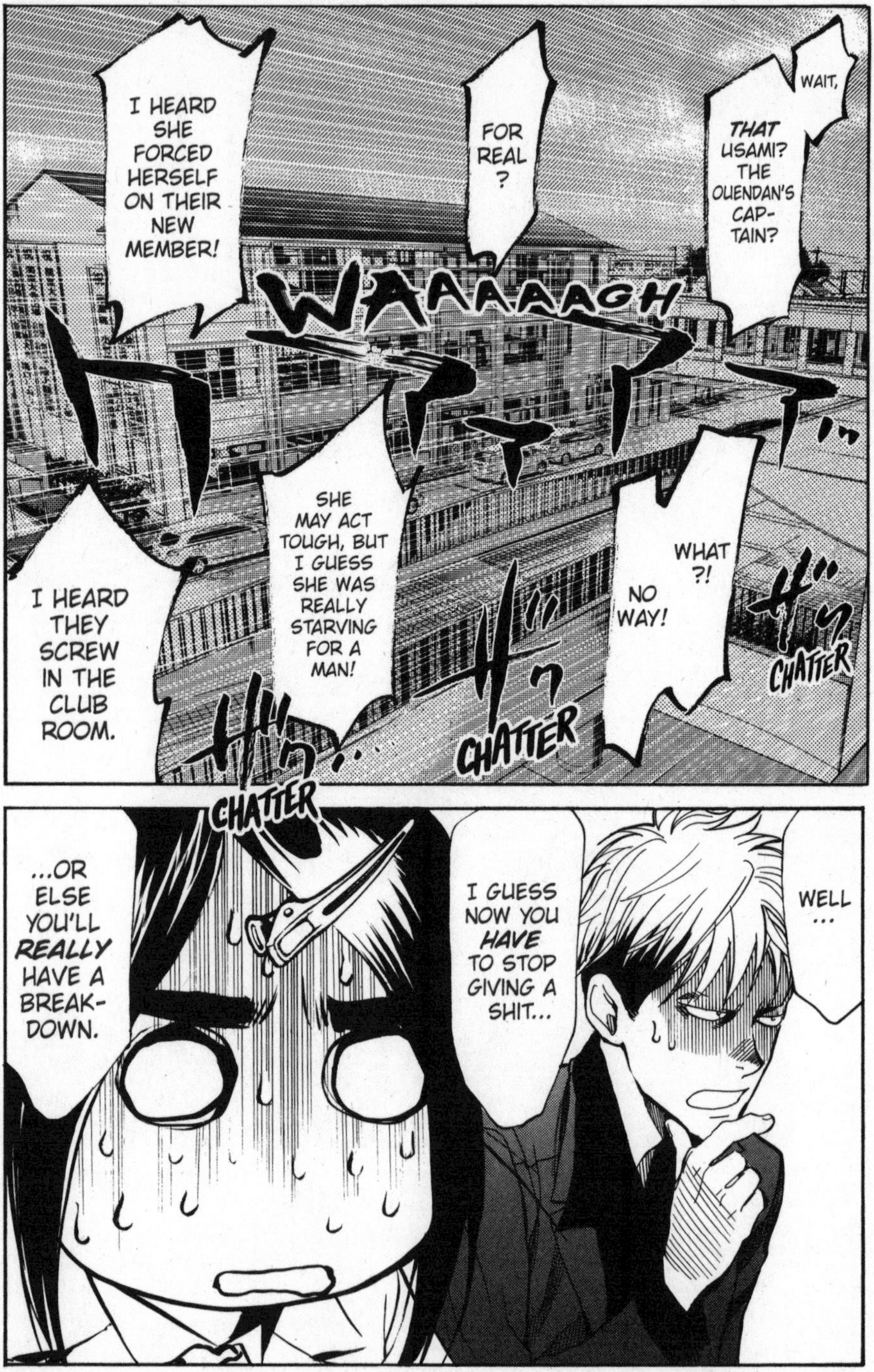
WAIT, THAT USAMI? THE OUENDAN'S CAP-TAIN?
FOR REAL?
I HEARD SHE FORCED HERSELF ON THEIR NEW MEMBER!
WAAAAAGH
WHAT?!
NO WAY!
CHATTER
SHE MAY ACT TOUGH, BUT I GUESS SHE WAS REALLY STARVING FOR A MAN!
CHATTER
I HEARD THEY SCREW IN THE CLUB ROOM.
CHATTER
WELL...
I GUESS NOW YOU HAVE TO STOP GIVING A SHIT...
...OR ELSE YOU'LL REALLY HAVE A BREAK-DOWN.

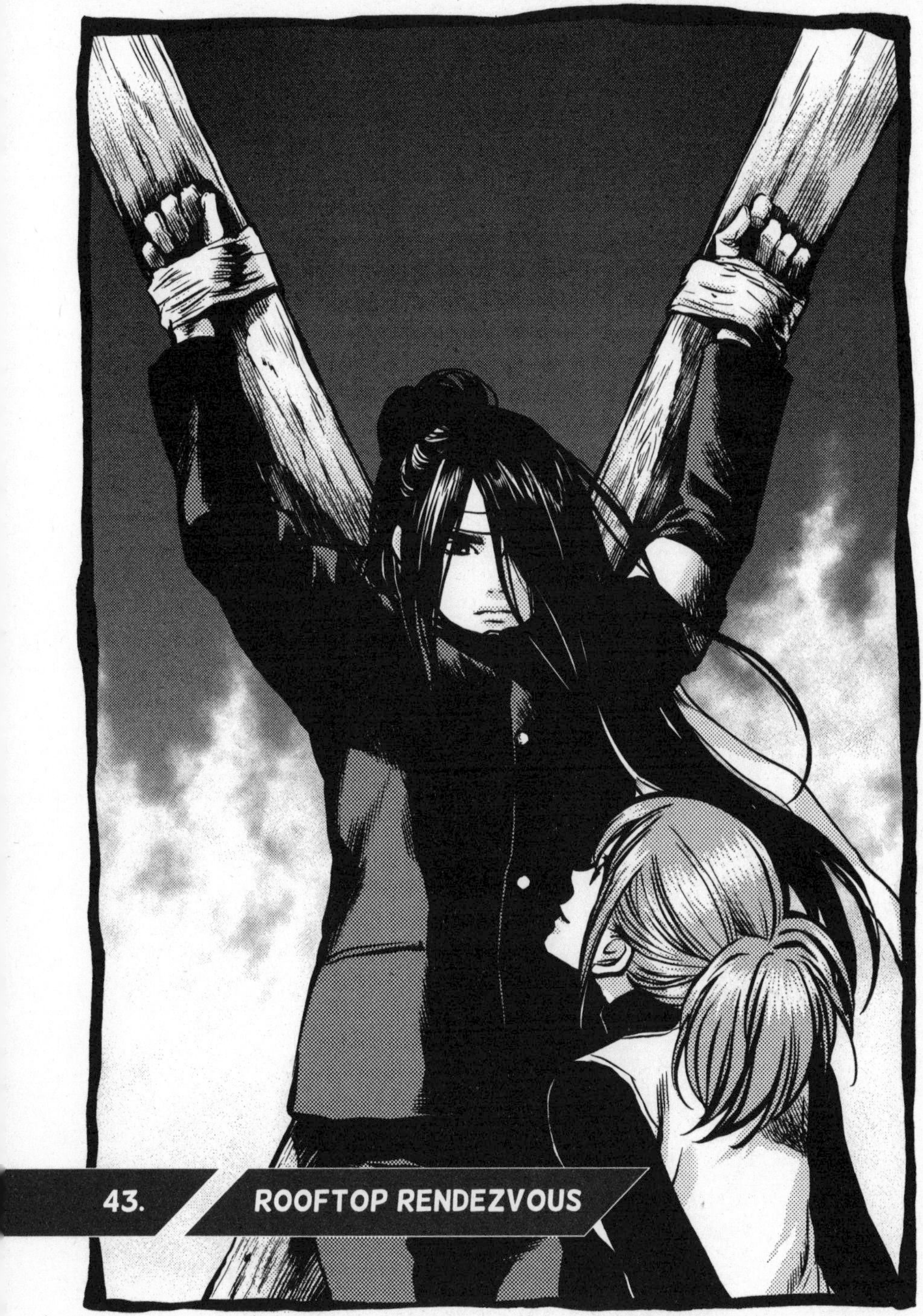
43.
ROOFTOP RENDEZVOUS

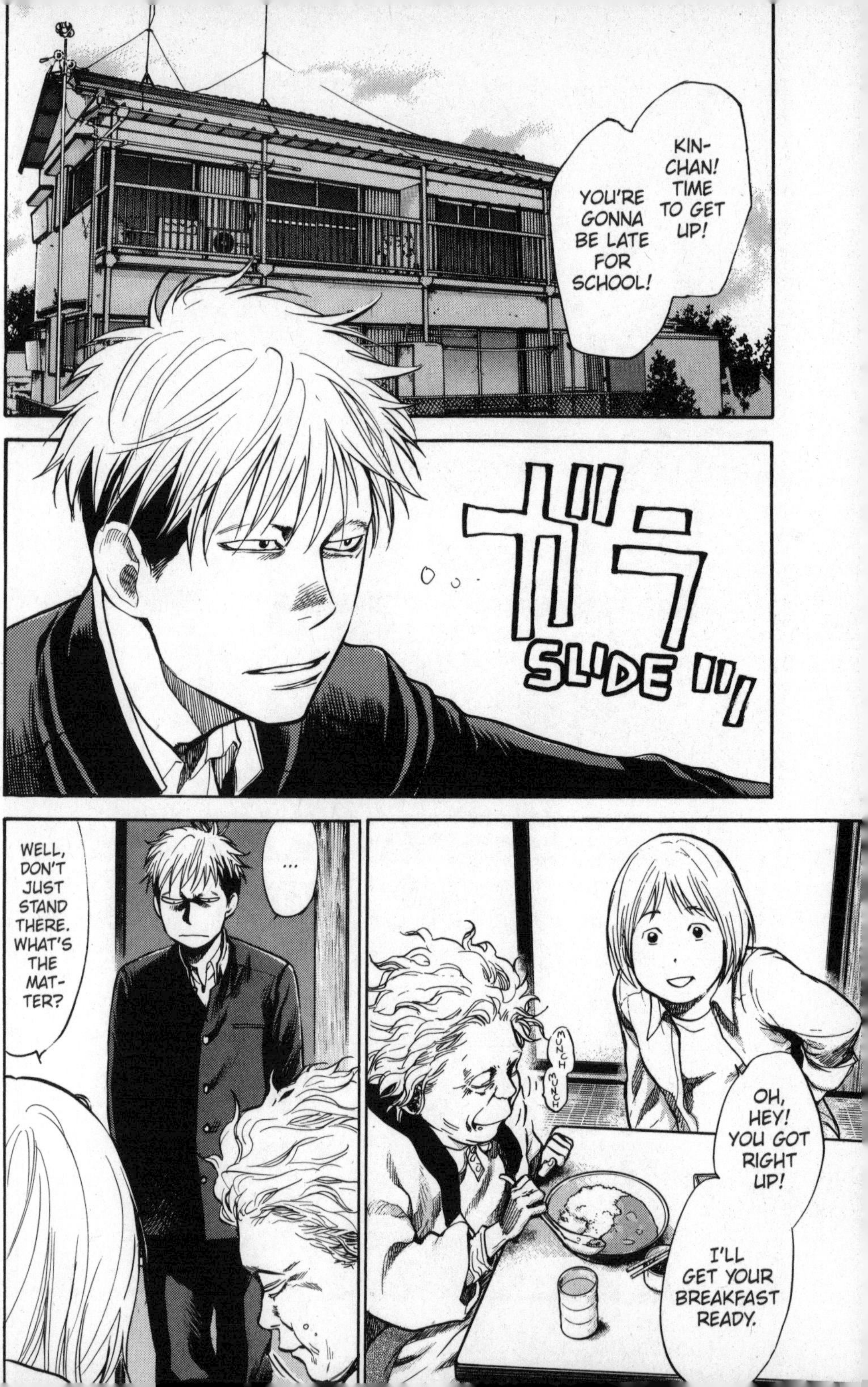
KIN-CHAN! TIME TO GET UP!
YOU'RE GONNA BE LATE FOR SCHOOL!
ガラ
SLIDE
OH, HEY! YOU GOT RIGHT UP!
I'LL GET YOUR BREAKFAST READY.
MUNCH
MUNCH
...
WELL, DON'T JUST STAND THERE. WHAT'S THE MAT-TER?

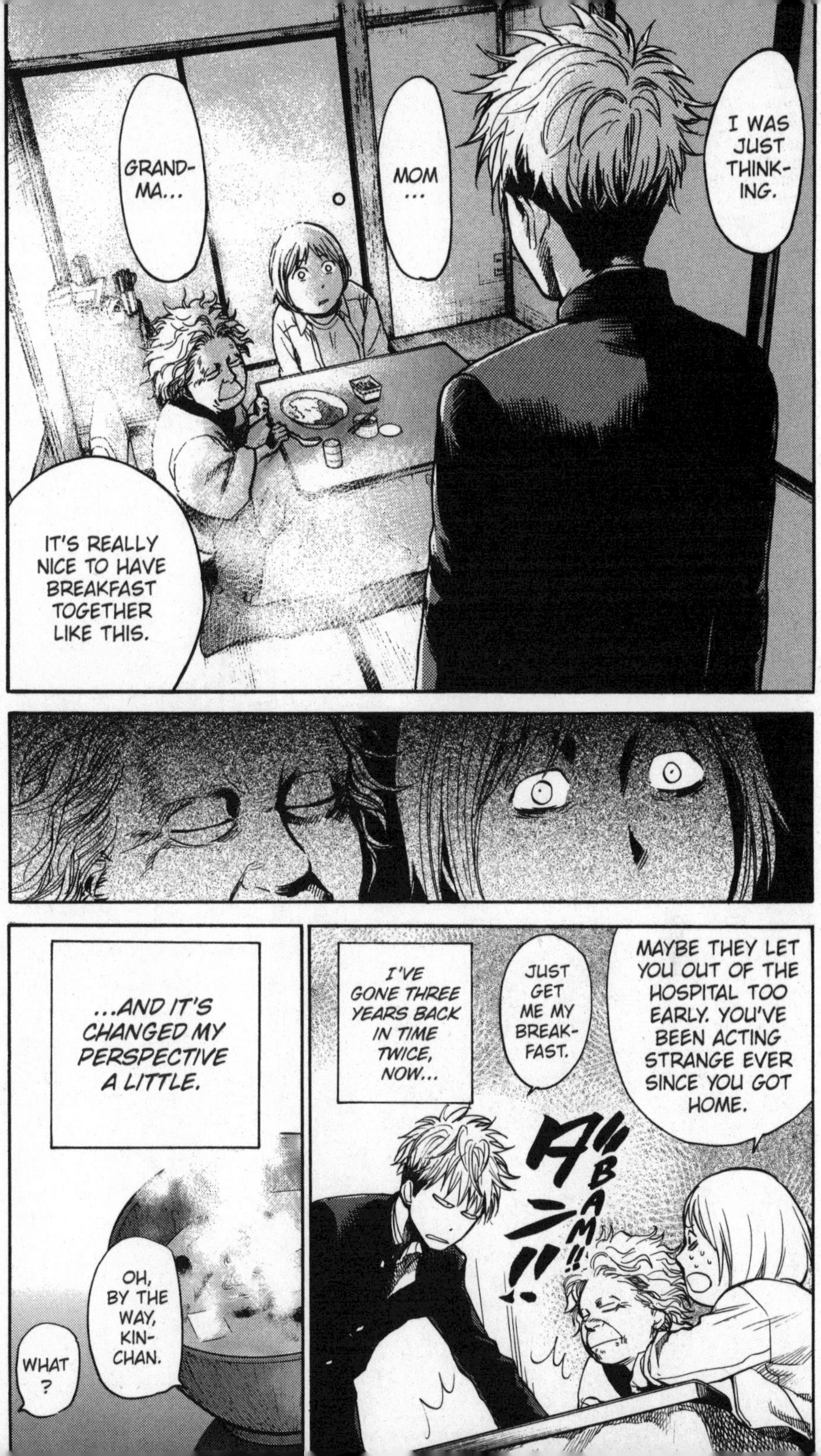
I WAS JUST THINKING.
MOM...
GRAND-MA...
IT'S REALLY NICE TO HAVE BREAKFAST TOGETHER LIKE THIS.
MAYBE THEY LET YOU OUT OF THE HOSPITAL TOO EARLY. YOU'VE BEEN ACTING STRANGE EVER SINCE YOU GOT HOME.
JUST GET ME MY BREAK-FAST.
I'VE GONE THREE YEARS BACK IN TIME TWICE, NOW...
BAM!!
...AND IT'S CHANGED MY PERSPECTIVE A LITTLE.
OH, BY THE WAY, KIN-CHAN.
WHAT?

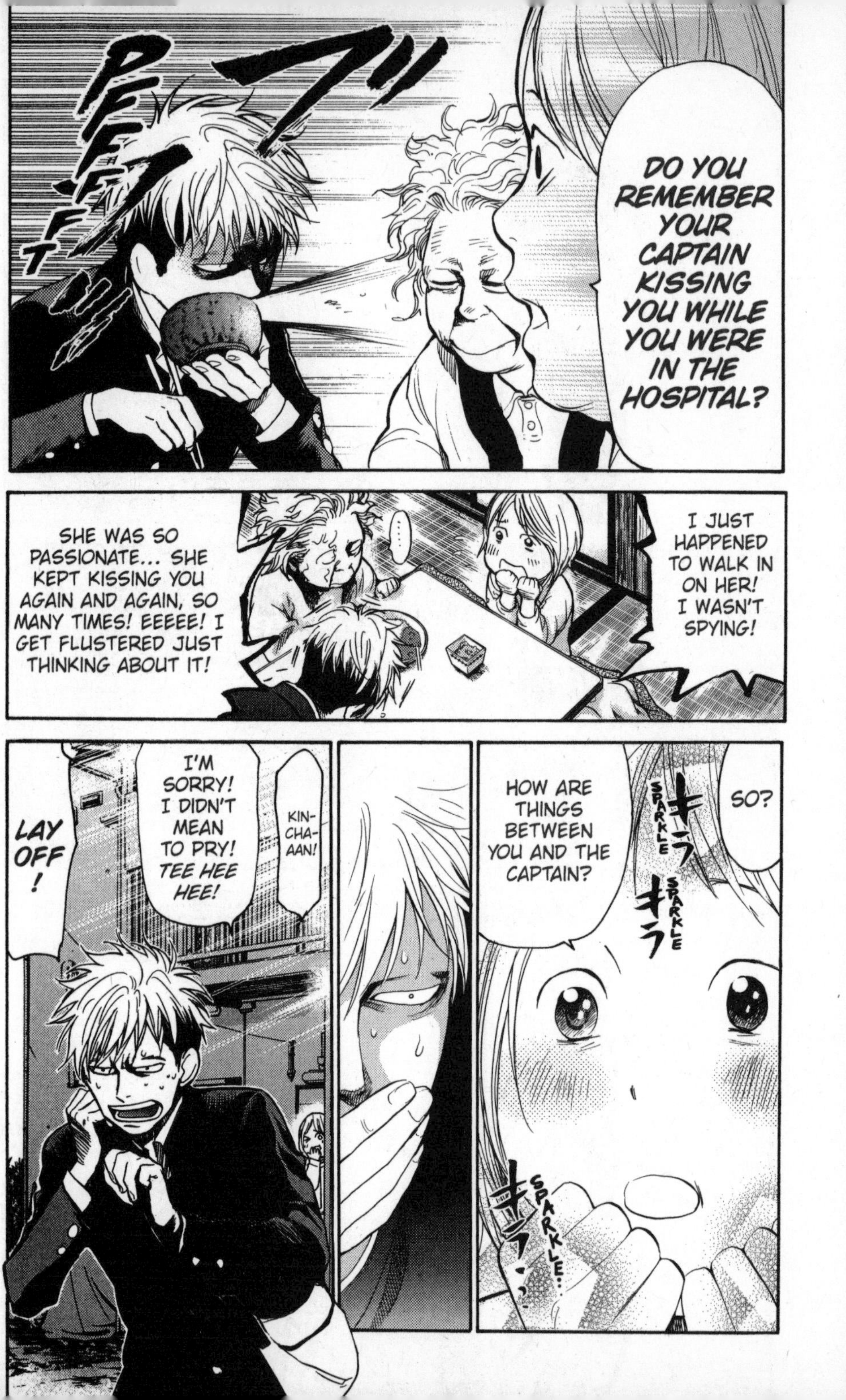
DO YOU REMEMBER YOUR CAPTAIN KISSING YOU WHILE YOU WERE IN THE HOSPITAL?
PFFFFT!!
I JUST HAPPENED TO WALK IN ON HER! I WASN'T SPYING!
...
SHE WAS SO PASSIONATE... SHE KEPT KISSING YOU AGAIN AND AGAIN, SO MANY TIMES! EEEEE! I GET FLUSTERED JUST THINKING ABOUT IT!
SO?
SPARKLE
SPARKLE
HOW ARE THINGS BETWEEN YOU AND THE CAPTAIN?
SPARKLE...
KIN-CHA-AAN!
I'M SORRY! I DIDN'T MEAN TO PRY! TEE HEE HEE!
LAY OFF!

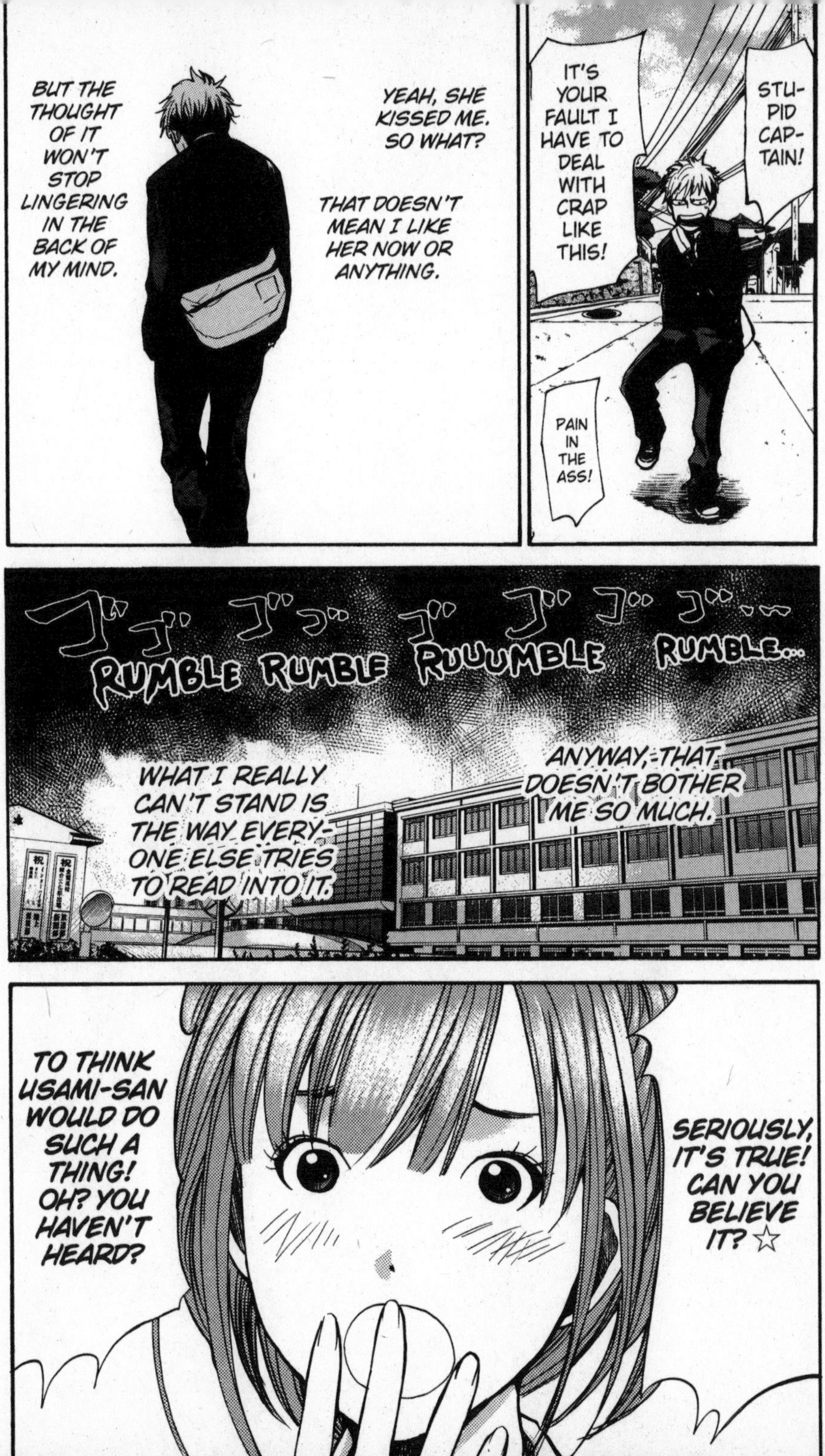
STU-PID CAP-TAIN!
IT'S YOUR FAULT I HAVE TO DEAL WITH CRAP LIKE THIS!
PAIN IN THE ASS!
YEAH, SHE KISSED ME. SO WHAT?
THAT DOESN'T MEAN I LIKE HER NOW OR ANYTHING.
BUT THE THOUGHT OF IT WON'T STOP LINGERING IN THE BACK OF MY MIND.
ゴゴ ゴゴ ゴ ゴ ゴ ゴ…
RUMBLE RUMBLE RUUUMBLE RUMBLE...
ANYWAY, THAT DOESN'T BOTHER ME SO MUCH.
WHAT I REALLY CAN'T STAND IS THE WAY EVERY-ONE ELSE TRIES TO READ INTO IT.
SERIOUSLY, IT'S TRUE! CAN YOU BELIEVE IT? ☆
TO THINK USAMI-SAN WOULD DO SUCH A THING! OH? YOU HAVEN'T HEARD?

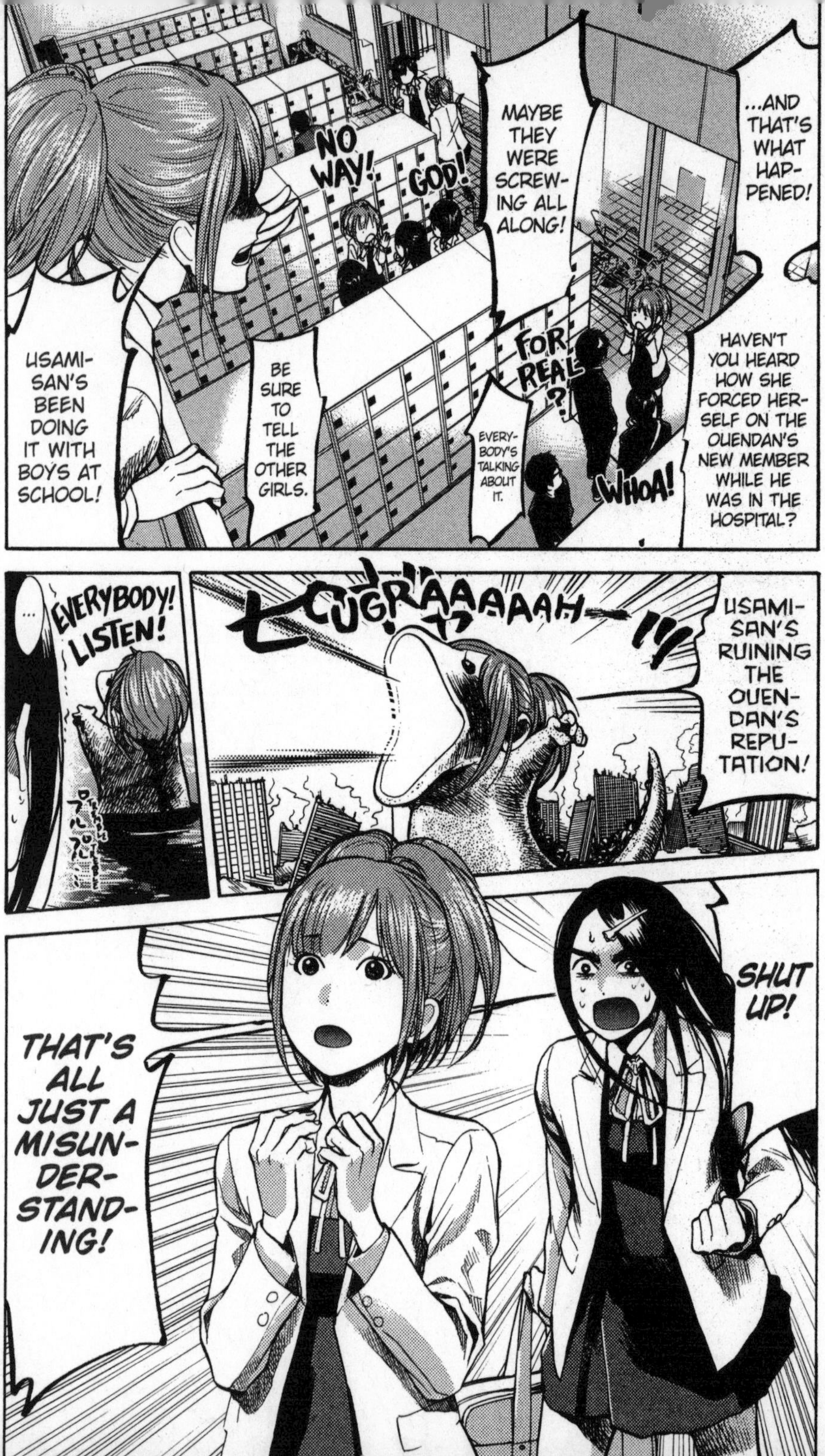
...AND THAT'S WHAT HAP-PENED!
HAVEN'T YOU HEARD HOW SHE FORCED HER-SELF ON THE OUENDAN'S NEW MEMBER WHILE HE WAS IN THE HOSPITAL?
MAYBE THEY WERE SCREW-ING ALL ALONG!
WHOA!
FOR REAL?
GOD!
NO WAY!
EVERY-BODY'S TALKING ABOUT IT.
BE SURE TO TELL THE OTHER GIRLS.
USAMI-SAN'S BEEN DOING IT WITH BOYS AT SCHOOL!
USAMI-SAN'S RUINING THE OUEN-DAN'S REPU-TATION!
GRAAAAAAH!!!
EVERYBODY! LISTEN!
...
SHUT UP!
THAT'S ALL JUST A MISUN-DER-STAND-ING!

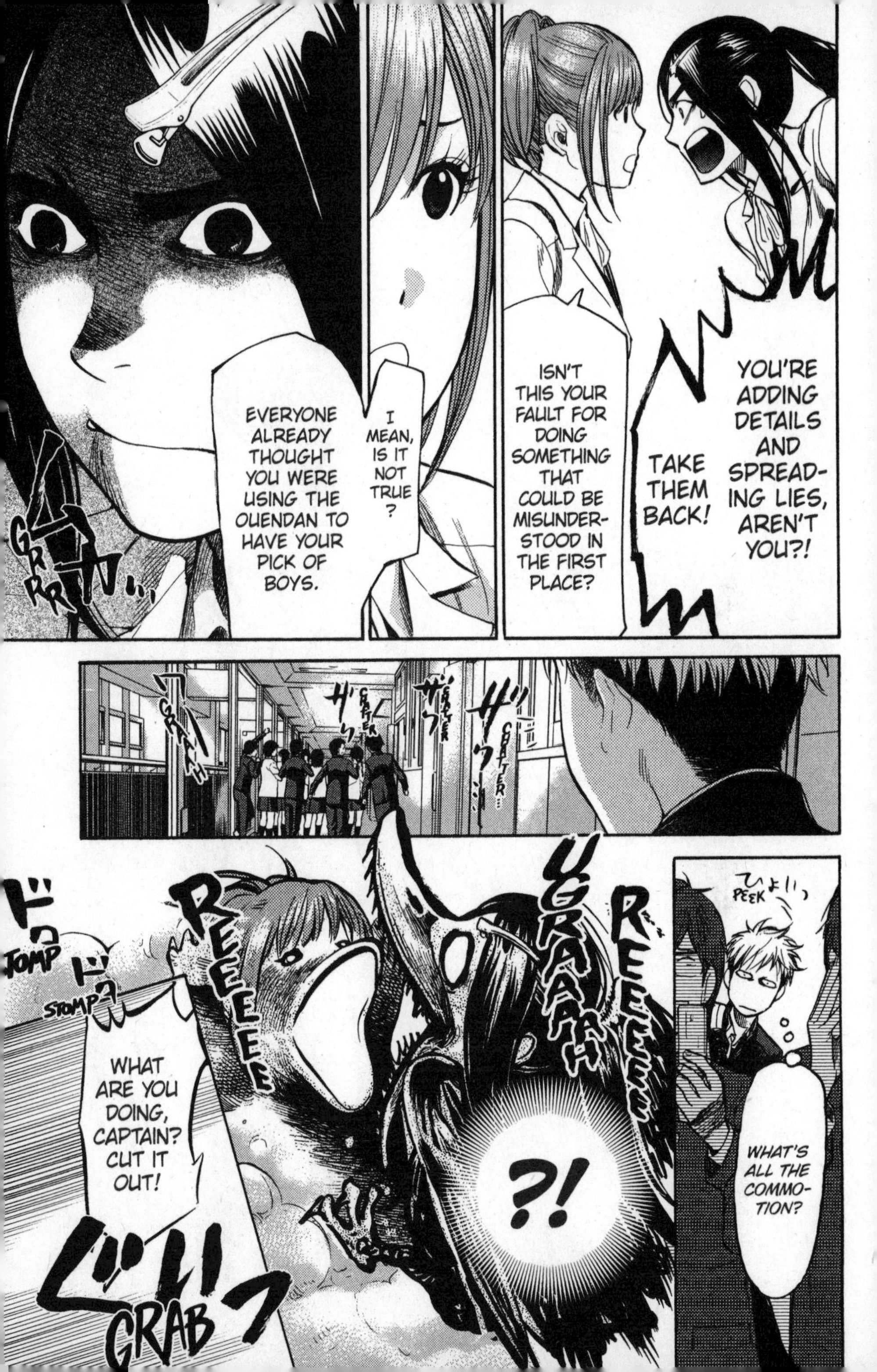
YOU'RE ADDING DETAILS AND SPREAD-ING LIES, AREN'T YOU?!
TAKE THEM BACK!
ISN'T THIS YOUR FAULT FOR DOING SOMETHING THAT COULD BE MISUNDER-STOOD IN THE FIRST PLACE?
I MEAN, IS IT NOT TRUE?
EVERYONE ALREADY THOUGHT YOU WERE USING THE OUENDAN TO HAVE YOUR PICK OF BOYS.
GRRR
PEEK
WHAT'S ALL THE COMMO-TION?
REEEEEE
UGRAAAH
REEEEEE
?!
TOMP
STOMP
WHAT ARE YOU DOING, CAPTAIN? CUT IT OUT!
GRAB

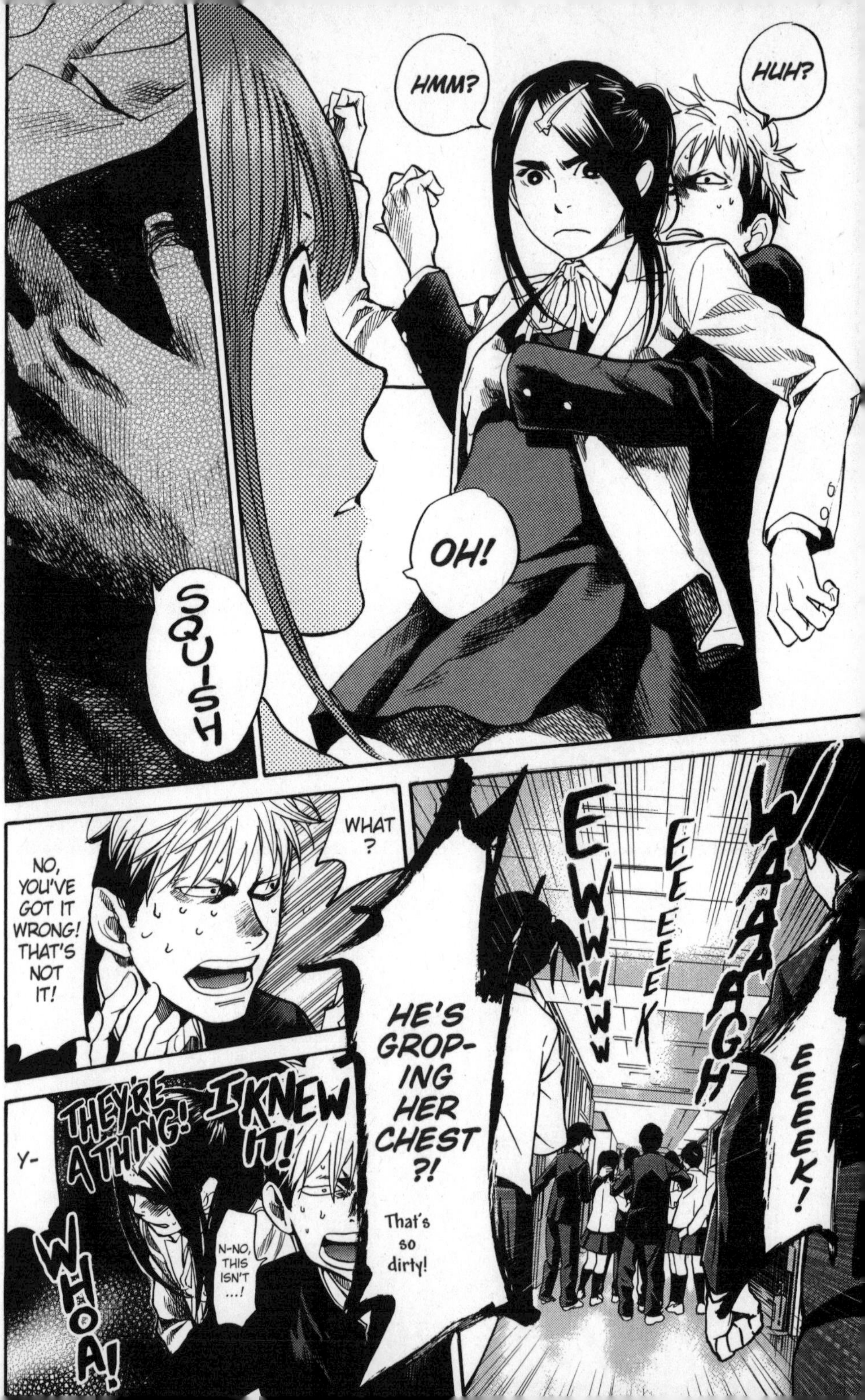
HUH?
HMM?
OH!
SQUISH
WAAAGH
EEEEEK!
EEEEEEK
EWWWWWW
HE'S GROPING HER CHEST?!
That's so dirty!
WHAT?
NO, YOU'VE GOT IT WRONG! THAT'S NOT IT!
I KNEW IT!
THEY'RE A THING!
Y-
N-NO, THIS ISN'T ...!
WHOA!

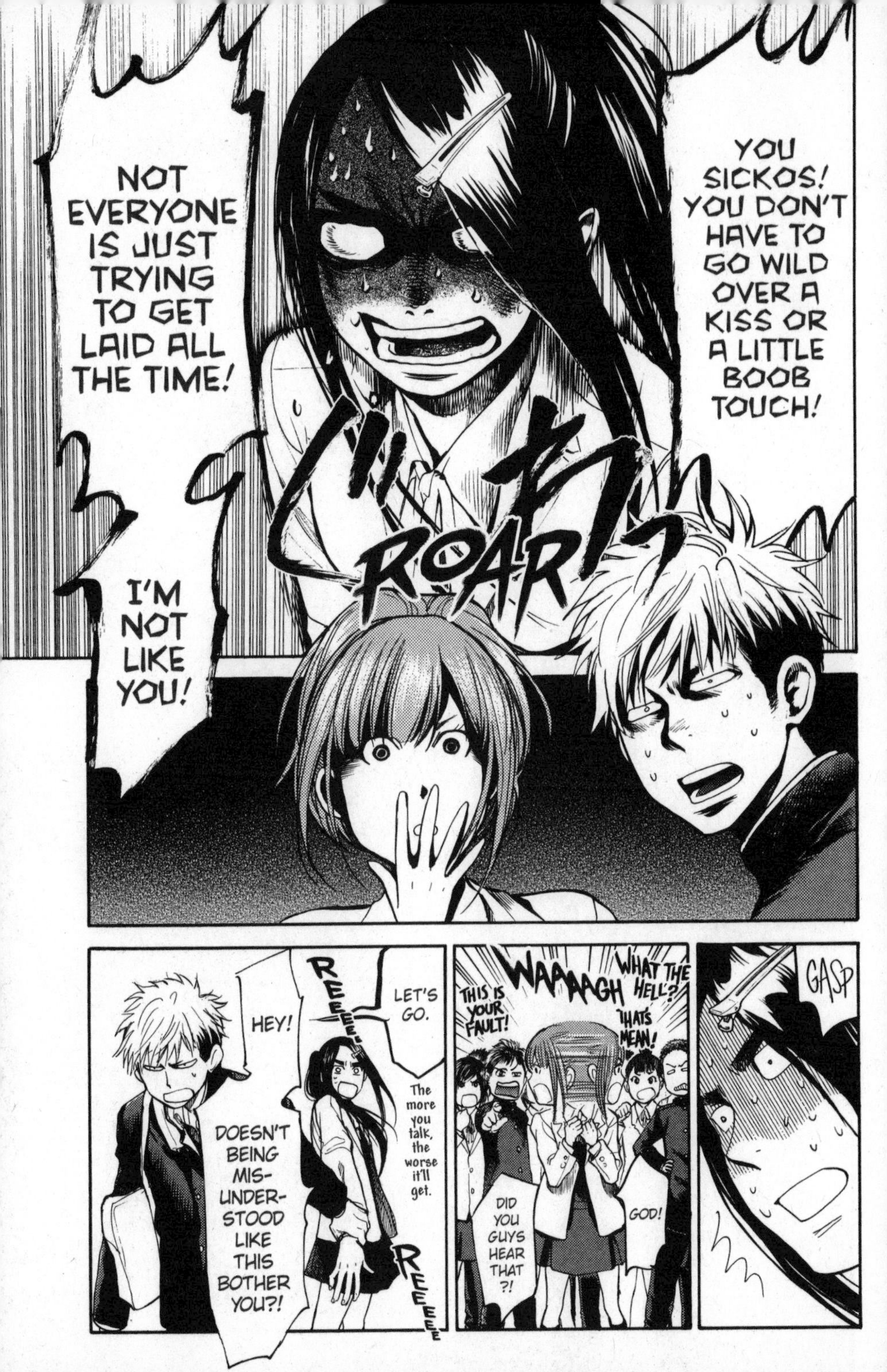
YOU SICKOS! YOU DON'T HAVE TO GO WILD OVER A KISS OR A LITTLE BOOB TOUCH!
NOT EVERYONE IS JUST TRYING TO GET LAID ALL THE TIME!
ROAR
I'M NOT LIKE YOU!
GASP
WHAT THE HELL?
WAAAAGH
THIS IS YOUR FAULT!
THAT'S MEAN!
GOD!
DID YOU GUYS HEAR THAT?!
LET'S GO.
REEEEE
HEY!
The more you talk, the worse it'll get.
DOESN'T BEING MIS-UNDER-STOOD LIKE THIS BOTHER YOU?!
REEEEE

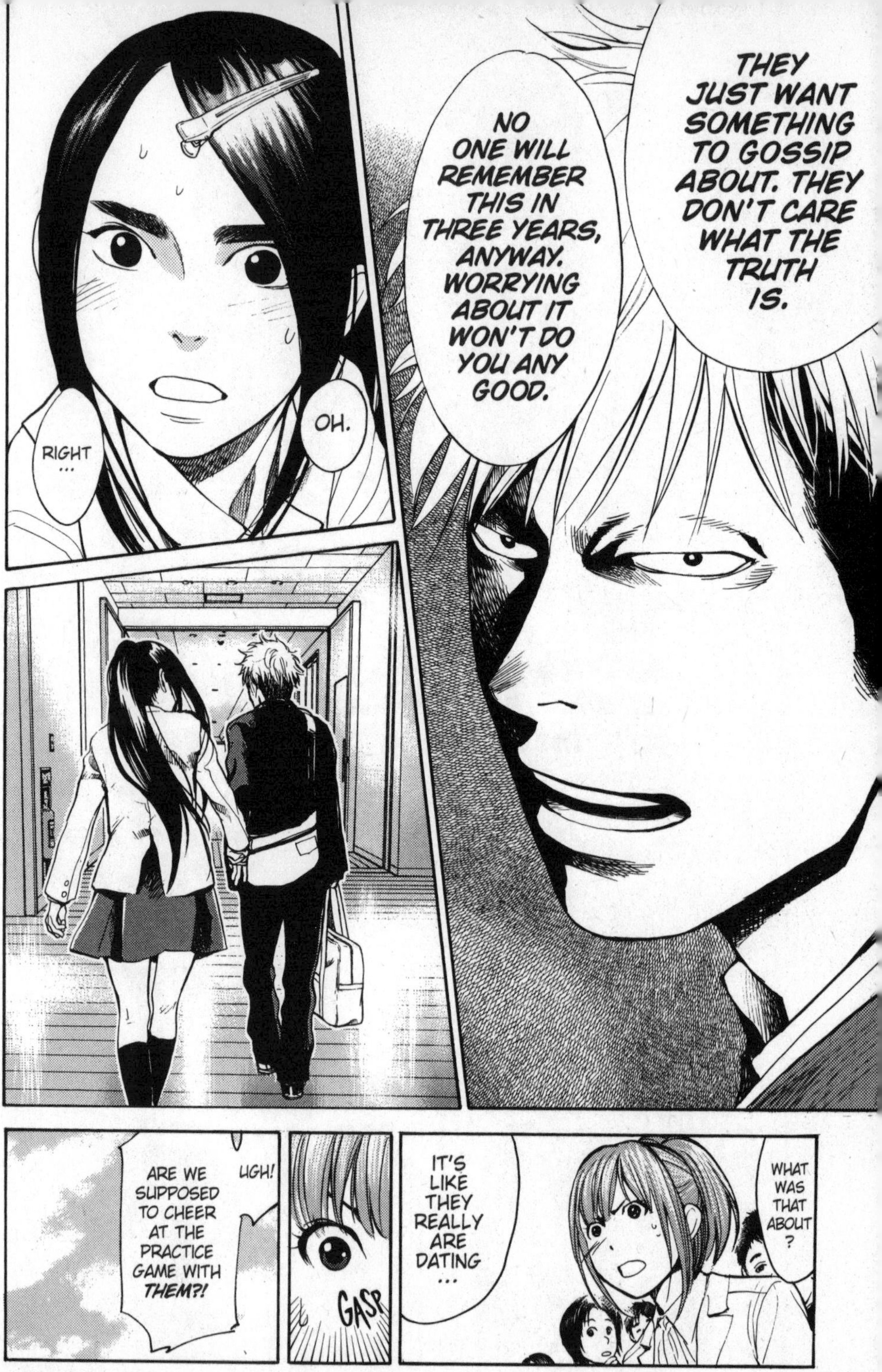
THEY JUST WANT SOMETHING TO GOSSIP ABOUT. THEY DON'T CARE WHAT THE TRUTH IS.
NO ONE WILL REMEMBER THIS IN THREE YEARS, ANYWAY. WORRYING ABOUT IT WON'T DO YOU ANY GOOD.
OH.
RIGHT...
WHAT WAS THAT ABOUT?
IT'S LIKE THEY REALLY ARE DATING...
GASP
UGH!
ARE WE SUPPOSED TO CHEER AT THE PRACTICE GAME WITH *THEM*?!

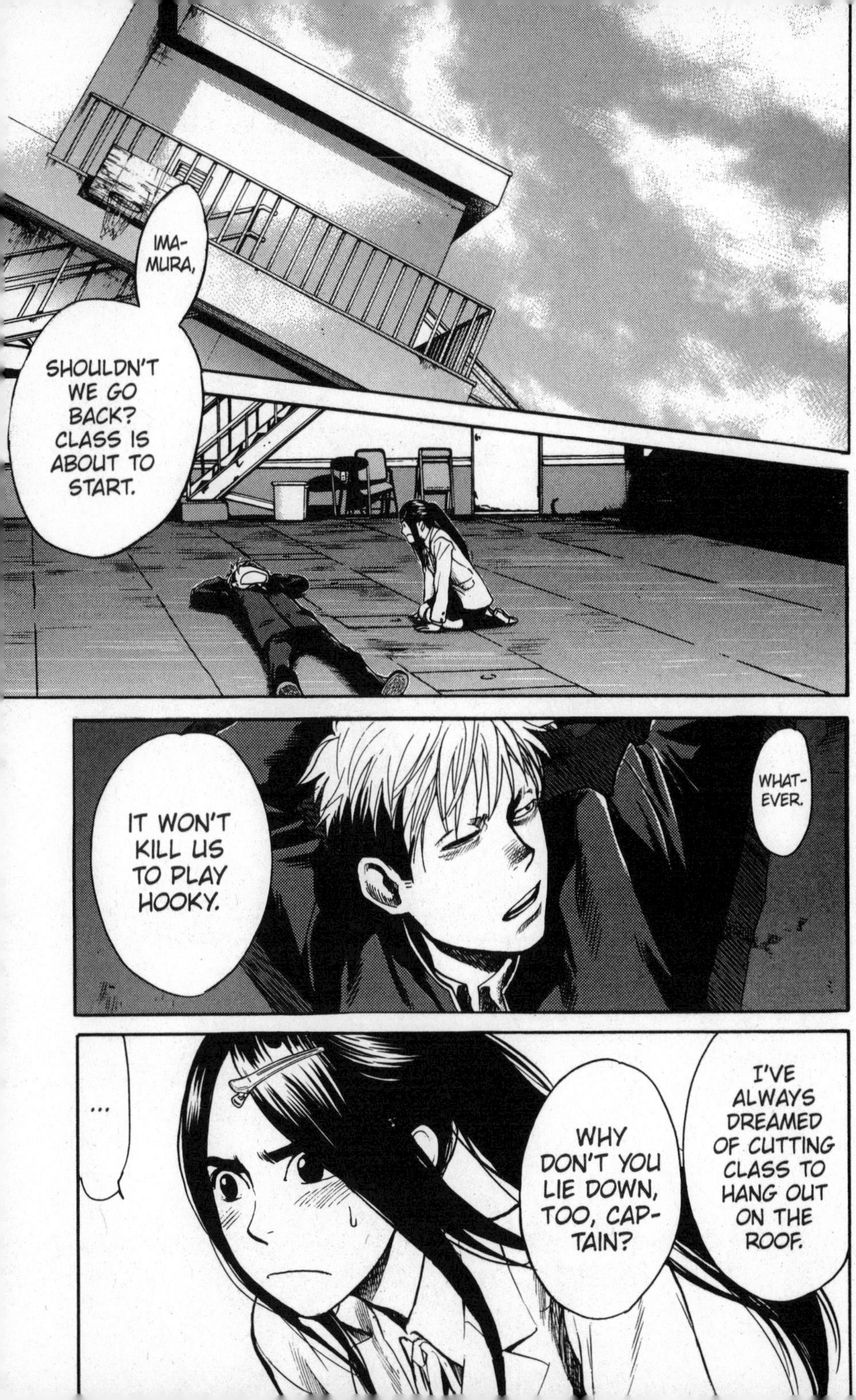
IMA-MURA,
SHOULDN'T WE GO BACK? CLASS IS ABOUT TO START.
WHAT-EVER.
IT WON'T KILL US TO PLAY HOOKY.
I'VE ALWAYS DREAMED OF CUTTING CLASS TO HANG OUT ON THE ROOF.
WHY DON'T YOU LIE DOWN, TOO, CAP-TAIN?
...

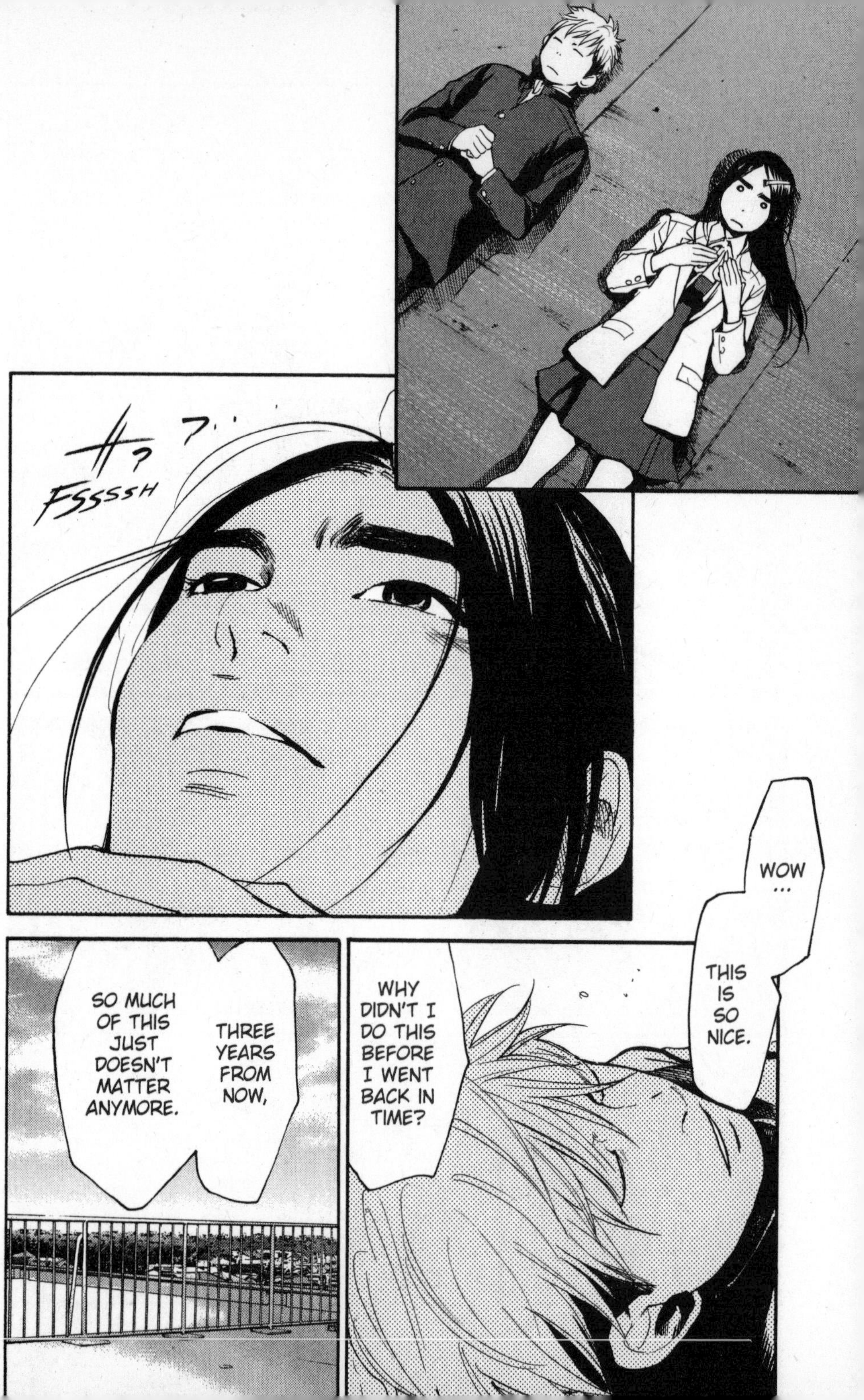
FSSSSH
WOW... THIS IS SO NICE.
WHY DIDN'T I DO THIS BEFORE I WENT BACK IN TIME?
THREE YEARS FROM NOW,
SO MUCH OF THIS JUST DOESN'T MATTER ANYMORE.

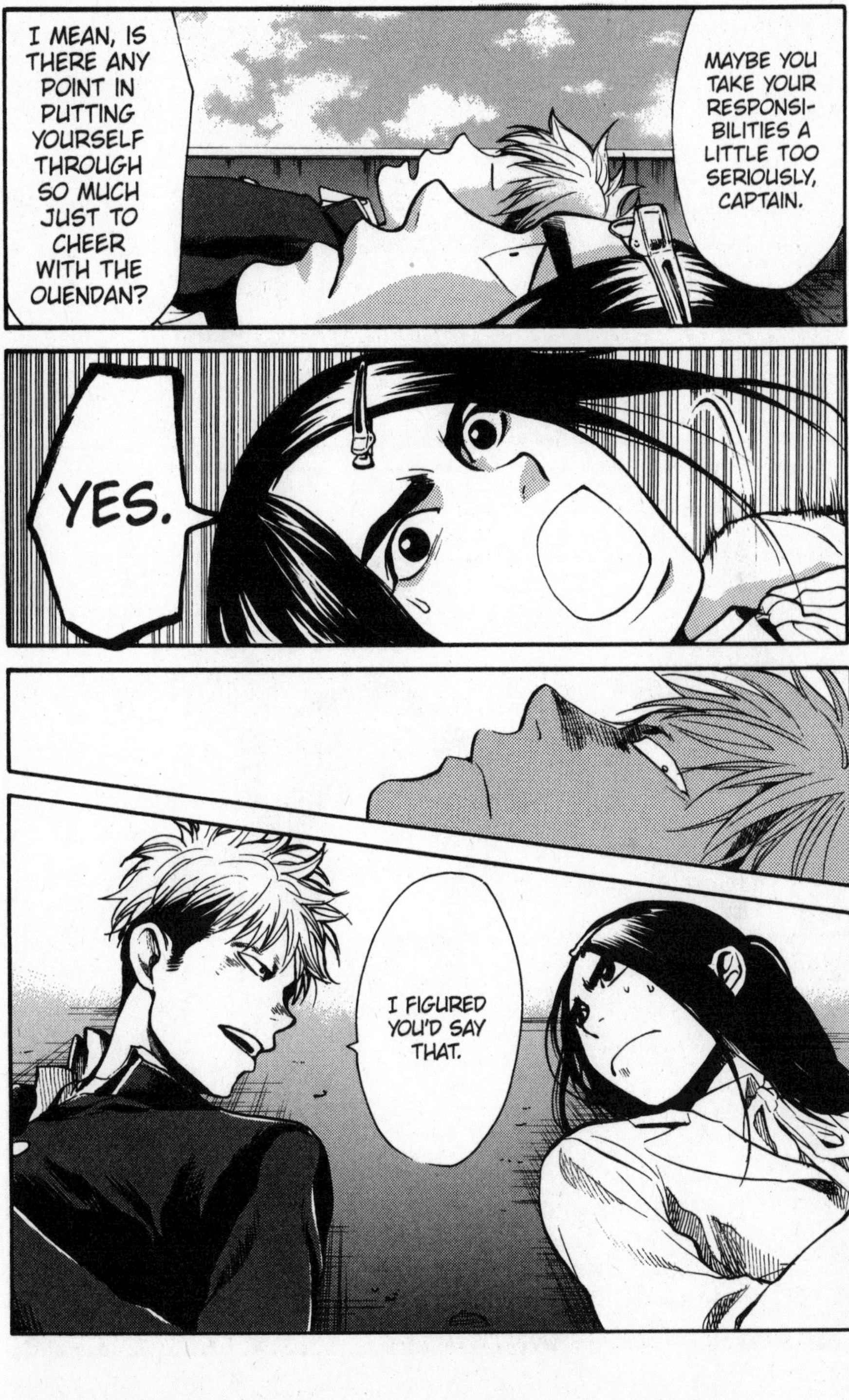
MAYBE YOU TAKE YOUR RESPONSI-BILITIES A LITTLE TOO SERIOUSLY, CAPTAIN.
I MEAN, IS THERE ANY POINT IN PUTTING YOURSELF THROUGH SO MUCH JUST TO CHEER WITH THE OUENDAN?
YES.
I FIGURED YOU'D SAY THAT.

SO,
YOU'LL DO WHATEVER IT TAKES TO BRING SOME LIFE BACK TO THE OUENDAN, RIGHT?
WHAT?
I MEAN, OF COURSE ...
THIS ISN'T ANY FUN. NOT LIKE THIS.
?

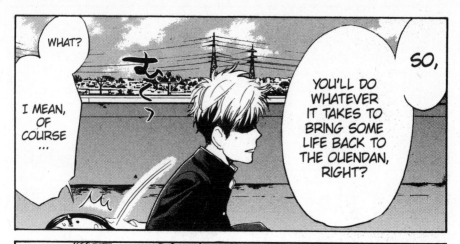

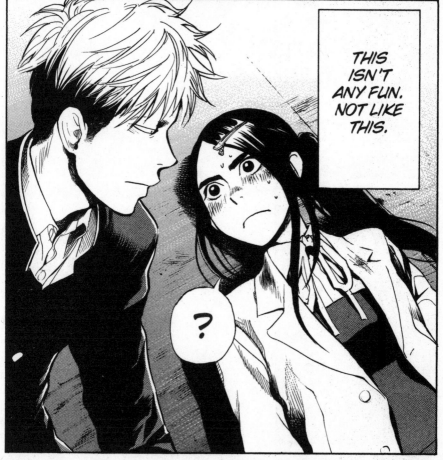

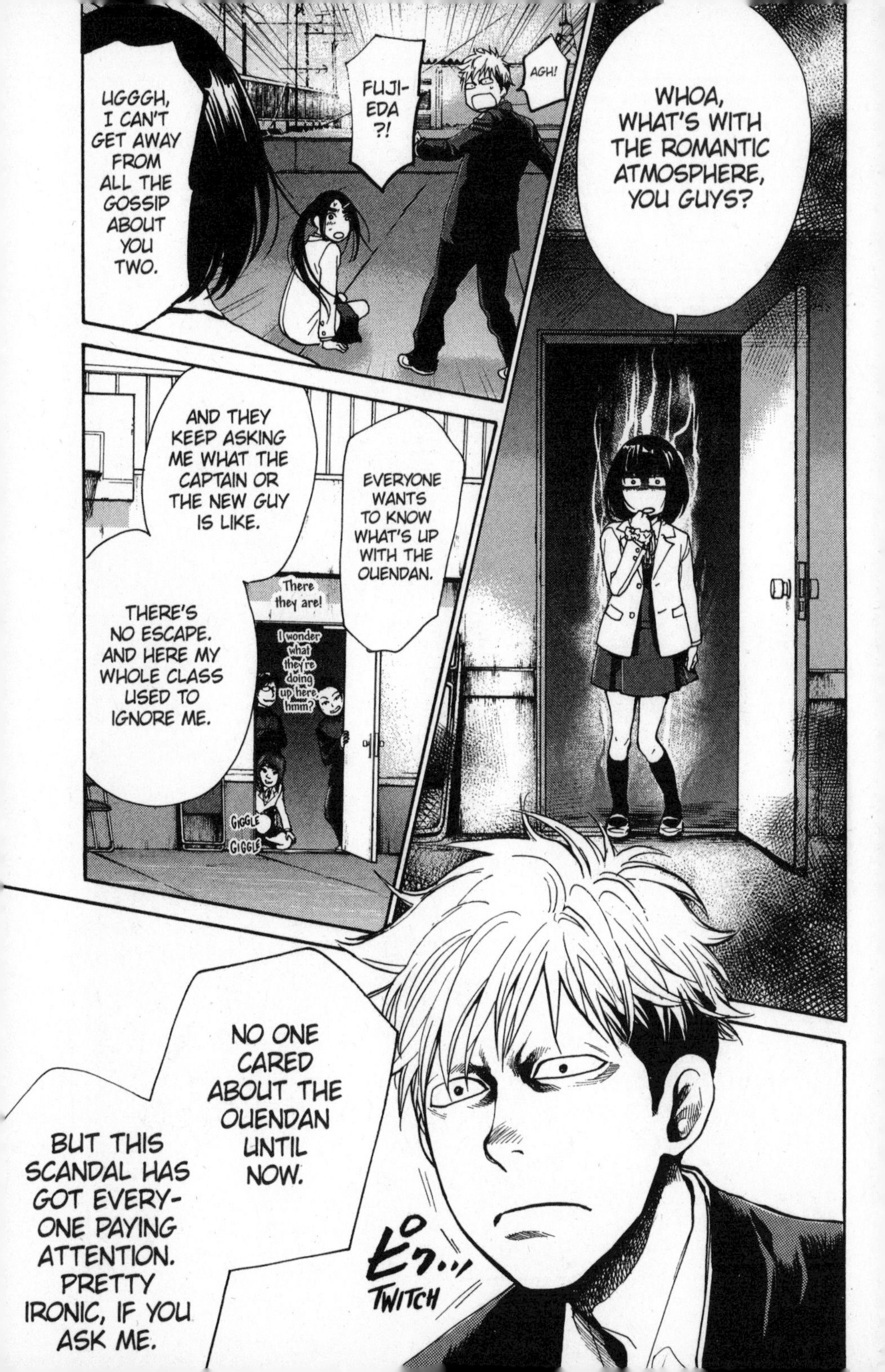
WHOA, WHAT'S WITH THE ROMANTIC ATMOSPHERE, YOU GUYS?
AGH!
FUJI-EDA?!
UGGGH, I CAN'T GET AWAY FROM ALL THE GOSSIP ABOUT YOU TWO.
EVERYONE WANTS TO KNOW WHAT'S UP WITH THE OUENDAN.
AND THEY KEEP ASKING ME WHAT THE CAPTAIN OR THE NEW GUY IS LIKE.
There they are!
I wonder what they're doing up here, hmm?
THERE'S NO ESCAPE. AND HERE MY WHOLE CLASS USED TO IGNORE ME.
GIGGLE
GIGGLE
NO ONE CARED ABOUT THE OUENDAN UNTIL NOW.
BUT THIS SCANDAL HAS GOT EVERY-ONE PAYING ATTENTION. PRETTY IRONIC, IF YOU ASK ME.
TWITCH

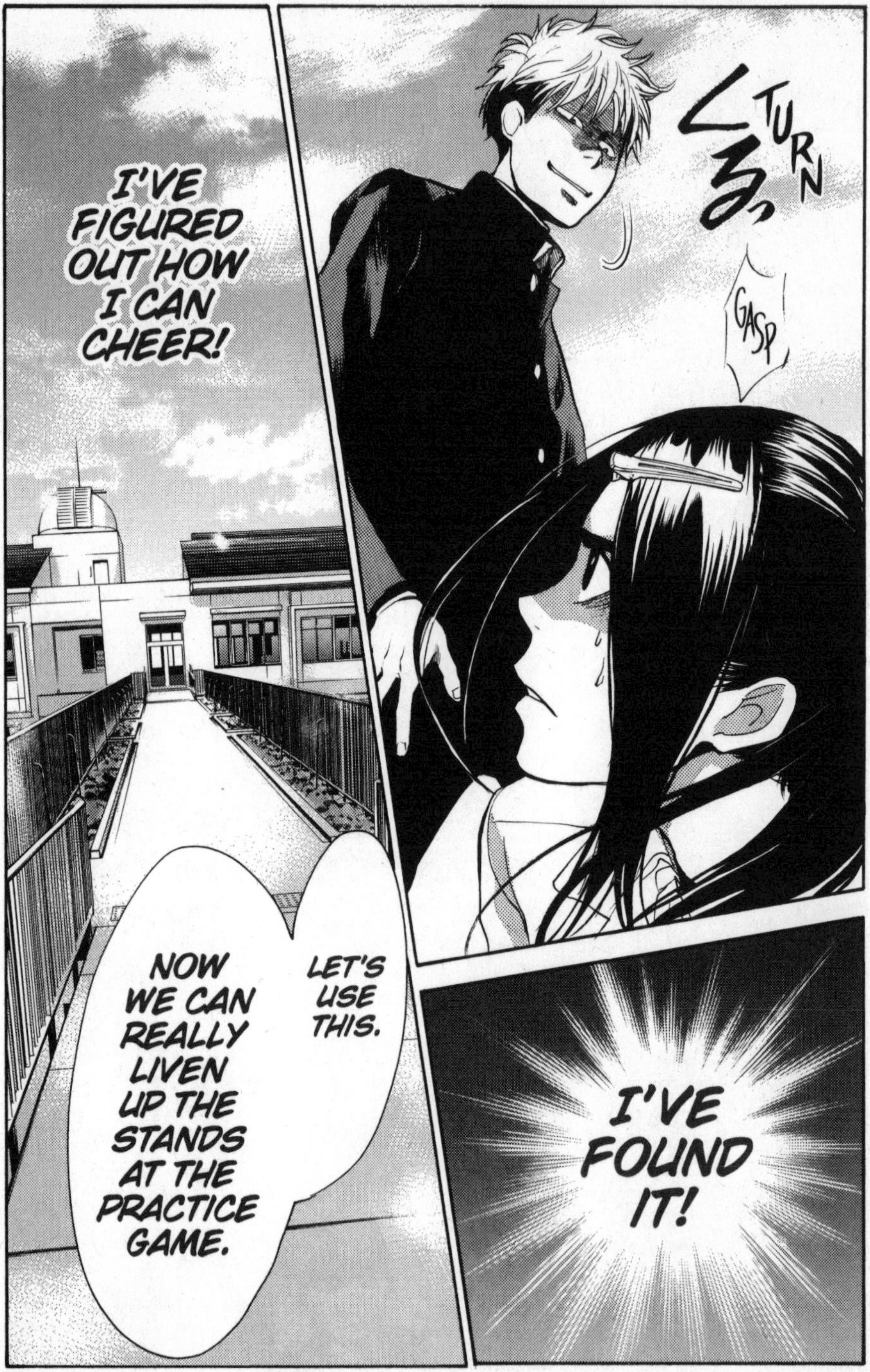
くるっ TURN
GASP
I'VE FOUND IT!
I'VE FIGURED OUT HOW I CAN CHEER!
LET'S USE THIS.
NOW WE CAN REALLY LIVEN UP THE STANDS AT THE PRACTICE GAME.

# 44. SECOND DO-OVER

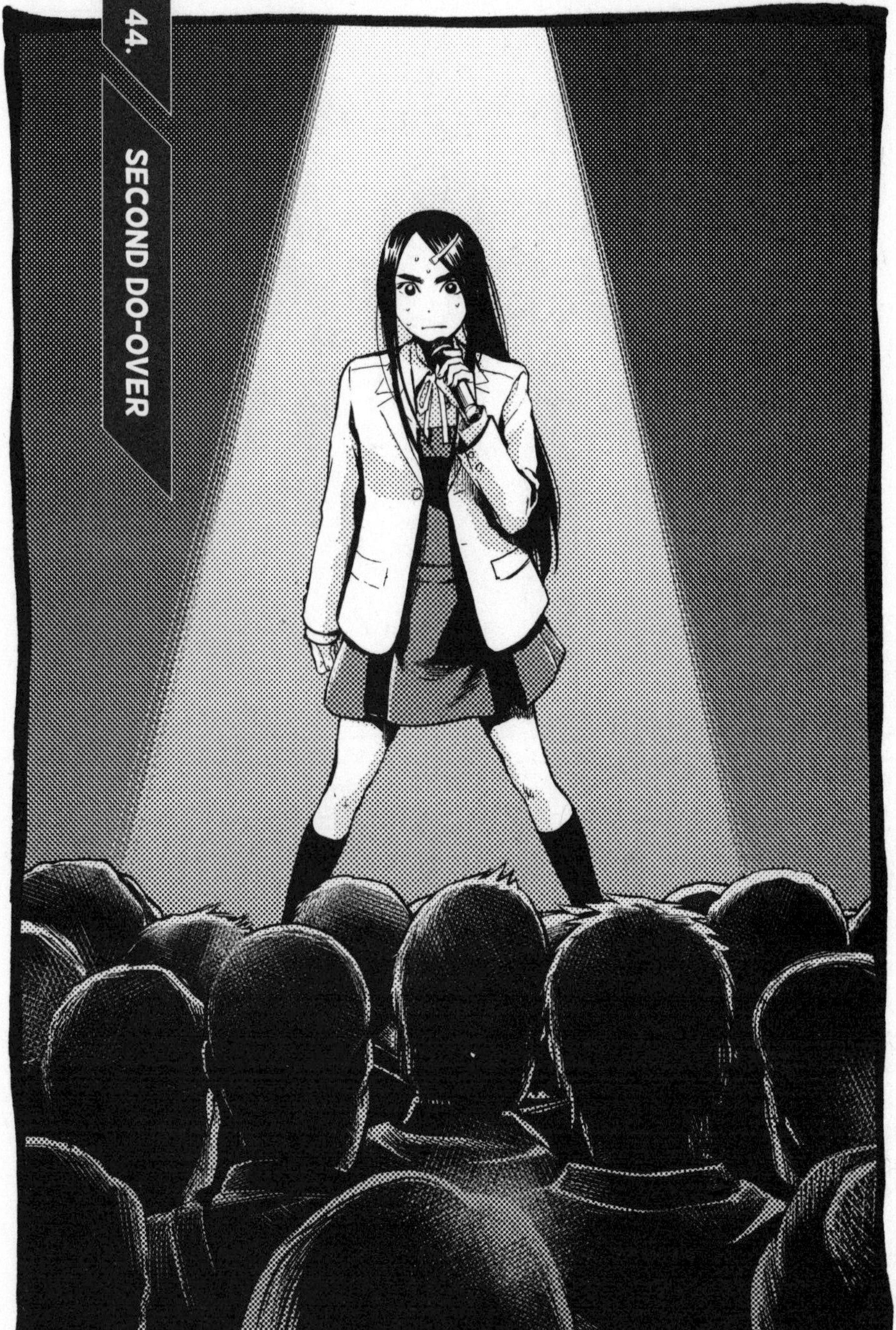

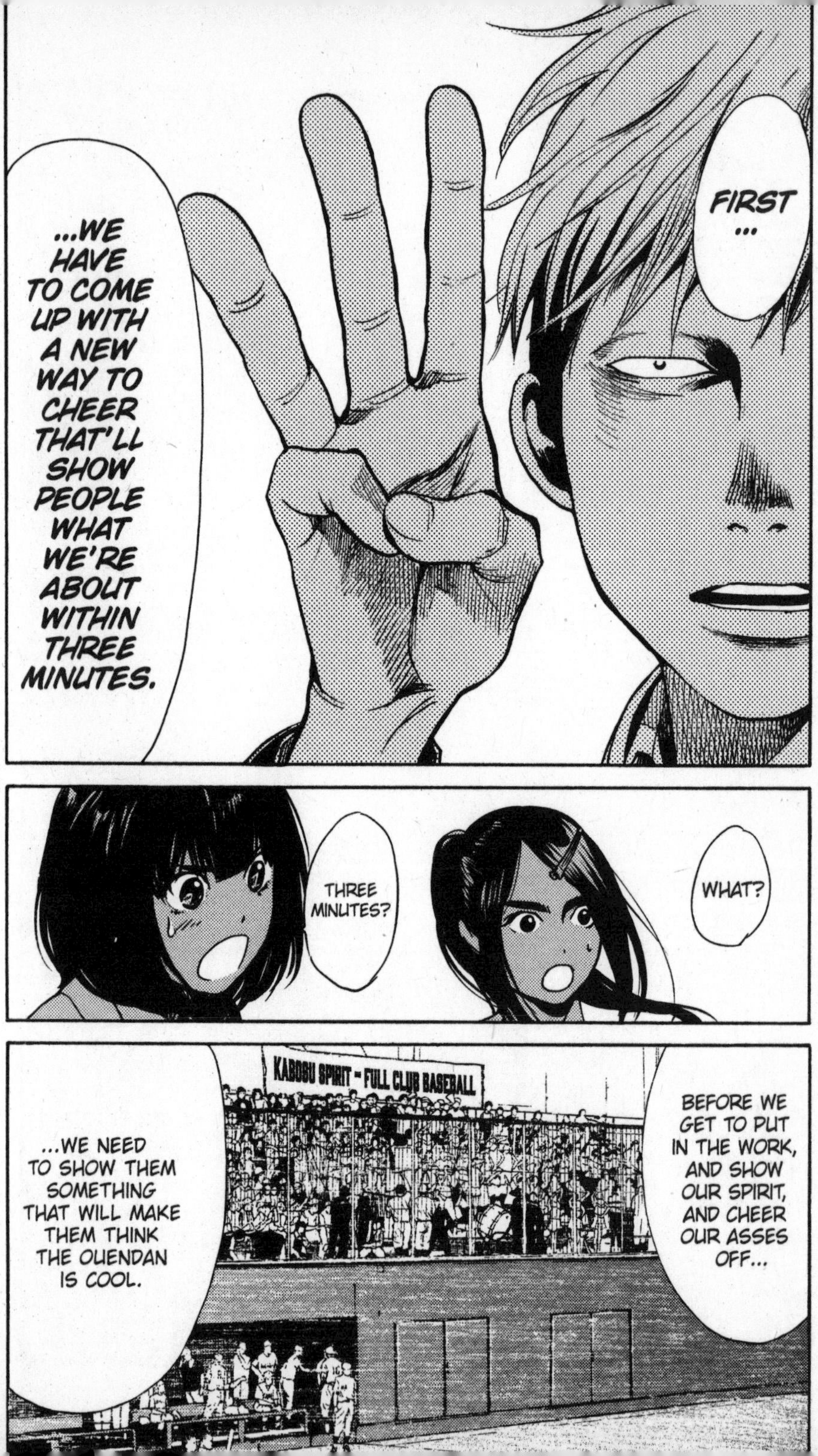
FIRST ...
...WE HAVE TO COME UP WITH A NEW WAY TO CHEER THAT'LL SHOW PEOPLE WHAT WE'RE ABOUT WITHIN THREE MINUTES.
WHAT?
THREE MINUTES?
BEFORE WE GET TO PUT IN THE WORK, AND SHOW OUR SPIRIT, AND CHEER OUR ASSES OFF...
KABOSU SPIRIT = FULL CLUB BASEBALL
...WE NEED TO SHOW THEM SOMETHING THAT WILL MAKE THEM THINK THE OUENDAN IS COOL.

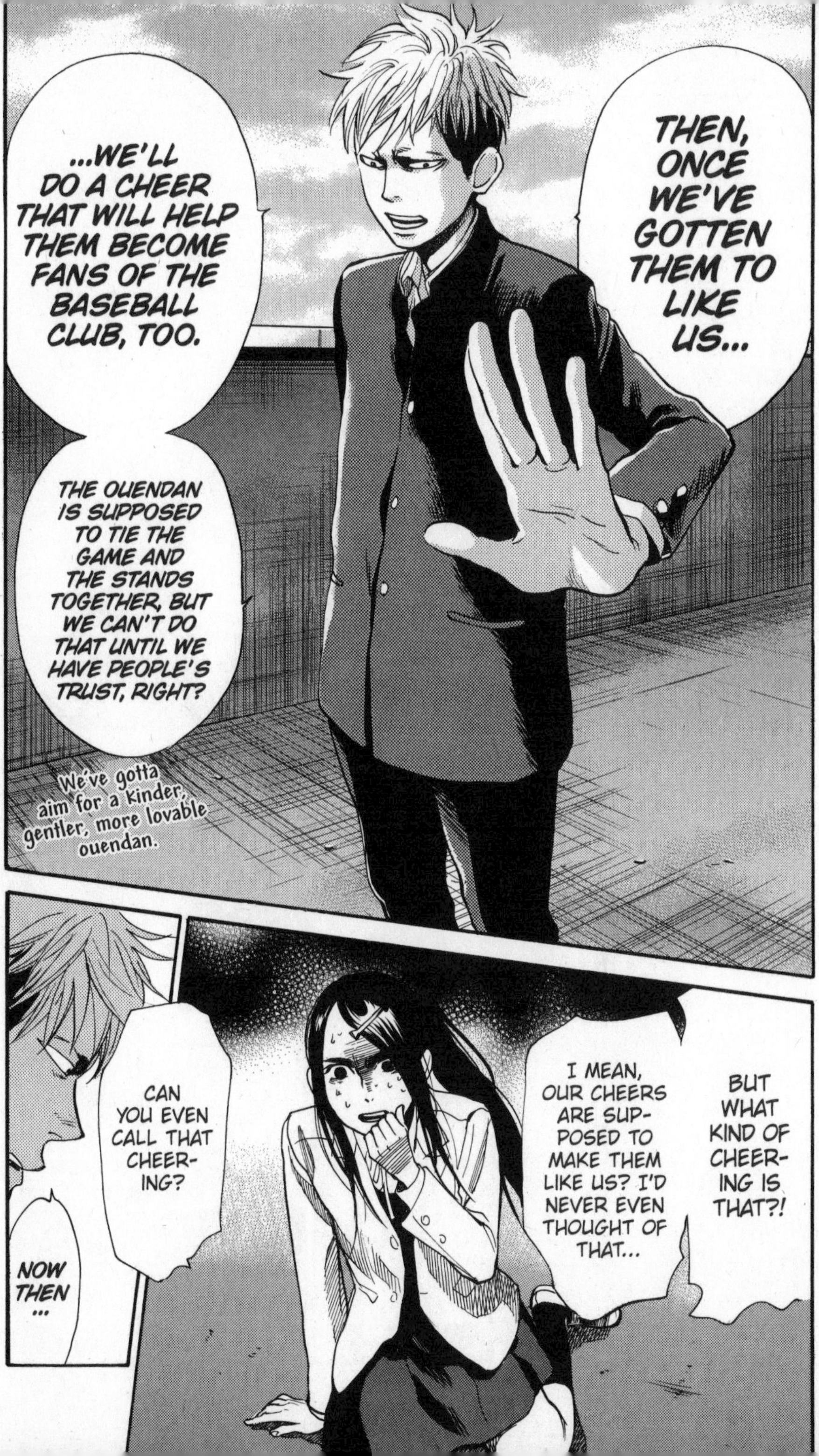
THEN, ONCE WE'VE GOTTEN THEM TO LIKE US...
...WE'LL DO A CHEER THAT WILL HELP THEM BECOME FANS OF THE BASEBALL CLUB, TOO.
THE OUENDAN IS SUPPOSED TO TIE THE GAME AND THE STANDS TOGETHER, BUT WE CAN'T DO THAT UNTIL WE HAVE PEOPLE'S TRUST, RIGHT?
We've gotta aim for a kinder, gentler, more lovable ouendan.
BUT WHAT KIND OF CHEERING IS THAT?!
I MEAN, OUR CHEERS ARE SUPPOSED TO MAKE THEM LIKE US? I'D NEVER EVEN THOUGHT OF THAT...
CAN YOU EVEN CALL THAT CHEERING?
NOW THEN...

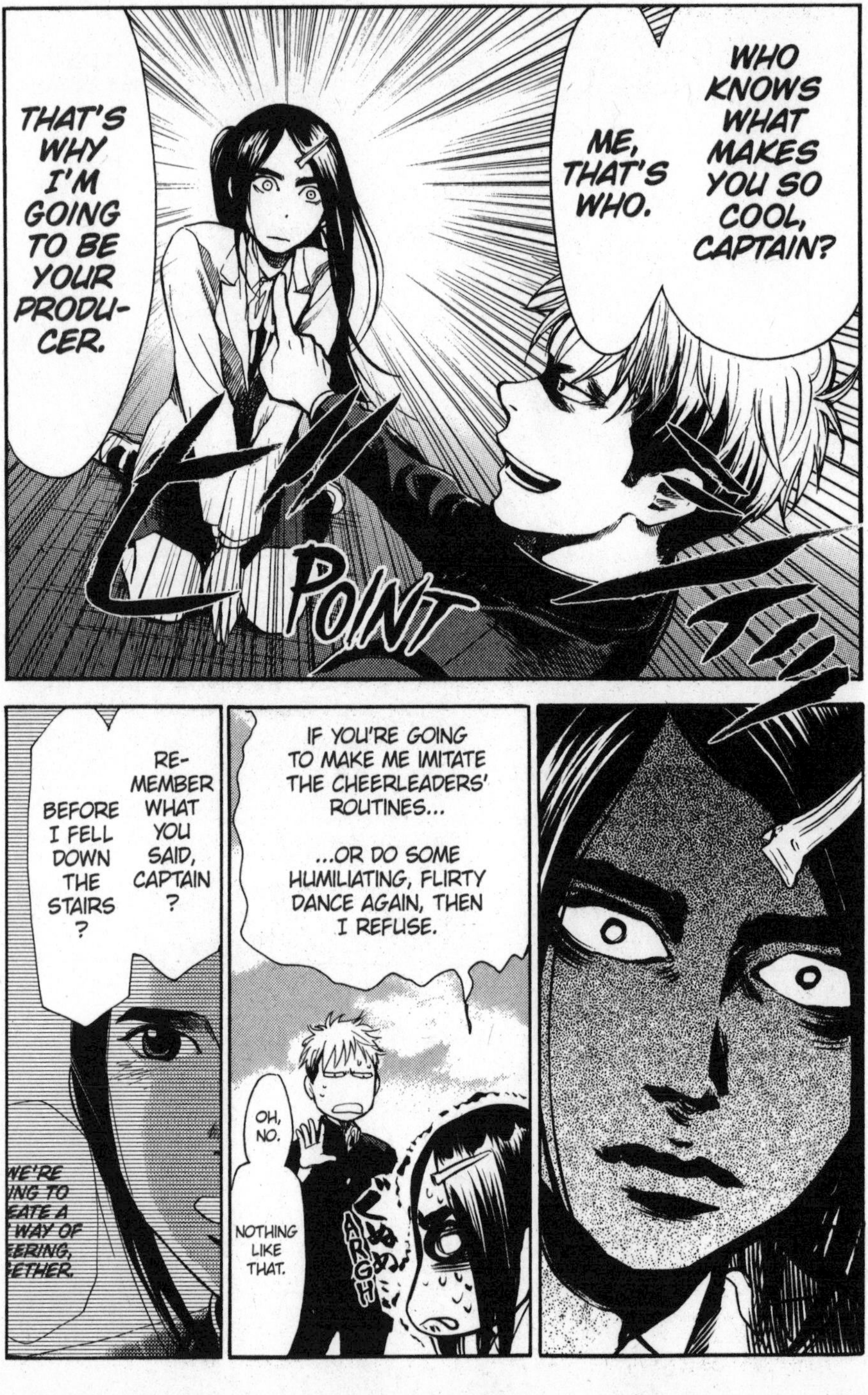
WHO KNOWS WHAT MAKES YOU SO COOL, CAPTAIN?
ME, THAT'S WHO.
THAT'S WHY I'M GOING TO BE YOUR PRODU-CER.
POINT
IF YOU'RE GOING TO MAKE ME IMITATE THE CHEERLEADERS' ROUTINES...
...OR DO SOME HUMILIATING, FLIRTY DANCE AGAIN, THEN I REFUSE.
OH, NO.
ARGH
NOTHING LIKE THAT.
RE-MEMBER WHAT YOU SAID, CAPTAIN?
BEFORE I FELL DOWN THE STAIRS?
E'RE ING TO EATE A WAY OF EERING, GETHER.

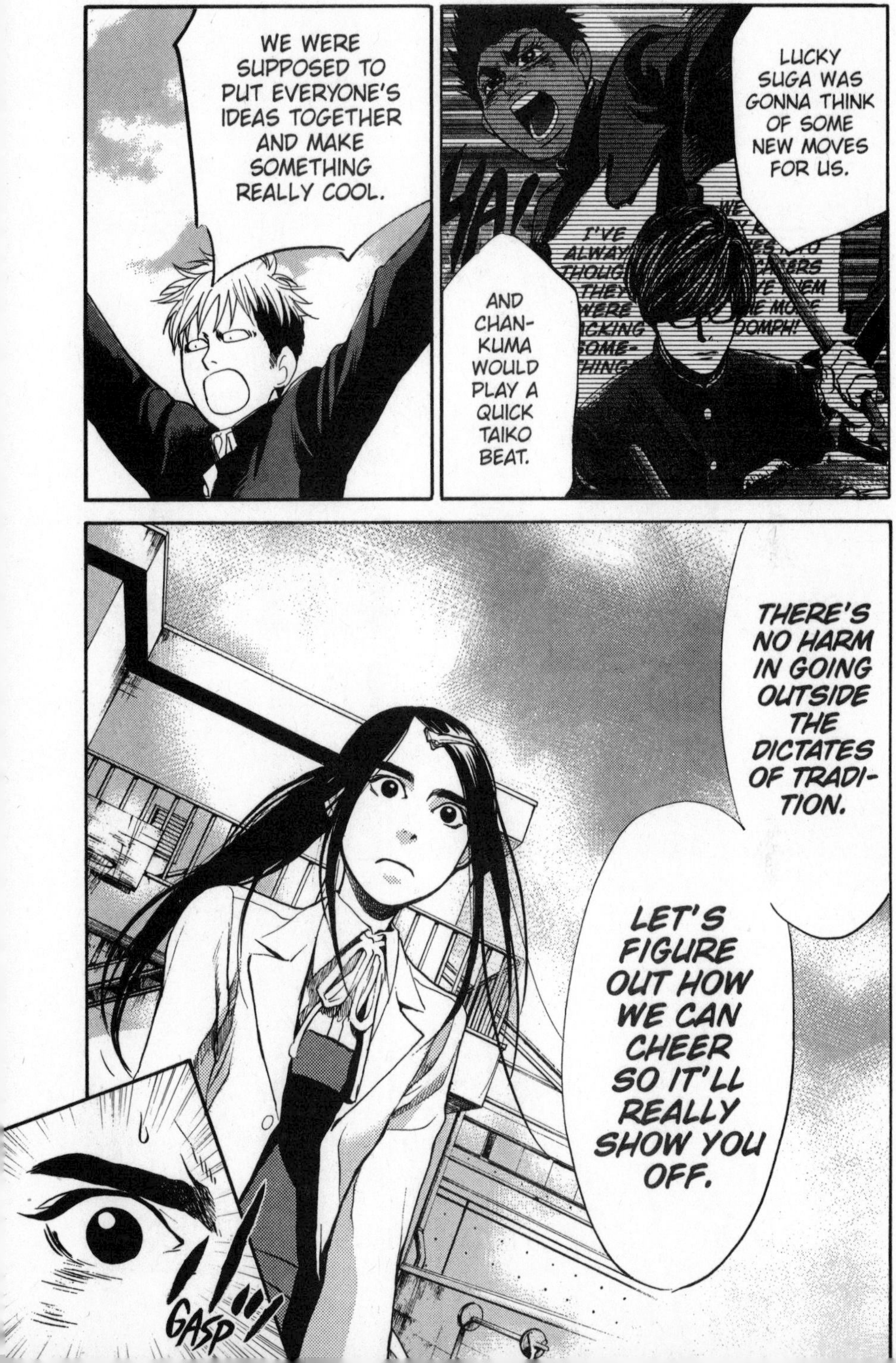
LUCKY SUGA WAS GONNA THINK OF SOME NEW MOVES FOR US.
AND CHAN-KUMA WOULD PLAY A QUICK TAIKO BEAT.
WE WERE SUPPOSED TO PUT EVERYONE'S IDEAS TOGETHER AND MAKE SOMETHING REALLY COOL.
THERE'S NO HARM IN GOING OUTSIDE THE DICTATES OF TRADITION.
LET'S FIGURE OUT HOW WE CAN CHEER SO IT'LL REALLY SHOW YOU OFF.
GASP

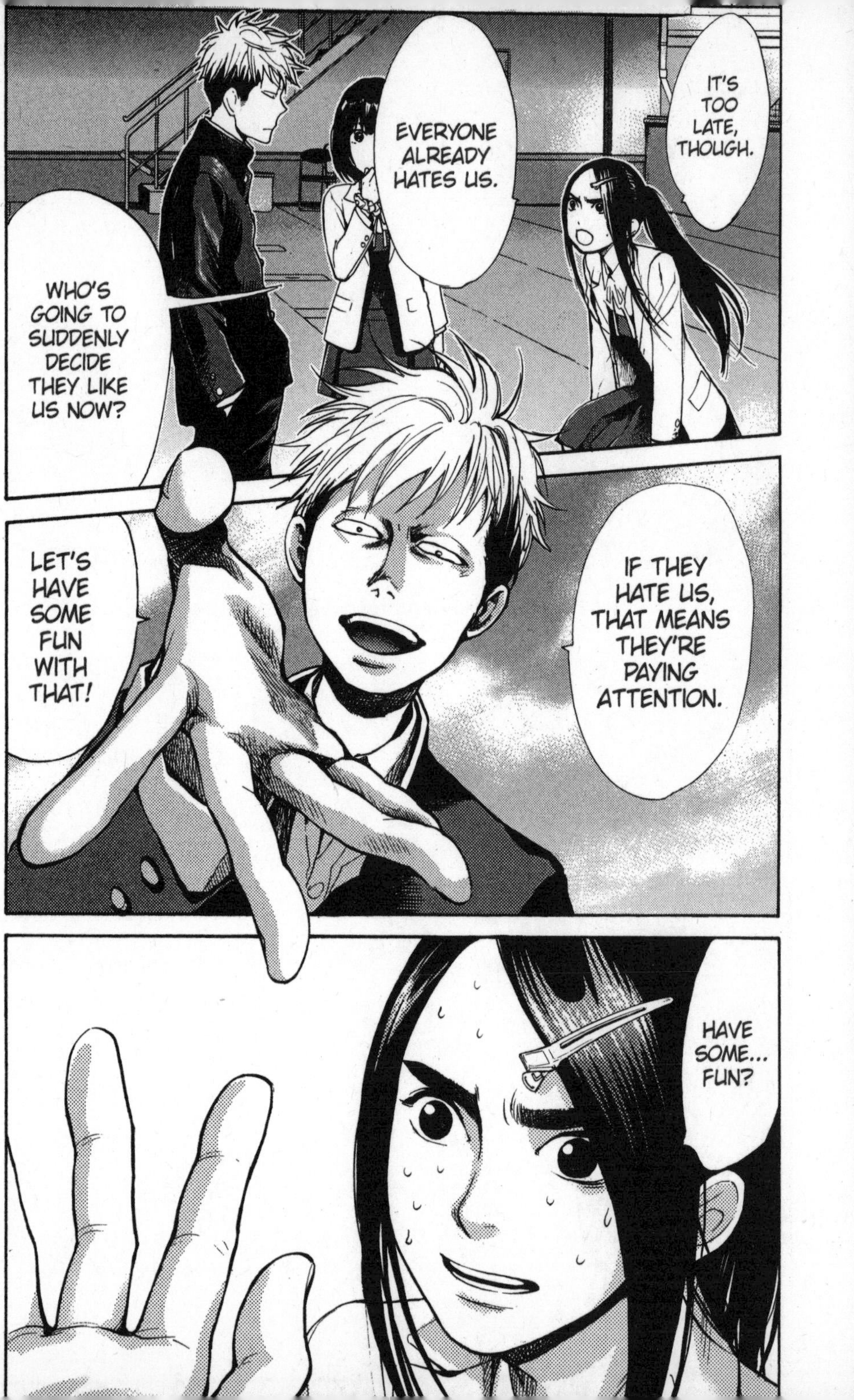
IT'S TOO LATE, THOUGH.
EVERYONE ALREADY HATES US.
WHO'S GOING TO SUDDENLY DECIDE THEY LIKE US NOW?
IF THEY HATE US, THAT MEANS THEY'RE PAYING ATTENTION.
LET'S HAVE SOME FUN WITH THAT!
HAVE SOME... FUN?

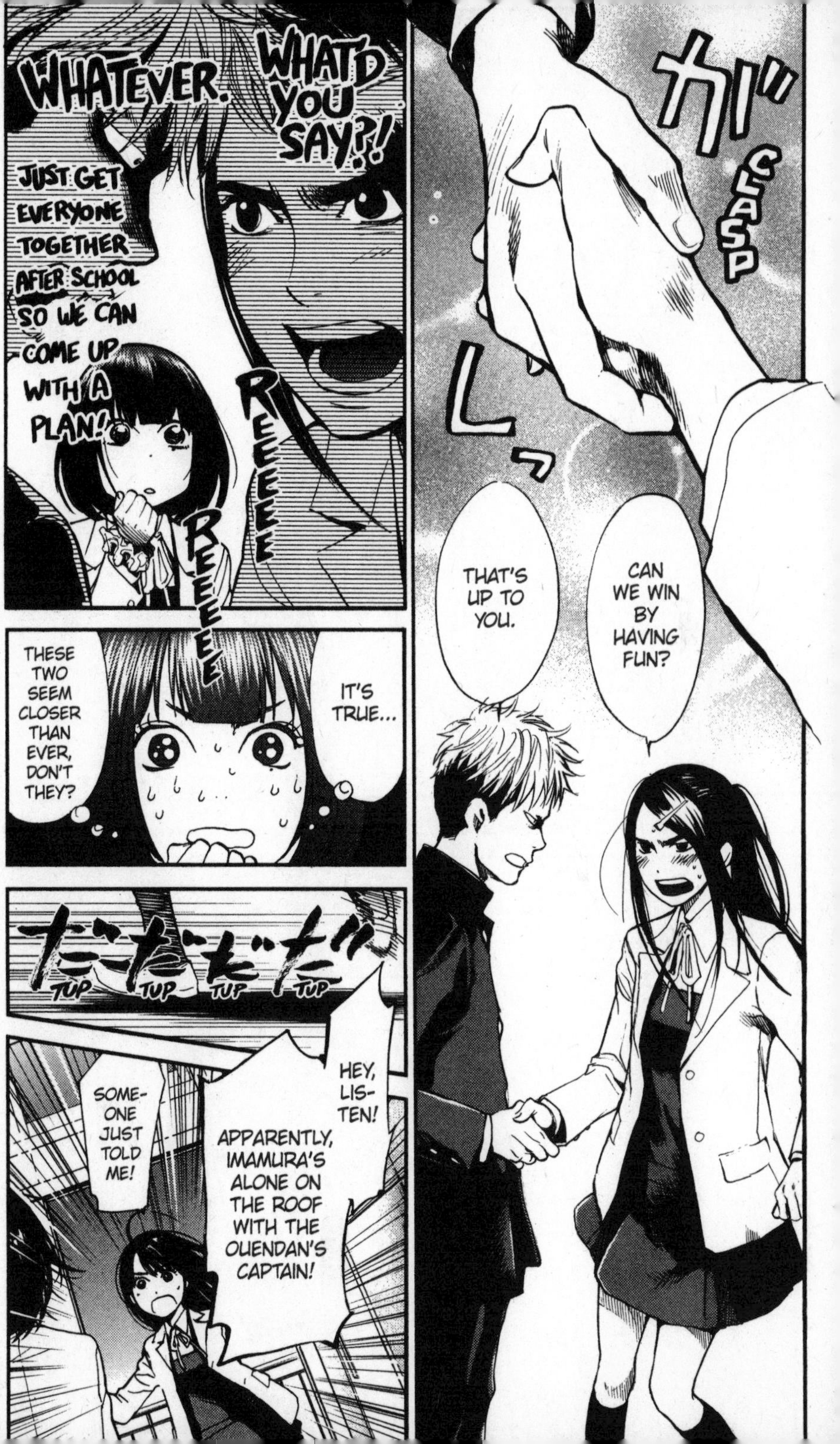
CLASP
CAN WE WIN BY HAVING FUN?
THAT'S UP TO YOU.
WHAT'D YOU SAY?!
WHATEVER.
JUST GET EVERYONE TOGETHER AFTER SCHOOL SO WE CAN COME UP WITH A PLAN!
REEEEEE
REEEEEE
IT'S TRUE...
THESE TWO SEEM CLOSER THAN EVER, DON'T THEY?
TUP TUP TUP TUP
HEY, LIS-TEN!
SOME-ONE JUST TOLD ME!
APPARENTLY, IMAMURA'S ALONE ON THE ROOF WITH THE OUENDAN'S CAPTAIN!

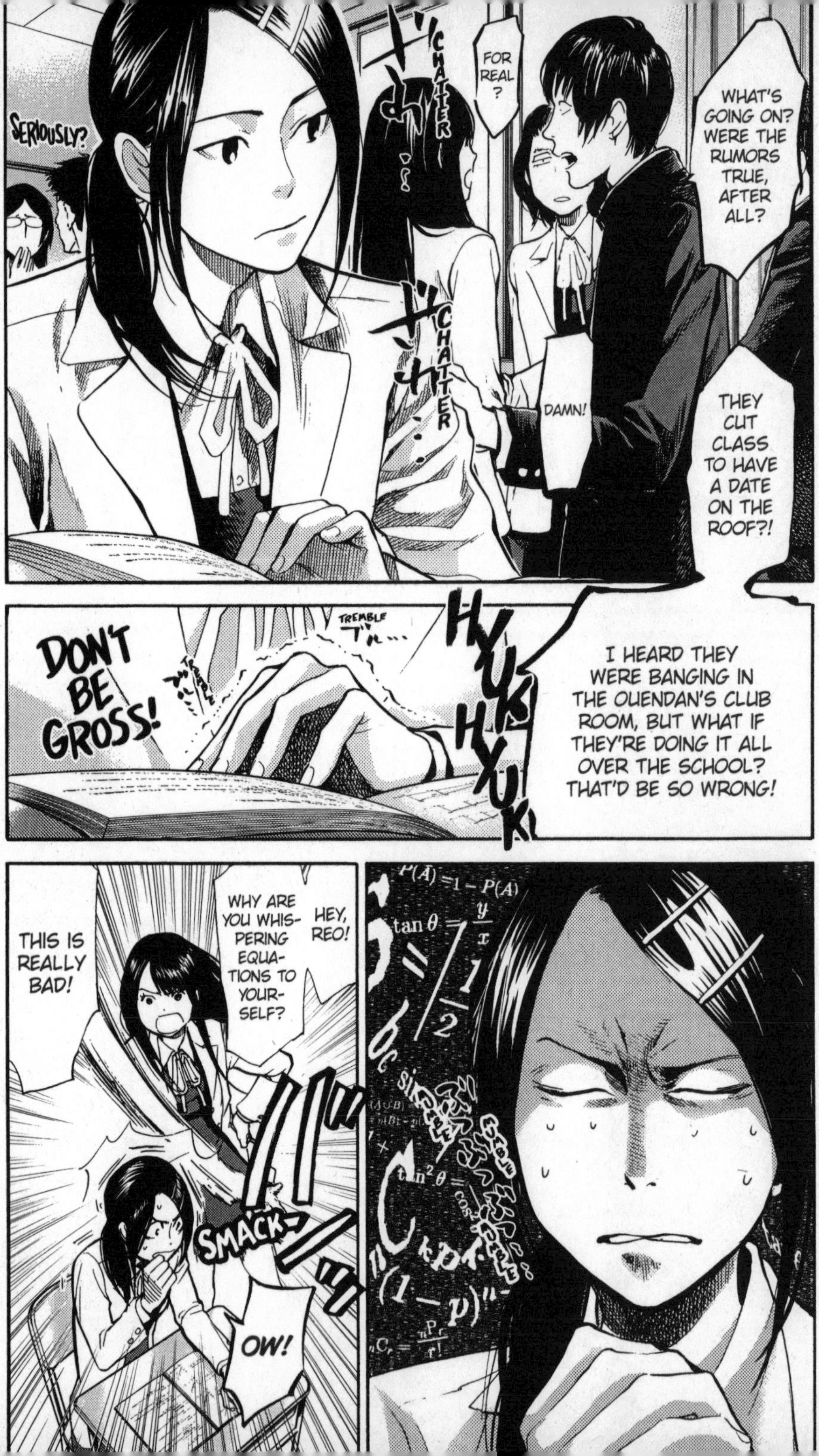

WHAT'S GOING ON? WERE THE RUMORS TRUE, AFTER ALL?
FOR REAL?
CHATTER
CHATTER
THEY CUT CLASS TO HAVE A DATE ON THE ROOF?!
DAMN!
SERIOUSLY?
I HEARD THEY WERE BANGING IN THE OUENDAN'S CLUB ROOM, BUT WHAT IF THEY'RE DOING IT ALL OVER THE SCHOOL? THAT'D BE SO WRONG!
HYUK HYUK HYUK
TREMBLE
TREMBLE
DON'T BE GROSS!
P(Ā) = 1 − P(A)
tan θ = y/x
HEY, REO!
WHY ARE YOU WHISPERING EQUATIONS TO YOURSELF?
THIS IS REALLY BAD!
SMACK
OW!

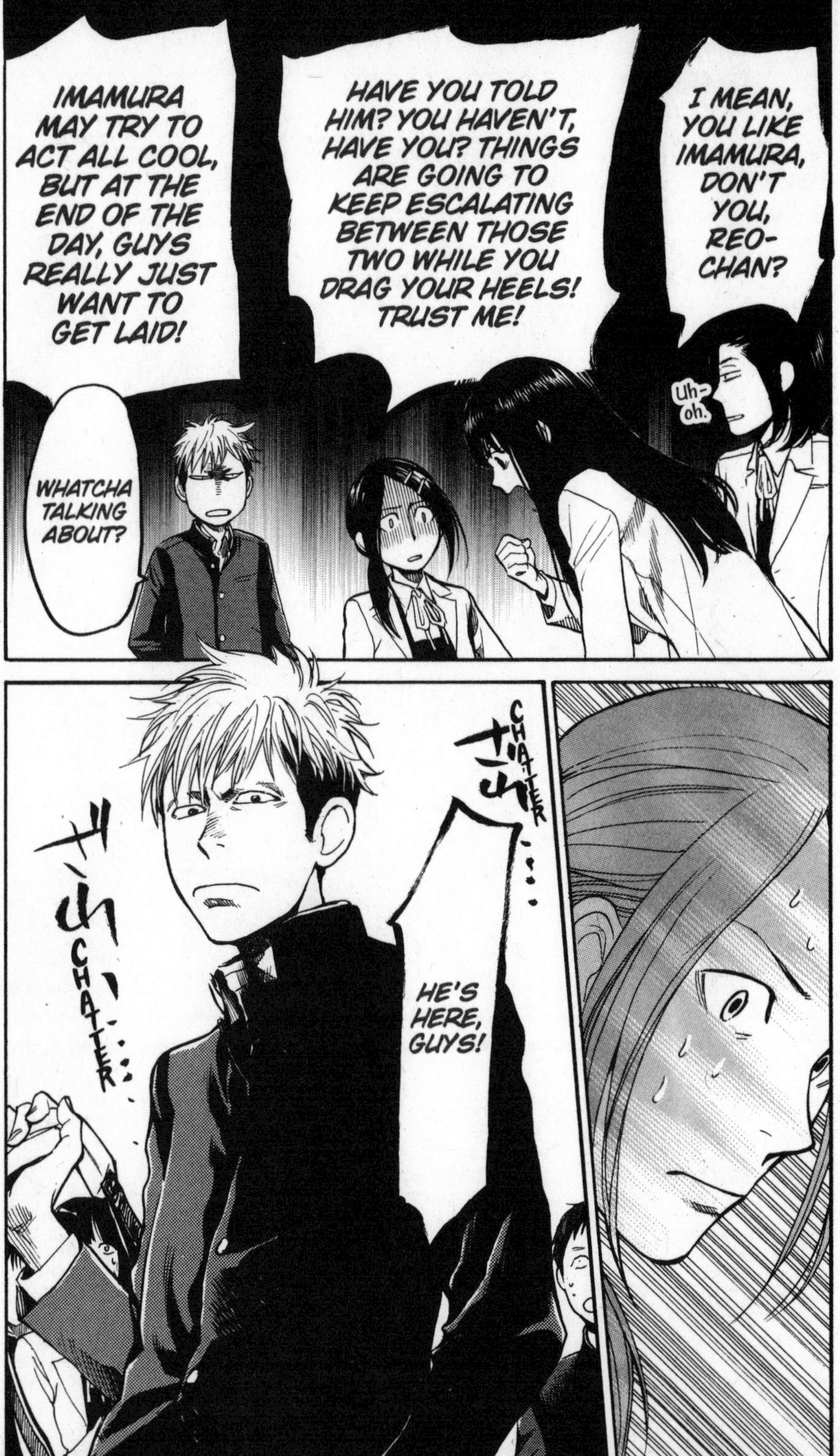
I MEAN, YOU LIKE IMAMURA, DON'T YOU, REO-CHAN?
HAVE YOU TOLD HIM? YOU HAVEN'T, HAVE YOU? THINGS ARE GOING TO KEEP ESCALATING BETWEEN THOSE TWO WHILE YOU DRAG YOUR HEELS! TRUST ME!
IMAMURA MAY TRY TO ACT ALL COOL, BUT AT THE END OF THE DAY, GUYS REALLY JUST WANT TO GET LAID!
Uh-oh.
WHATCHA TALKING ABOUT?
CHATTER
HE'S HERE, GUYS!
CHATTER

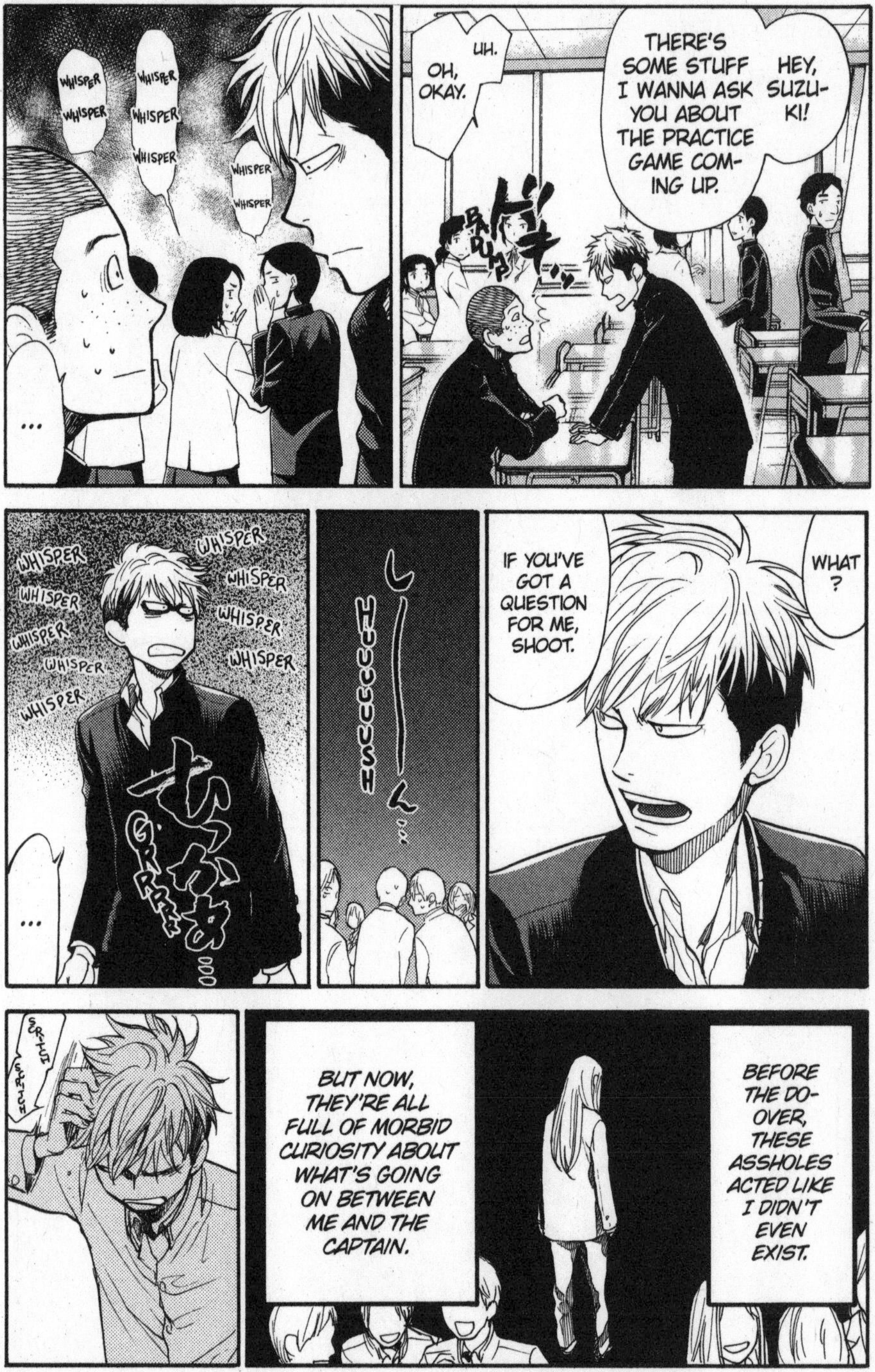
HEY, SUZUKI!
THERE'S SOME STUFF I WANNA ASK YOU ABOUT THE PRACTICE GAME COMING UP.
BA-DUMP
UH. OH, OKAY.
WHISPER WHISPER
WHISPER WHISPER WHISPER
WHISPER WHISPER
...
WHAT?
IF YOU'VE GOT A QUESTION FOR ME, SHOOT.
HUUUUUUSH
WHISPER WHISPER WHISPER WHISPER WHISPER WHISPER WHISPER WHISPER WHISPER
GRRRR
...
BEFORE THE DO-OVER, THESE ASSHOLES ACTED LIKE I DIDN'T EVEN EXIST.
BUT NOW, THEY'RE ALL FULL OF MORBID CURIOSITY ABOUT WHAT'S GOING ON BETWEEN ME AND THE CAPTAIN.
SCRITCH SCRITCH

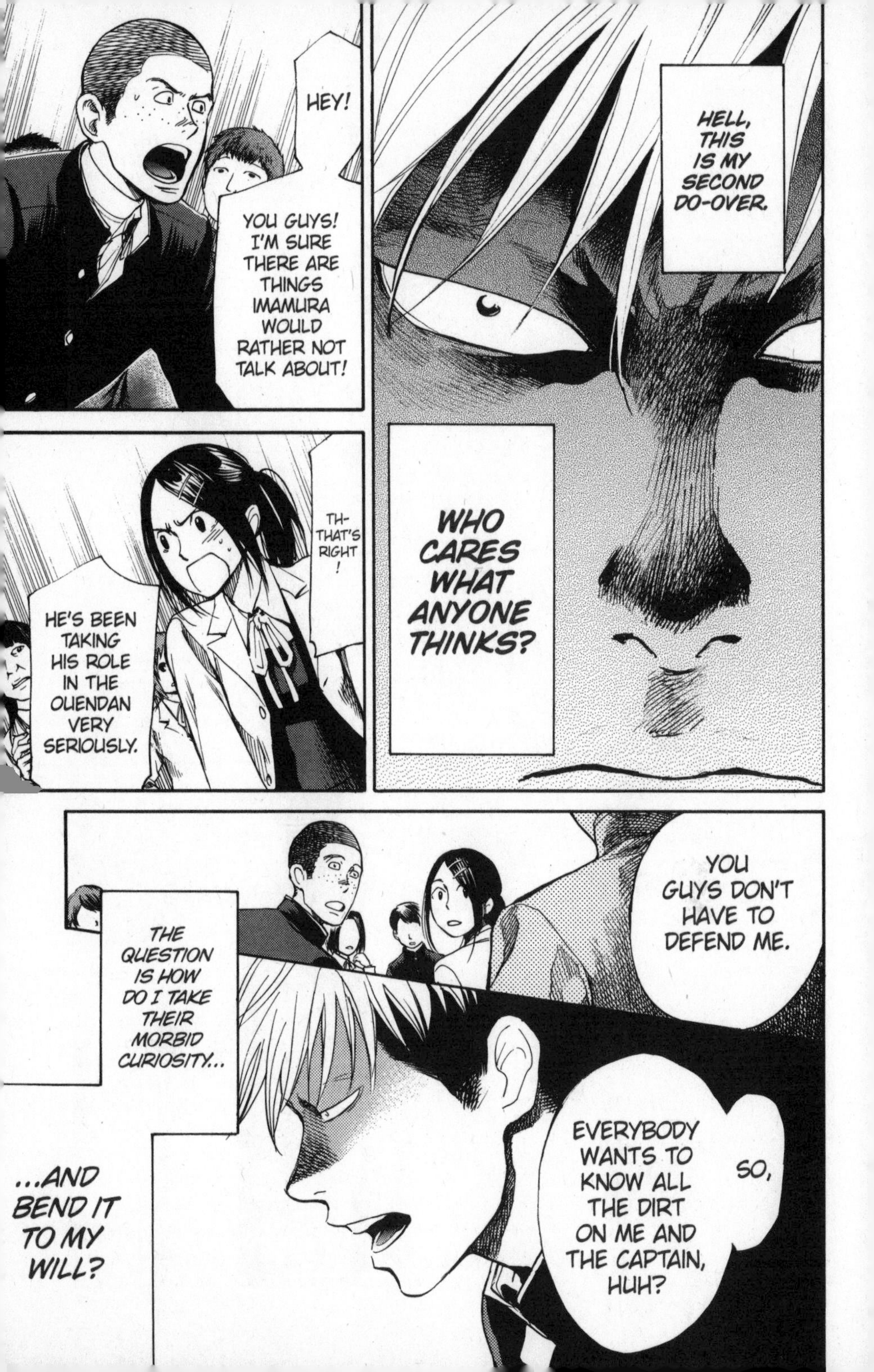
HELL, THIS IS MY SECOND DO-OVER.
WHO CARES WHAT ANYONE THINKS?
HEY!
YOU GUYS! I'M SURE THERE ARE THINGS IMAMURA WOULD RATHER NOT TALK ABOUT!
TH-THAT'S RIGHT!
HE'S BEEN TAKING HIS ROLE IN THE OUENDAN VERY SERIOUSLY.
YOU GUYS DON'T HAVE TO DEFEND ME.
SO,
EVERYBODY WANTS TO KNOW ALL THE DIRT ON ME AND THE CAPTAIN, HUH?
THE QUESTION IS HOW DO I TAKE THEIR MORBID CURIOSITY...
...AND BEND IT TO MY WILL?

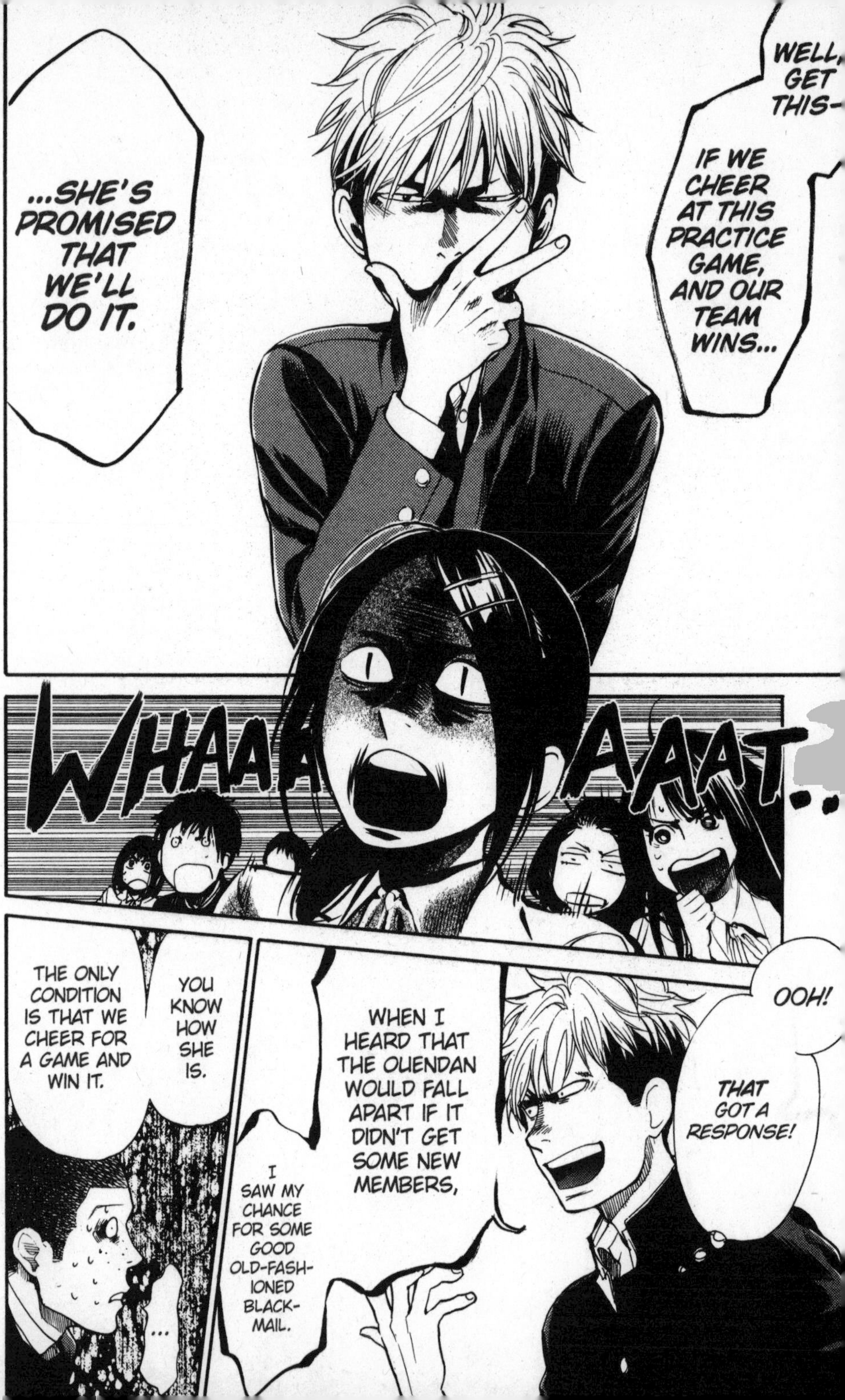
WELL, GET THIS-
IF WE CHEER AT THIS PRACTICE GAME, AND OUR TEAM WINS...
...SHE'S PROMISED THAT WE'LL DO IT.
WHAAA AAAT..
OOH!
THAT GOT A RESPONSE!
WHEN I HEARD THAT THE OUENDAN WOULD FALL APART IF IT DIDN'T GET SOME NEW MEMBERS,
I SAW MY CHANCE FOR SOME GOOD OLD-FASHIONED BLACKMAIL.
YOU KNOW HOW SHE IS.
THE ONLY CONDITION IS THAT WE CHEER FOR A GAME AND WIN IT.
...

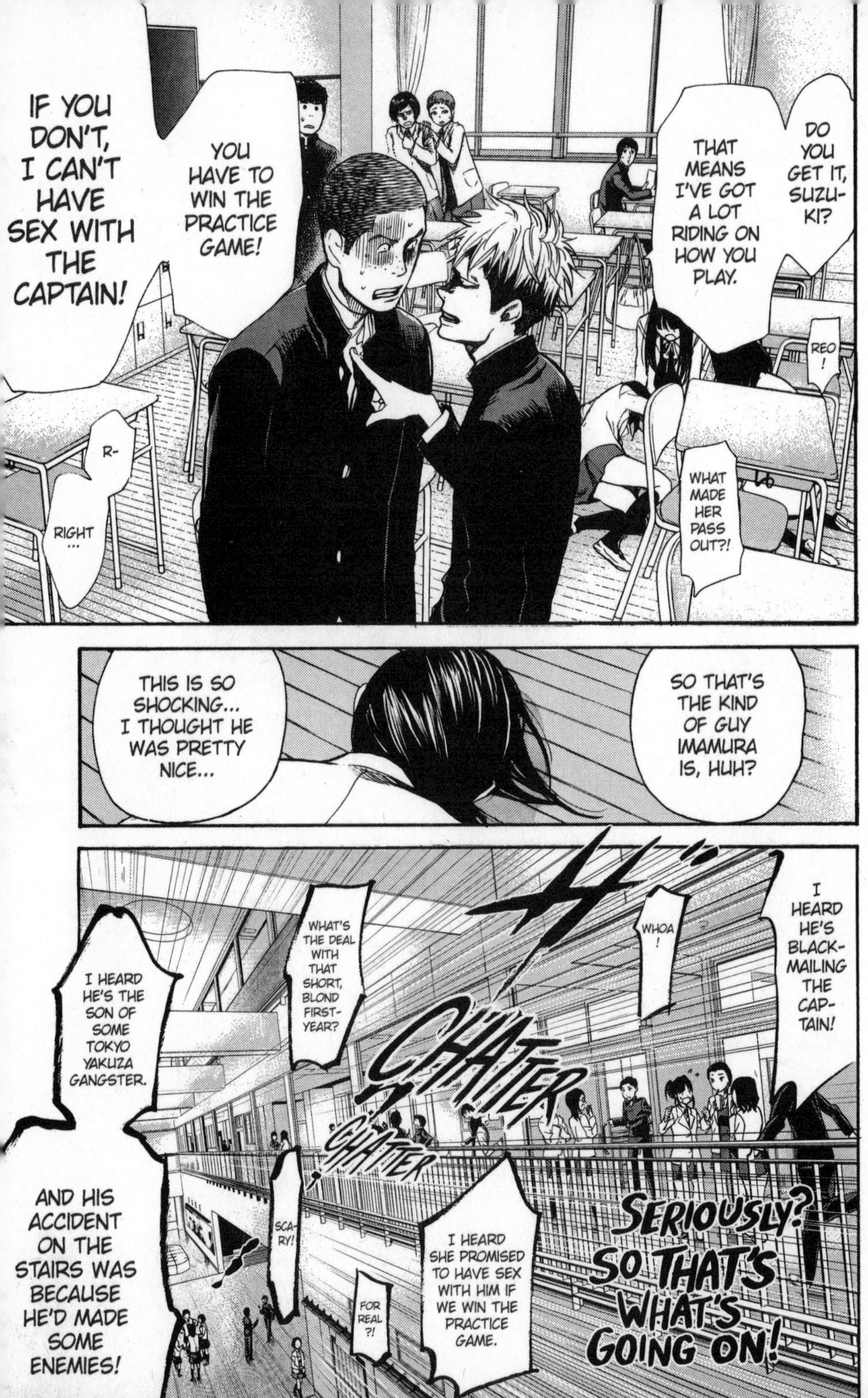
DO YOU GET IT, SUZUKI?
THAT MEANS I'VE GOT A LOT RIDING ON HOW YOU PLAY.
YOU HAVE TO WIN THE PRACTICE GAME!
IF YOU DON'T, I CAN'T HAVE SEX WITH THE CAPTAIN!
REO!
WHAT MADE HER PASS OUT?!
R-
RIGHT...
SO THAT'S THE KIND OF GUY IMAMURA IS, HUH?
THIS IS SO SHOCKING... I THOUGHT HE WAS PRETTY NICE...
I HEARD HE'S BLACKMAILING THE CAPTAIN!
WHOA!
WHAT'S THE DEAL WITH THAT SHORT, BLOND FIRST-YEAR?
I HEARD HE'S THE SON OF SOME TOKYO YAKUZA GANGSTER.
CHATTER
CHATTER
SERIOUSLY? SO THAT'S WHAT'S GOING ON!
I HEARD SHE PROMISED TO HAVE SEX WITH HIM IF WE WIN THE PRACTICE GAME.
FOR REAL?!
SCARY!
AND HIS ACCIDENT ON THE STAIRS WAS BECAUSE HE'D MADE SOME ENEMIES!

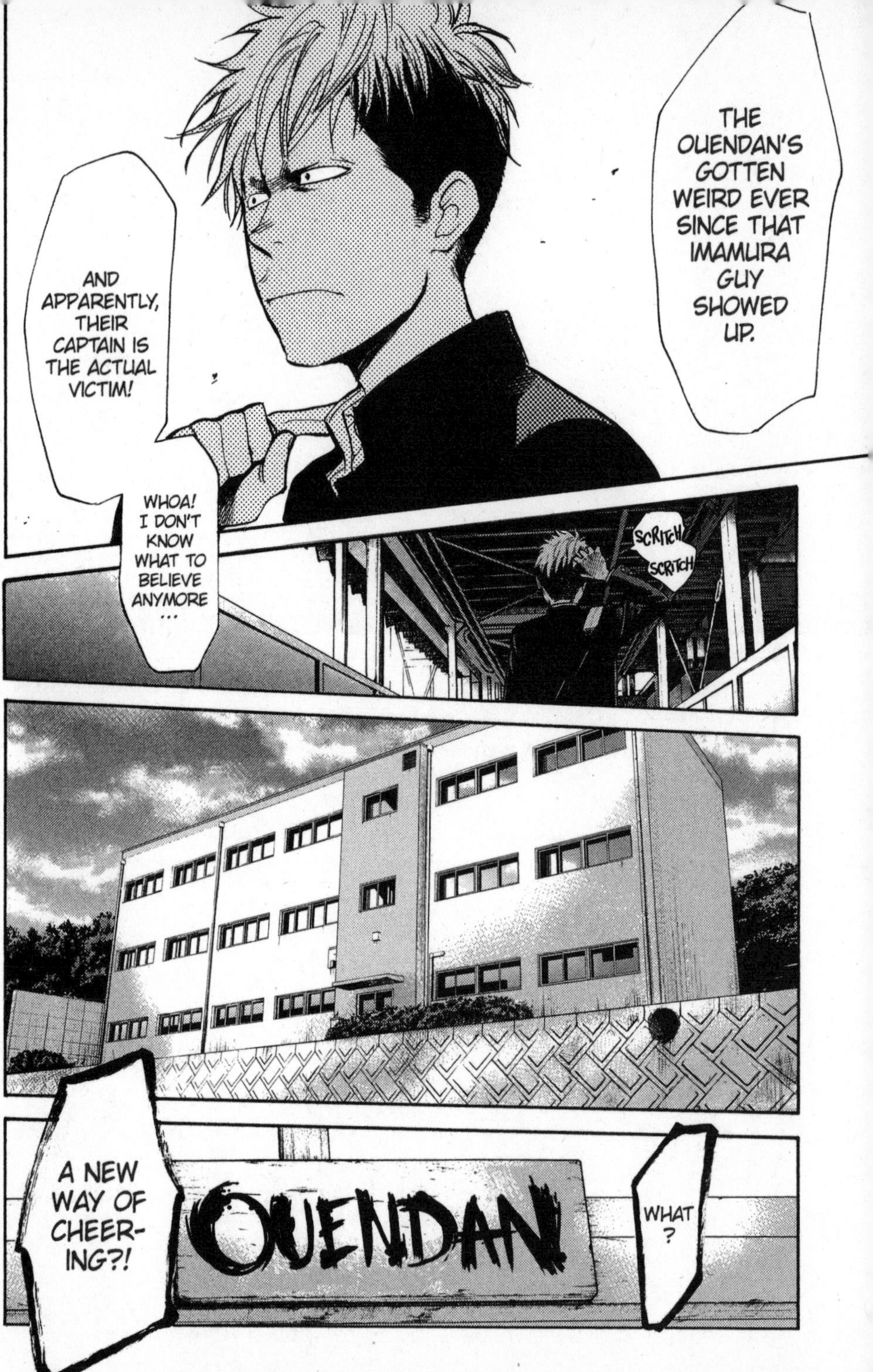
THE OUENDAN'S GOTTEN WEIRD EVER SINCE THAT IMAMURA GUY SHOWED UP.
AND APPARENTLY, THEIR CAPTAIN IS THE ACTUAL VICTIM!
SCRITCH SCRITCH
WHOA! I DON'T KNOW WHAT TO BELIEVE ANYMORE ...
WHAT?
OUENDAN
A NEW WAY OF CHEER-ING?!

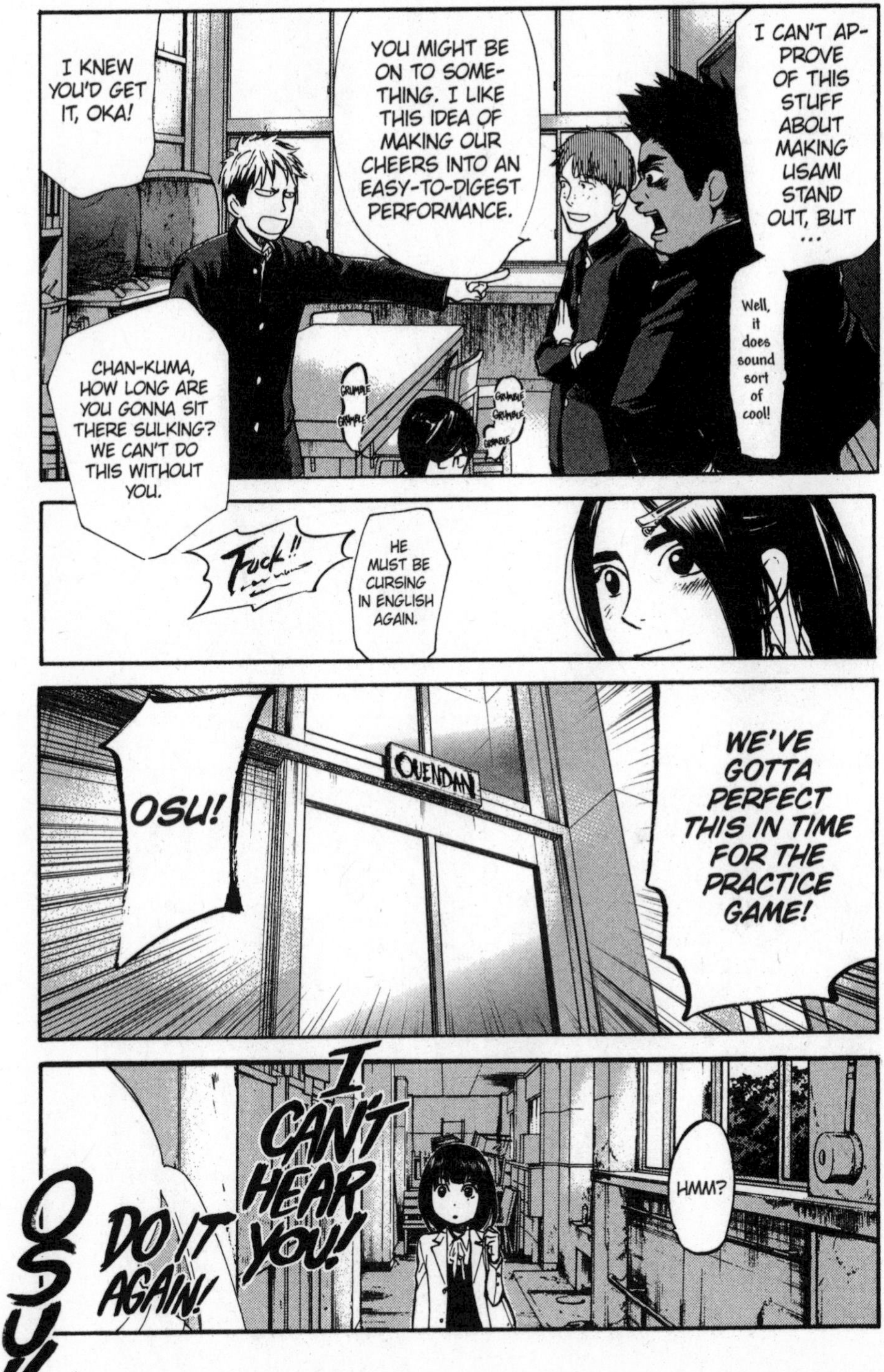
I CAN'T APPROVE OF THIS STUFF ABOUT MAKING USAMI STAND OUT, BUT ...
Well, it does sound sort of cool!
YOU MIGHT BE ON TO SOMETHING. I LIKE THIS IDEA OF MAKING OUR CHEERS INTO AN EASY-TO-DIGEST PERFORMANCE.
I KNEW YOU'D GET IT, OKA!
CHAN-KUMA, HOW LONG ARE YOU GONNA SIT THERE SULKING? WE CAN'T DO THIS WITHOUT YOU.
GRUMBLE GRUMBLE
GRUMBLE GRUMBLE GRUMBLE
Fuck!!
HE MUST BE CURSING IN ENGLISH AGAIN.
OUENDAN
WE'VE GOTTA PERFECT THIS IN TIME FOR THE PRACTICE GAME!
OSU!
HMM?
I CAN'T HEAR YOU!
DO IT AGAIN!
OSU!!

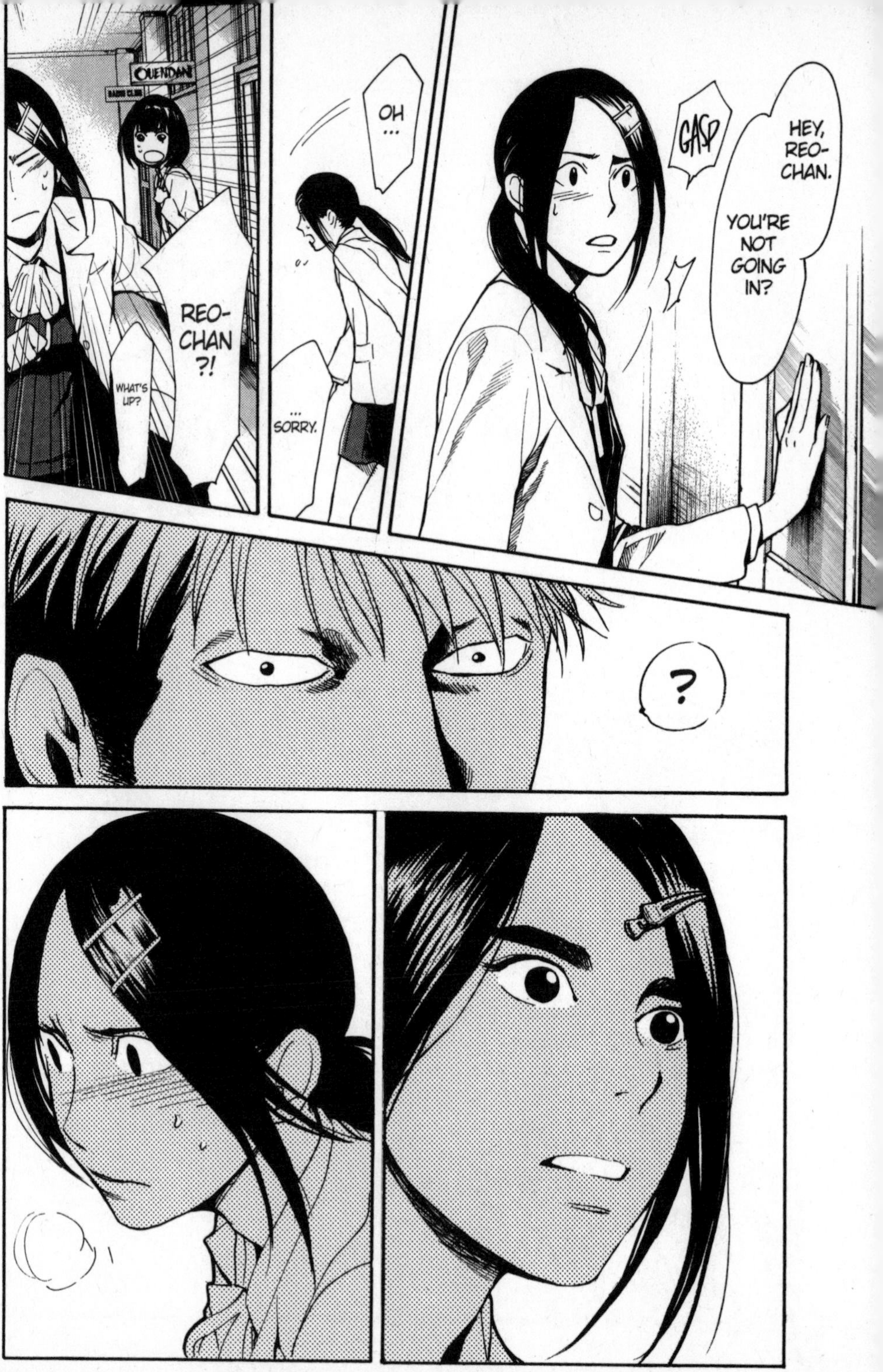
HEY, REO-CHAN.
YOU'RE NOT GOING IN?
GASP
OH ...
... SORRY.
OUENDAN
REO-CHAN ?!
WHAT'S UP?
?

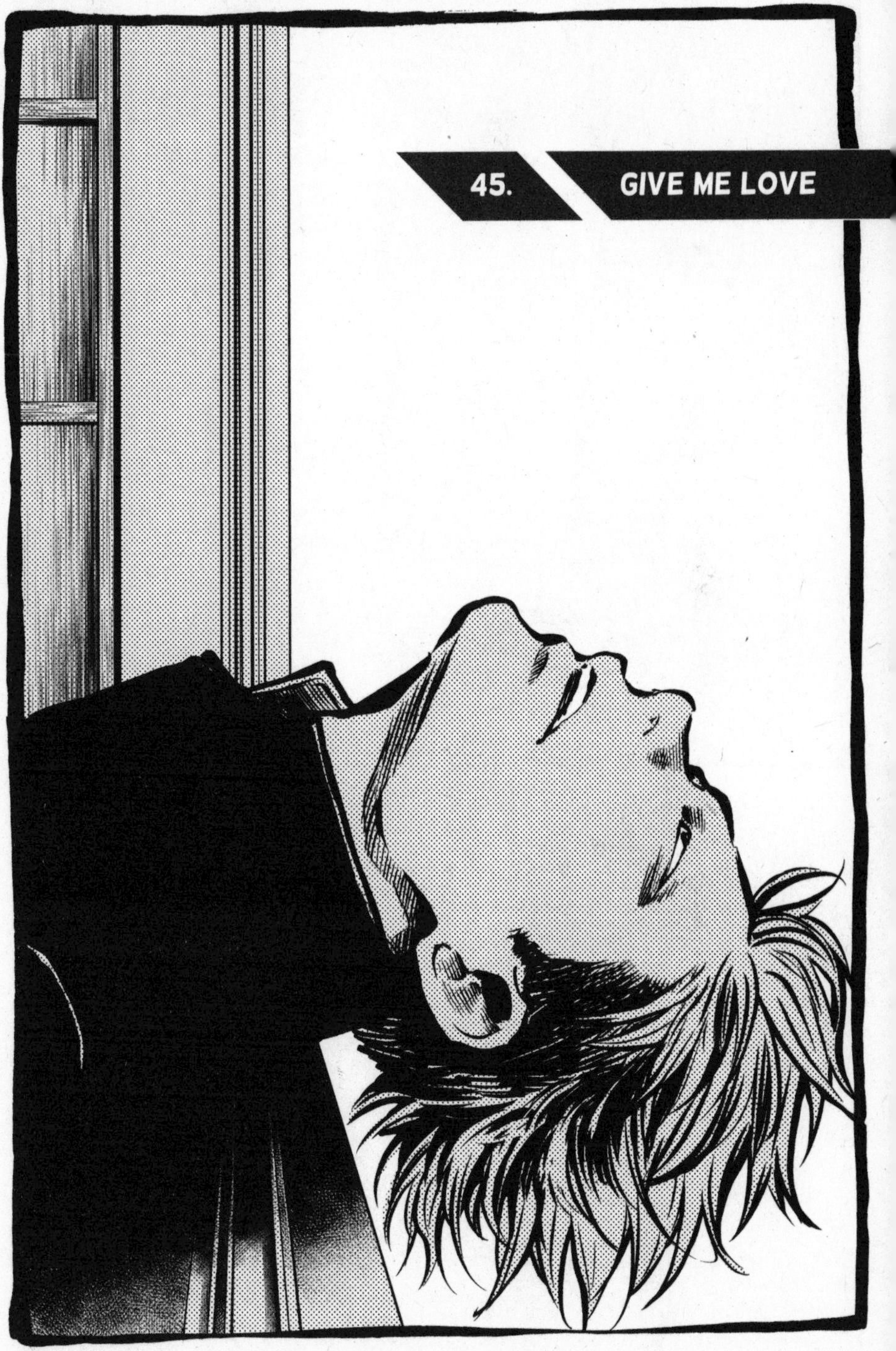
45.
GIVE ME LOVE

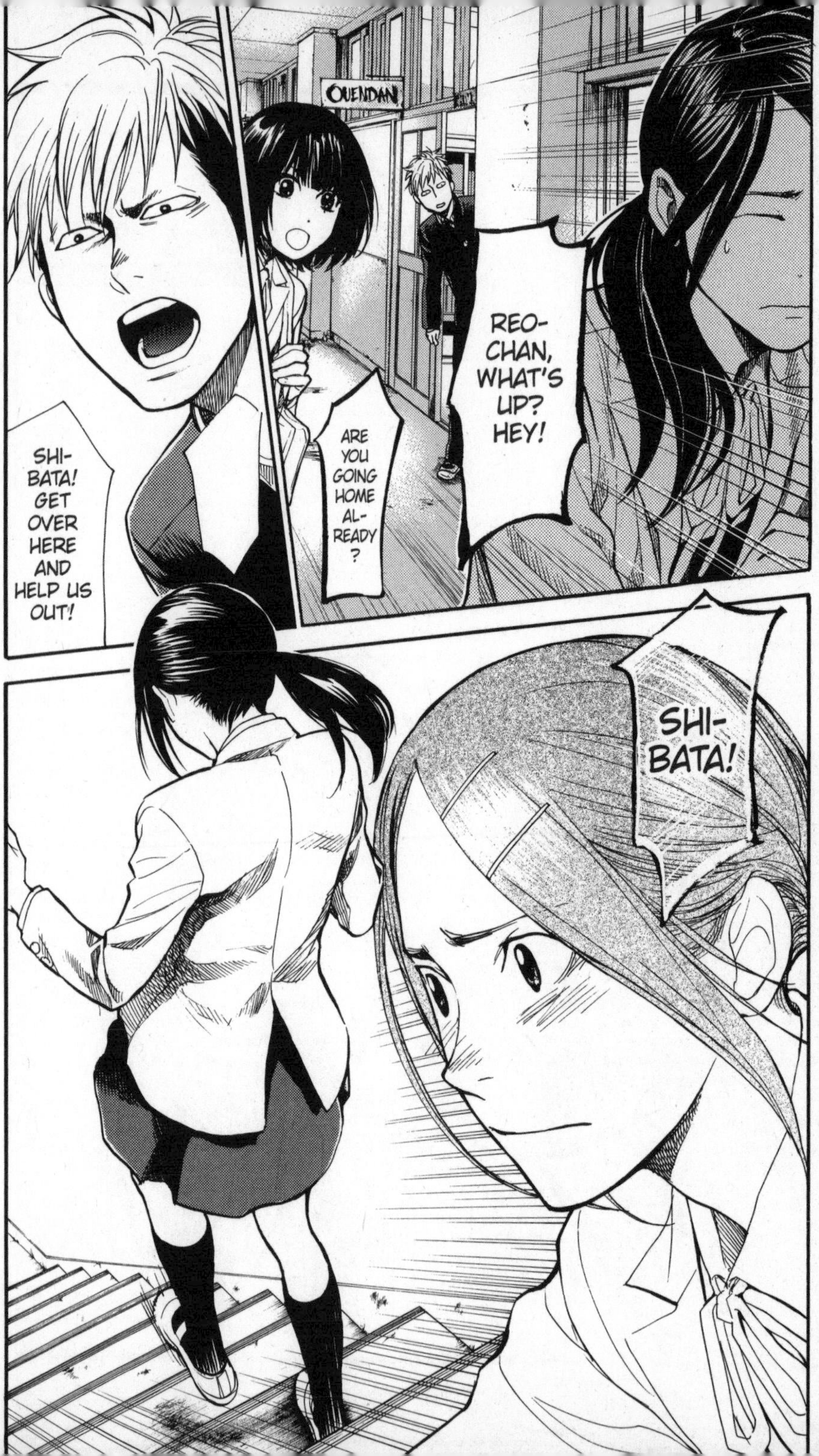
OUENDAN
REO-CHAN, WHAT'S UP? HEY!
ARE YOU GOING HOME AL-READY?
SHI-BATA! GET OVER HERE AND HELP US OUT!
SHI-BATA!

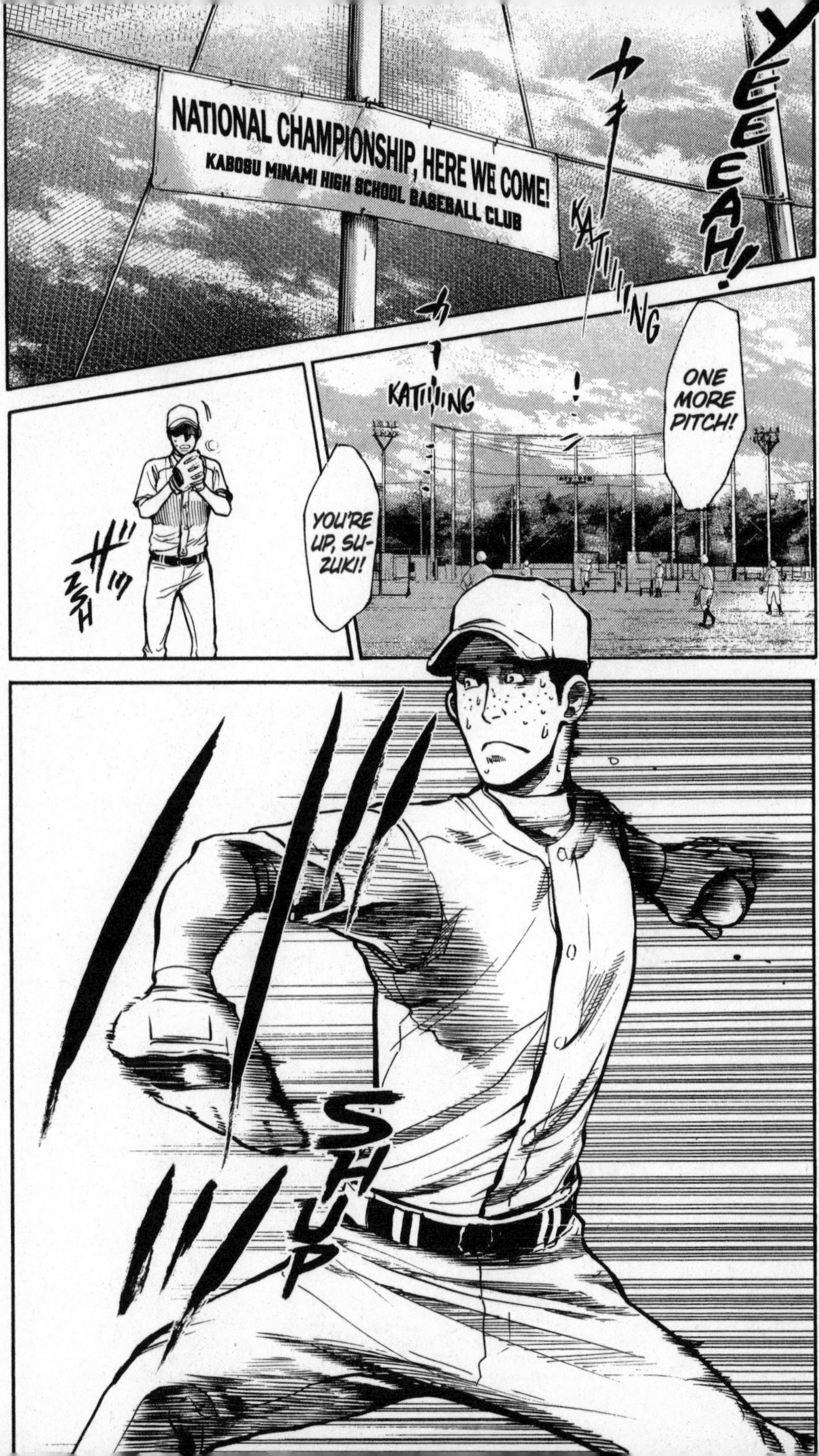
NATIONAL CHAMPIONSHIP, HERE WE COME!
KABOSU MINAMI HIGH SCHOOL BASEBALL CLUB
YEEEEAH!
KATIIIING
ONE MORE PITCH!
KATIIIING
YOU'RE UP, SU-ZUKI!
ZSH
SHUP

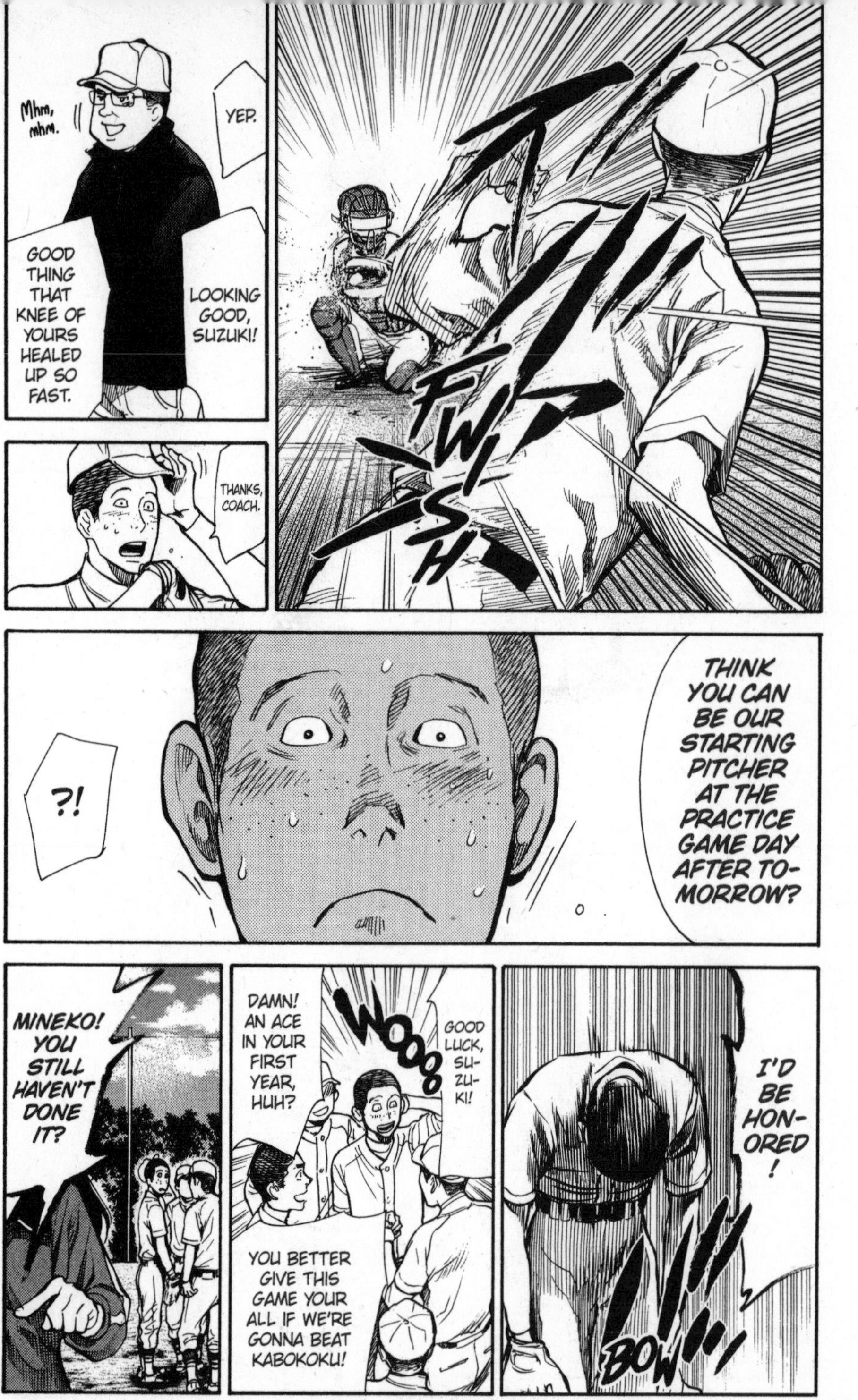
FWISH
YEP.
Mhm, mhm.
LOOKING GOOD, SUZUKI!
GOOD THING THAT KNEE OF YOURS HEALED UP SO FAST.
THANKS, COACH.
THINK YOU CAN BE OUR STARTING PITCHER AT THE PRACTICE GAME DAY AFTER TO-MORROW?
?!
I'D BE HON-ORED!
BOW!!!
GOOD LUCK, SU-ZU-KI!
WOOO
DAMN! AN ACE IN YOUR FIRST YEAR, HUH?
YOU BETTER GIVE THIS GAME YOUR ALL IF WE'RE GONNA BEAT KABOKOKU!
MINEKO! YOU STILL HAVEN'T DONE IT?

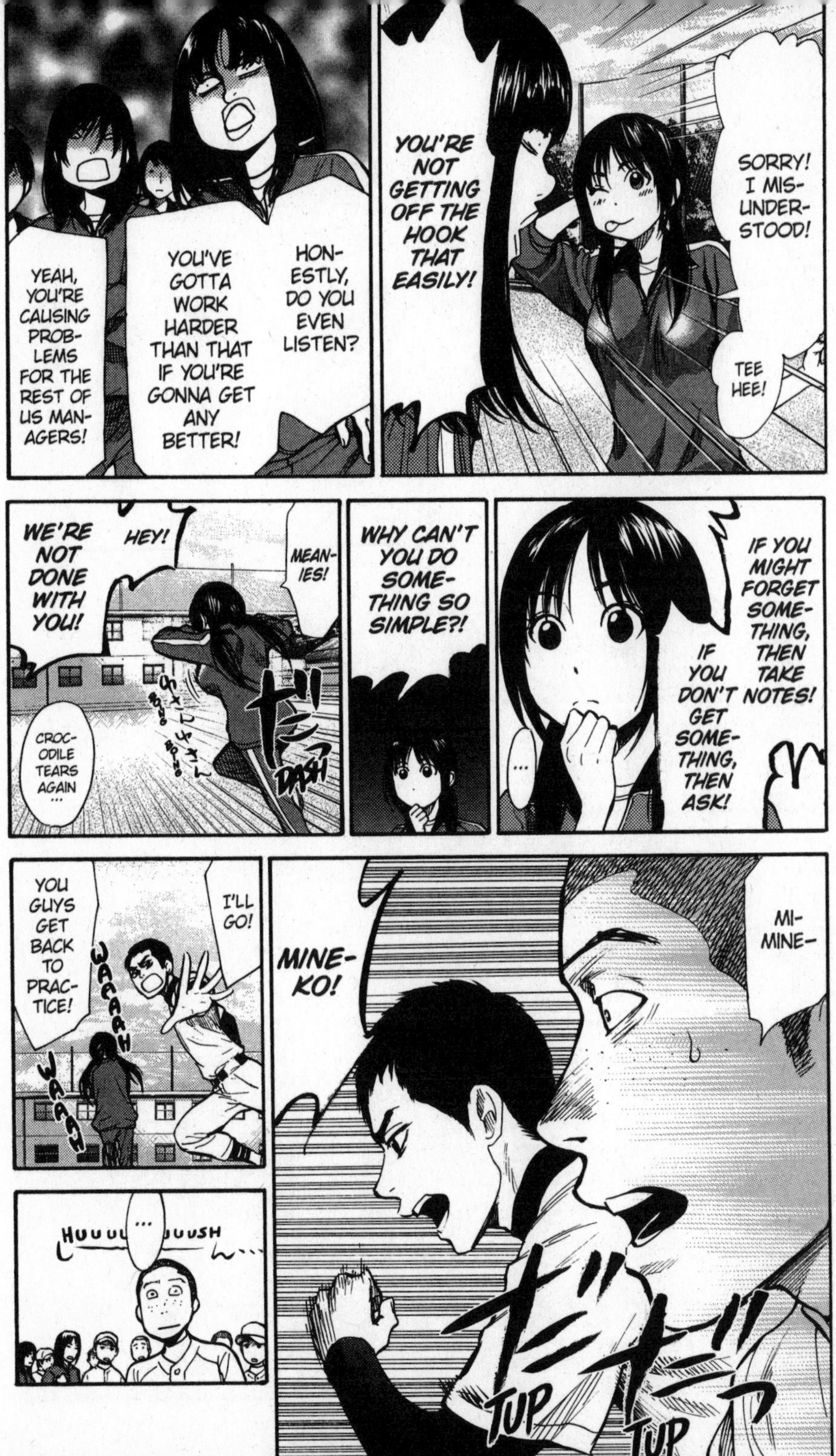
SORRY! I MISUNDERSTOOD!
TEE HEE!
YOU'RE NOT GETTING OFF THE HOOK THAT EASILY!
HONESTLY, DO YOU EVEN LISTEN?
YOU'VE GOTTA WORK HARDER THAN THAT IF YOU'RE GONNA GET ANY BETTER!
YEAH, YOU'RE CAUSING PROBLEMS FOR THE REST OF US MANAGERS!
IF YOU MIGHT FORGET SOMETHING, THEN TAKE NOTES!
IF YOU DON'T GET SOMETHING, THEN ASK!
...
WHY CAN'T YOU DO SOMETHING SO SIMPLE?!
MEANIES!
HEY!
WE'RE NOT DONE WITH YOU!
DASH
BOING BOING
CROCODILE TEARS AGAIN...
MI-MINE-
MINE-KO!
TUP TUP
I'LL GO!
YOU GUYS GET BACK TO PRACTICE!
WAAAAH WAAAAH
...
HUUUU...UUUSH

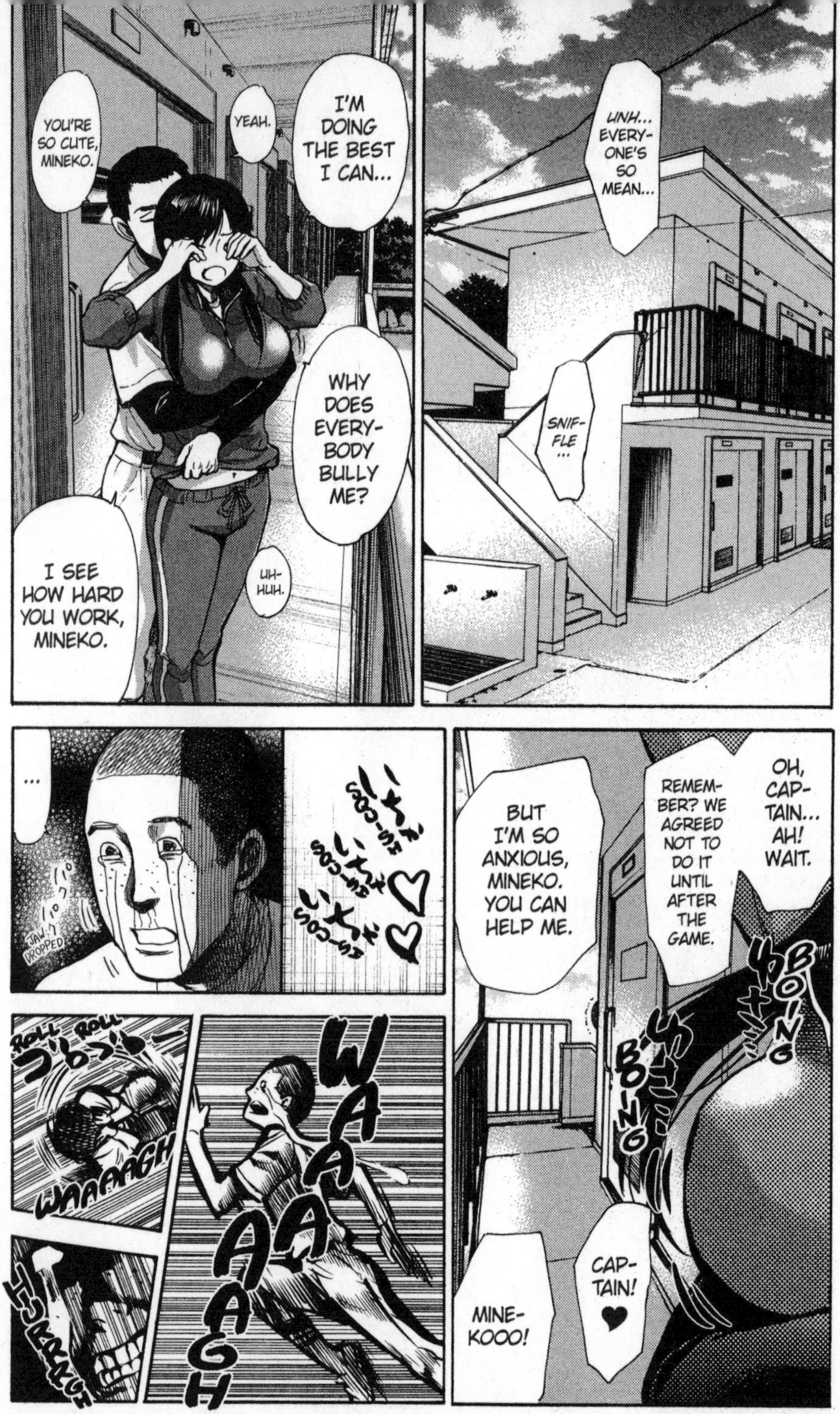
UNH... EVERY-ONE'S SO MEAN...
SNIF-FLE...
I'M DOING THE BEST I CAN...
YEAH.
YOU'RE SO CUTE, MINEKO.
WHY DOES EVERY-BODY BULLY ME?
UH-HUH.
I SEE HOW HARD YOU WORK, MINEKO.
OH, CAP-TAIN... AH! WAIT.
REMEM-BER? WE AGREED NOT TO DO IT UNTIL AFTER THE GAME.
BUT I'M SO ANXIOUS, MINEKO. YOU CAN HELP ME.
BOING
BOING
CAP-TAIN! ♥
MINE-KOOO!
SCO-SCO
SCO-SCO ♥
SCO-SCO ♥
...
JAW DROPPED
WAAAAAGH
ROLL ROLL
WAAAAGH
HURRRGH

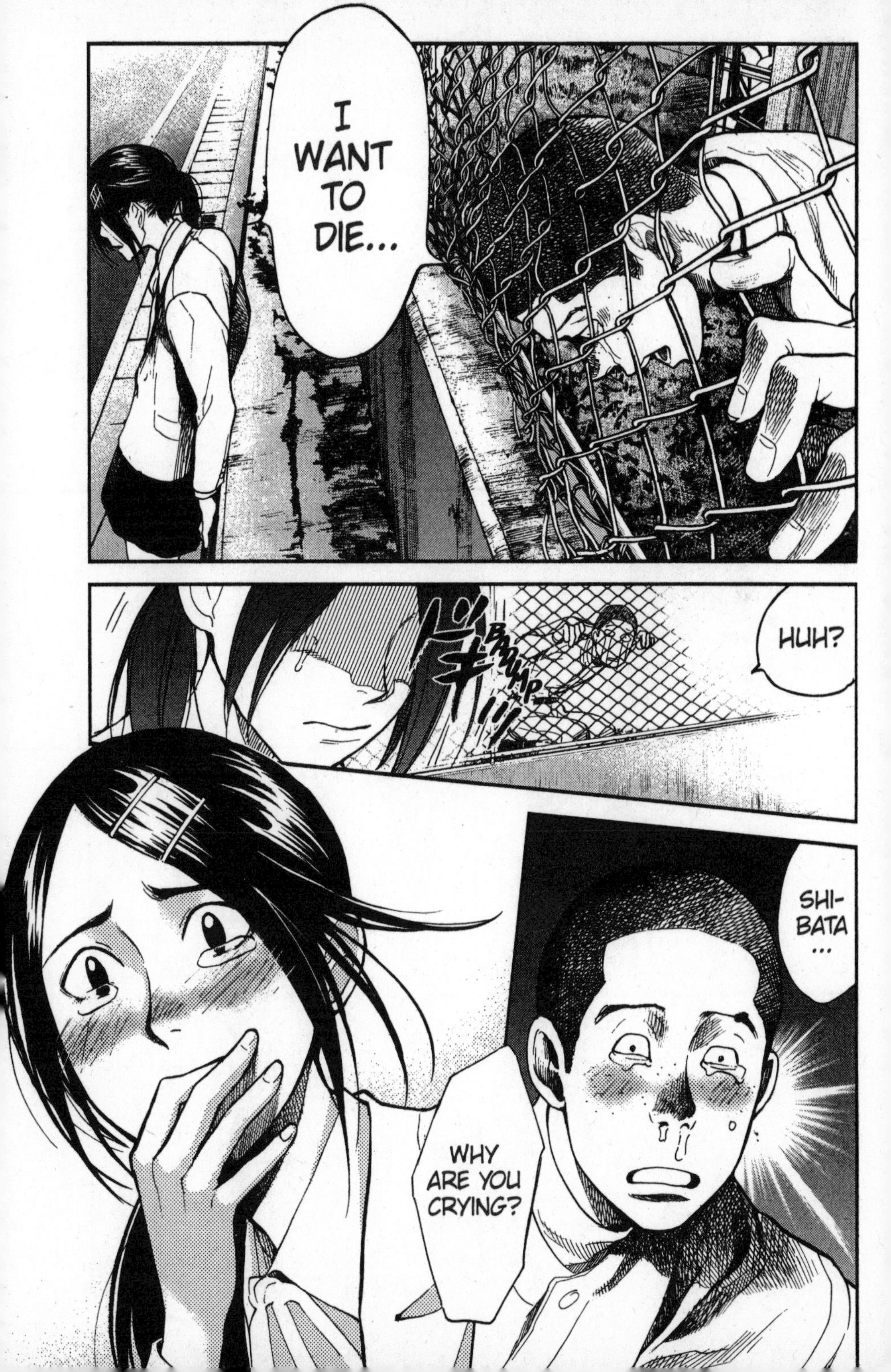
I WANT TO DIE...
HUH?
BADUMP
SHI-BATA...
WHY ARE YOU CRYING?

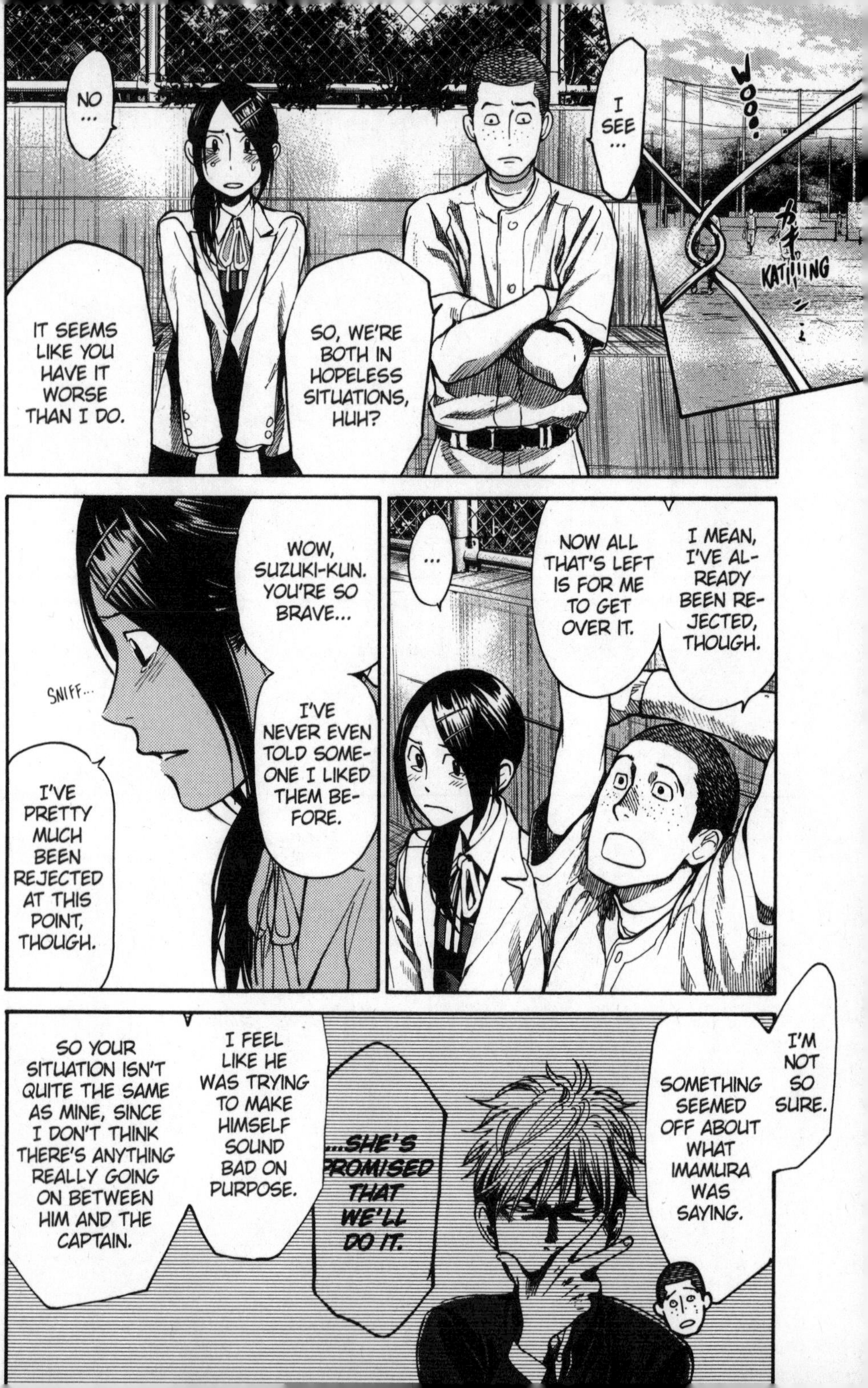
WOOO...
KATIIIING
I SEE ...
NO ...
SO, WE'RE BOTH IN HOPELESS SITUATIONS, HUH?
IT SEEMS LIKE YOU HAVE IT WORSE THAN I DO.
I MEAN, I'VE ALREADY BEEN REJECTED, THOUGH.
NOW ALL THAT'S LEFT IS FOR ME TO GET OVER IT.
...
WOW, SUZUKI-KUN. YOU'RE SO BRAVE...
I'VE NEVER EVEN TOLD SOMEONE I LIKED THEM BEFORE.
SNIFF...
I'VE PRETTY MUCH BEEN REJECTED AT THIS POINT, THOUGH.
I'M NOT SO SURE.
SOMETHING SEEMED OFF ABOUT WHAT IMAMURA WAS SAYING.
...SHE'S PROMISED THAT WE'LL DO IT.
I FEEL LIKE HE WAS TRYING TO MAKE HIMSELF SOUND BAD ON PURPOSE.
SO YOUR SITUATION ISN'T QUITE THE SAME AS MINE, SINCE I DON'T THINK THERE'S ANYTHING REALLY GOING ON BETWEEN HIM AND THE CAPTAIN.

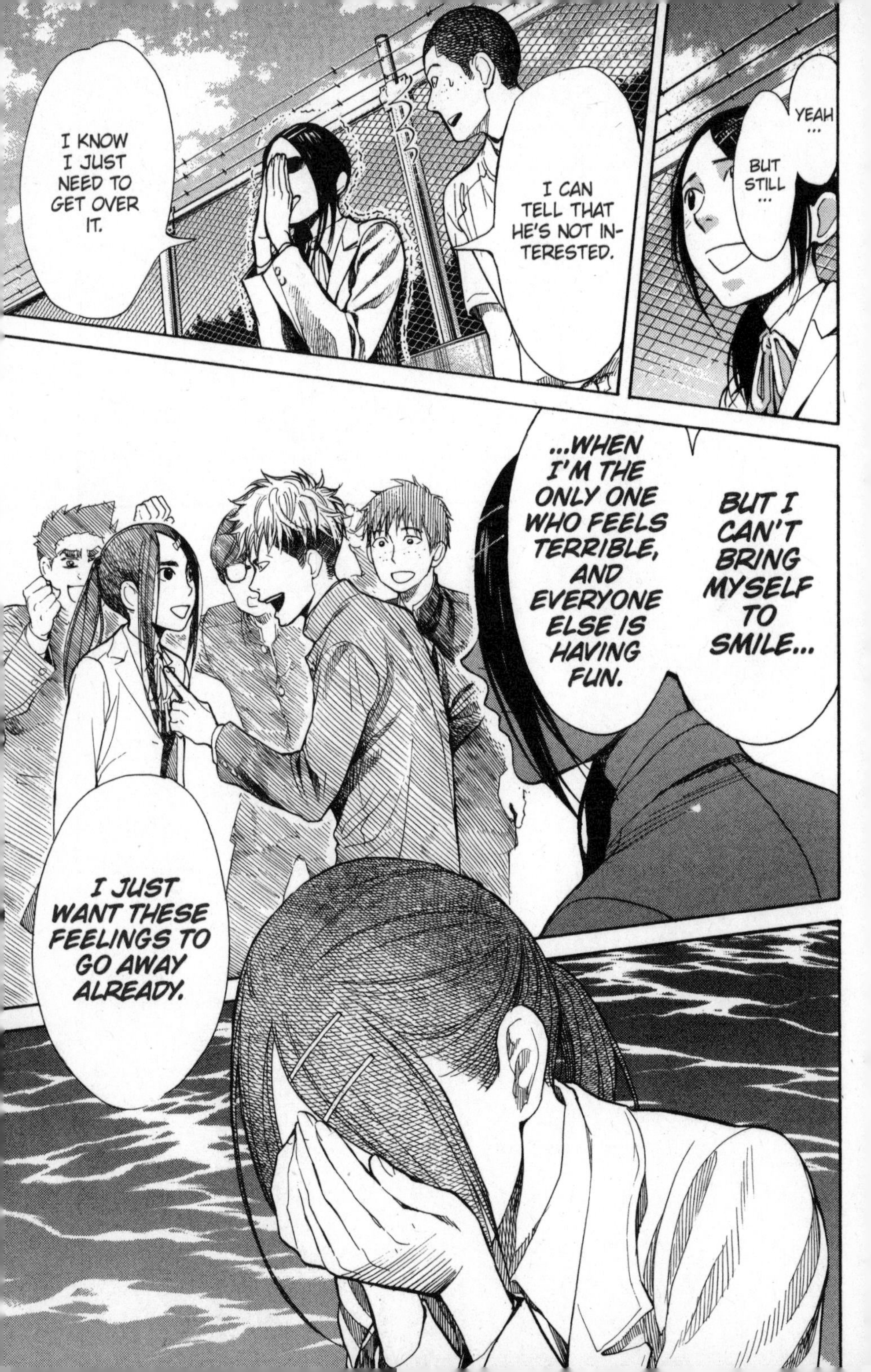
YEAH ... BUT STILL ...
I CAN TELL THAT HE'S NOT INTERESTED.
I KNOW I JUST NEED TO GET OVER IT.
BUT I CAN'T BRING MYSELF TO SMILE...
...WHEN I'M THE ONLY ONE WHO FEELS TERRIBLE, AND EVERYONE ELSE IS HAVING FUN.
I JUST WANT THESE FEELINGS TO GO AWAY ALREADY.

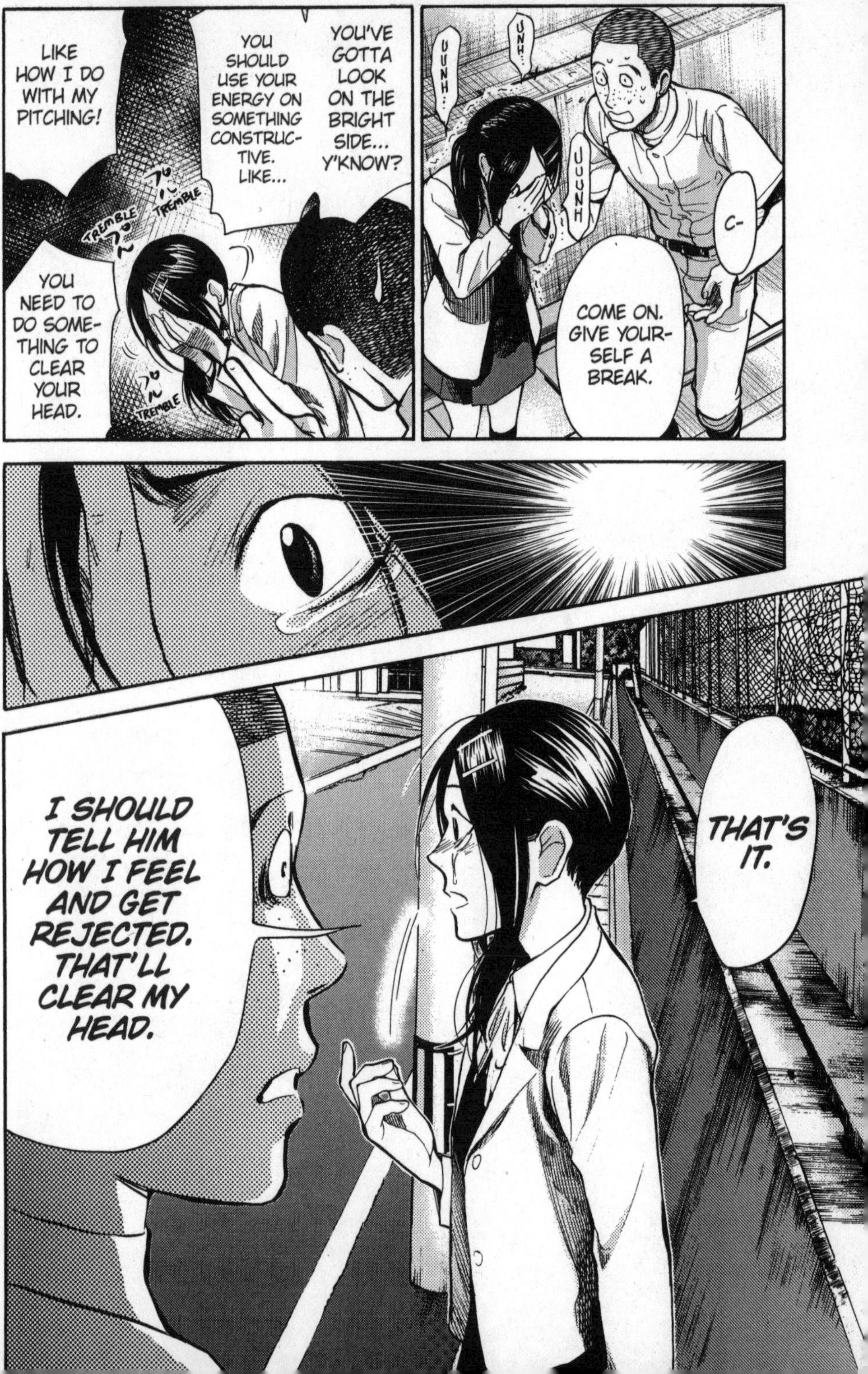
UNH...
UUNH...
UUUNH
C-
COME ON. GIVE YOURSELF A BREAK.
YOU'VE GOTTA LOOK ON THE BRIGHT SIDE... Y'KNOW?
YOU SHOULD USE YOUR ENERGY ON SOMETHING CONSTRUCTIVE. LIKE...
LIKE HOW I DO WITH MY PITCHING!
TREMBLE
TREMBLE
TREMBLE
YOU NEED TO DO SOMETHING TO CLEAR YOUR HEAD.
THAT'S IT.
I SHOULD TELL HIM HOW I FEEL AND GET REJECTED. THAT'LL CLEAR MY HEAD.

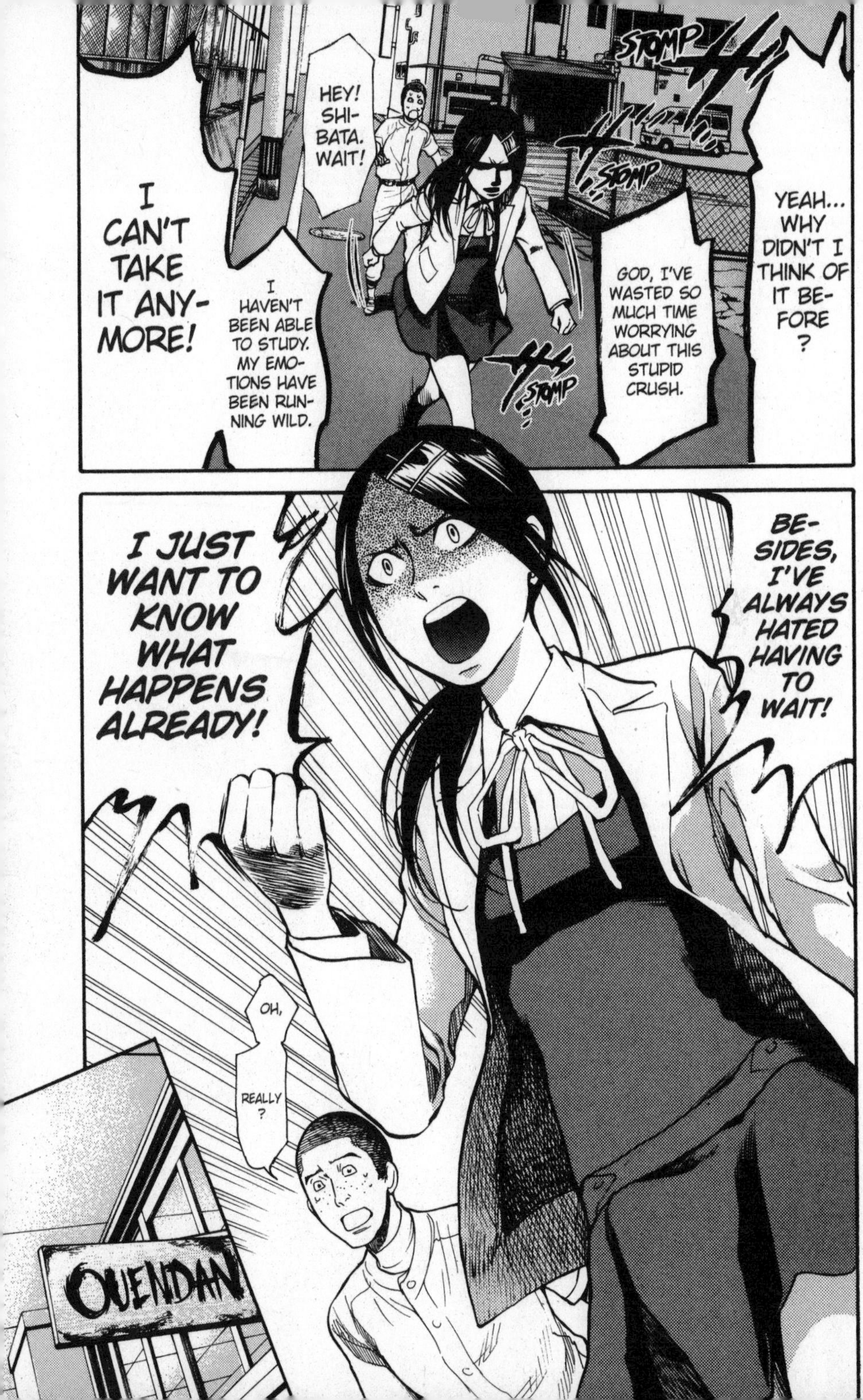

STOMP
YEAH... WHY DIDN'T I THINK OF IT BEFORE?
GOD, I'VE WASTED SO MUCH TIME WORRYING ABOUT THIS STUPID CRUSH.
STOMP
HEY! SHIBATA. WAIT!
STOMP
I HAVEN'T BEEN ABLE TO STUDY. MY EMOTIONS HAVE BEEN RUNNING WILD.
I CAN'T TAKE IT ANYMORE!
BESIDES, I'VE ALWAYS HATED HAVING TO WAIT!
I JUST WANT TO KNOW WHAT HAPPENS ALREADY!
OH, REALLY?
OUENDAN

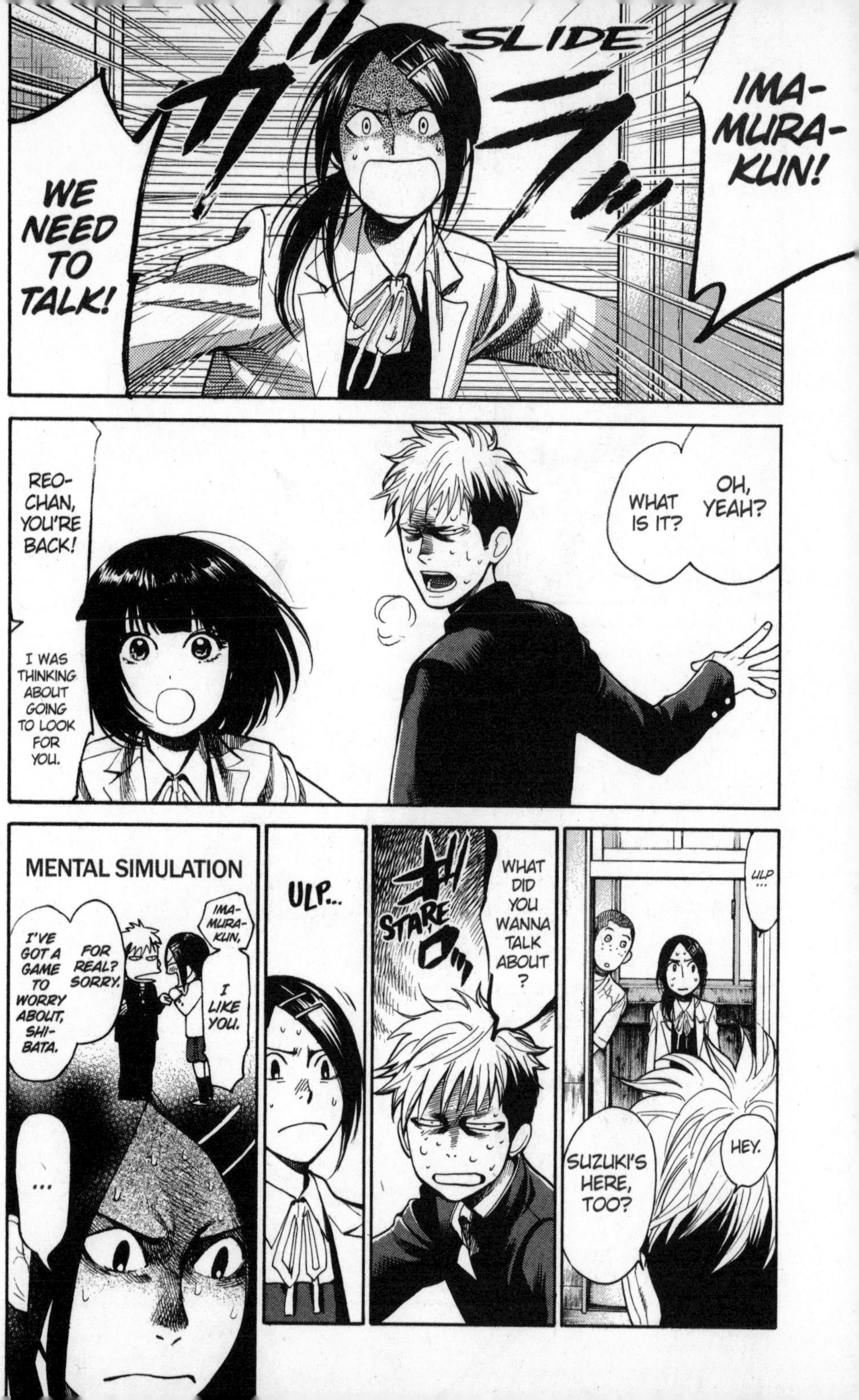
SLIDE
IMA-MURA-KUN!
WE NEED TO TALK!
OH, YEAH? WHAT IS IT?
REO-CHAN, YOU'RE BACK!
I WAS THINKING ABOUT GOING TO LOOK FOR YOU.
ULP...
HEY.
SUZUKI'S HERE, TOO?
WHAT DID YOU WANNA TALK ABOUT?
STARE
ULP...
MENTAL SIMULATION
IMA-MURA-KUN, I LIKE YOU.
FOR REAL? SORRY.
I'VE GOT A GAME TO WORRY ABOUT, SHIBATA.
...

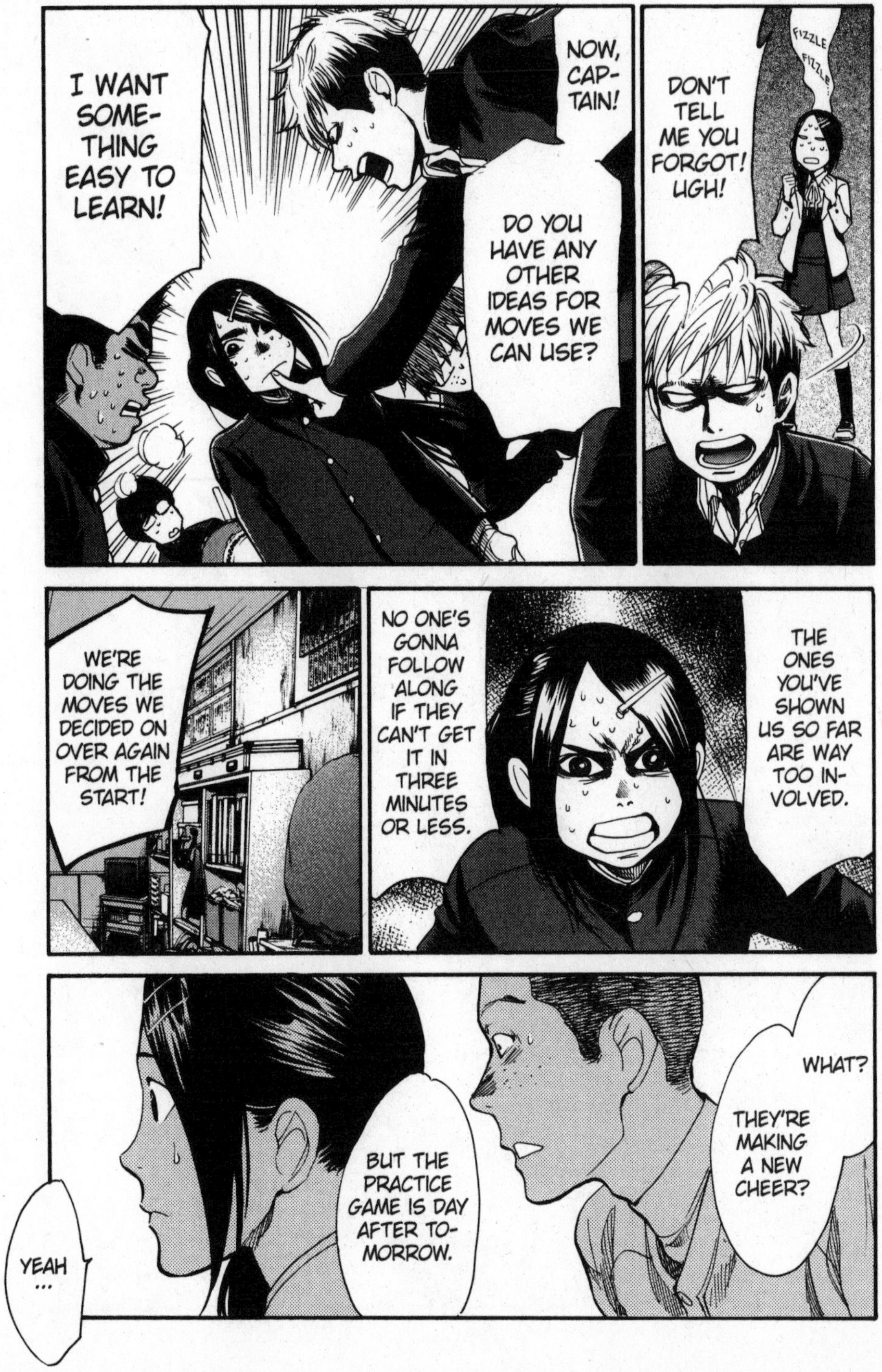
FIZZLE FIZZLE
DON'T TELL ME YOU FORGOT! UGH!
NOW, CAP-TAIN!
DO YOU HAVE ANY OTHER IDEAS FOR MOVES WE CAN USE?
I WANT SOME-THING EASY TO LEARN!
THE ONES YOU'VE SHOWN US SO FAR ARE WAY TOO IN-VOLVED.
NO ONE'S GONNA FOLLOW ALONG IF THEY CAN'T GET IT IN THREE MINUTES OR LESS.
WE'RE DOING THE MOVES WE DECIDED ON OVER AGAIN FROM THE START!
WHAT?
THEY'RE MAKING A NEW CHEER?
BUT THE PRACTICE GAME IS DAY AFTER TO-MORROW.
YEAH ...

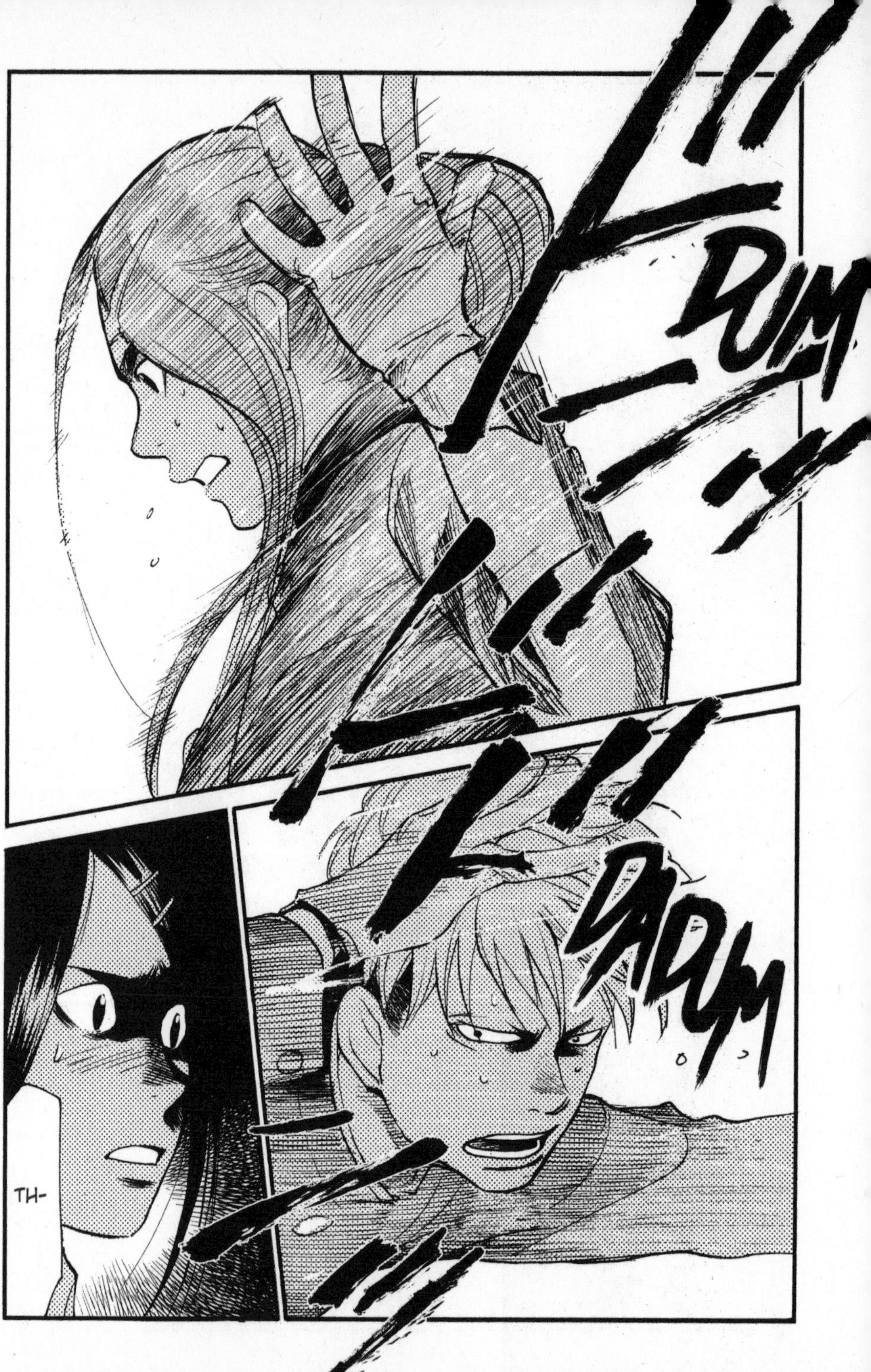
DUM
DADUM
TH-

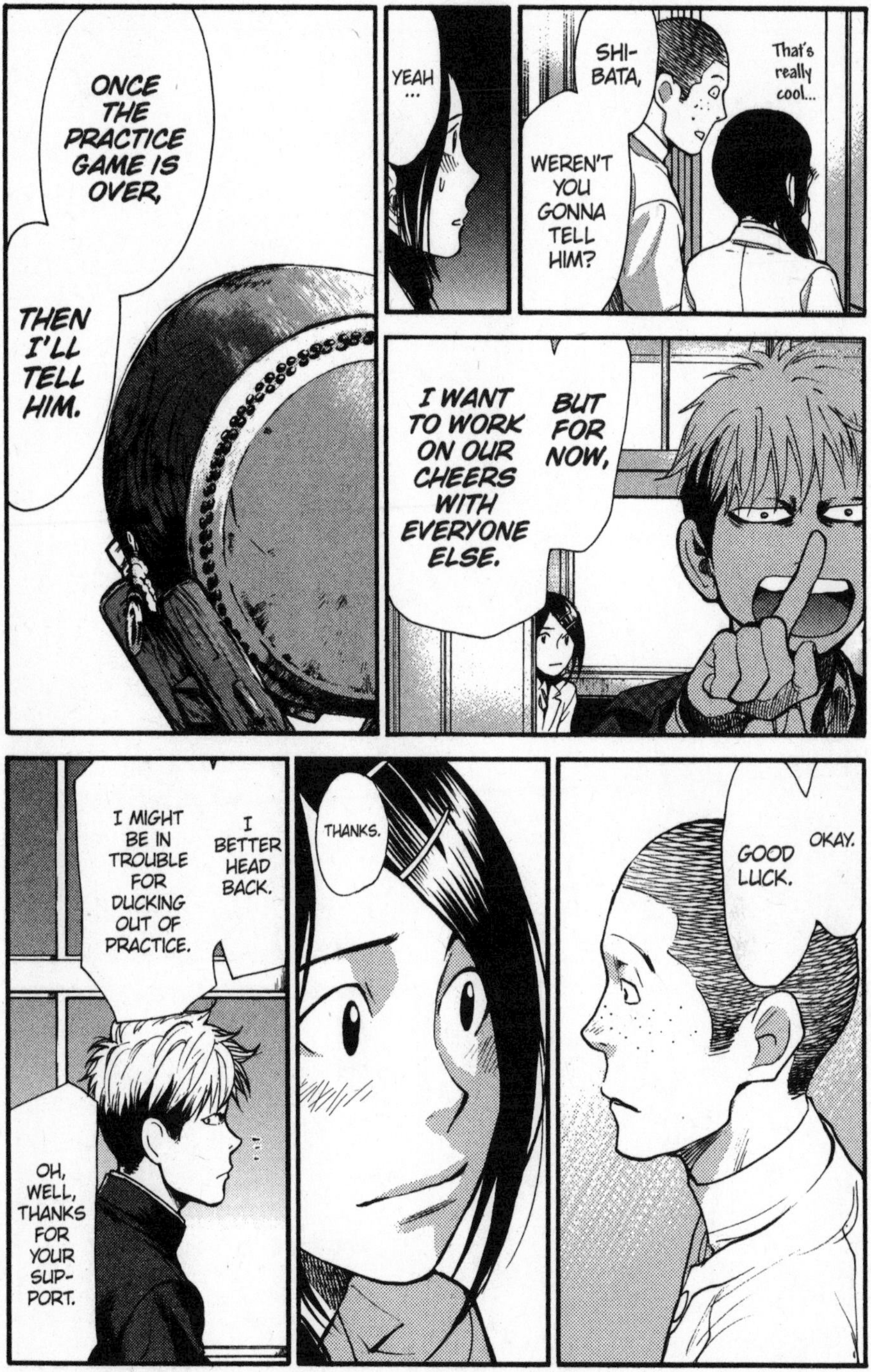
That's really cool...
SHIBATA, WEREN'T YOU GONNA TELL HIM?
YEAH...
BUT FOR NOW,
I WANT TO WORK ON OUR CHEERS WITH EVERYONE ELSE.
ONCE THE PRACTICE GAME IS OVER,
THEN I'LL TELL HIM.
OKAY.
GOOD LUCK.
THANKS.
I BETTER HEAD BACK.
I MIGHT BE IN TROUBLE FOR DUCKING OUT OF PRACTICE.
OH, WELL, THANKS FOR YOUR SUPPORT.

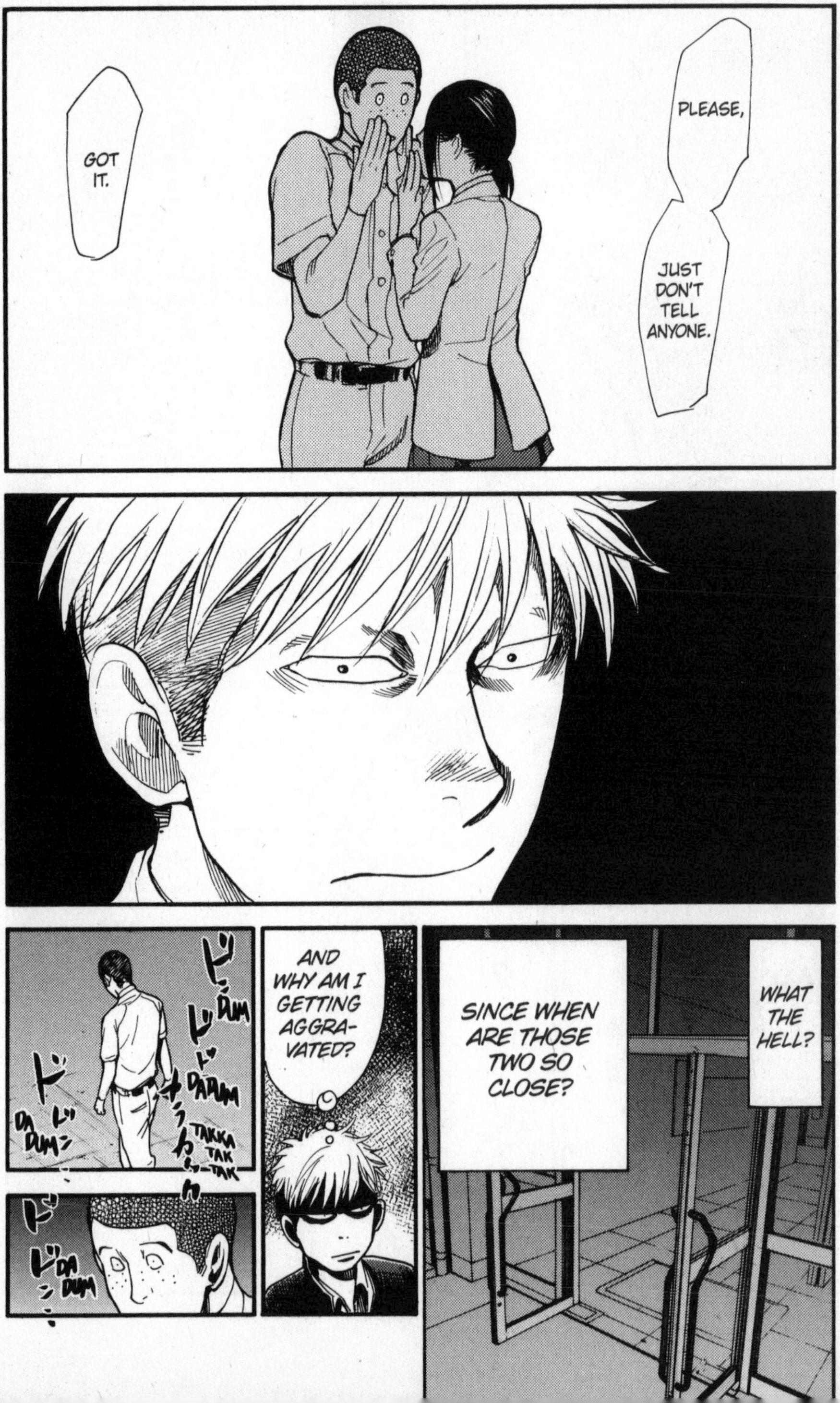
PLEASE,
JUST DON'T TELL ANYONE.
GOT IT.
WHAT THE HELL?
SINCE WHEN ARE THOSE TWO SO CLOSE?
AND WHY AM I GETTING AGGRA-VATED?
DUM
DADUM
TAKKA TAK TAK
DA DUM
DA DUM

DUM
DADUM...
TAKKA TAK TAK
BWA HA HA...
QUIT SCREWING AROUND!
SO, SHIBATA LIKES IMAMURA, HUH?
DADUM
MAKES SENSE. HE'S A GOOD GUY.
DUM
DUM...
DADUM
DUM
KATIIIIING
WOOO...
I GUESS I'LL NEED SOME LUCK OF MY OWN.

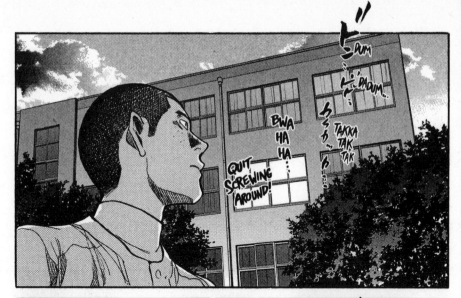

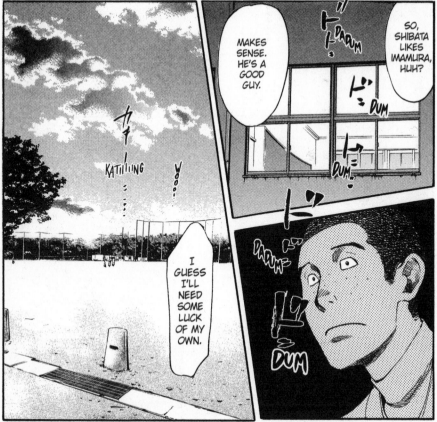

Again!!
アゲイン!!

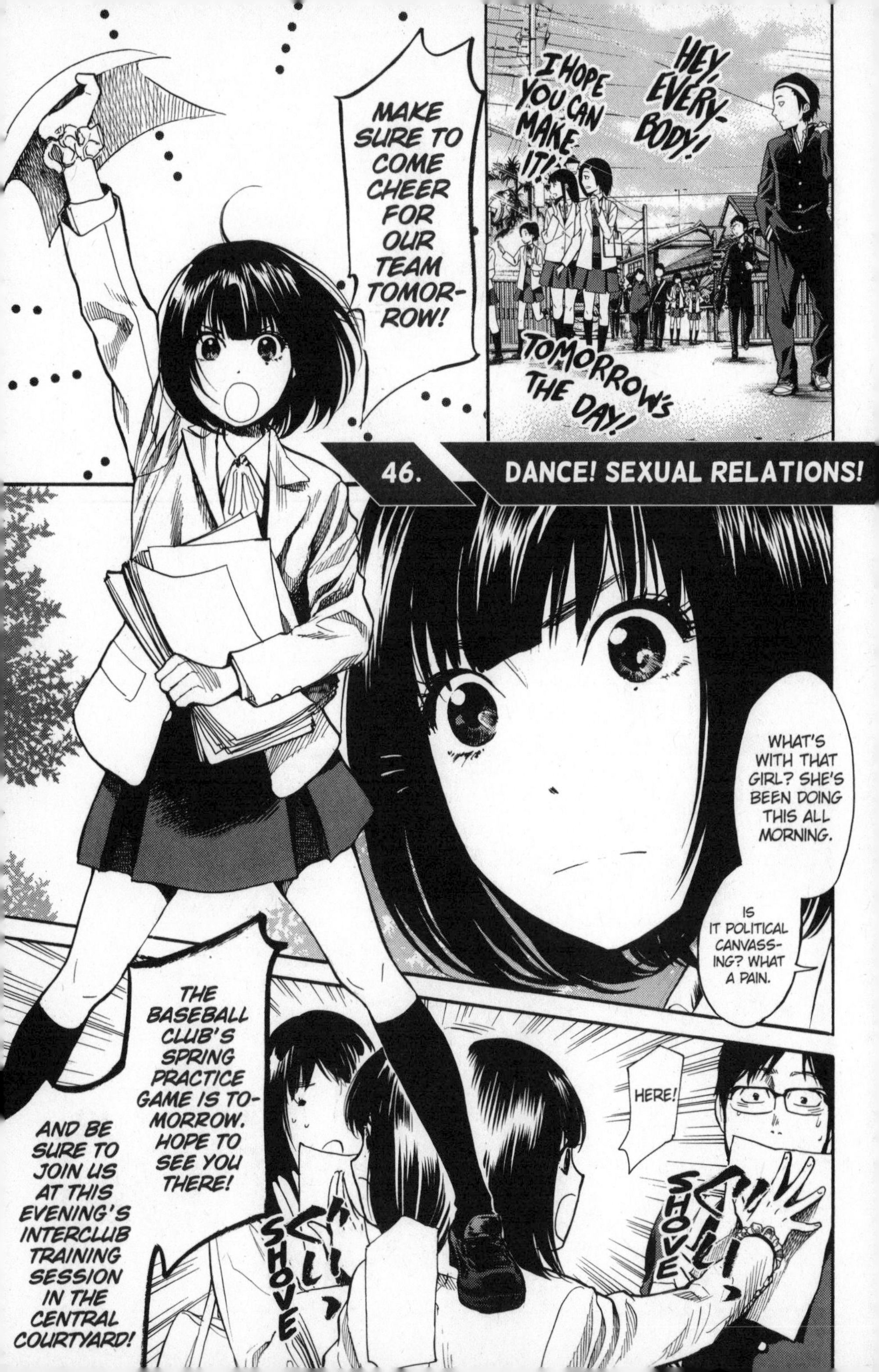
HEY, EVERYBODY!
I HOPE YOU CAN MAKE IT!
TOMORROW'S THE DAY!
46. DANCE! SEXUAL RELATIONS!
WHAT'S WITH THAT GIRL? SHE'S BEEN DOING THIS ALL MORNING.
IS IT POLITICAL CANVASSING? WHAT A PAIN.
HERE!
SHOVE
SHOVE
MAKE SURE TO COME CHEER FOR OUR TEAM TOMORROW!
THE BASEBALL CLUB'S SPRING PRACTICE GAME IS TOMORROW. HOPE TO SEE YOU THERE!
AND BE SURE TO JOIN US AT THIS EVENING'S INTERCLUB TRAINING SESSION IN THE CENTRAL COURTYARD!

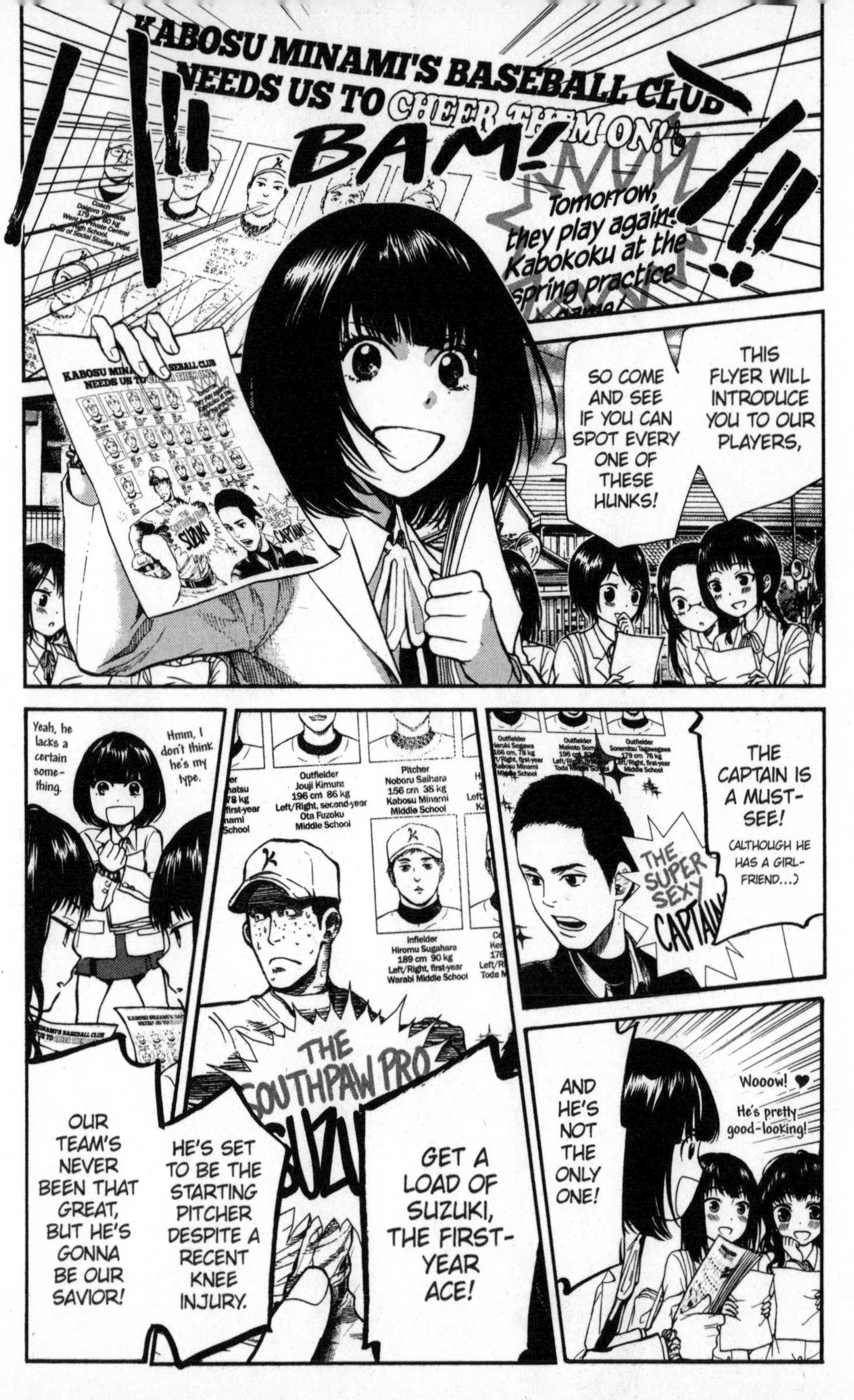
KABOSU MINAMI'S BASEBALL CLUB NEEDS US TO CHEER THEM ON!
BAM!
Tomorrow, they play against Kabokoku at the spring practice
THIS FLYER WILL INTRODUCE YOU TO OUR PLAYERS,
SO COME AND SEE IF YOU CAN SPOT EVERY ONE OF THESE HUNKS!
THE CAPTAIN IS A MUST-SEE!
(ALTHOUGH HE HAS A GIRLFRIEND...)
THE SUPER SEXY
Outfielder Haruki Segawa 166 cm, 78 kg Left/Right, first-year Kabosu Minami Middle School
Outfielder Jouji Kimura 196 cm 86 kg Left/Right, second-year Ota Fuzoku Middle School
Pitcher Noboru Saihara 156 cm 35 kg Kabosu Minami Middle School
Infielder Hiromu Sugahara 189 cm 90 kg Left/Right, first-year Warabi Middle School
Hmm, I don't think he's my type.
Yeah, he lacks a certain something.
Wooow! ♥
He's pretty good-looking!
AND HE'S NOT THE ONLY ONE!
GET A LOAD OF SUZUKI, THE FIRST-YEAR ACE!
THE SOUTHPAW PRO
HE'S SET TO BE THE STARTING PITCHER DESPITE A RECENT KNEE INJURY.
OUR TEAM'S NEVER BEEN THAT GREAT, BUT HE'S GONNA BE OUR SAVIOR!

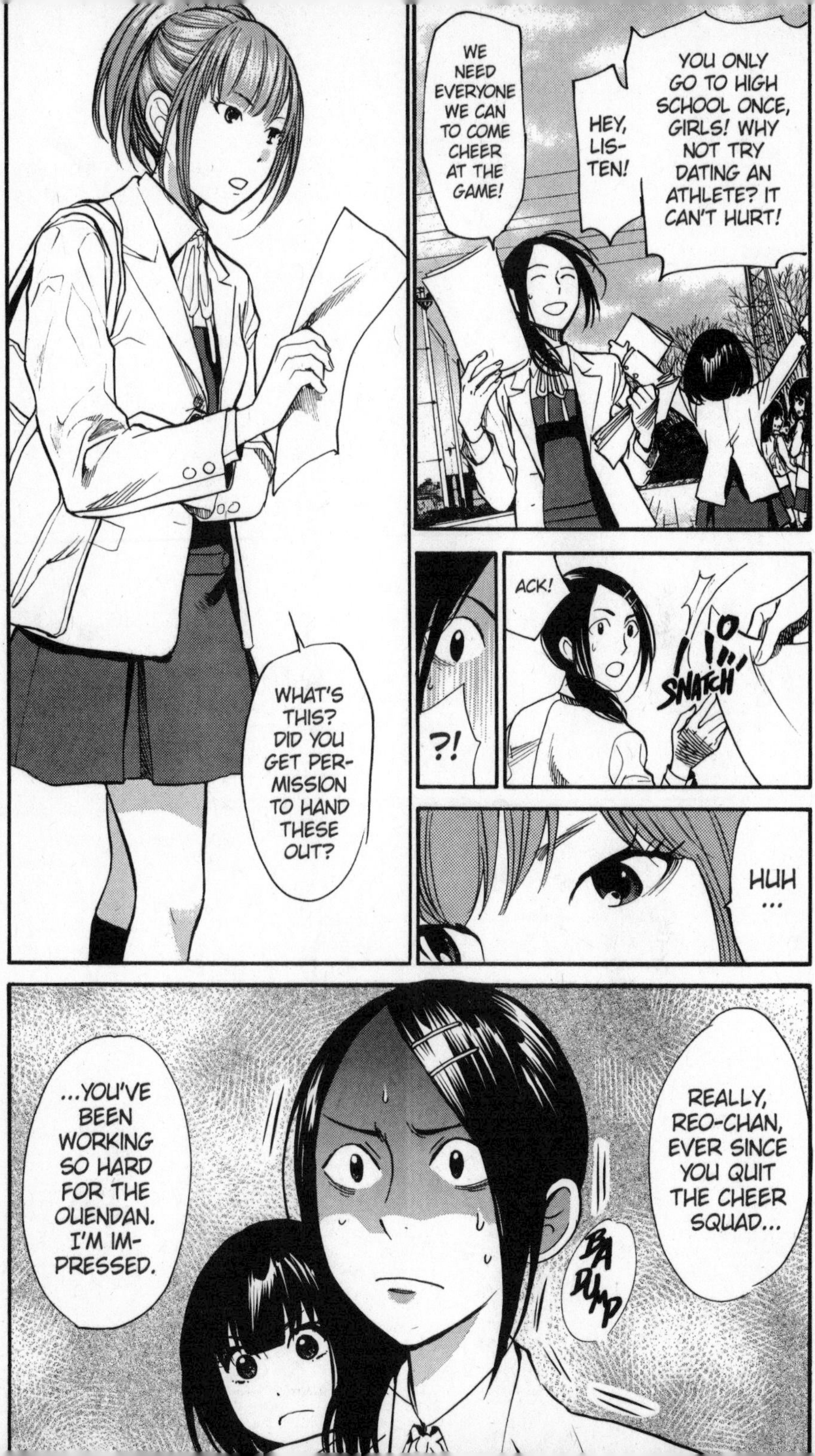
YOU ONLY GO TO HIGH SCHOOL ONCE, GIRLS! WHY NOT TRY DATING AN ATHLETE? IT CAN'T HURT!
HEY, LIS-TEN!
WE NEED EVERYONE WE CAN TO COME CHEER AT THE GAME!
SNATCH
ACK!
?!
HUH...
WHAT'S THIS? DID YOU GET PER-MISSION TO HAND THESE OUT?
REALLY, REO-CHAN, EVER SINCE YOU QUIT THE CHEER SQUAD...
BA DUMP
...YOU'VE BEEN WORKING SO HARD FOR THE OUENDAN. I'M IM-PRESSED.

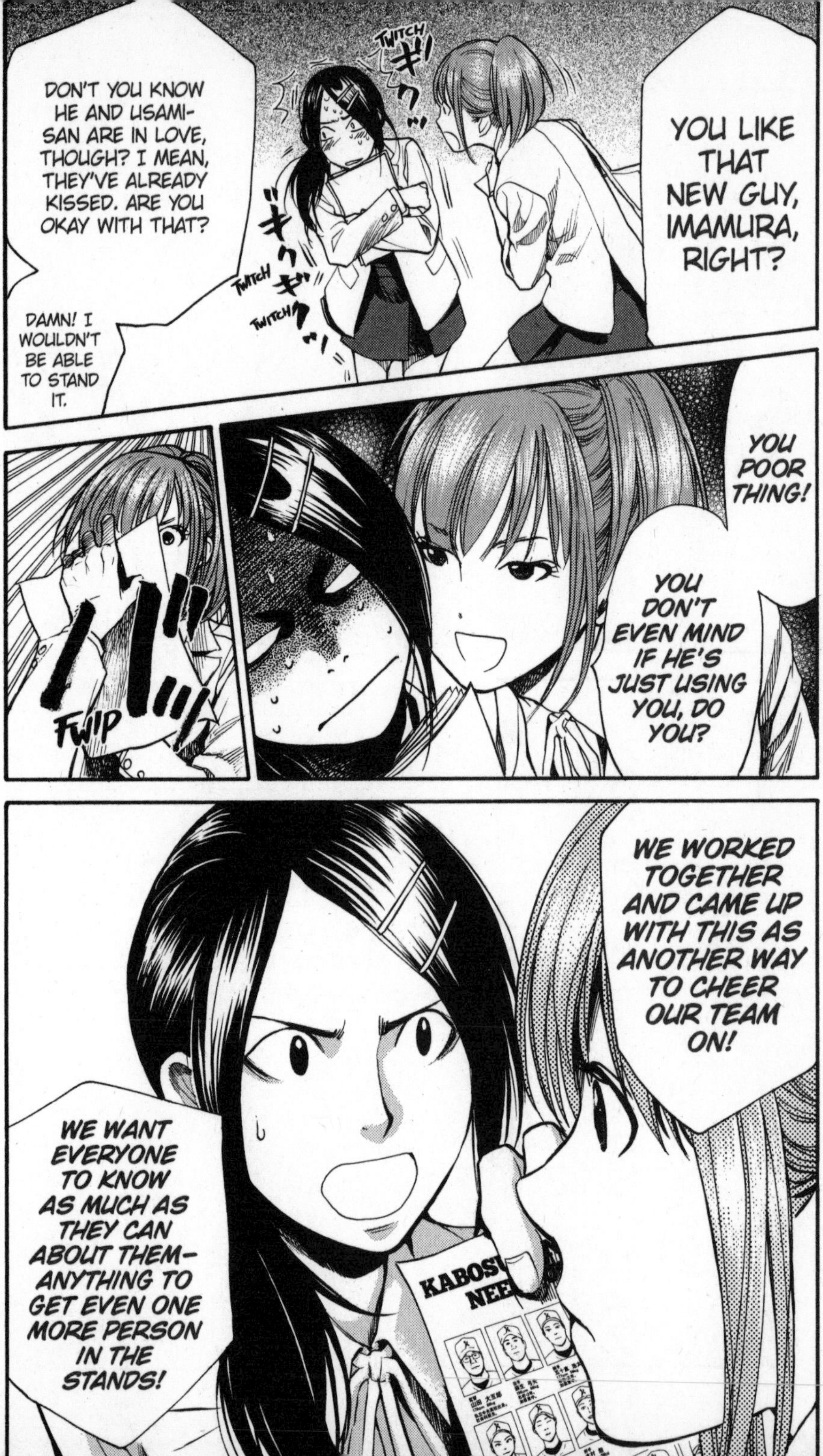
YOU LIKE THAT NEW GUY, IMAMURA, RIGHT?
TWITCH
TWITCH
TWITCH
DON'T YOU KNOW HE AND USAMI-SAN ARE IN LOVE, THOUGH? I MEAN, THEY'VE ALREADY KISSED. ARE YOU OKAY WITH THAT?
DAMN! I WOULDN'T BE ABLE TO STAND IT.
YOU POOR THING!
YOU DON'T EVEN MIND IF HE'S JUST USING YOU, DO YOU?
FWIP
WE WORKED TOGETHER AND CAME UP WITH THIS AS ANOTHER WAY TO CHEER OUR TEAM ON!
WE WANT EVERYONE TO KNOW AS MUCH AS THEY CAN ABOUT THEM—ANYTHING TO GET EVEN ONE MORE PERSON IN THE STANDS!

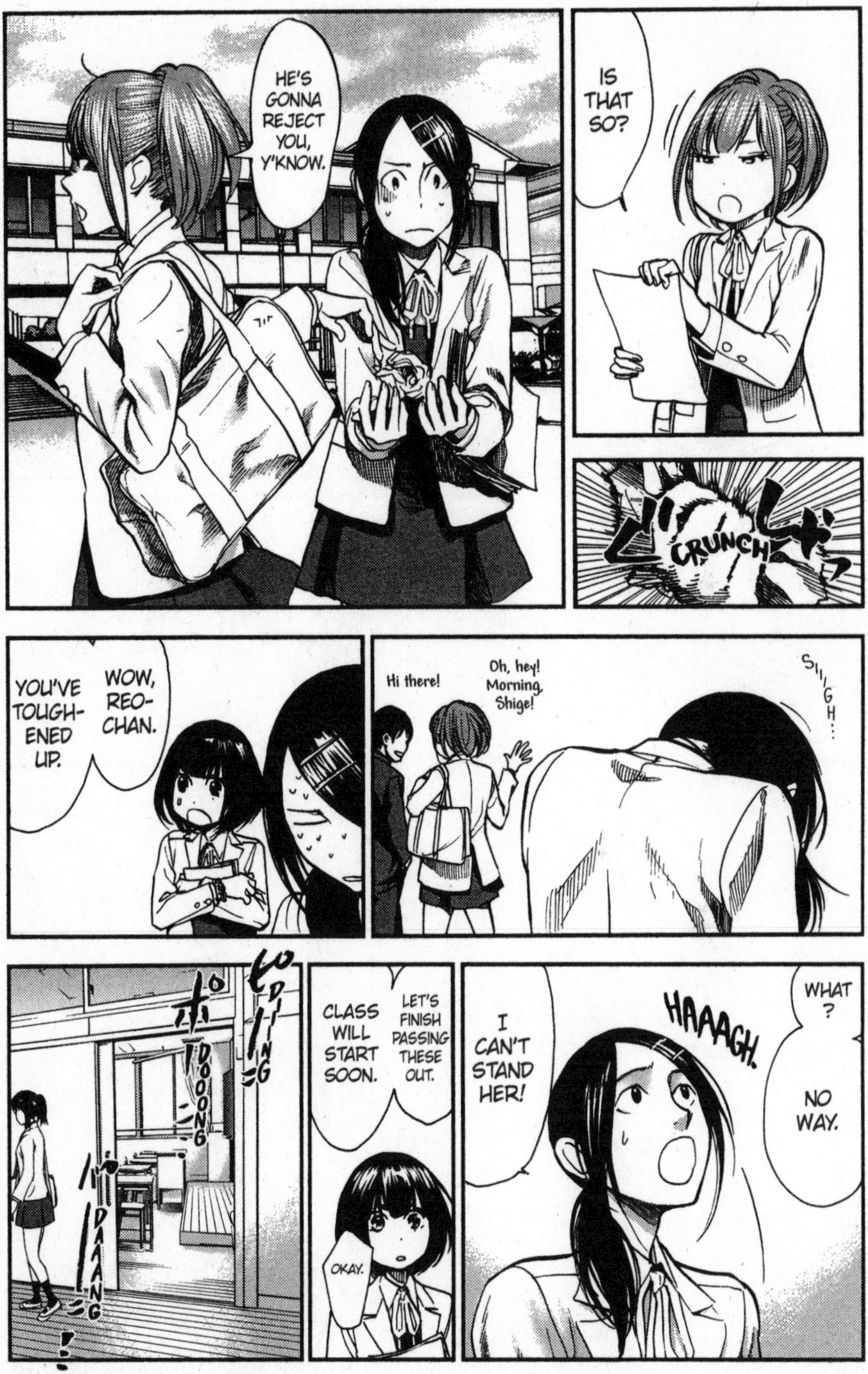
IS THAT SO?
CRUNCH
HE'S GONNA REJECT YOU, Y'KNOW.
SIIIGH...
Oh, hey! Morning, Shige!
Hi there!
WOW, REO-CHAN.
YOU'VE TOUGHENED UP.
WHAT? NO WAY.
HAAAGH.
I CAN'T STAND HER!
LET'S FINISH PASSING THESE OUT.
CLASS WILL START SOON.
OKAY.
DIIING
DOOONG
DAAANG

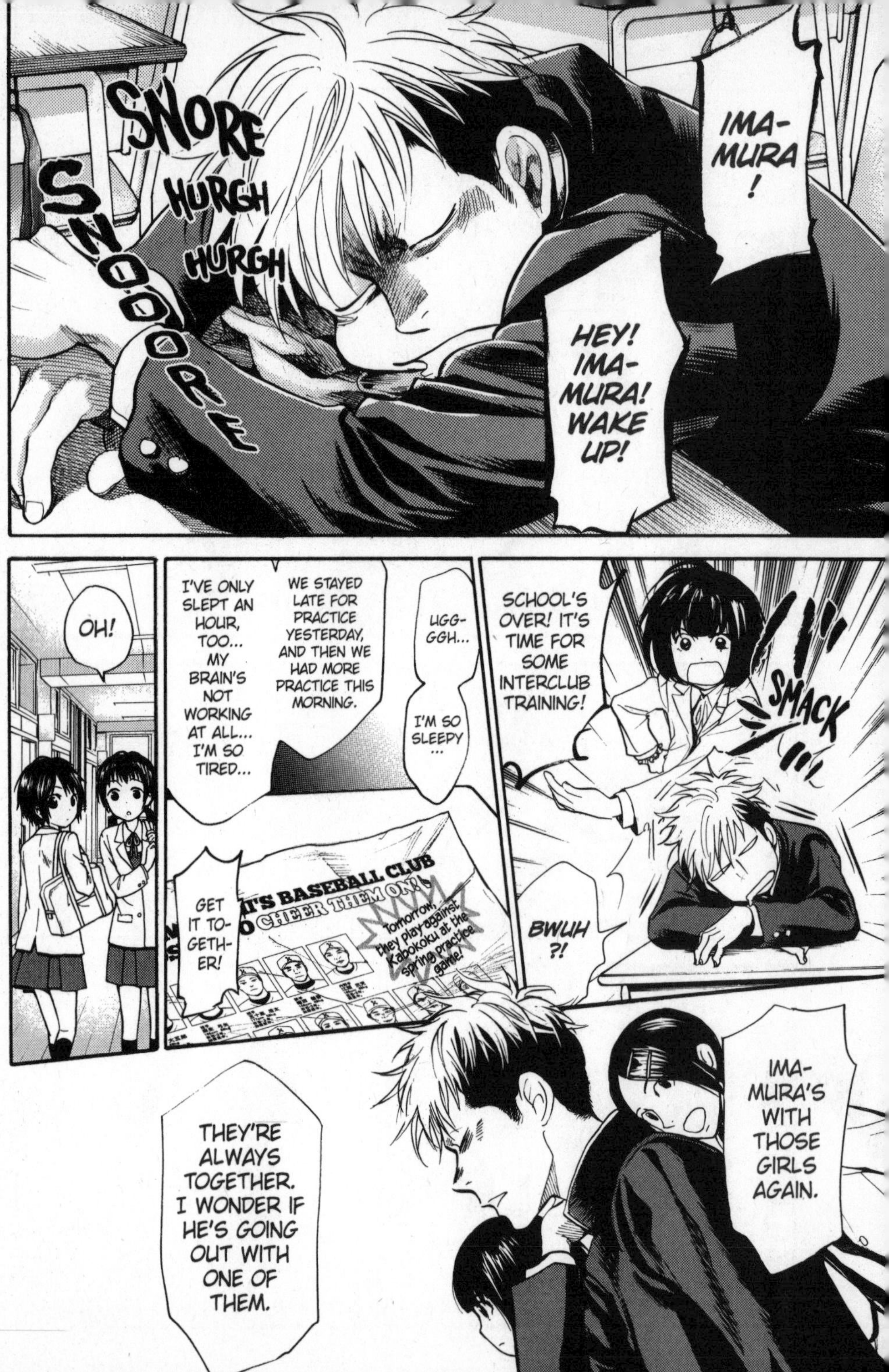
IMA-MURA!
HEY! IMA-MURA! WAKE UP!
SNORE
HURGH HURGH
SNOOORE
SCHOOL'S OVER! IT'S TIME FOR SOME INTERCLUB TRAINING!
SMACK
BWUH?!
UGG-GGH...
I'M SO SLEEPY...
WE STAYED LATE FOR PRACTICE YESTERDAY, AND THEN WE HAD MORE PRACTICE THIS MORNING.
I'VE ONLY SLEPT AN HOUR, TOO... MY BRAIN'S NOT WORKING AT ALL... I'M SO TIRED...
'S BASEBALL CLUB
CHEER THEM ON!
Tomorrow, they play against Kabokoku at the spring practice game!
GET IT TO-GETH-ER!
OH!
IMA-MURA'S WITH THOSE GIRLS AGAIN.
THEY'RE ALWAYS TOGETHER. I WONDER IF HE'S GOING OUT WITH ONE OF THEM.

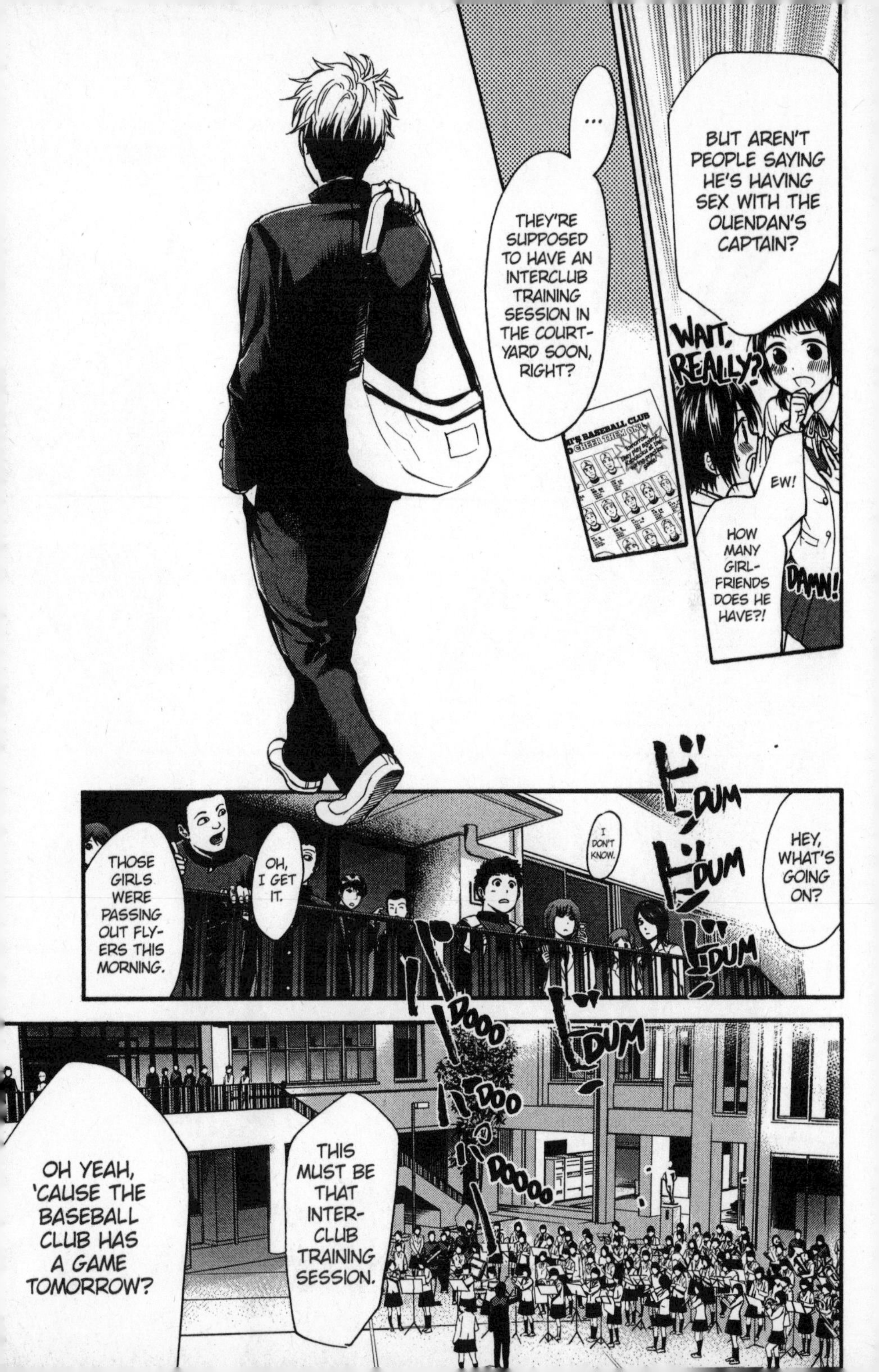
BUT AREN'T PEOPLE SAYING HE'S HAVING SEX WITH THE OUENDAN'S CAPTAIN?
WAIT, REALLY?
EW!
HOW MANY GIRL-FRIENDS DOES HE HAVE?!
DAMN!
...
THEY'RE SUPPOSED TO HAVE AN INTERCLUB TRAINING SESSION IN THE COURT-YARD SOON, RIGHT?
HEY, WHAT'S GOING ON?
DUM
DUM
DUM
I DON'T KNOW.
OH, I GET IT.
THOSE GIRLS WERE PASSING OUT FLY-ERS THIS MORNING.
DUM
DOOO
DOO
DOOOO
THIS MUST BE THAT INTER-CLUB TRAINING SESSION.
OH YEAH, 'CAUSE THE BASEBALL CLUB HAS A GAME TOMORROW?

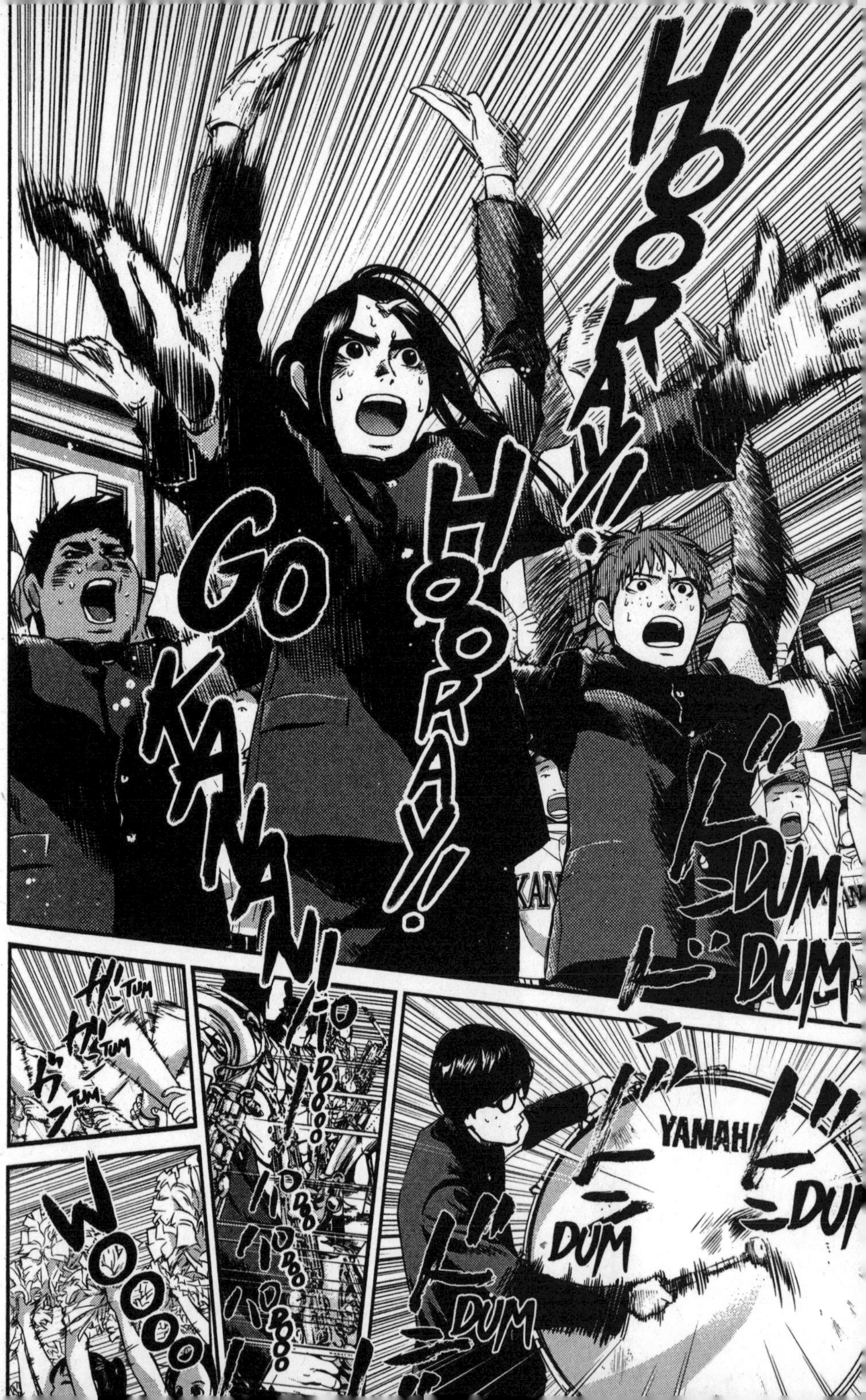
HOORAY!!
HOORAY!!
GO KANAN!!
DUM
DUM
YAMAH
DUM
DUM
DUM
DUM
TUM
TUM
TUM
WOOOOO

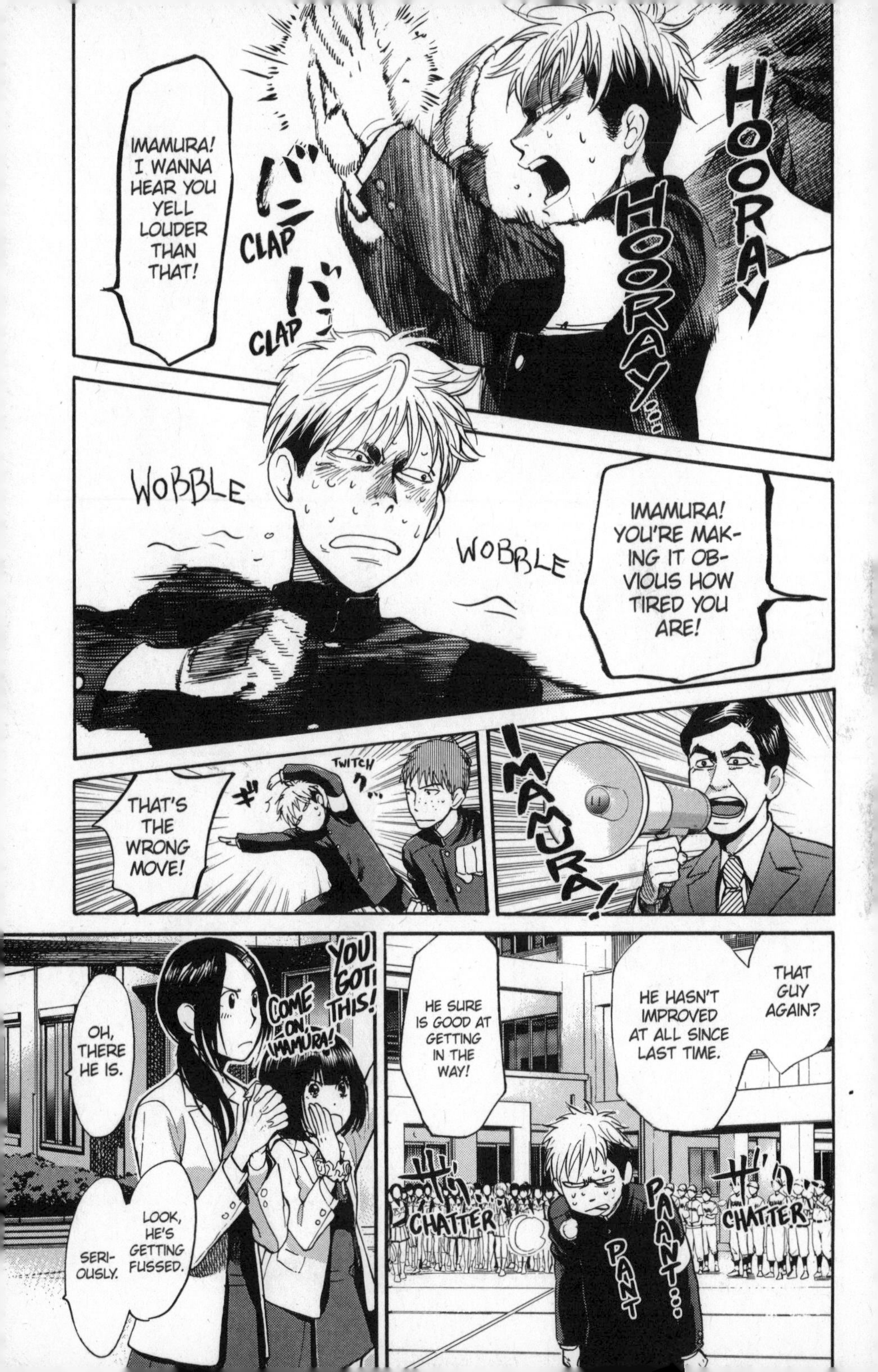
HOORAY
HOORAY...
CLAP
CLAP
IMAMURA! I WANNA HEAR YOU YELL LOUDER THAN THAT!
IMAMURA! YOU'RE MAK-ING IT OB-VIOUS HOW TIRED YOU ARE!
WOBBLE
WOBBLE
IMAMURA!
TWITCH
THAT'S THE WRONG MOVE!
THAT GUY AGAIN?
HE HASN'T IMPROVED AT ALL SINCE LAST TIME.
HE SURE IS GOOD AT GETTING IN THE WAY!
CHATTER
PANT PANT...
CHATTER
YOU GOT THIS!
COME ON, IMAMURA!
OH, THERE HE IS.
LOOK, HE'S GETTING FUSSED.
SERI-OUSLY.

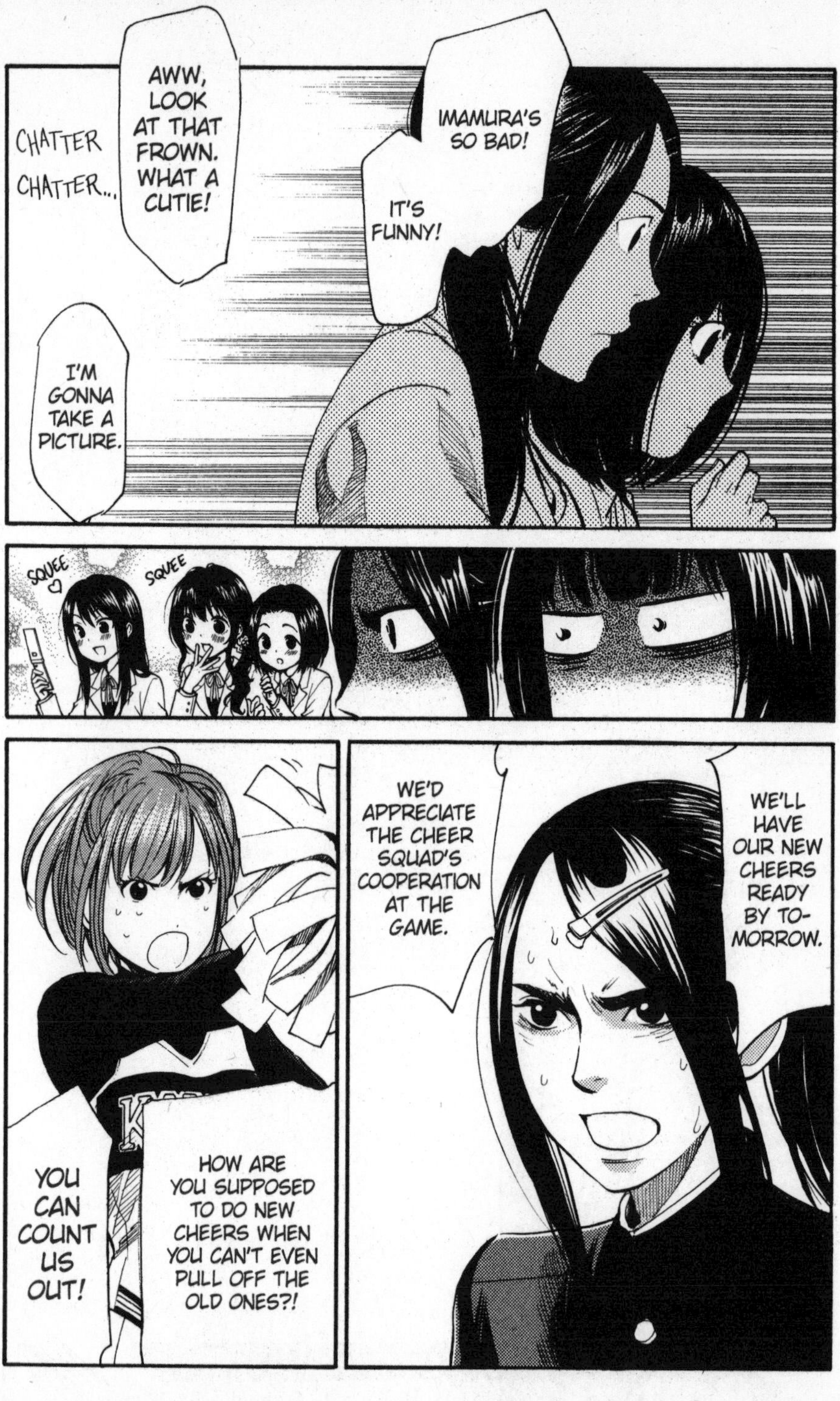
IMAMURA'S SO BAD!
IT'S FUNNY!
AWW, LOOK AT THAT FROWN. WHAT A CUTIE!
CHATTER CHATTER...
I'M GONNA TAKE A PICTURE.
SQUEE
SQUEE ♡
WE'LL HAVE OUR NEW CHEERS READY BY TO-MORROW.
WE'D APPRECIATE THE CHEER SQUAD'S COOPERATION AT THE GAME.
HOW ARE YOU SUPPOSED TO DO NEW CHEERS WHEN YOU CAN'T EVEN PULL OFF THE OLD ONES?!
YOU CAN COUNT US OUT!

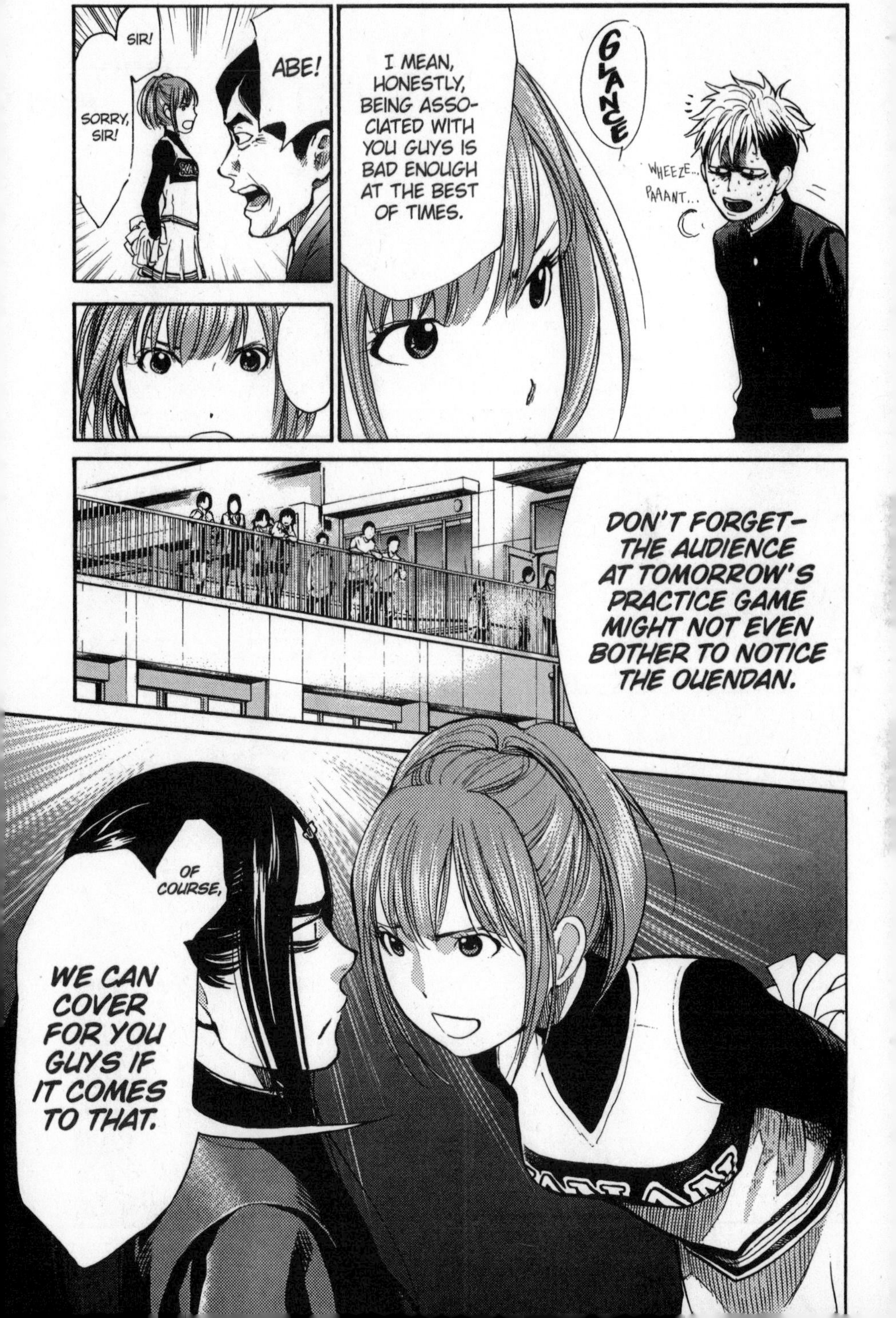

GLANCE
WHEEZE... PAAANT...
I MEAN, HONESTLY, BEING ASSOCIATED WITH YOU GUYS IS BAD ENOUGH AT THE BEST OF TIMES.
ABE!
SIR!
SORRY, SIR!
DON'T FORGET-THE AUDIENCE AT TOMORROW'S PRACTICE GAME MIGHT NOT EVEN BOTHER TO NOTICE THE OUENDAN.
OF COURSE,
WE CAN COVER FOR YOU GUYS IF IT COMES TO THAT.

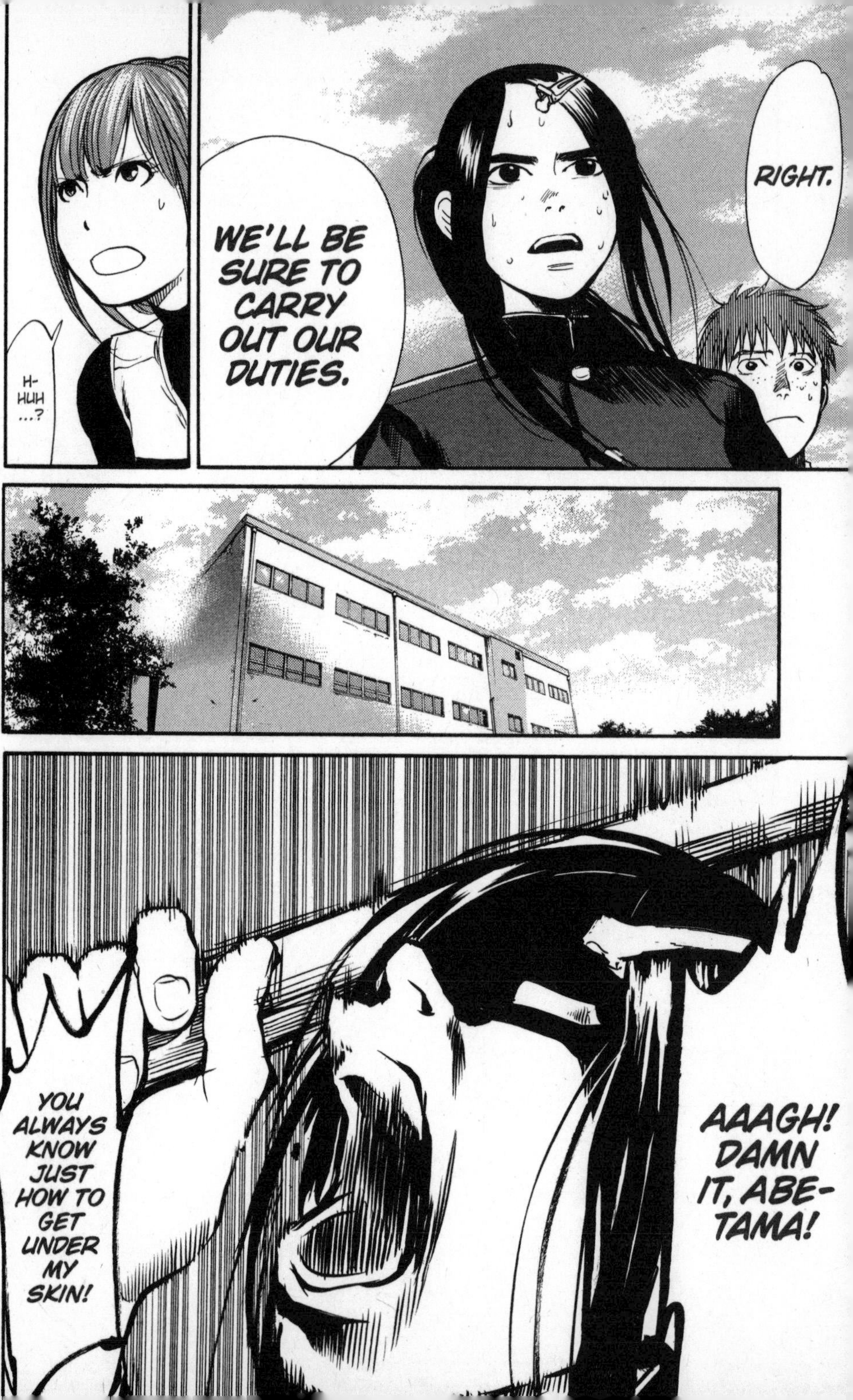
RIGHT.
WE'LL BE SURE TO CARRY OUT OUR DUTIES.
H-HUH ...?
AAAGH! DAMN IT, ABE-TAMA!
YOU ALWAYS KNOW JUST HOW TO GET UNDER MY SKIN!

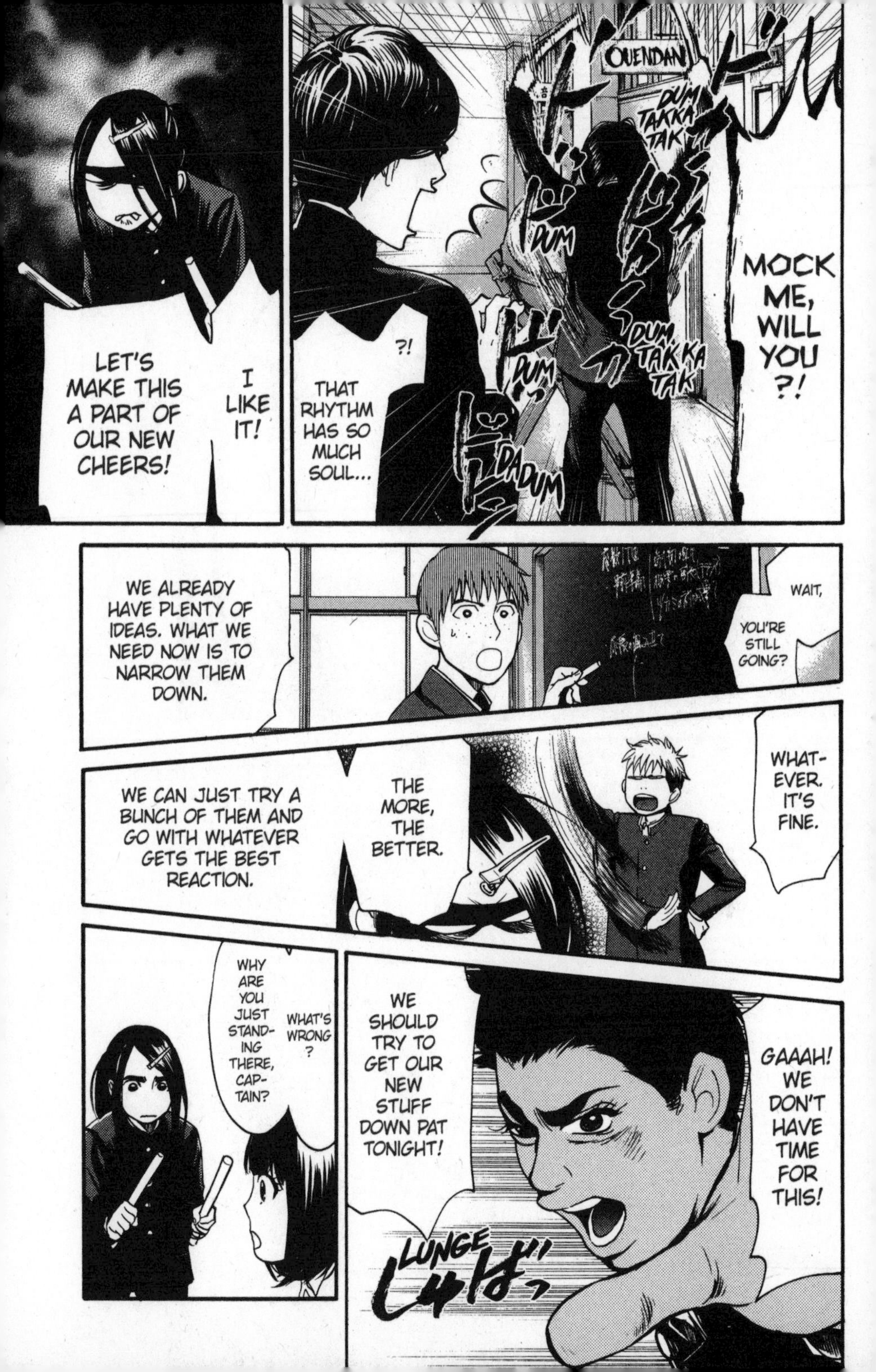
OUENDAN
DUM TAKKA TAK
MOCK ME, WILL YOU?!
DUM
DUM TAK KA TAK
DUM
DADUM
?!
THAT RHYTHM HAS SO MUCH SOUL...
I LIKE IT!
LET'S MAKE THIS A PART OF OUR NEW CHEERS!
WAIT,
YOU'RE STILL GOING?
WE ALREADY HAVE PLENTY OF IDEAS. WHAT WE NEED NOW IS TO NARROW THEM DOWN.
WHATEVER. IT'S FINE.
THE MORE, THE BETTER.
WE CAN JUST TRY A BUNCH OF THEM AND GO WITH WHATEVER GETS THE BEST REACTION.
GAAAH! WE DON'T HAVE TIME FOR THIS!
WE SHOULD TRY TO GET OUR NEW STUFF DOWN PAT TONIGHT!
LUNGE
WHAT'S WRONG?
WHY ARE YOU JUST STANDING THERE, CAPTAIN?

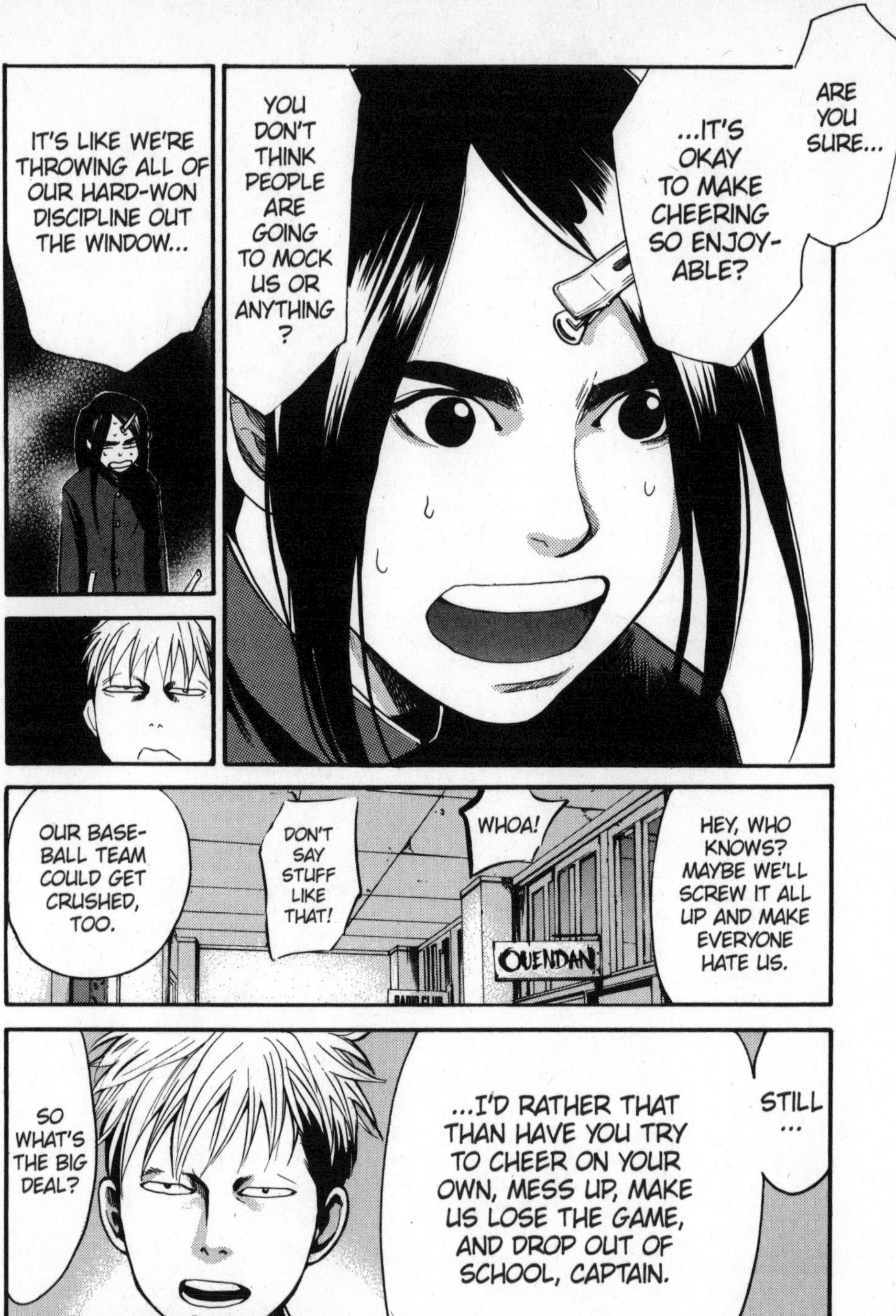

ARE YOU SURE...
...IT'S OKAY TO MAKE CHEERING SO ENJOYABLE?
YOU DON'T THINK PEOPLE ARE GOING TO MOCK US OR ANYTHING?
IT'S LIKE WE'RE THROWING ALL OF OUR HARD-WON DISCIPLINE OUT THE WINDOW...
HEY, WHO KNOWS? MAYBE WE'LL SCREW IT ALL UP AND MAKE EVERYONE HATE US.
OUENDAN
WHOA!
DON'T SAY STUFF LIKE THAT!
OUR BASEBALL TEAM COULD GET CRUSHED, TOO.
STILL...
...I'D RATHER THAT THAN HAVE YOU TRY TO CHEER ON YOUR OWN, MESS UP, MAKE US LOSE THE GAME, AND DROP OUT OF SCHOOL, CAPTAIN.
SO WHAT'S THE BIG DEAL?

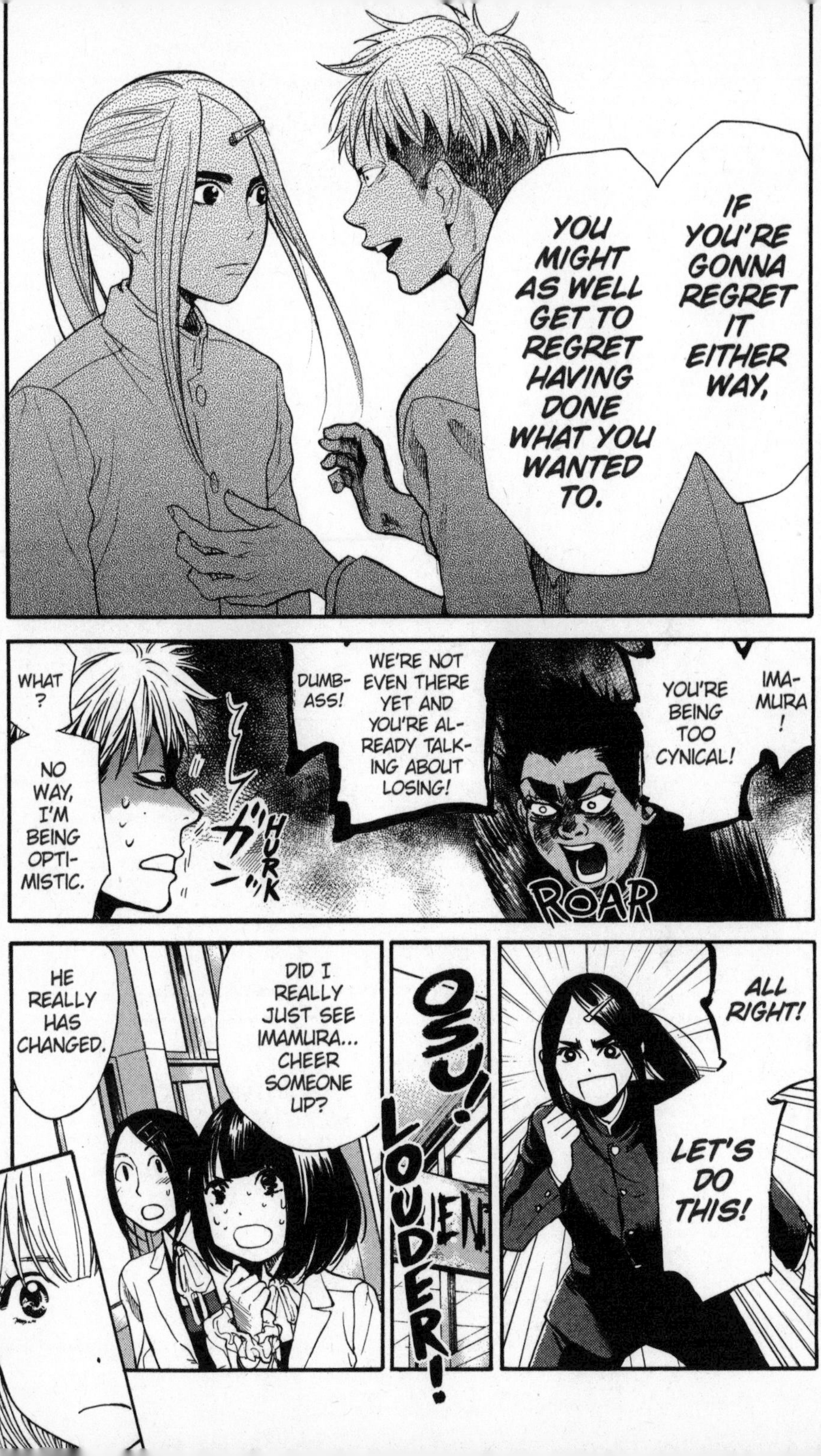
IF YOU'RE GONNA REGRET IT EITHER WAY,
YOU MIGHT AS WELL GET TO REGRET HAVING DONE WHAT YOU WANTED TO.
IMAMURA!
YOU'RE BEING TOO CYNICAL!
WE'RE NOT EVEN THERE YET AND YOU'RE ALREADY TALKING ABOUT LOSING!
DUMBASS!
ROAR
HURK
WHAT?
NO WAY, I'M BEING OPTIMISTIC.
ALL RIGHT!
LET'S DO THIS!
OSU!!
LOUDER!
DID I REALLY JUST SEE IMAMURA... CHEER SOMEONE UP?
HE REALLY HAS CHANGED.

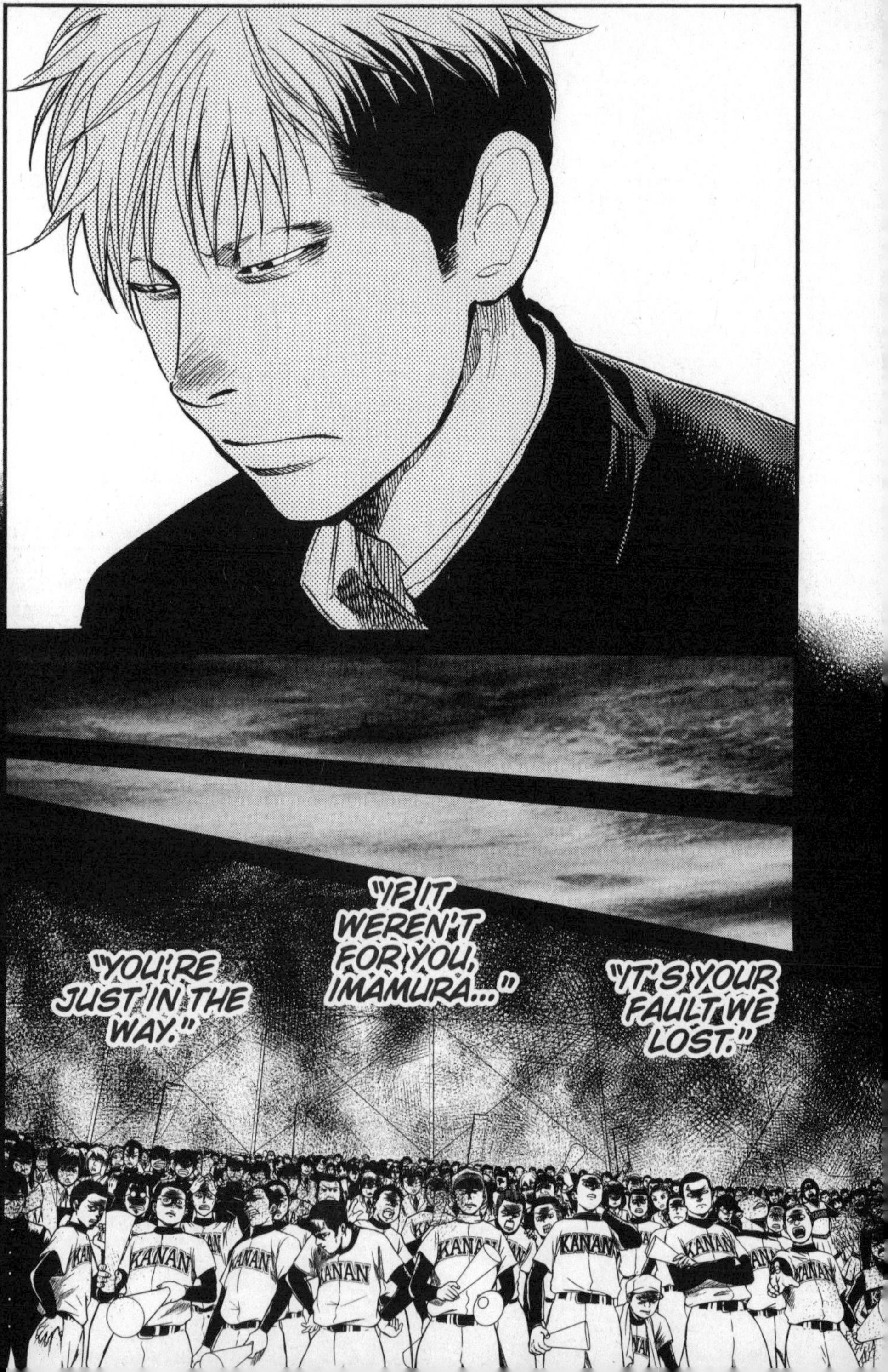
"IT'S YOUR FAULT WE LOST."
"IF IT WEREN'T FOR YOU, IMAMURA..."
"YOU'RE JUST IN THE WAY."

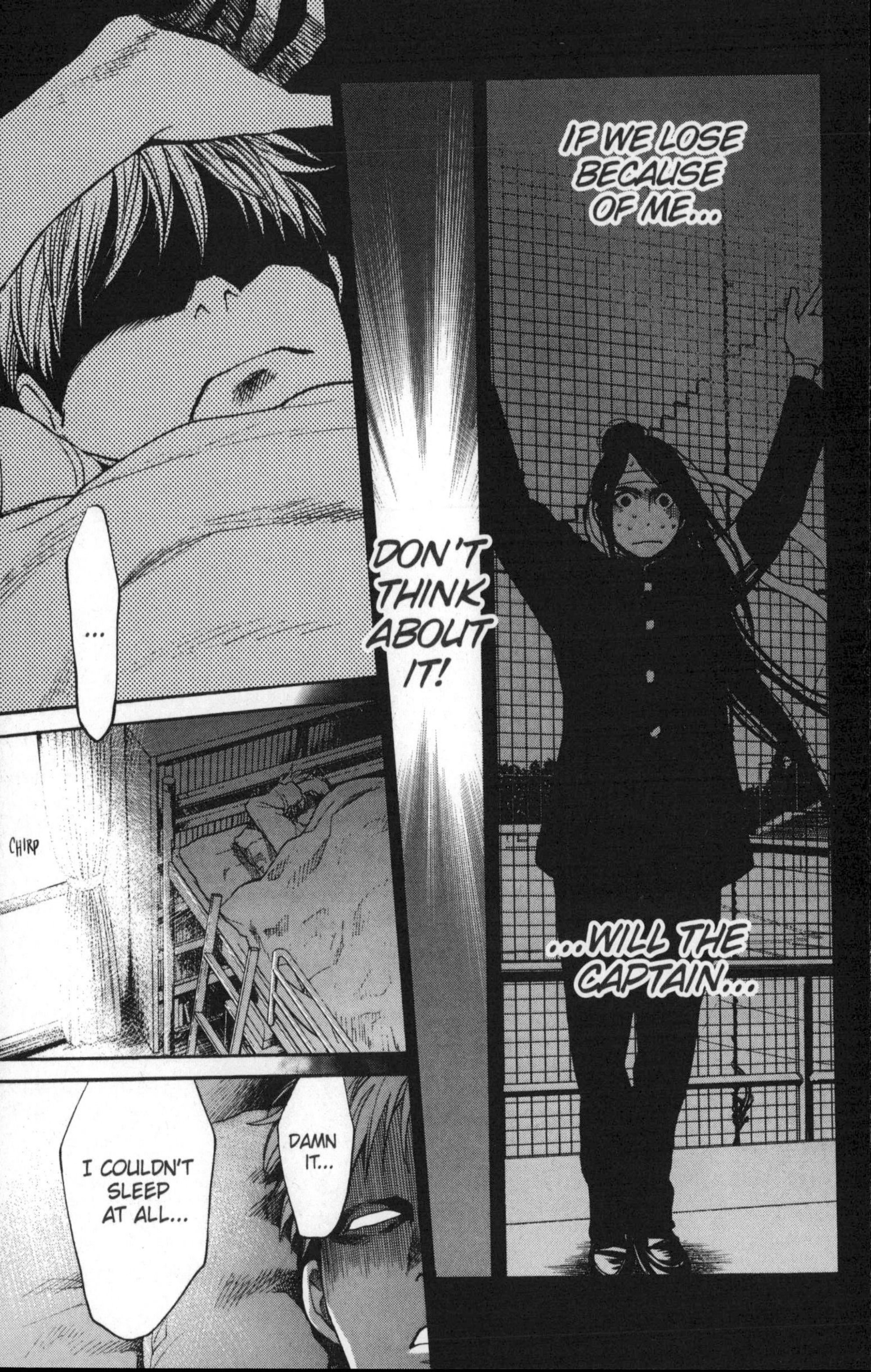
IF WE LOSE BECAUSE OF ME...
...WILL THE CAPTAIN...
DON'T THINK ABOUT IT!
...
CHIRP
DAMN IT...
I COULDN'T SLEEP AT ALL...

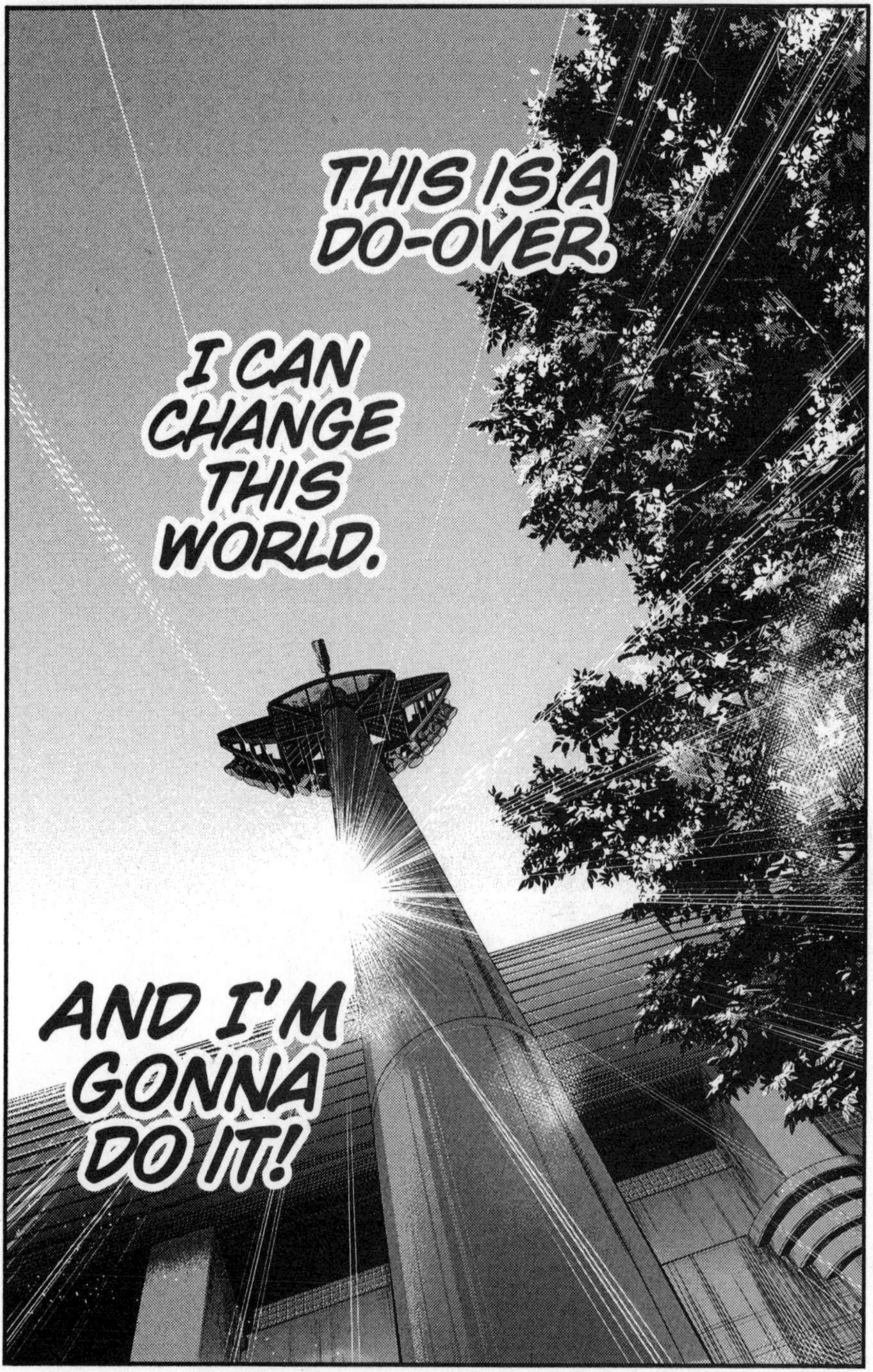
THIS IS A DO-OVER.
I CAN CHANGE THIS WORLD.
AND I'M GONNA DO IT!

# 47. CHECK OUT WHO'S CHECKING IN

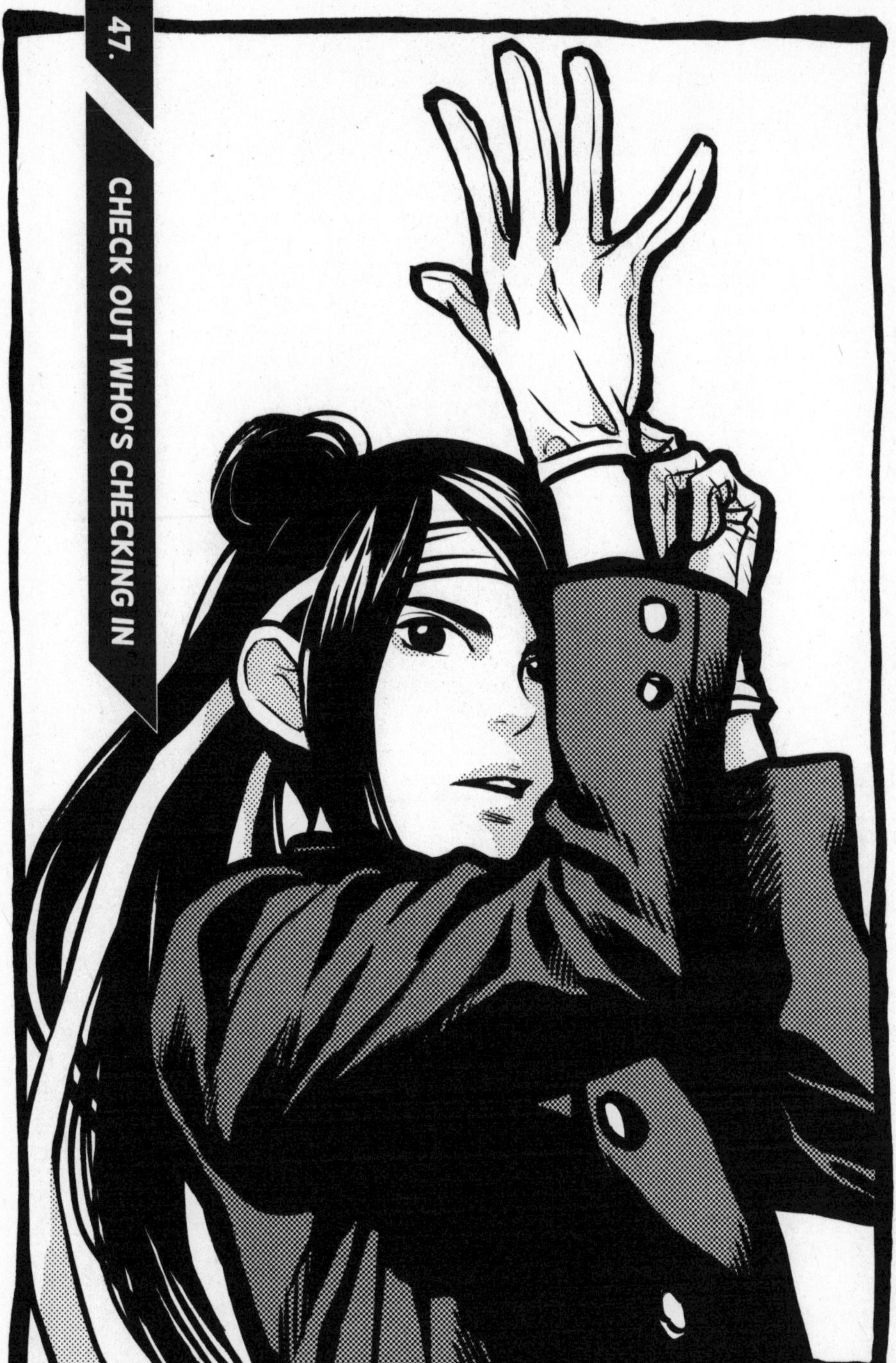

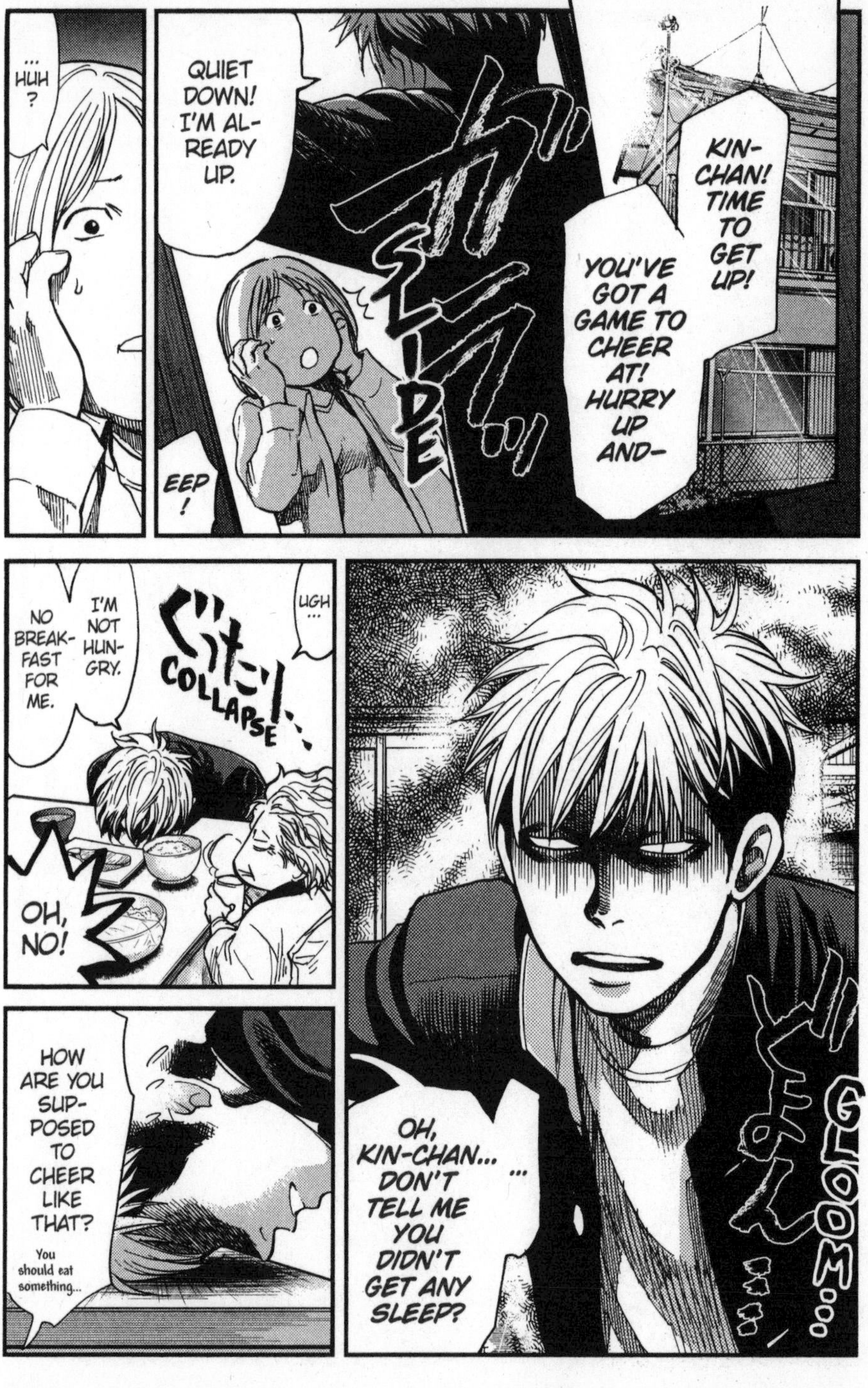
KIN-CHAN! TIME TO GET UP!
YOU'VE GOT A GAME TO CHEER AT! HURRY UP AND-
SLIDE
QUIET DOWN! I'M ALREADY UP.
EEP!
... HUH?
GLOOM...
...
OH, KIN-CHAN... DON'T TELL ME YOU DIDN'T GET ANY SLEEP?
UGH...
COLLAPSE
I'M NOT HUNGRY.
NO BREAKFAST FOR ME.
OH, NO!
HOW ARE YOU SUPPOSED TO CHEER LIKE THAT?
You should eat something...

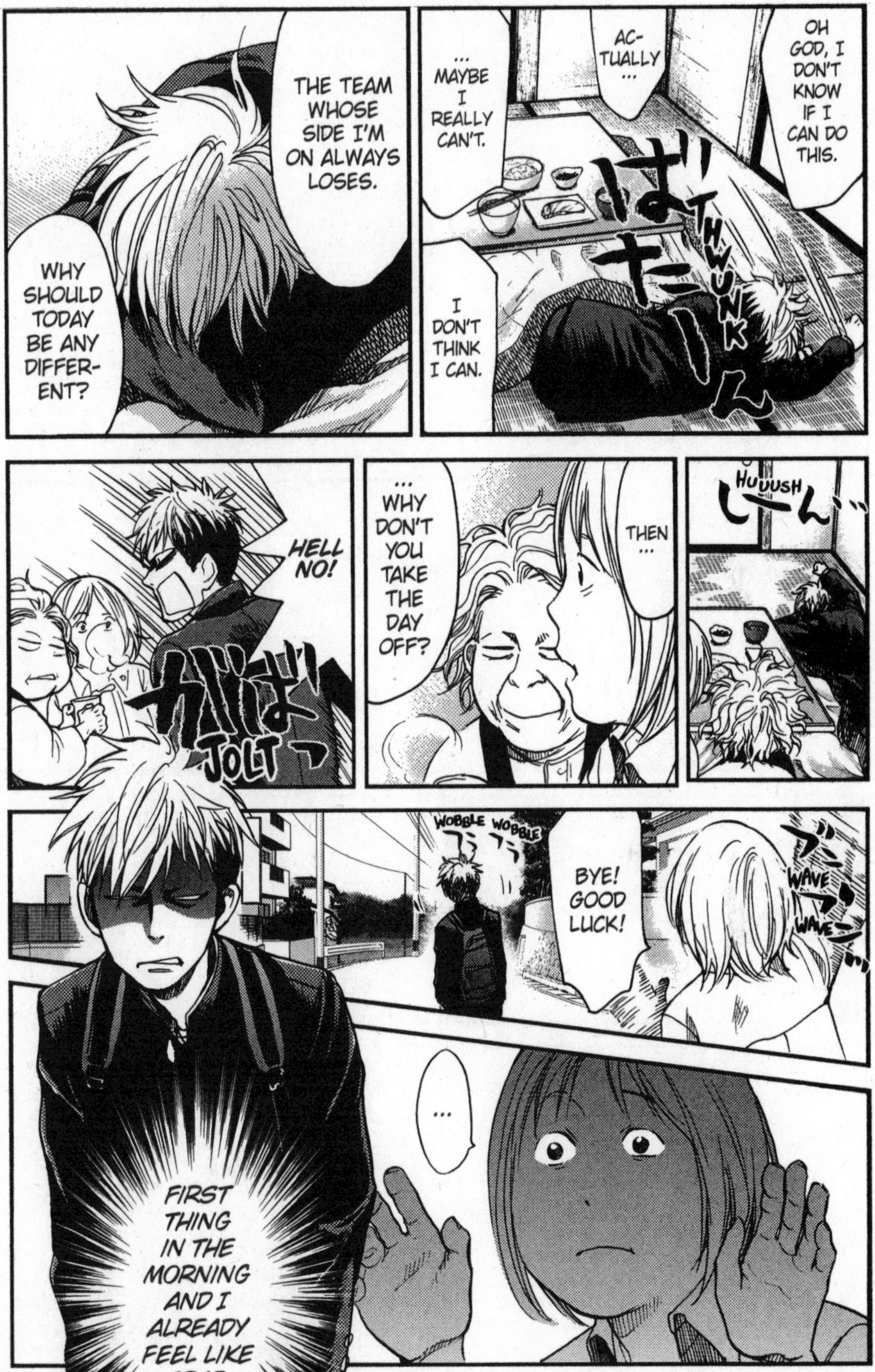
OH GOD, I DON'T KNOW IF I CAN DO THIS.
ACTUALLY ...
... MAYBE I REALLY CAN'T.
ばたーん
THWUNK
I DON'T THINK I CAN.
THE TEAM WHOSE SIDE I'M ON ALWAYS LOSES.
WHY SHOULD TODAY BE ANY DIFFERENT?
じーん
HUUUSH
THEN ...
... WHY DON'T YOU TAKE THE DAY OFF?
HELL NO!
がばっ
JOLT
WAVE WAVE
BYE! GOOD LUCK!
WOBBLE WOBBLE
...
FIRST THING IN THE MORNING AND I ALREADY FEEL LIKE CRAP.

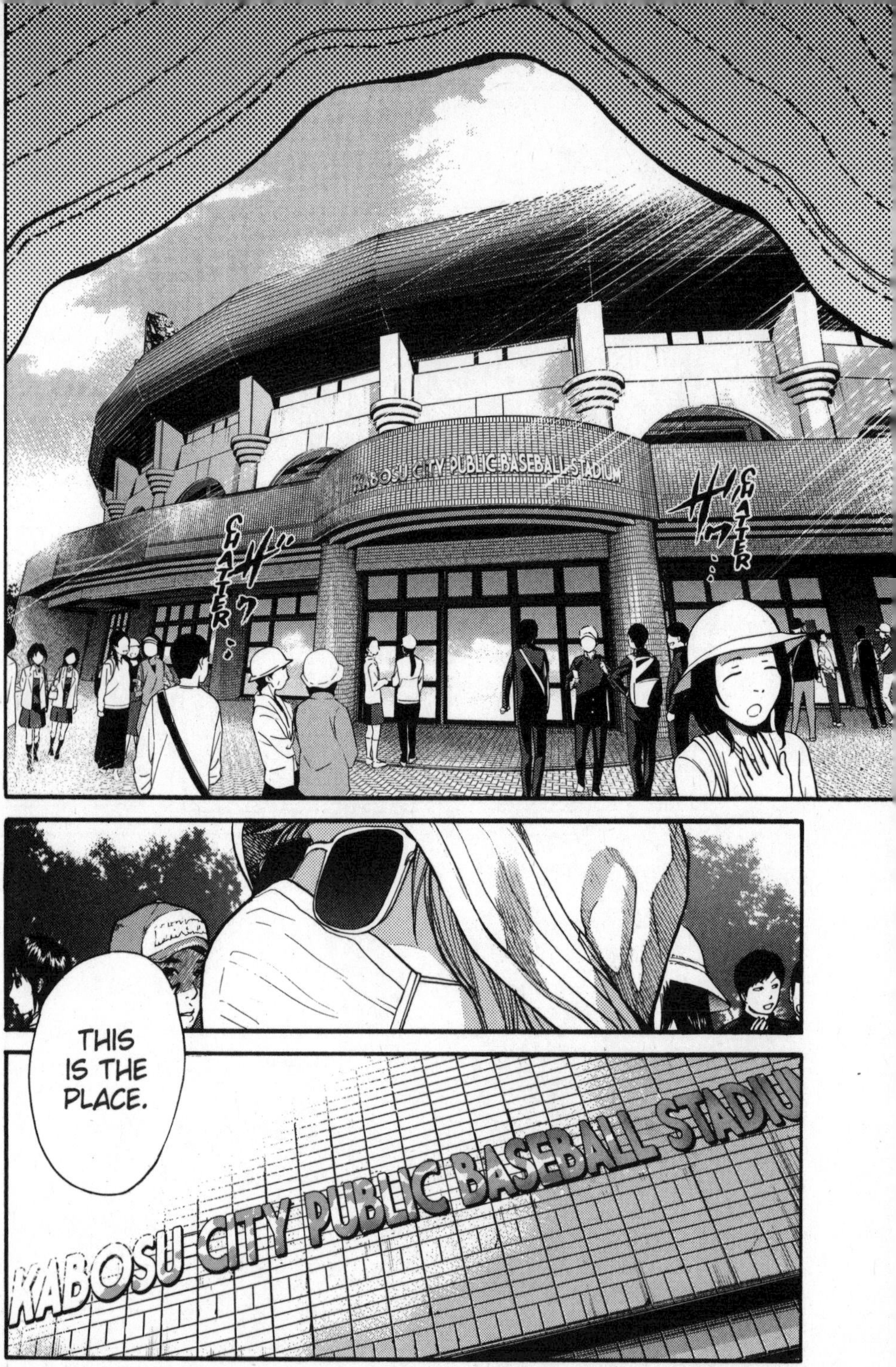
KABOSU CITY PUBLIC BASEBALL STADIUM
CHATTER
CHATTER
THIS IS THE PLACE.
KABOSU CITY PUBLIC BASEBALL STADIU

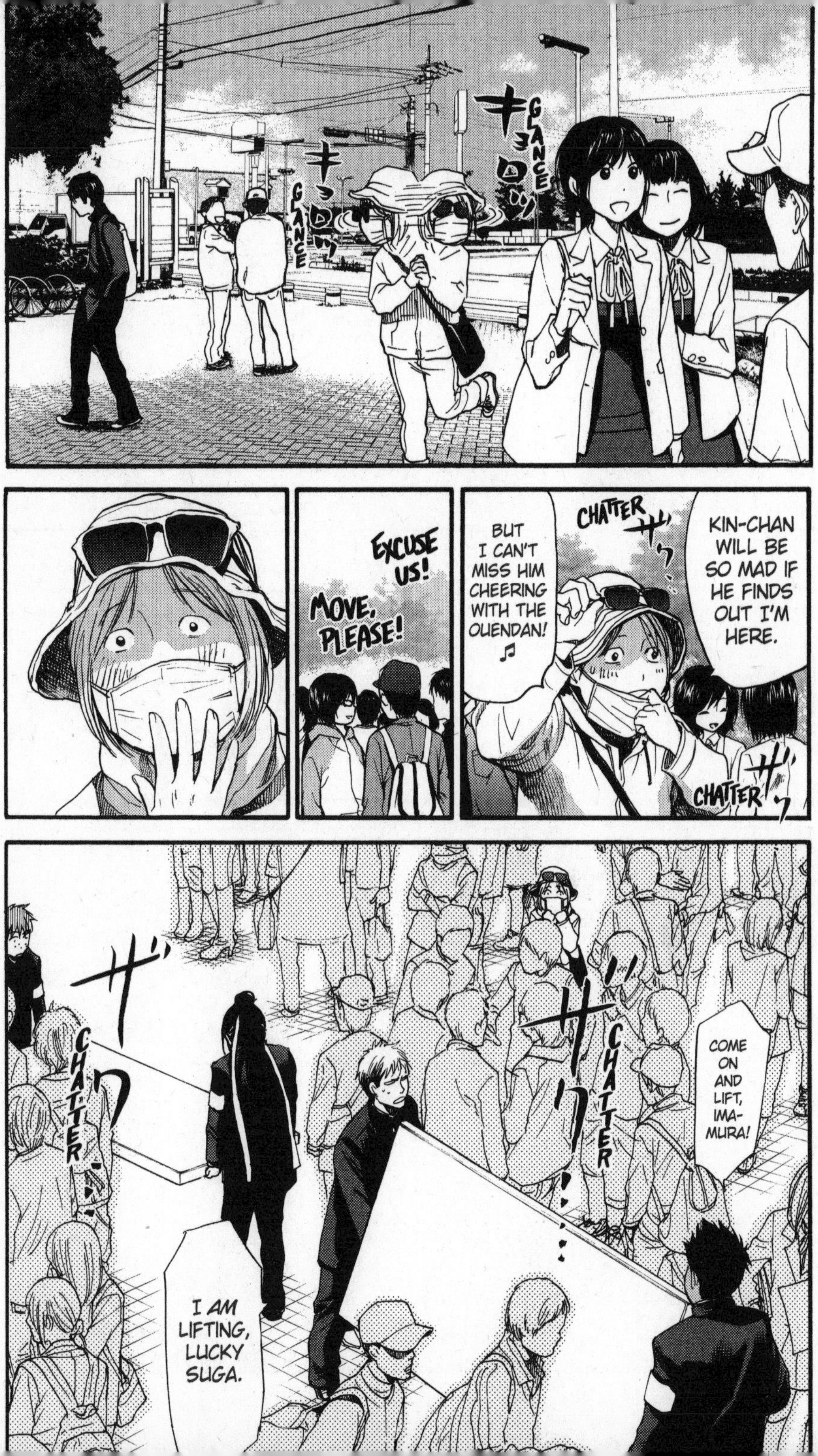
GLANCE
GLANCE
KIN-CHAN WILL BE SO MAD IF HE FINDS OUT I'M HERE.
CHATTER
BUT I CAN'T MISS HIM CHEERING WITH THE OUENDAN! ♪
CHATTER
EXCUSE US!
MOVE, PLEASE!
CHATTER
COME ON AND LIFT, IMA-MURA!
CHATTER
I AM LIFTING, LUCKY SUGA.

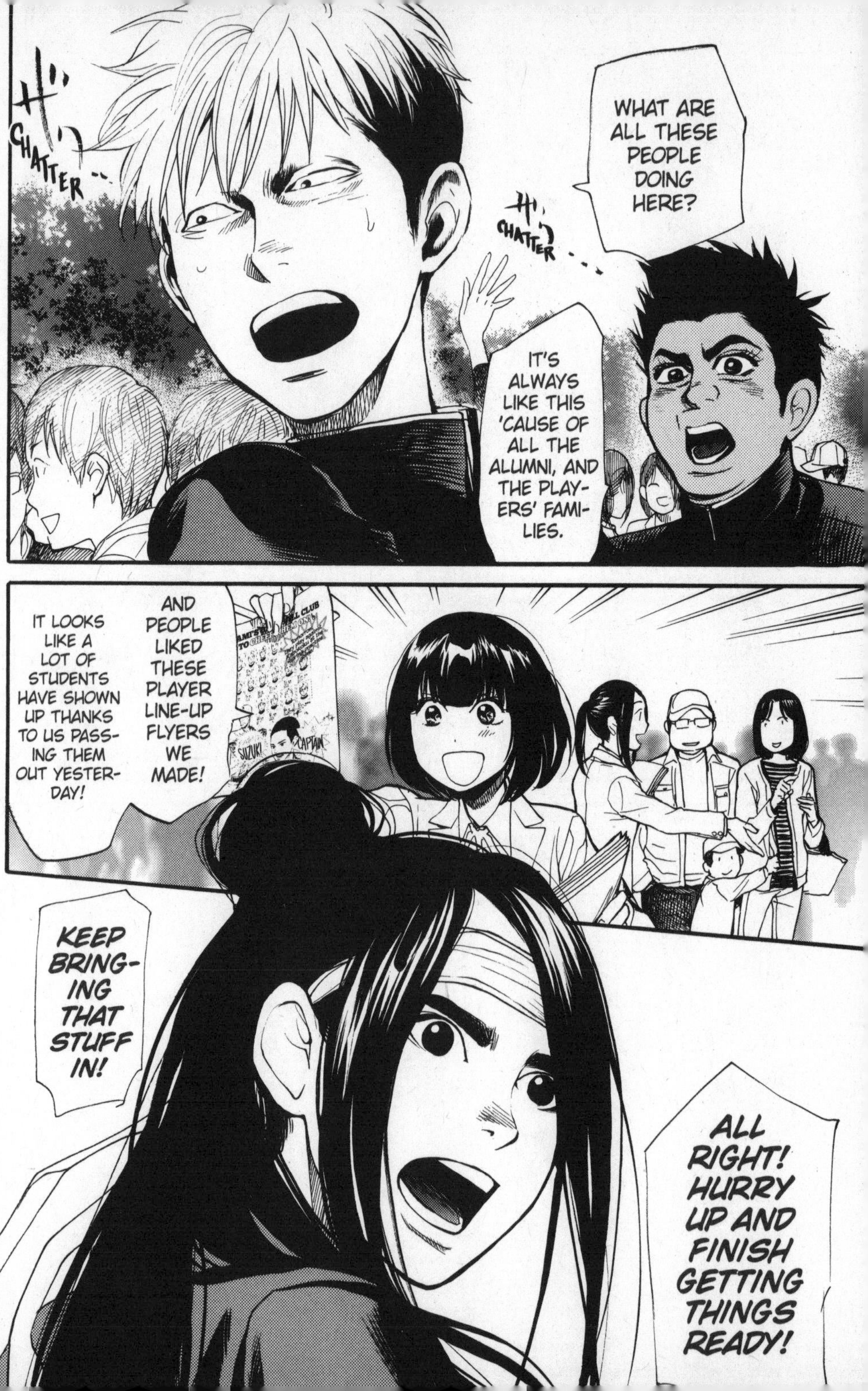
WHAT ARE ALL THESE PEOPLE DOING HERE?
CHATTER...
IT'S ALWAYS LIKE THIS 'CAUSE OF ALL THE ALUMNI, AND THE PLAYERS' FAMILIES.
CHATTER...
AND PEOPLE LIKED THESE PLAYER LINE-UP FLYERS WE MADE!
IT LOOKS LIKE A LOT OF STUDENTS HAVE SHOWN UP THANKS TO US PASSING THEM OUT YESTERDAY!
SUZUKI
CAPTAIN
ALL RIGHT! HURRY UP AND FINISH GETTING THINGS READY!
KEEP BRINGING THAT STUFF IN!

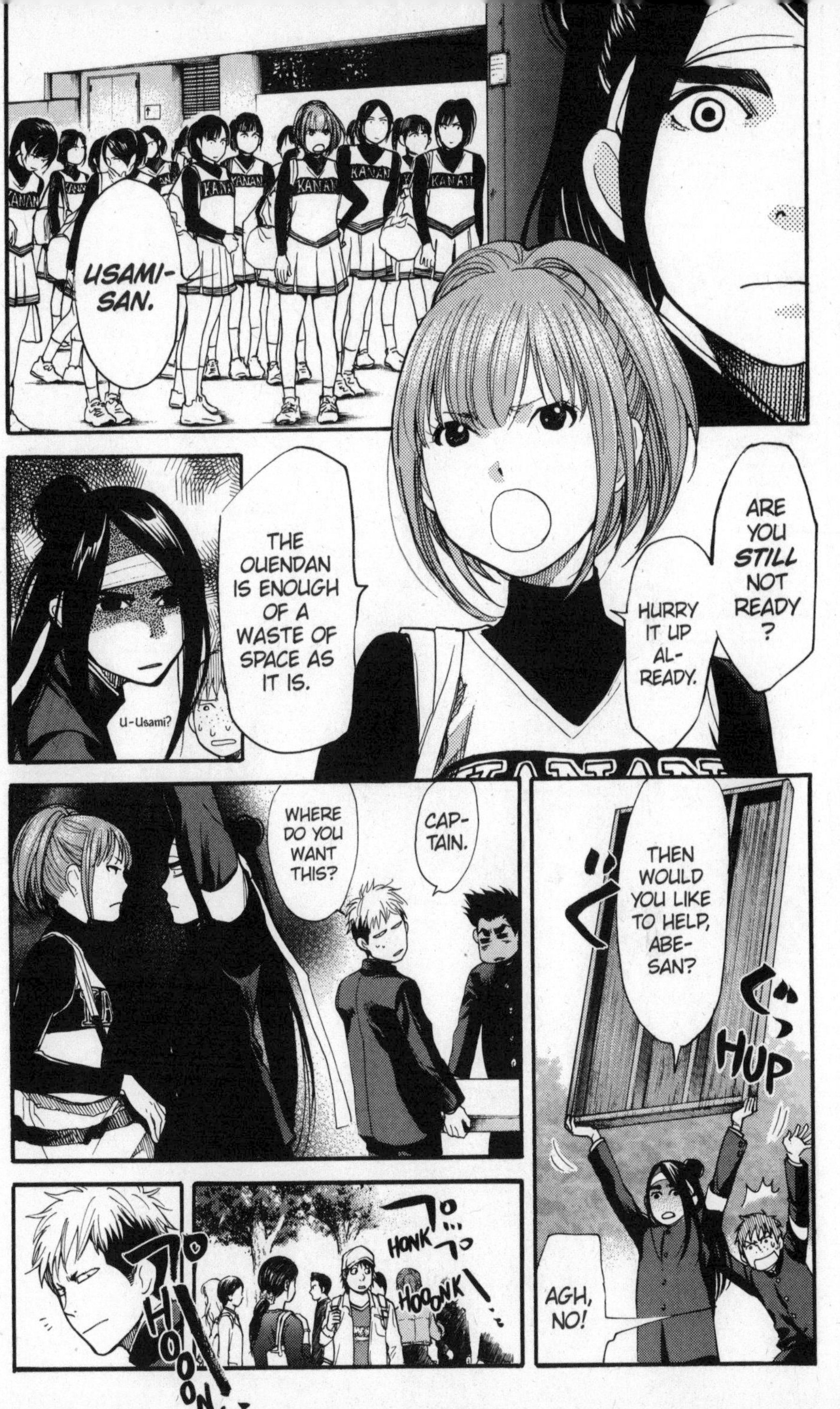
USAMI-SAN.
ARE YOU STILL NOT READY?
HURRY IT UP AL-READY.
THE OUENDAN IS ENOUGH OF A WASTE OF SPACE AS IT IS.
U-Usami?
THEN WOULD YOU LIKE TO HELP, ABE-SAN?
HUP
AGH, NO!
CAP-TAIN.
WHERE DO YOU WANT THIS?
HONK
HOOONK
HOOOONK

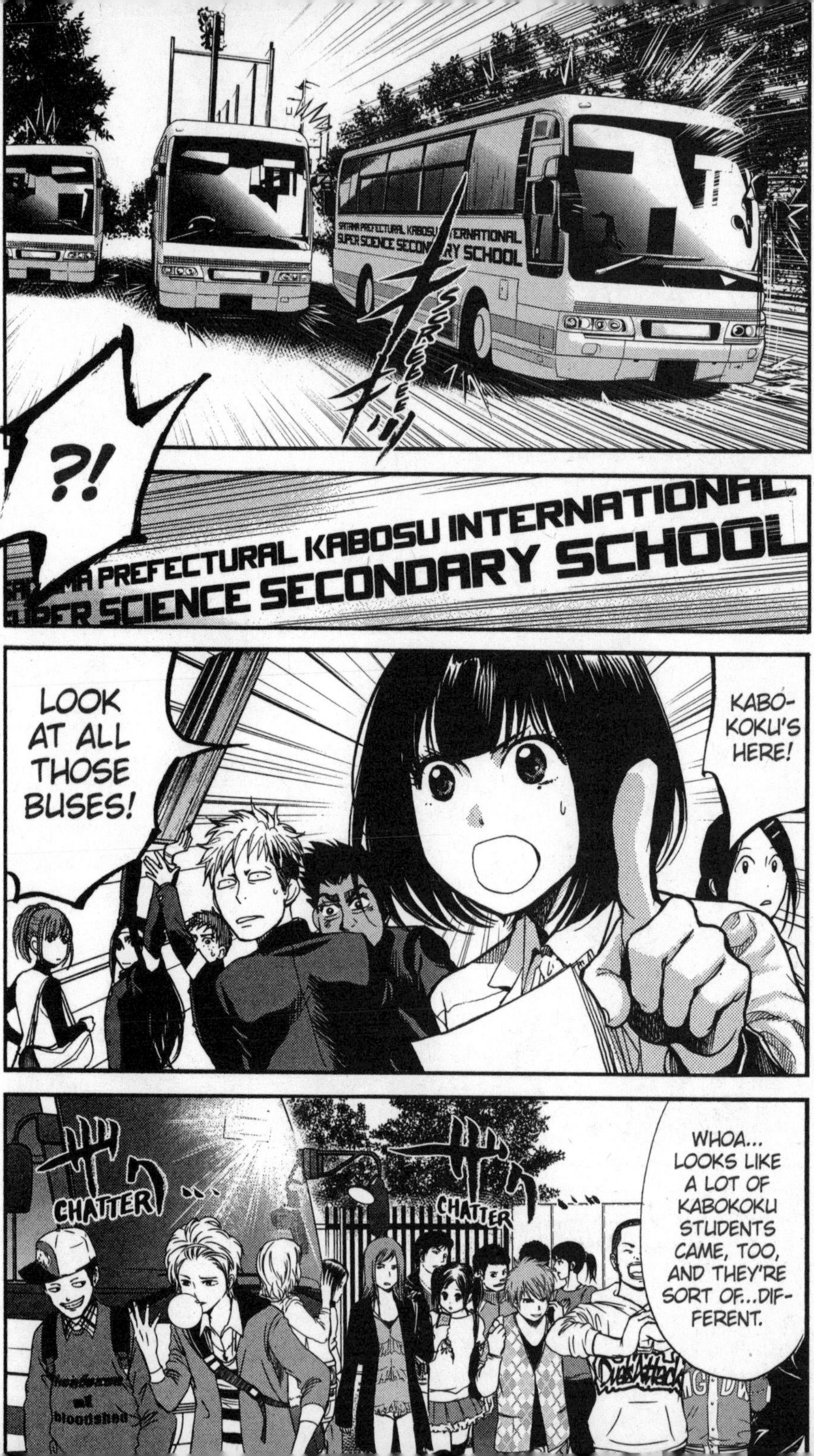

SAITAMA PREFECTURAL KABOSU INTERNATIONAL
SUPER SCIENCE SECONDARY SCHOOL
SCREEEE
?!
PREFECTURAL KABOSU INTERNATIONAL
SCIENCE SECONDARY SCHOOL
KABO-KOKU'S HERE!
LOOK AT ALL THOSE BUSES!
WHOA... LOOKS LIKE A LOT OF KABOKOKU STUDENTS CAME, TOO, AND THEY'RE SORT OF...DIF-FERENT.
CHATTER
CHATTER
bloodshed

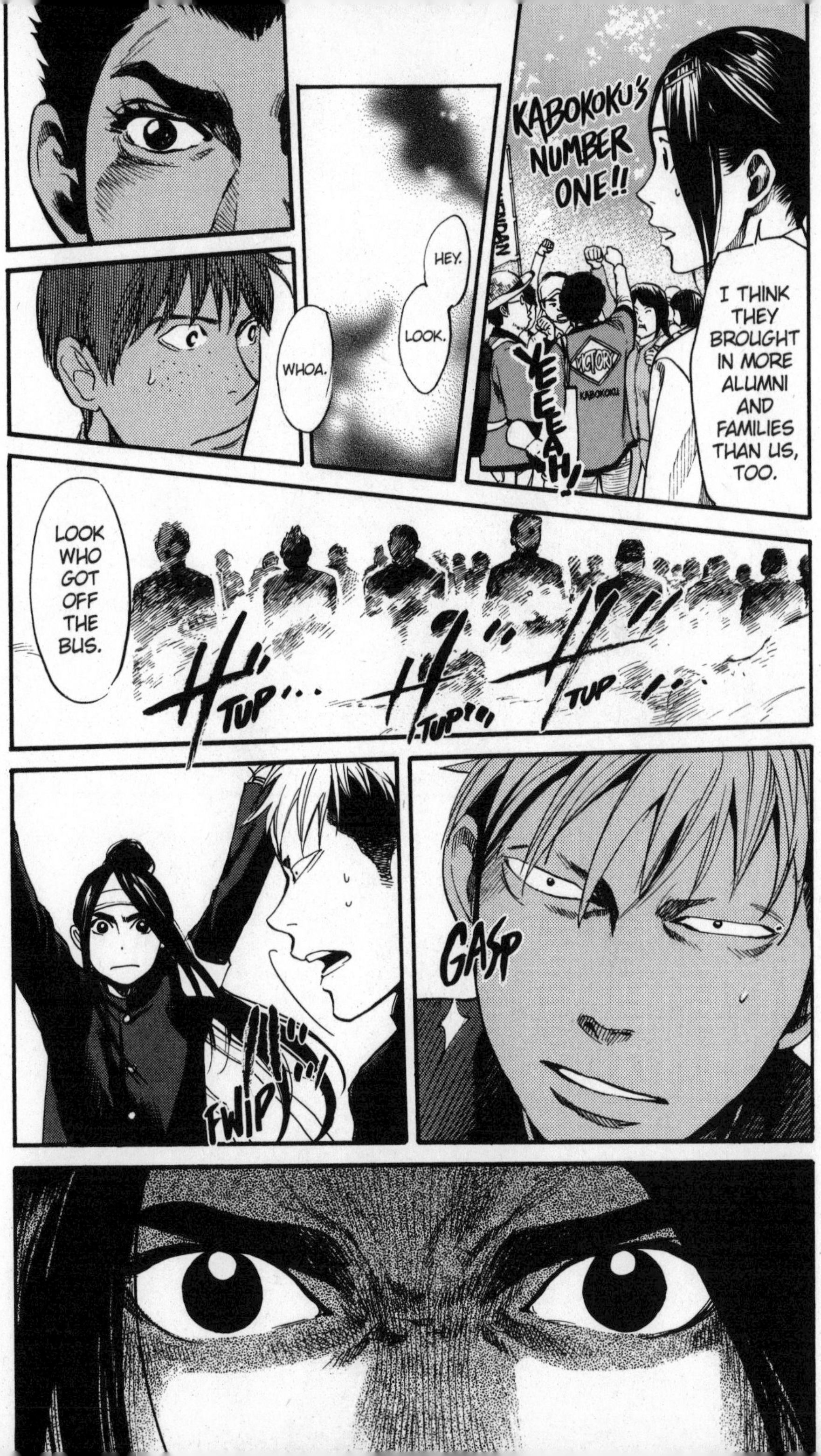

KABOKOKU'S NUMBER ONE!!
YEEEEAH!!
VICTORY
KABOKOKU
I THINK THEY BROUGHT IN MORE ALUMNI AND FAMILIES THAN US, TOO.
HEY.
LOOK.
WHOA.
LOOK WHO GOT OFF THE BUS.
TUP...
TUP...
TUP...
GASP
FWIP

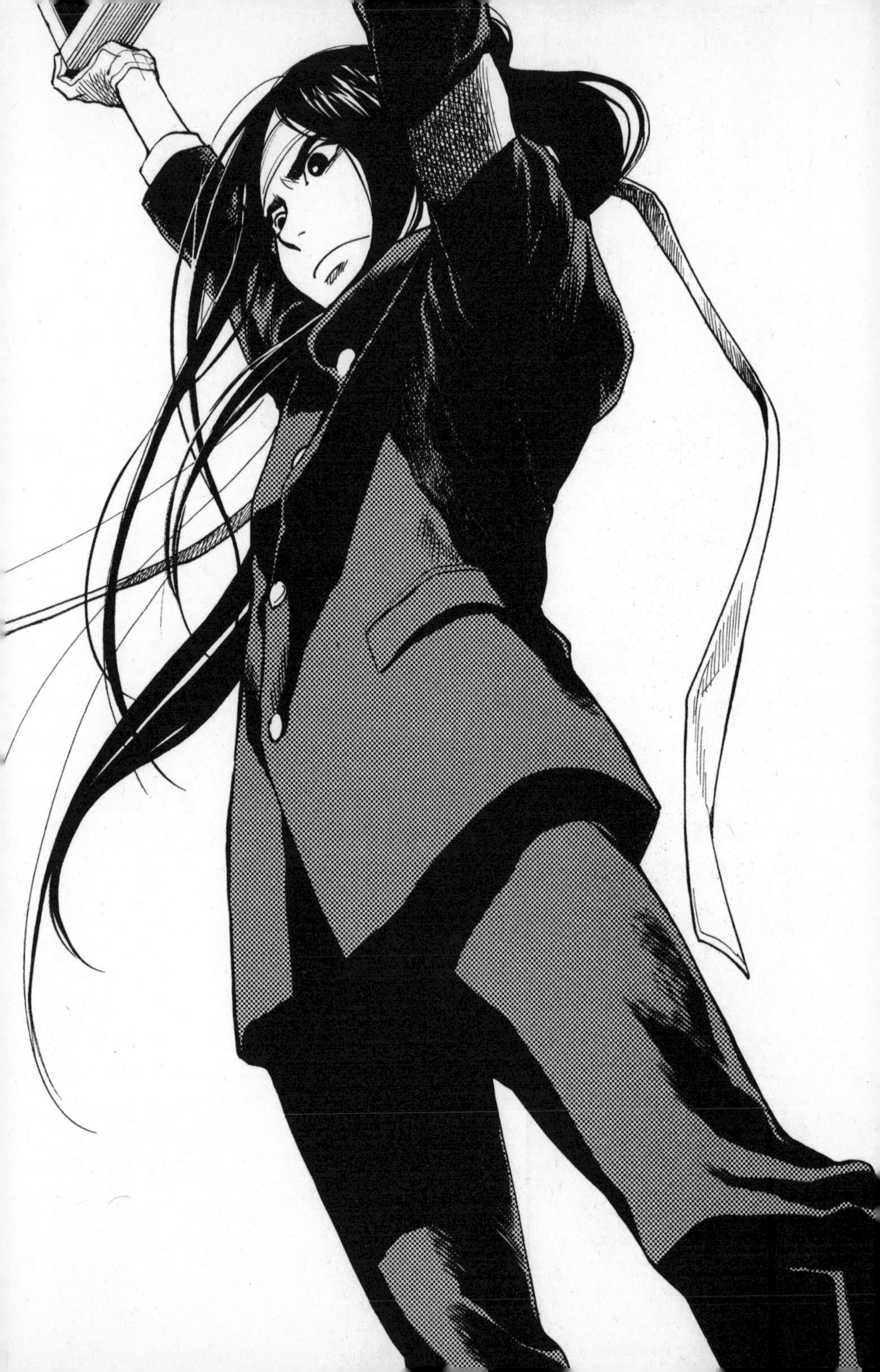

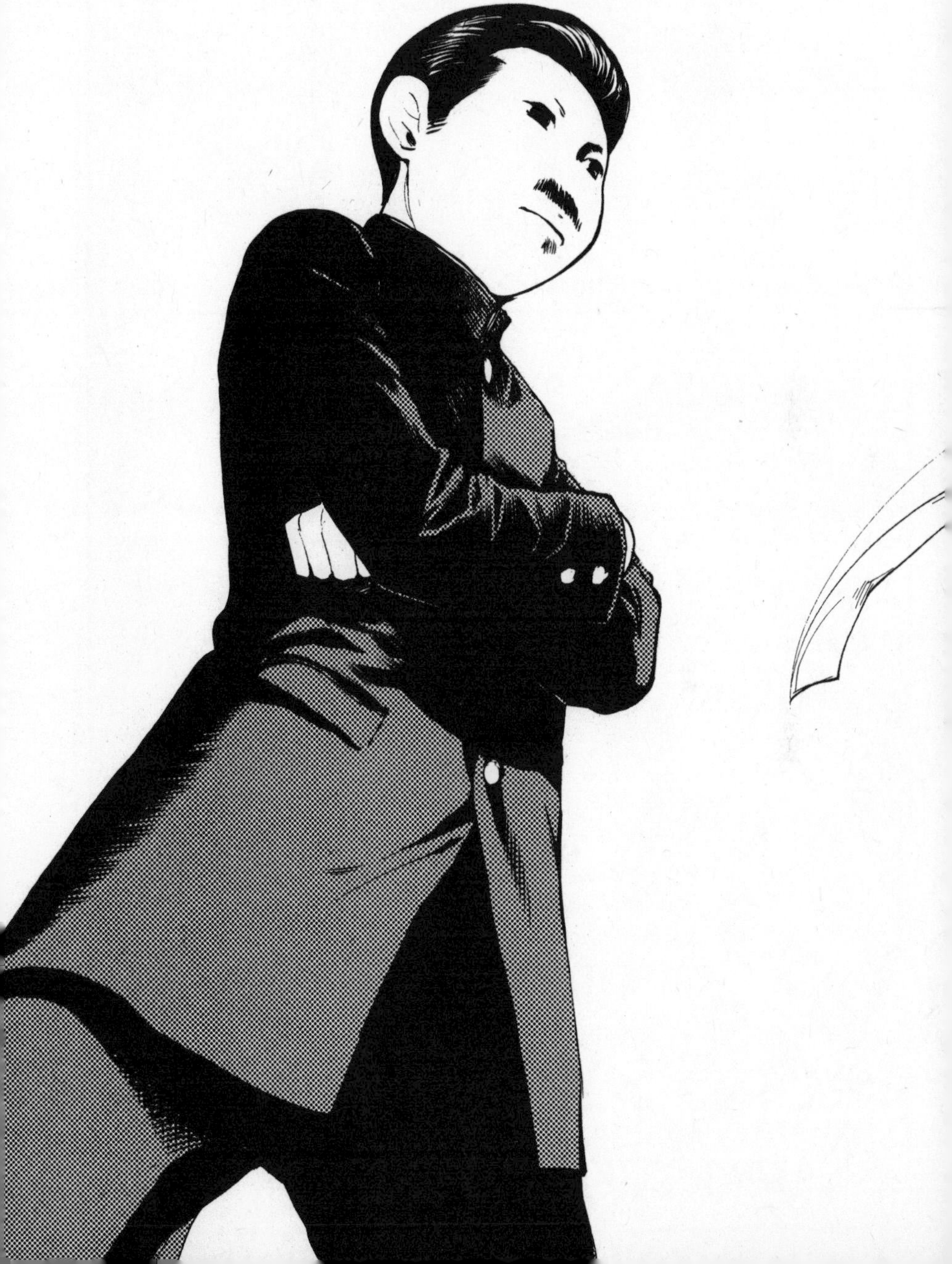

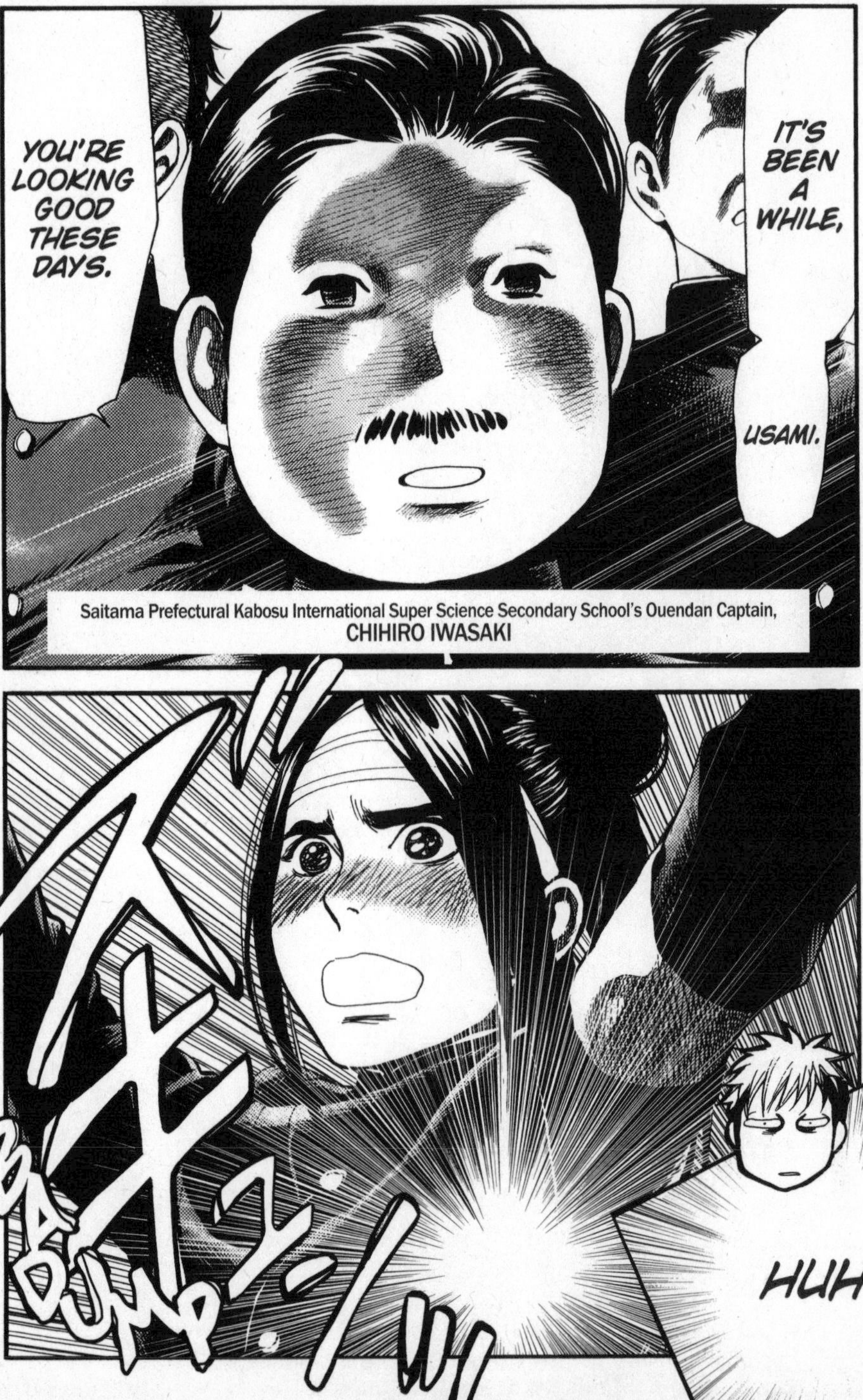
IT'S BEEN A WHILE,
USAMI.
YOU'RE LOOKING GOOD THESE DAYS.
Saitama Prefectural Kabosu International Super Science Secondary School's Ouendan Captain, CHIHIRO IWASAKI
BA DUMP
HUH?!

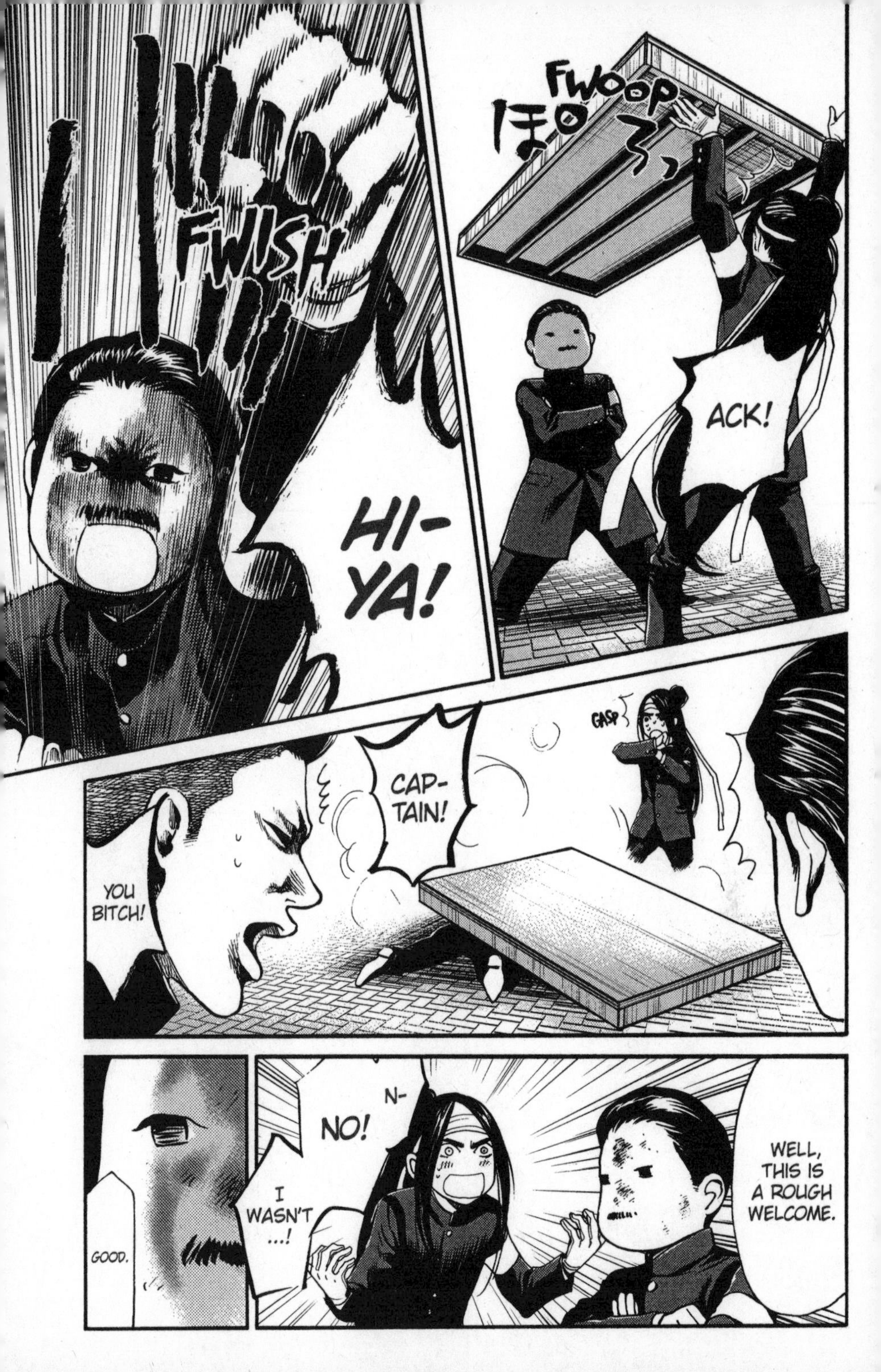
FWOOP
ACK!
FWISH
HI-YA!
GASP
CAP-TAIN!
YOU BITCH!
WELL, THIS IS A ROUGH WELCOME.
N- NO!
I WASN'T ...!
GOOD.

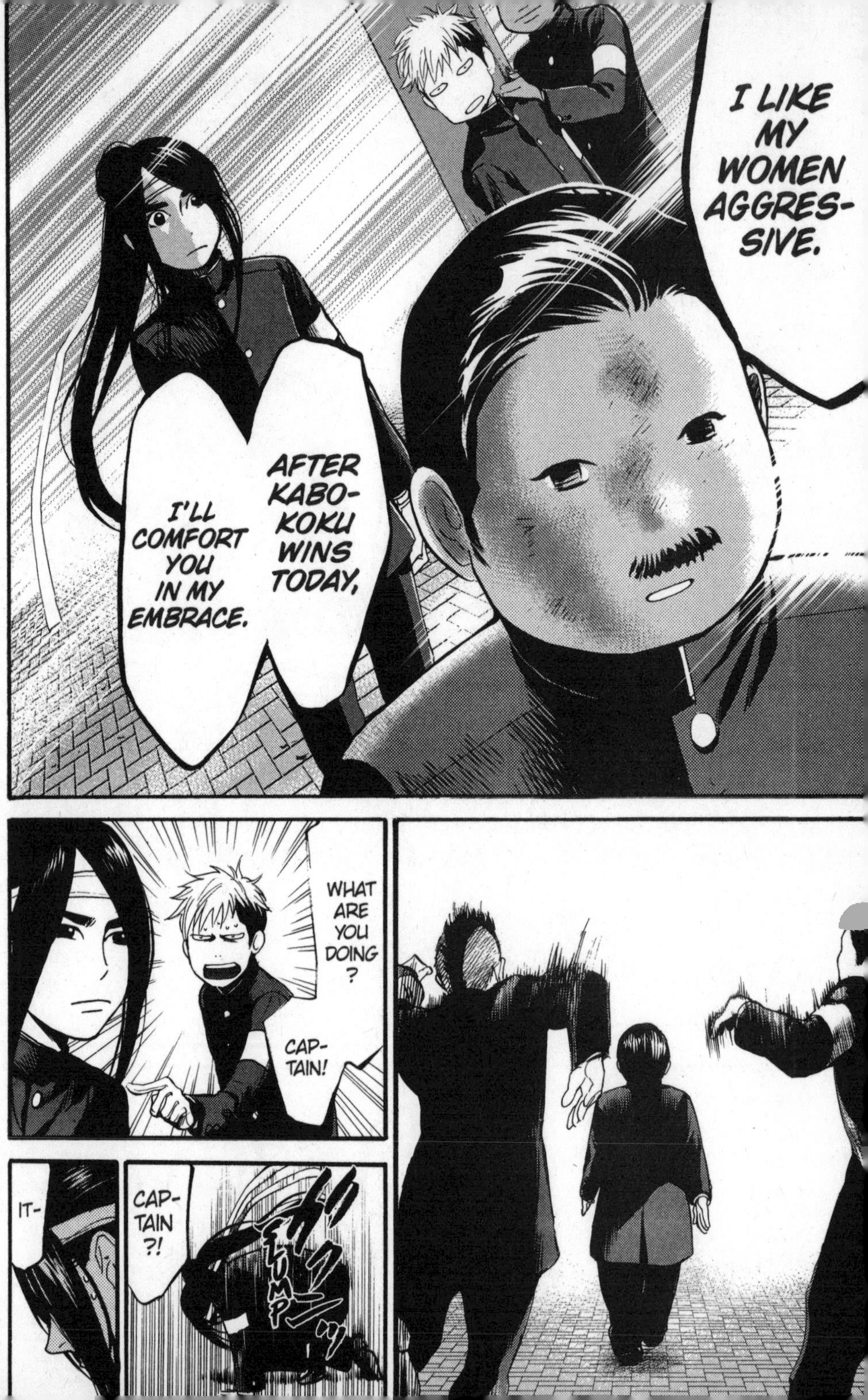
I LIKE MY WOMEN AGGRESSIVE.
AFTER KABOKOKU WINS TODAY,
I'LL COMFORT YOU IN MY EMBRACE.
WHAT ARE YOU DOING?
CAPTAIN!
CAPTAIN?!
FLUMP
IT-

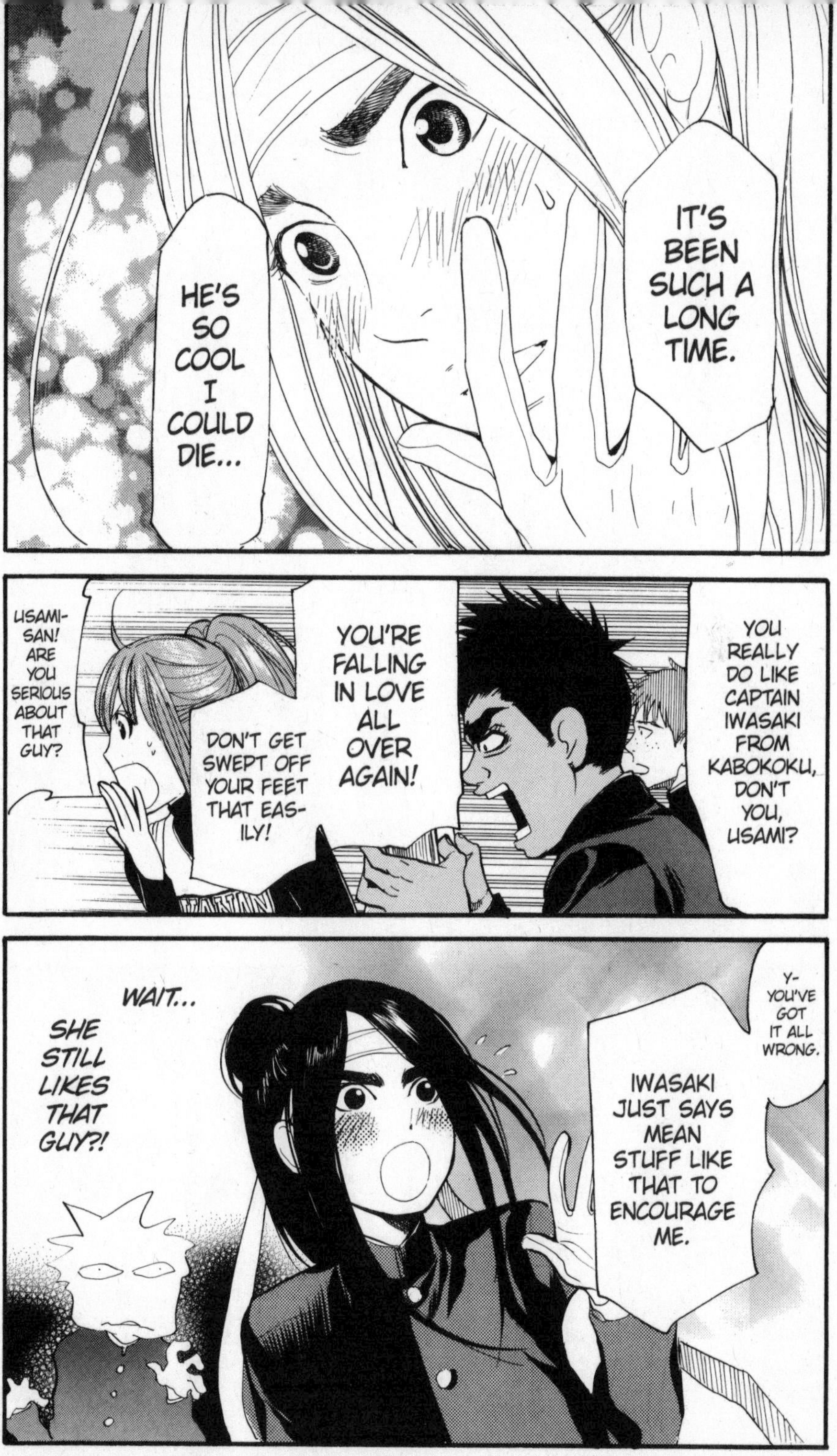
IT'S BEEN SUCH A LONG TIME.
HE'S SO COOL I COULD DIE...
YOU REALLY DO LIKE CAPTAIN IWASAKI FROM KABOKOKU, DON'T YOU, USAMI?
YOU'RE FALLING IN LOVE ALL OVER AGAIN!
DON'T GET SWEPT OFF YOUR FEET THAT EAS-ILY!
USAMI-SAN! ARE YOU SERIOUS ABOUT THAT GUY?
Y-YOU'VE GOT IT ALL WRONG.
IWASAKI JUST SAYS MEAN STUFF LIKE THAT TO ENCOURAGE ME.
WAIT...
SHE STILL LIKES THAT GUY?!

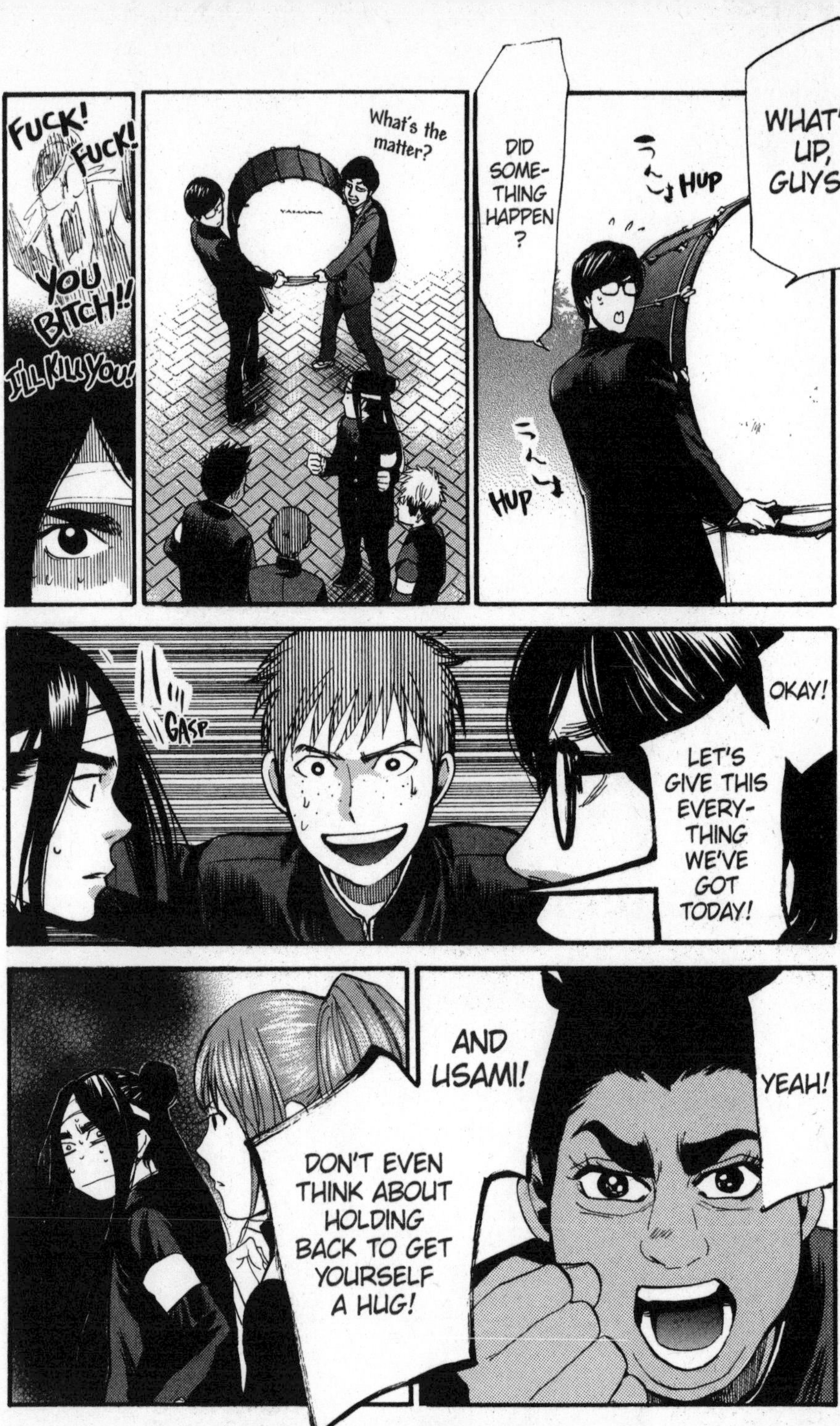
WHAT'S UP, GUYS?
HUP
DID SOMETHING HAPPEN?
HUP
What's the matter?
FUCK! FUCK!
YOU BITCH!!
I'LL KILL YOU!
OKAY!
LET'S GIVE THIS EVERYTHING WE'VE GOT TODAY!
GASP
YEAH!
AND USAMI!
DON'T EVEN THINK ABOUT HOLDING BACK TO GET YOURSELF A HUG!

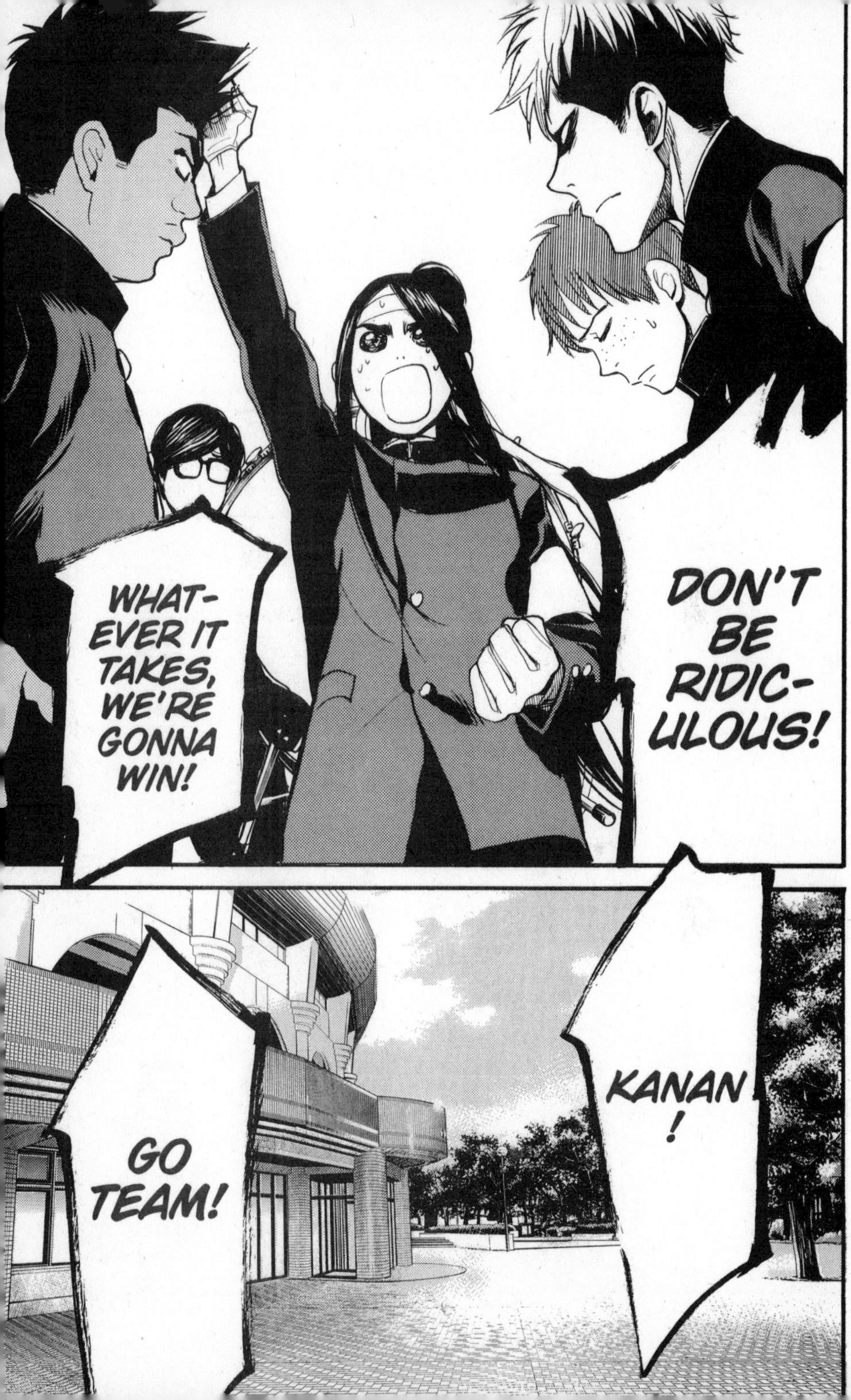
DON'T BE RIDIC-ULOUS!
WHAT-EVER IT TAKES, WE'RE GONNA WIN!
KANAN!
GO TEAM!

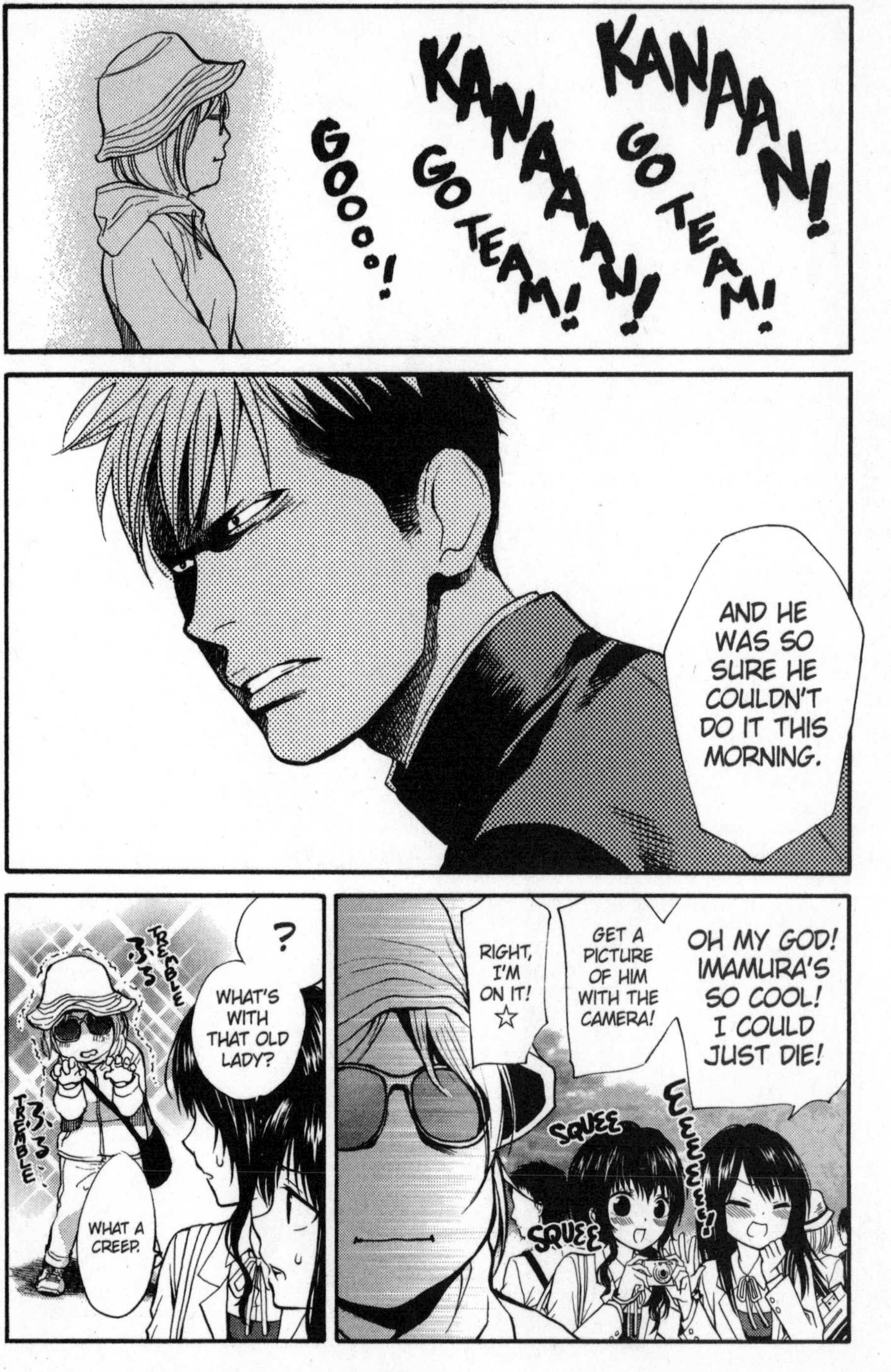
KANAAAN!
GO TEAM!
KANAAAAN!
GO TEAM!
GOOoo!
AND HE WAS SO SURE HE COULDN'T DO IT THIS MORNING.
OH MY GOD! IMAMURA'S SO COOL! I COULD JUST DIE!
GET A PICTURE OF HIM WITH THE CAMERA!
RIGHT, I'M ON IT! ☆
EEEEEE!
SQUEE
SQUEE
?
WHAT'S WITH THAT OLD LADY?
TREMBLE
TREMBLE
WHAT A CREEP.

# 48. THE WEIRDO OUENDAN FIVE

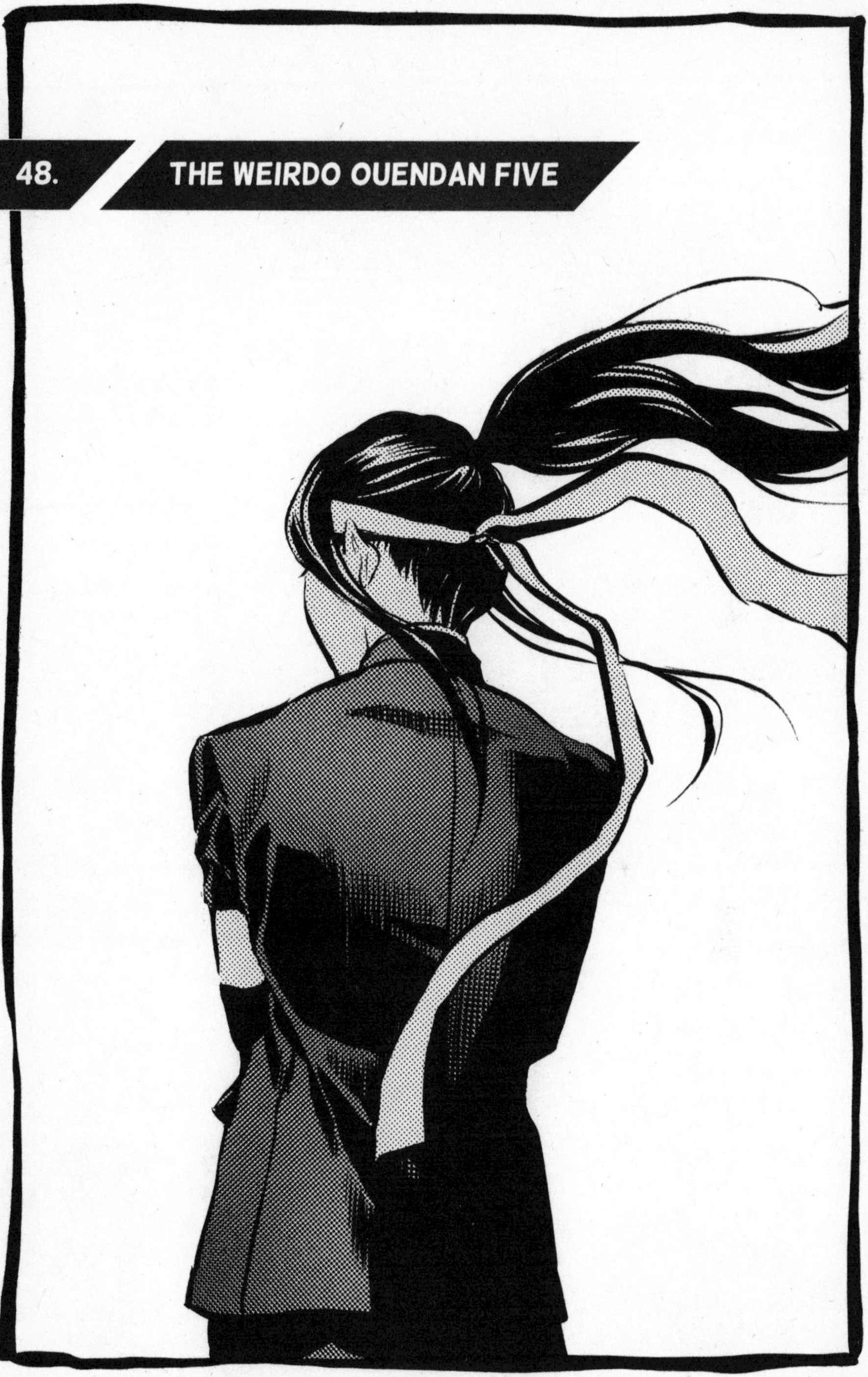

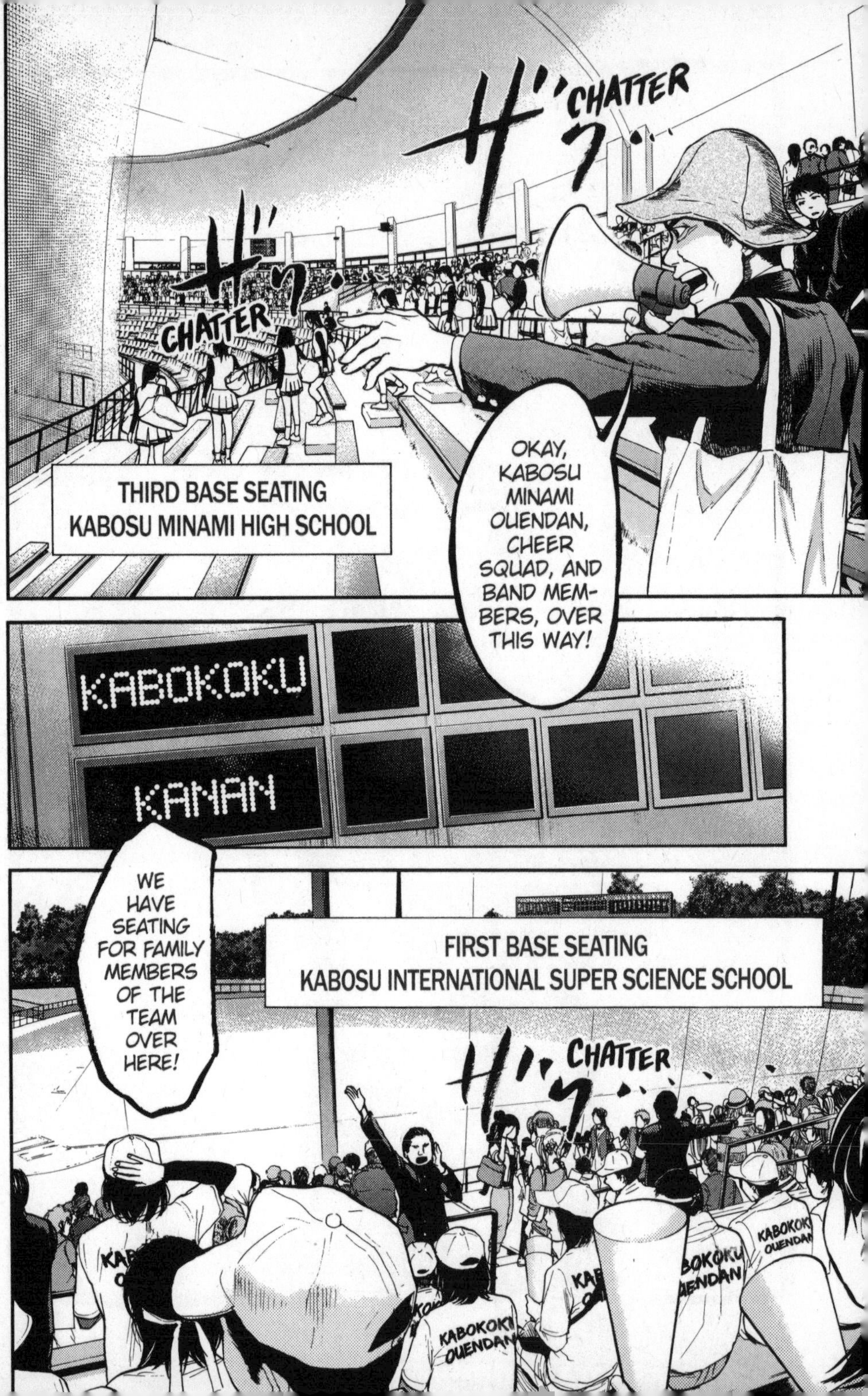
CHATTER
OKAY, KABOSU MINAMI OUENDAN, CHEER SQUAD, AND BAND MEMBERS, OVER THIS WAY!
CHATTER
THIRD BASE SEATING
KABOSU MINAMI HIGH SCHOOL
KABOKOKU
KANAN
FIRST BASE SEATING
KABOSU INTERNATIONAL SUPER SCIENCE SCHOOL
WE HAVE SEATING FOR FAMILY MEMBERS OF THE TEAM OVER HERE!
CHATTER
KABOKOKU OUENDAN
KABOKOKU OUENDAN

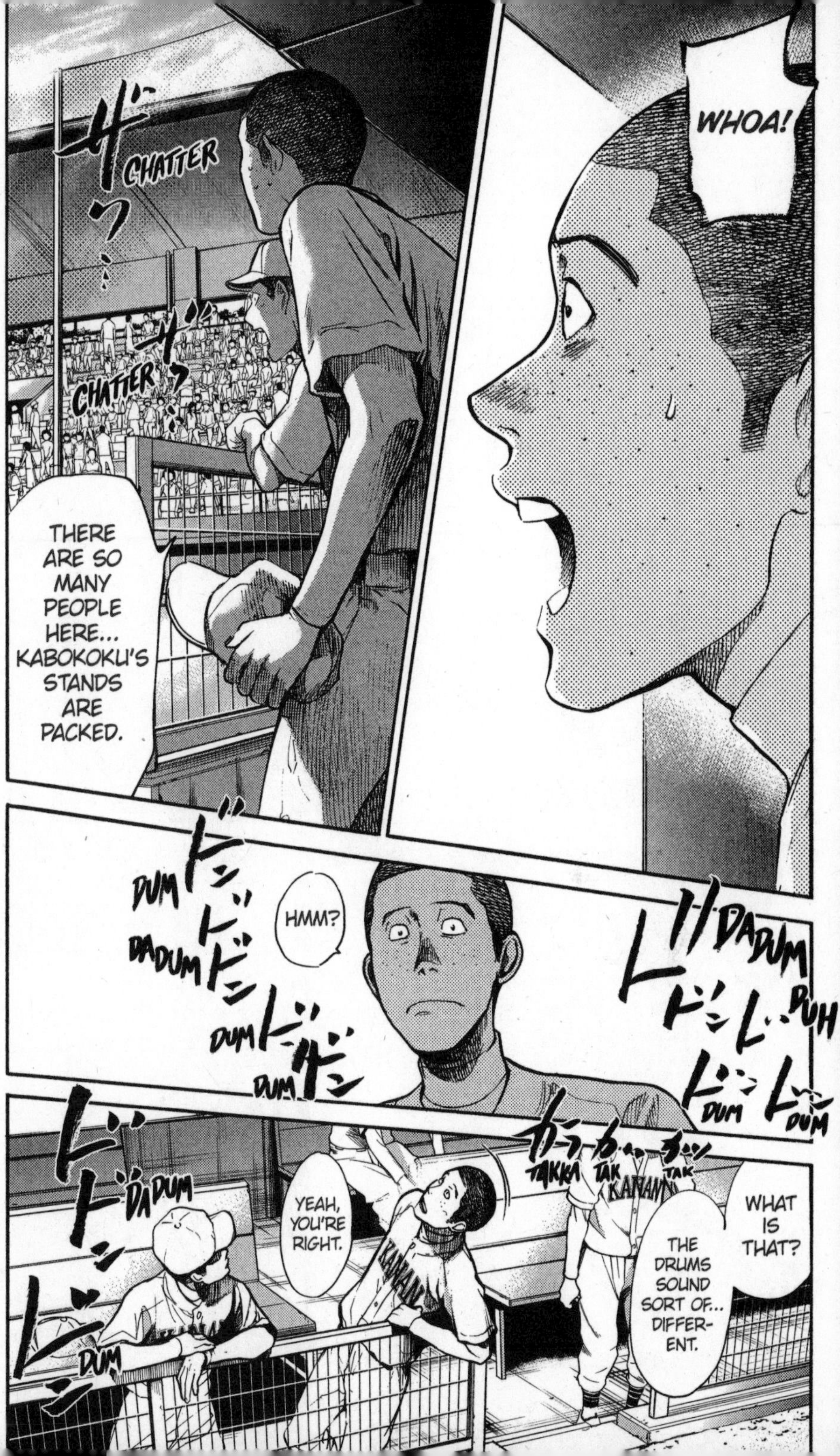
WHOA!
CHATTER
CHATTER
THERE ARE SO MANY PEOPLE HERE... KABOKOKU'S STANDS ARE PACKED.
DADUM
DUH
DUM
DUM
HMM?
DUM
DADUM
DUM
DUM
WHAT IS THAT?
THE DRUMS SOUND SORT OF... DIFFER-ENT.
TAKKA
TAK
TAK
KANAN
YEAH, YOU'RE RIGHT.
DADUM
DUM

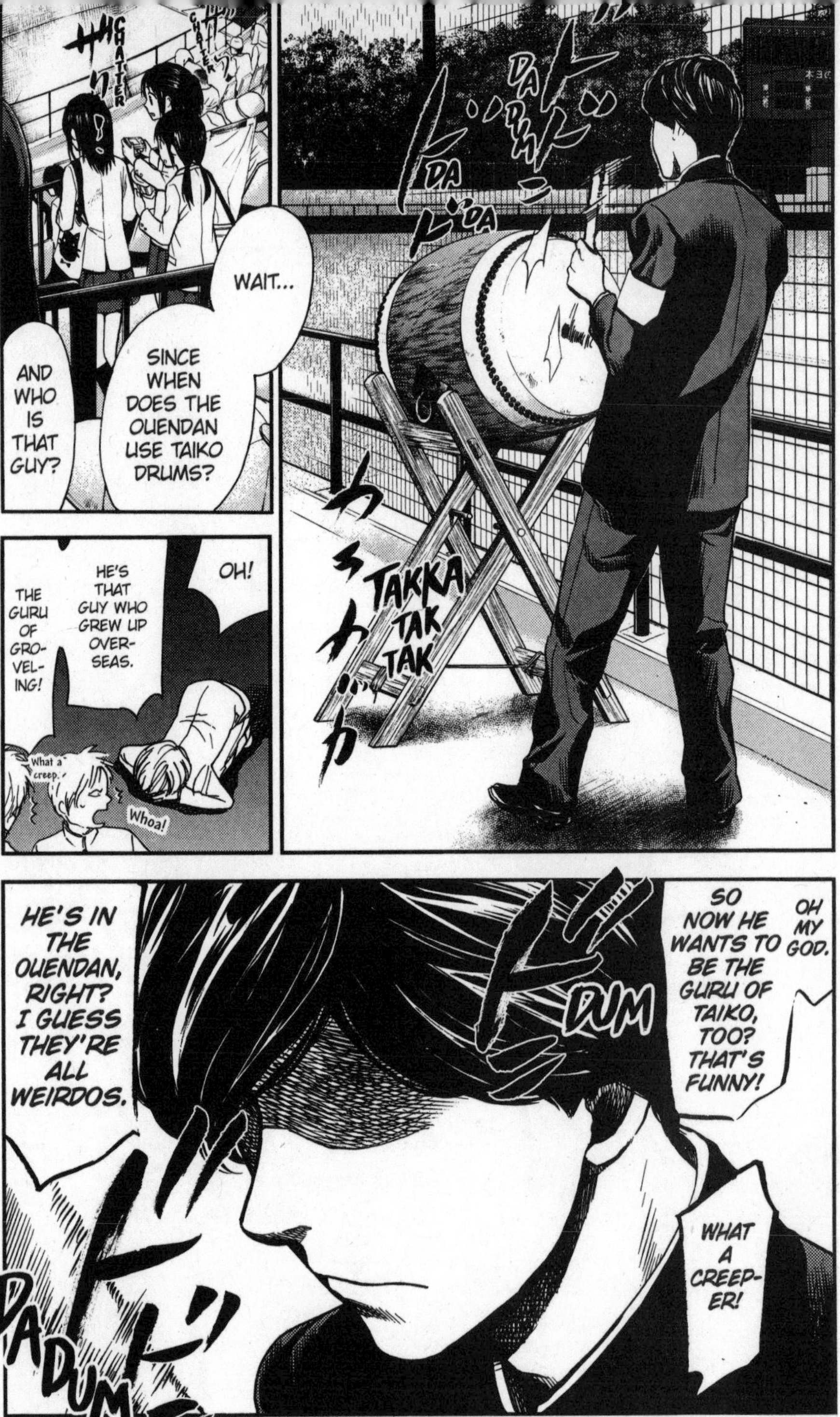
DA DUM
DA DA
TAKKA TAK TAK
CHATTER
CHATTER
WAIT...
SINCE WHEN DOES THE OUENDAN USE TAIKO DRUMS?
AND WHO IS THAT GUY?
OH!
HE'S THAT GUY WHO GREW UP OVER-SEAS.
THE GURU OF GRO-VEL-ING!
What a creep.
Whoa!
OH MY GOD.
SO NOW HE WANTS TO BE THE GURU OF TAIKO, TOO? THAT'S FUNNY!
DUM
HE'S IN THE OUENDAN, RIGHT? I GUESS THEY'RE ALL WEIRDOS.
WHAT A CREEP-ER!
DADUM

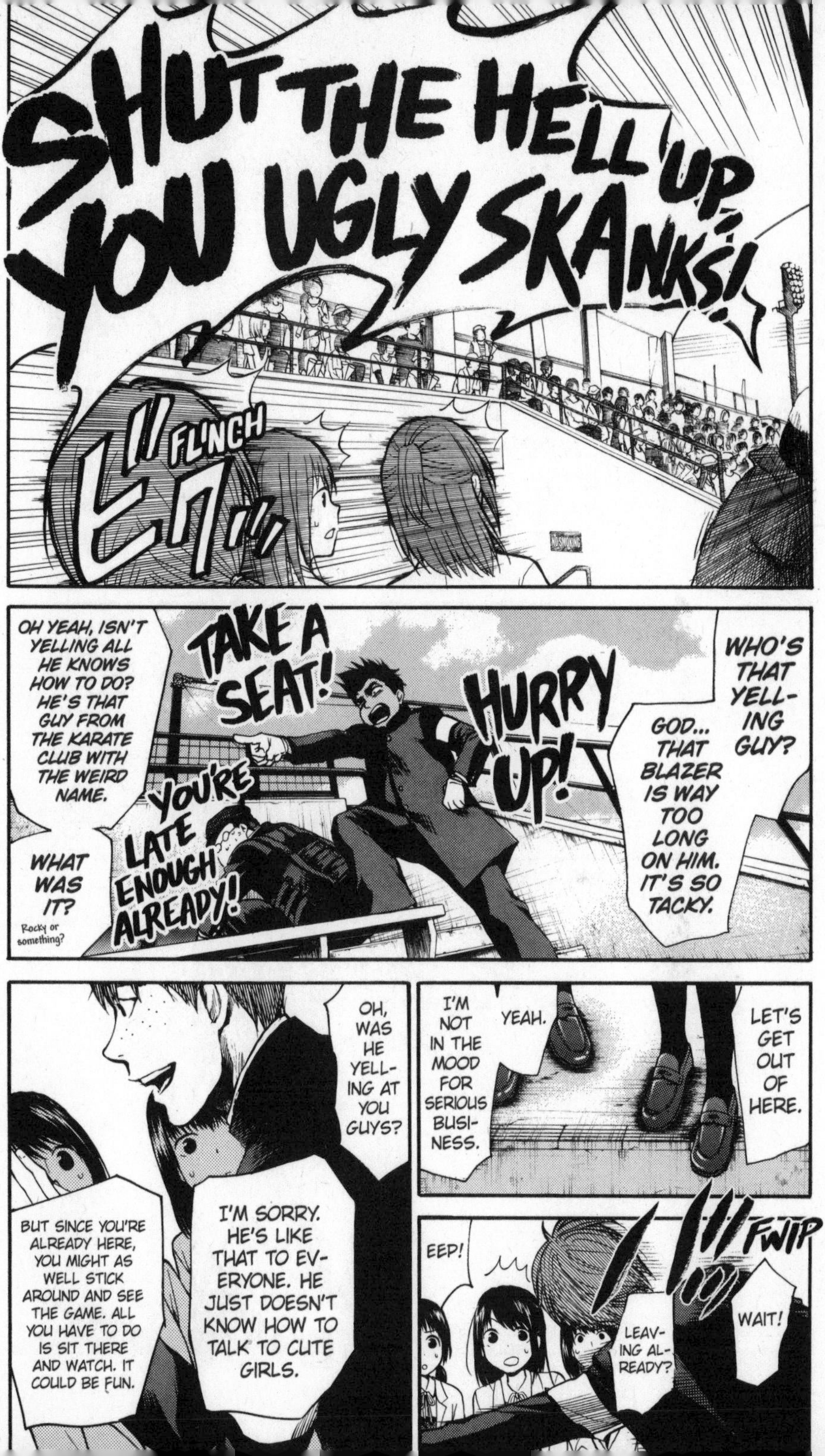
SHUT THE HELL UP YOU UGLY SKANKS!!
ヒッ
FLINCH
WHO'S THAT YELLING GUY?
GOD... THAT BLAZER IS WAY TOO LONG ON HIM. IT'S SO TACKY.
HURRY UP!
TAKE A SEAT!
YOU'RE LATE ENOUGH ALREADY!
OH YEAH, ISN'T YELLING ALL HE KNOWS HOW TO DO? HE'S THAT GUY FROM THE KARATE CLUB WITH THE WEIRD NAME.
WHAT WAS IT?
Rocky or something?
LET'S GET OUT OF HERE.
YEAH.
I'M NOT IN THE MOOD FOR SERIOUS BUSINESS.
FWIP
WAIT!
LEAVING ALREADY?
EEP!
OH, WAS HE YELLING AT YOU GUYS?
I'M SORRY. HE'S LIKE THAT TO EVERYONE. HE JUST DOESN'T KNOW HOW TO TALK TO CUTE GIRLS.
BUT SINCE YOU'RE ALREADY HERE, YOU MIGHT AS WELL STICK AROUND AND SEE THE GAME. ALL YOU HAVE TO DO IS SIT THERE AND WATCH. IT COULD BE FUN.

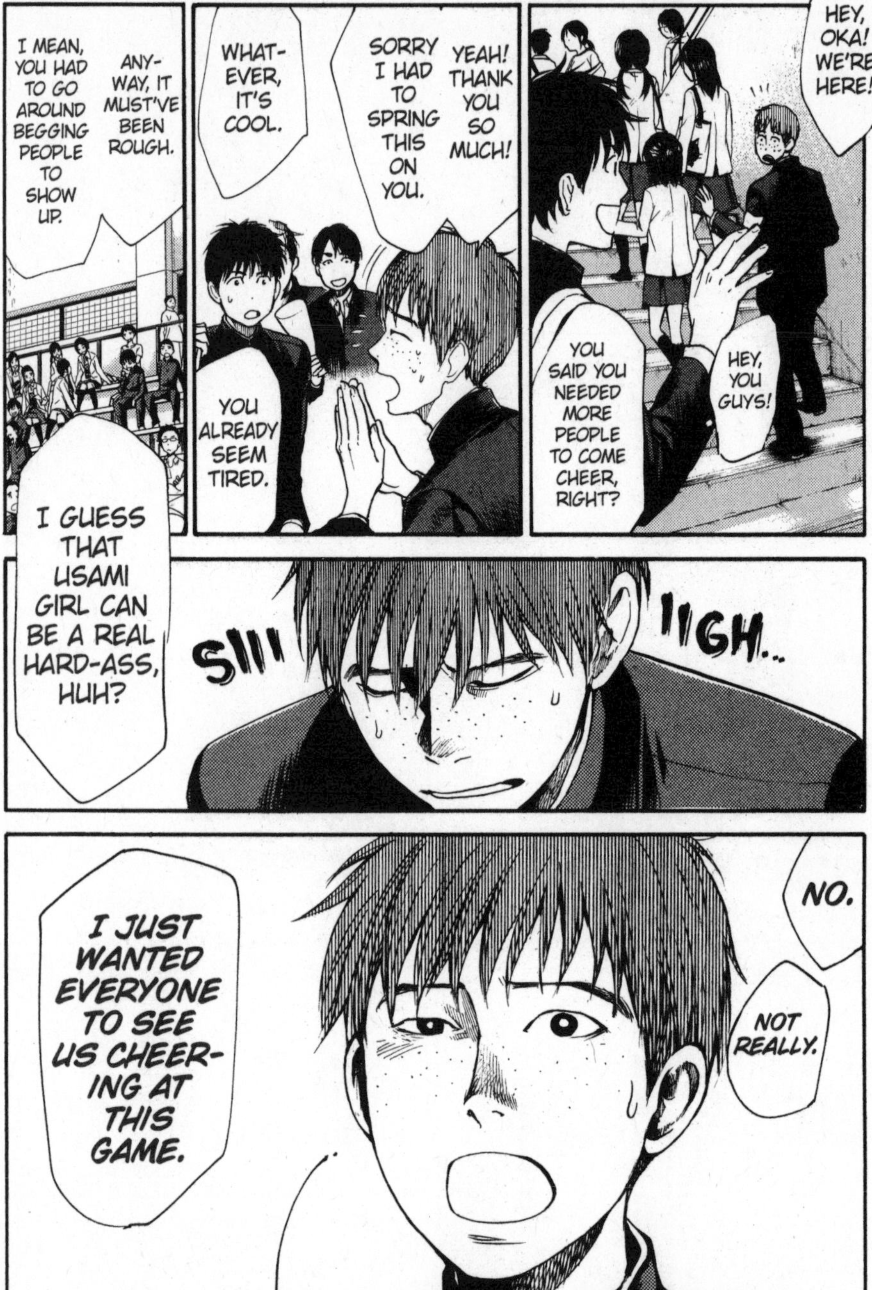
HEY, OKA! WE'RE HERE!
HEY, YOU GUYS!
YOU SAID YOU NEEDED MORE PEOPLE TO COME CHEER, RIGHT?
YEAH! THANK YOU SO MUCH!
SORRY I HAD TO SPRING THIS ON YOU.
WHAT-EVER, IT'S COOL.
YOU ALREADY SEEM TIRED.
ANY-WAY, IT MUST'VE BEEN ROUGH.
I MEAN, YOU HAD TO GO AROUND BEGGING PEOPLE TO SHOW UP.
I GUESS THAT USAMI GIRL CAN BE A REAL HARD-ASS, HUH?
SIIIIGH...
NO.
NOT REALLY.
I JUST WANTED EVERYONE TO SEE US CHEER-ING AT THIS GAME.

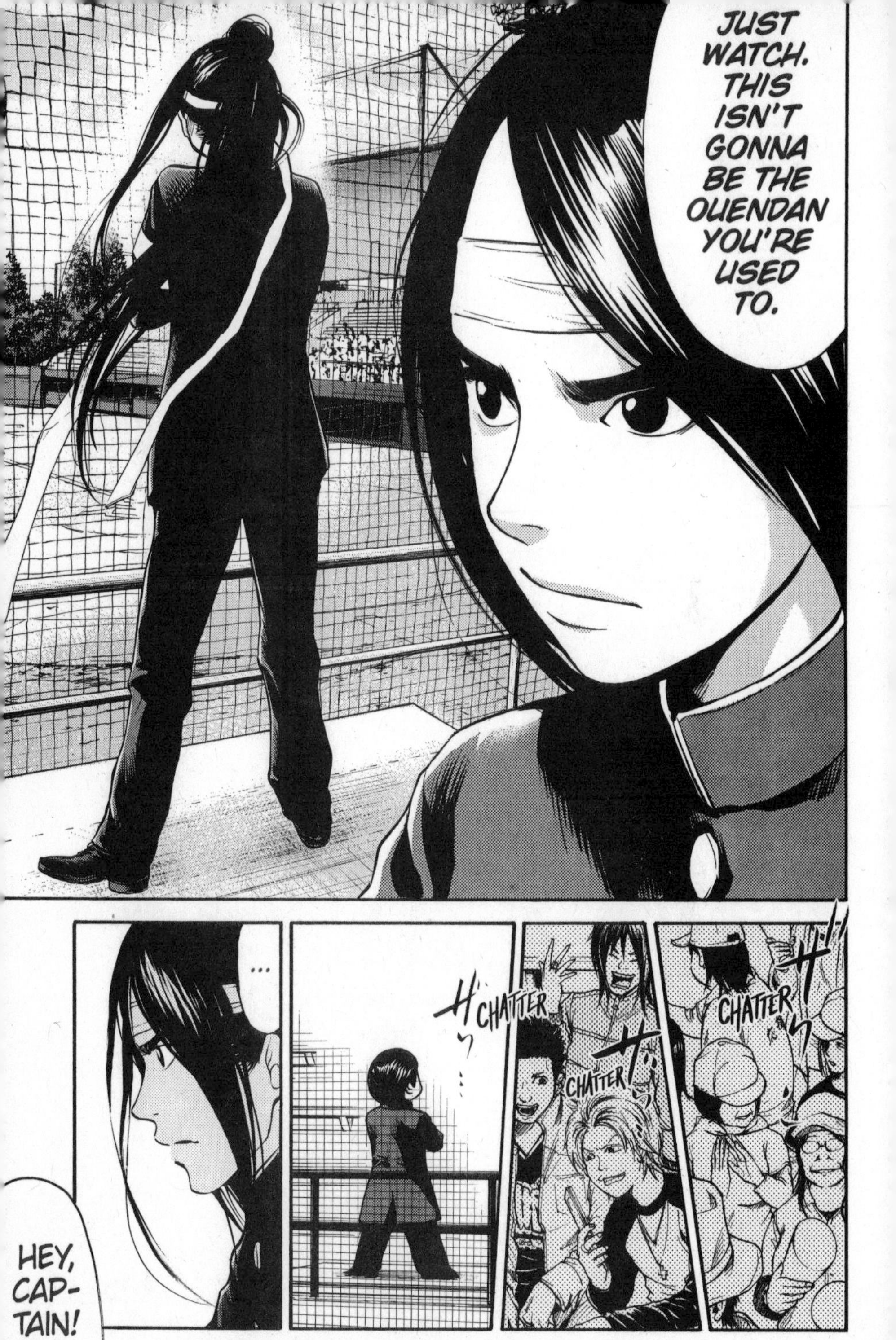
JUST WATCH. THIS ISN'T GONNA BE THE OUENDAN YOU'RE USED TO.
CHATTER
CHATTER
CHATTER
...
HEY, CAP-TAIN!

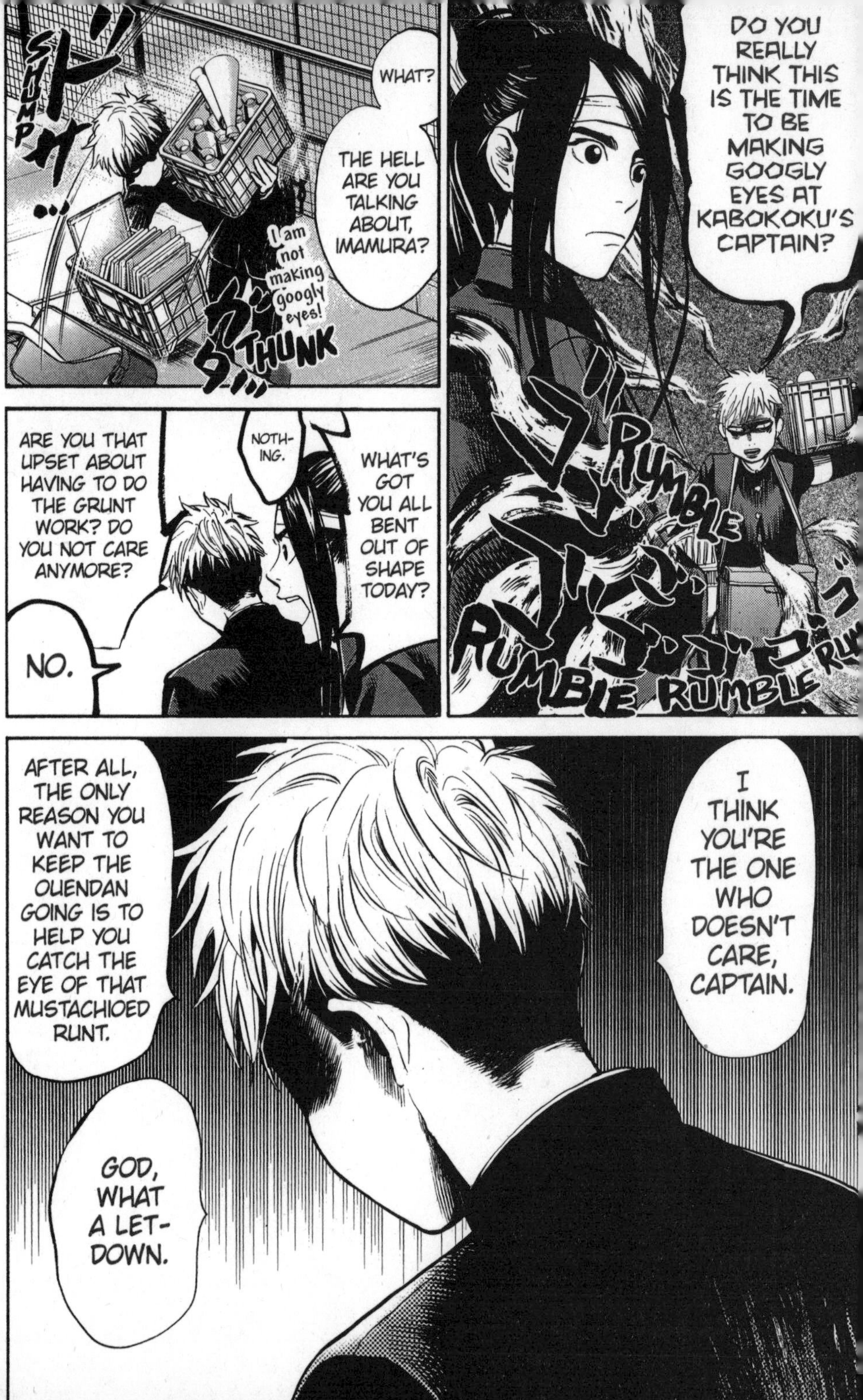
DO YOU REALLY THINK THIS IS THE TIME TO BE MAKING GOOGLY EYES AT KABOKOKU'S CAPTAIN?
RUMBLE
RUMBLE RUMBLE RUMBLE RU
WHAT?
THE HELL ARE YOU TALKING ABOUT, IMAMURA?
I am not making googly eyes!
THUNK
SHUMP
WHAT'S GOT YOU ALL BENT OUT OF SHAPE TODAY?
NOTHING.
ARE YOU THAT UPSET ABOUT HAVING TO DO THE GRUNT WORK? DO YOU NOT CARE ANYMORE?
NO.
I THINK YOU'RE THE ONE WHO DOESN'T CARE, CAPTAIN.
AFTER ALL, THE ONLY REASON YOU WANT TO KEEP THE OUENDAN GOING IS TO HELP YOU CATCH THE EYE OF THAT MUSTACHIOED RUNT.
GOD, WHAT A LET-DOWN.

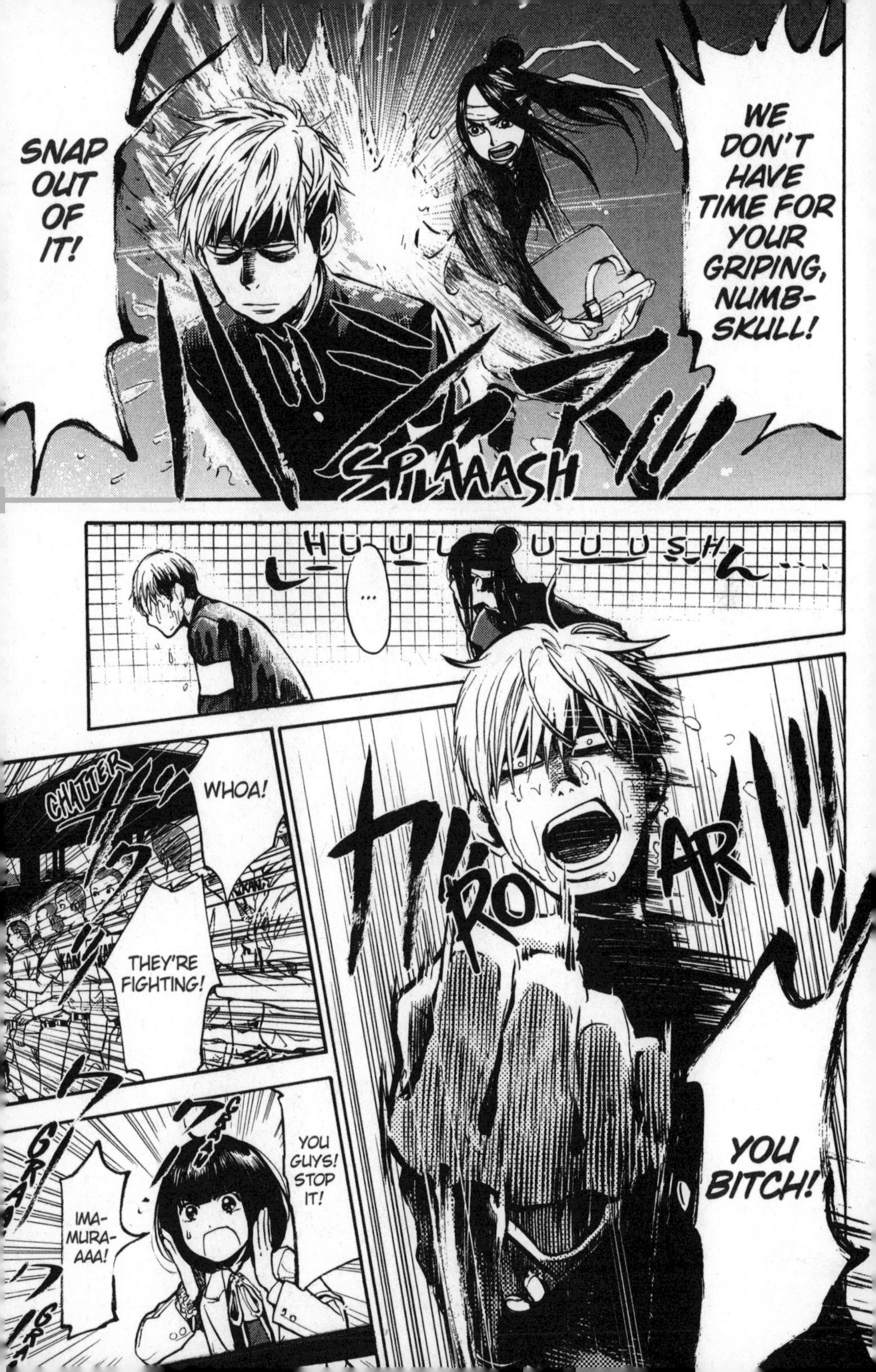
WE DON'T HAVE TIME FOR YOUR GRIPING, NUMB-SKULL!
SNAP OUT OF IT!
SPILAAASH
HUUUUUUSH...
...
ROAR!!!
YOU BITCH!
WHOA!
CHATTER
THEY'RE FIGHTING!
YOU GUYS! STOP IT!
IMA-MURA-AAA!
GRA
GRA

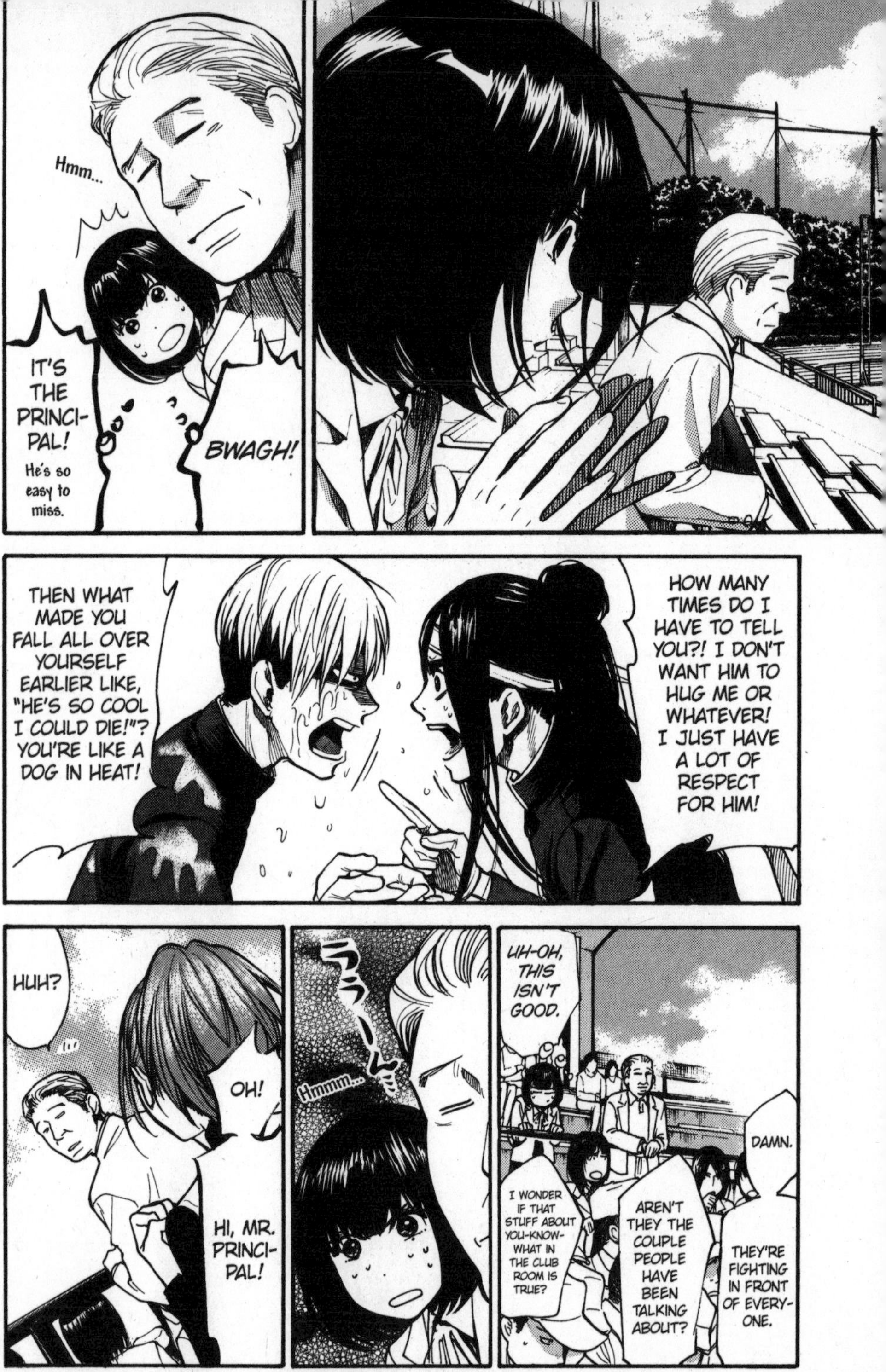
Hmm...
IT'S THE PRINCIPAL!
He's so easy to miss.
BWAGH!
HOW MANY TIMES DO I HAVE TO TELL YOU?! I DON'T WANT HIM TO HUG ME OR WHATEVER! I JUST HAVE A LOT OF RESPECT FOR HIM!
THEN WHAT MADE YOU FALL ALL OVER YOURSELF EARLIER LIKE, "HE'S SO COOL I COULD DIE!"? YOU'RE LIKE A DOG IN HEAT!
UH-OH, THIS ISN'T GOOD.
DAMN.
THEY'RE FIGHTING IN FRONT OF EVERY-ONE.
AREN'T THEY THE COUPLE PEOPLE HAVE BEEN TALKING ABOUT?
I WONDER IF THAT STUFF ABOUT YOU-KNOW-WHAT IN THE CLUB ROOM IS TRUE?
Hmmm...
HUH?
OH!
HI, MR. PRINCI-PAL!

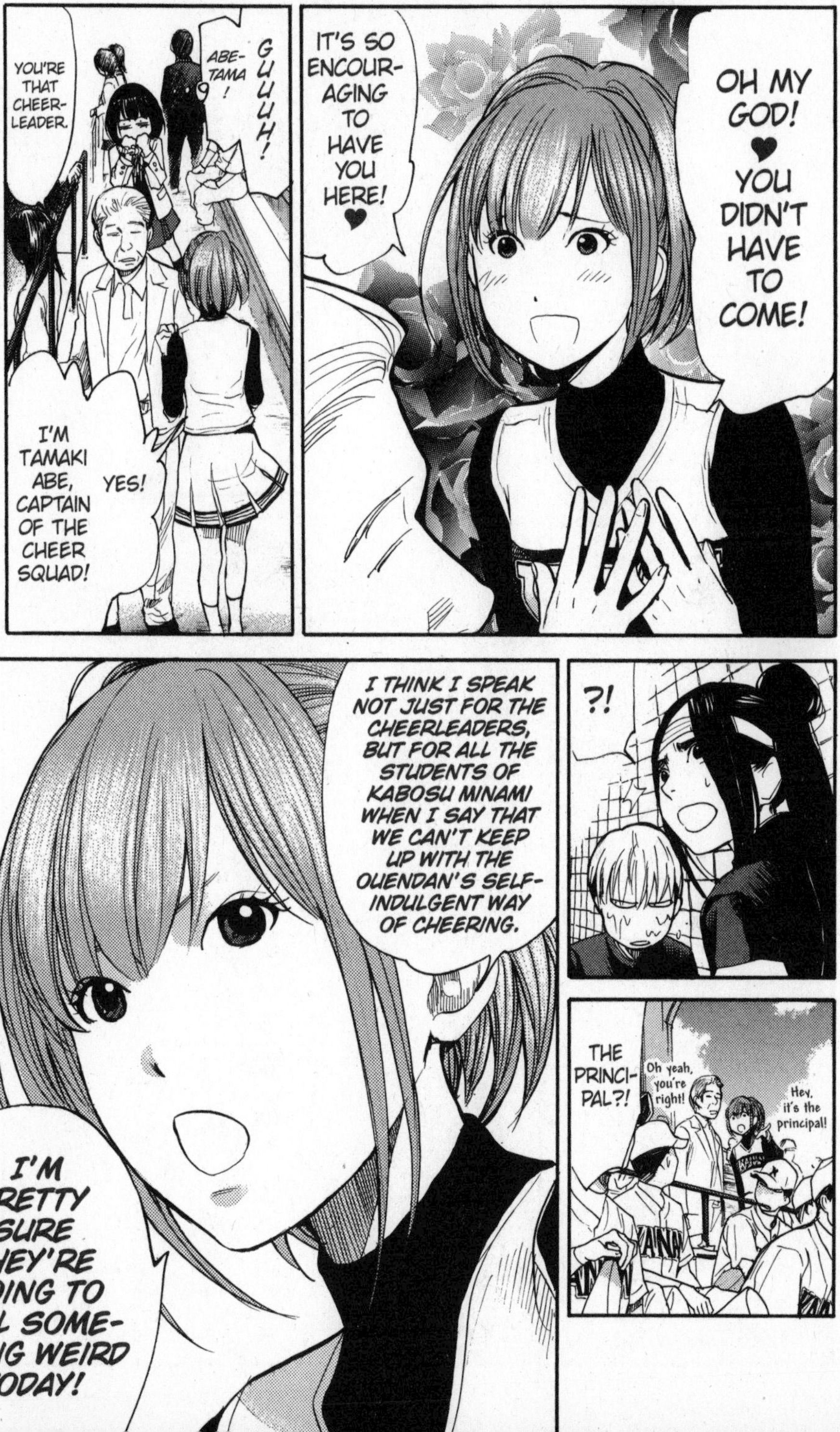
OH MY GOD! ♥ YOU DIDN'T HAVE TO COME!
IT'S SO ENCOURAGING TO HAVE YOU HERE! ♥
GUUUH!
ABE-TAMA!
YOU'RE THAT CHEERLEADER.
YES!
I'M TAMAKI ABE, CAPTAIN OF THE CHEER SQUAD!
?!
Hey, it's the principal!
Oh yeah, you're right!
THE PRINCIPAL?!
I THINK I SPEAK NOT JUST FOR THE CHEERLEADERS, BUT FOR ALL THE STUDENTS OF KABOSU MINAMI WHEN I SAY THAT WE CAN'T KEEP UP WITH THE OUENDAN'S SELF-INDULGENT WAY OF CHEERING.
I'M PRETTY SURE THEY'RE GOING TO PULL SOMETHING WEIRD TODAY!

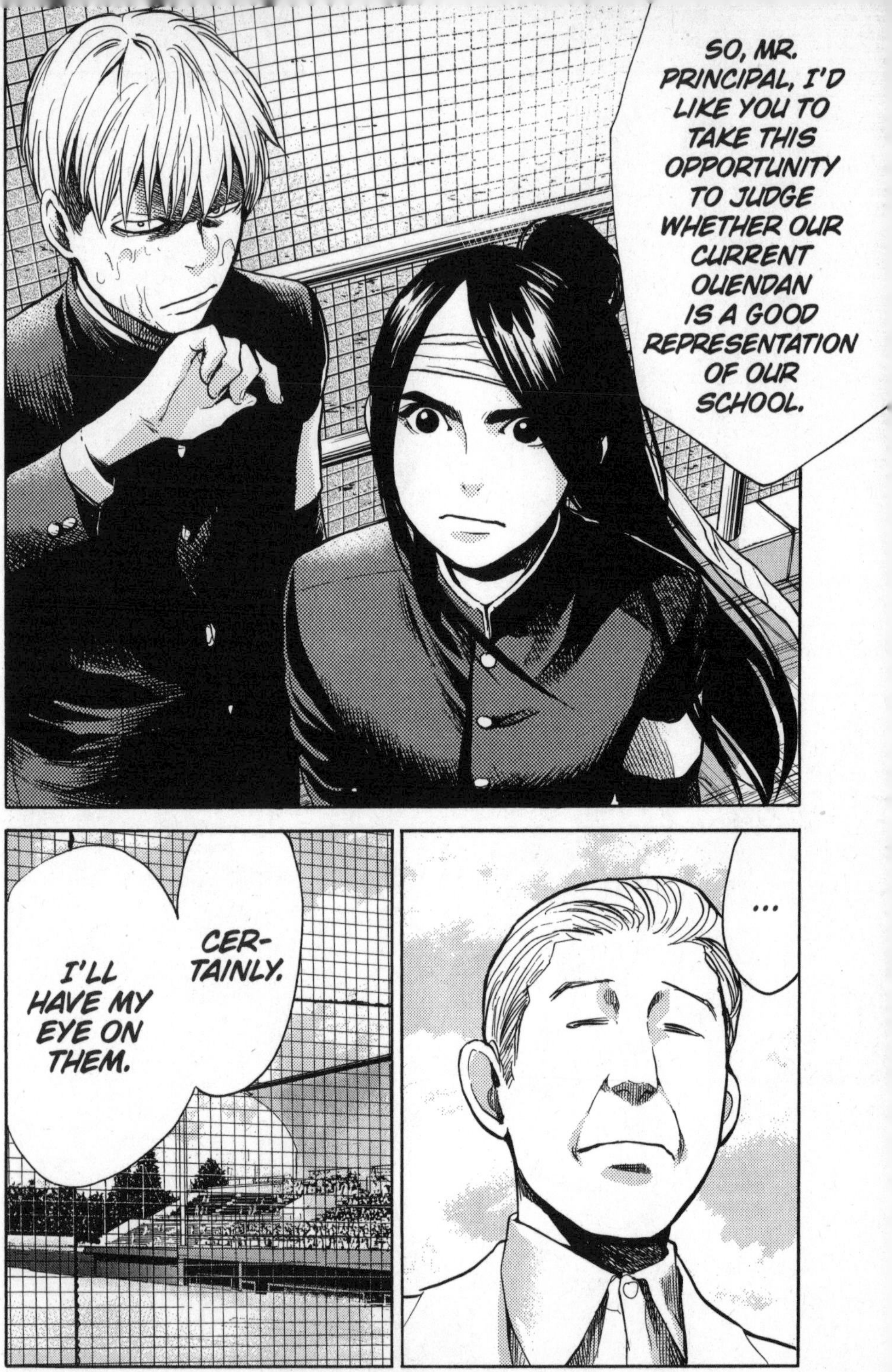
SO, MR. PRINCIPAL, I'D LIKE YOU TO TAKE THIS OPPORTUNITY TO JUDGE WHETHER OUR CURRENT OUENDAN IS A GOOD REPRESENTATION OF OUR SCHOOL.
...
CER-TAINLY.
I'LL HAVE MY EYE ON THEM.

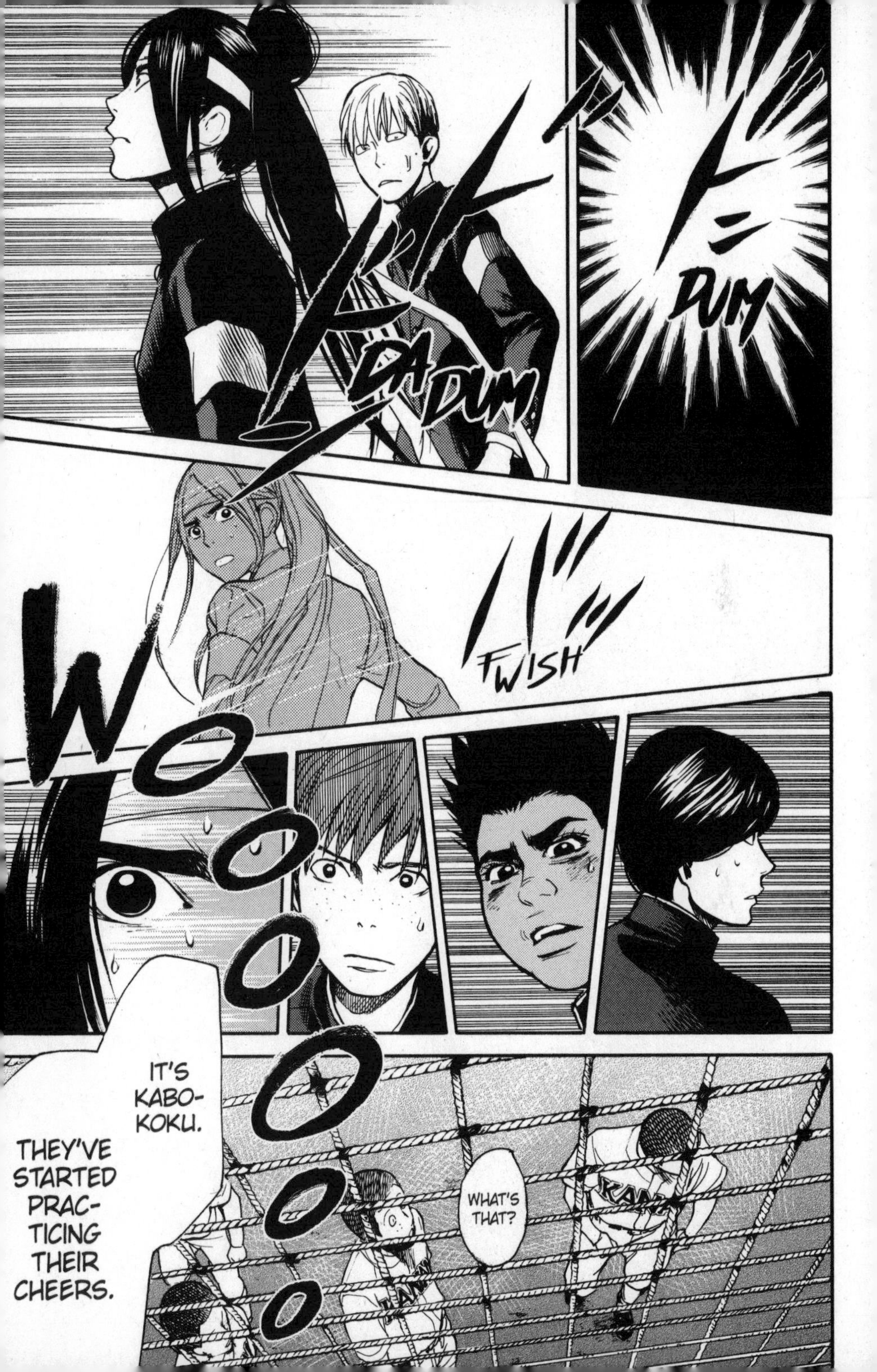
DUM
DA DUM
FWISH
WOOOOOOO
WHAT'S THAT?
IT'S KABO-KOKU.
THEY'VE STARTED PRAC-TICING THEIR CHEERS.

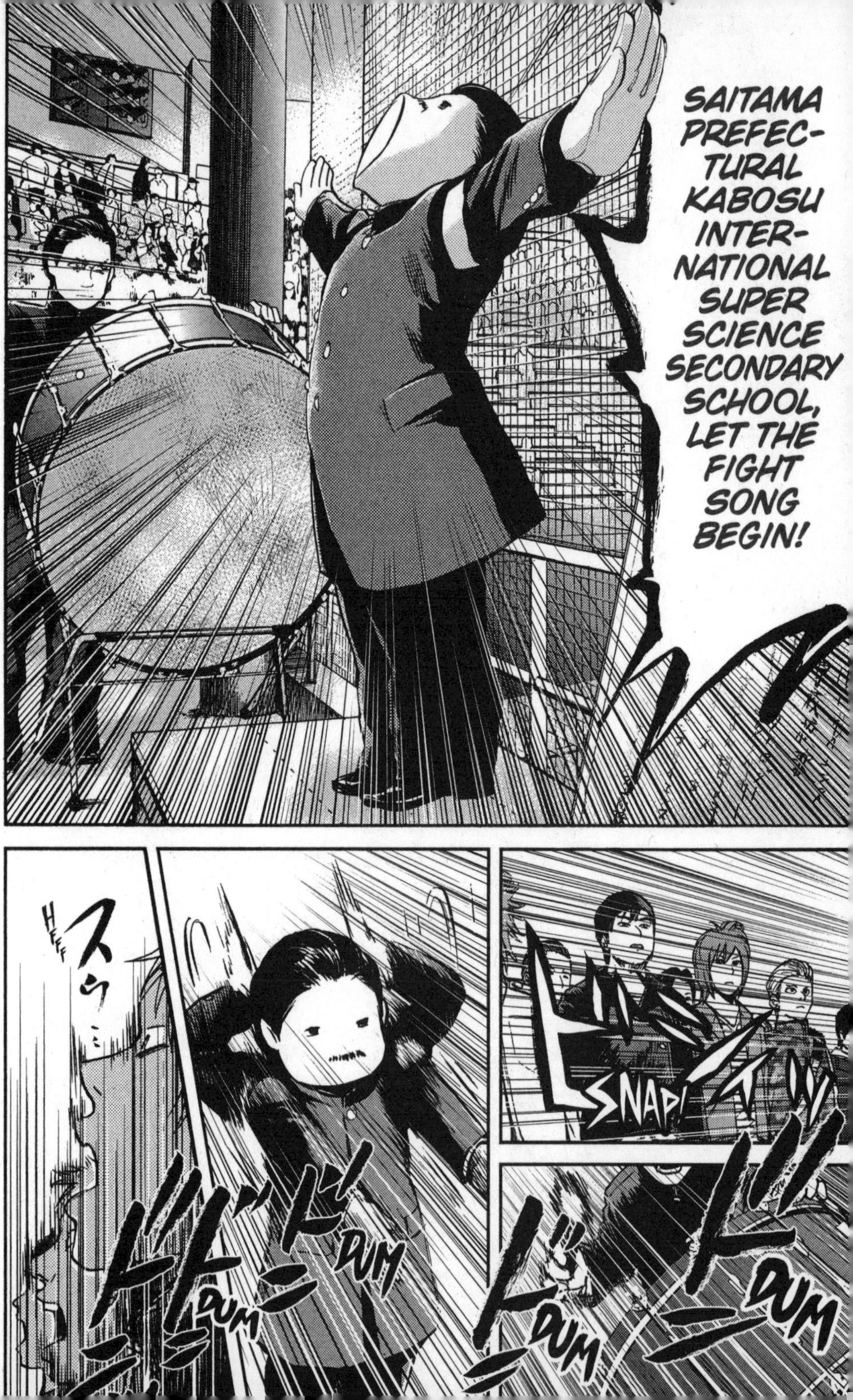
SAITAMA PREFECTURAL KABOSU INTERNATIONAL SUPER SCIENCE SECONDARY SCHOOL, LET THE FIGHT SONG BEGIN!
SNAP!
DUM
DUM
DUM
DUM
DUM
HFF

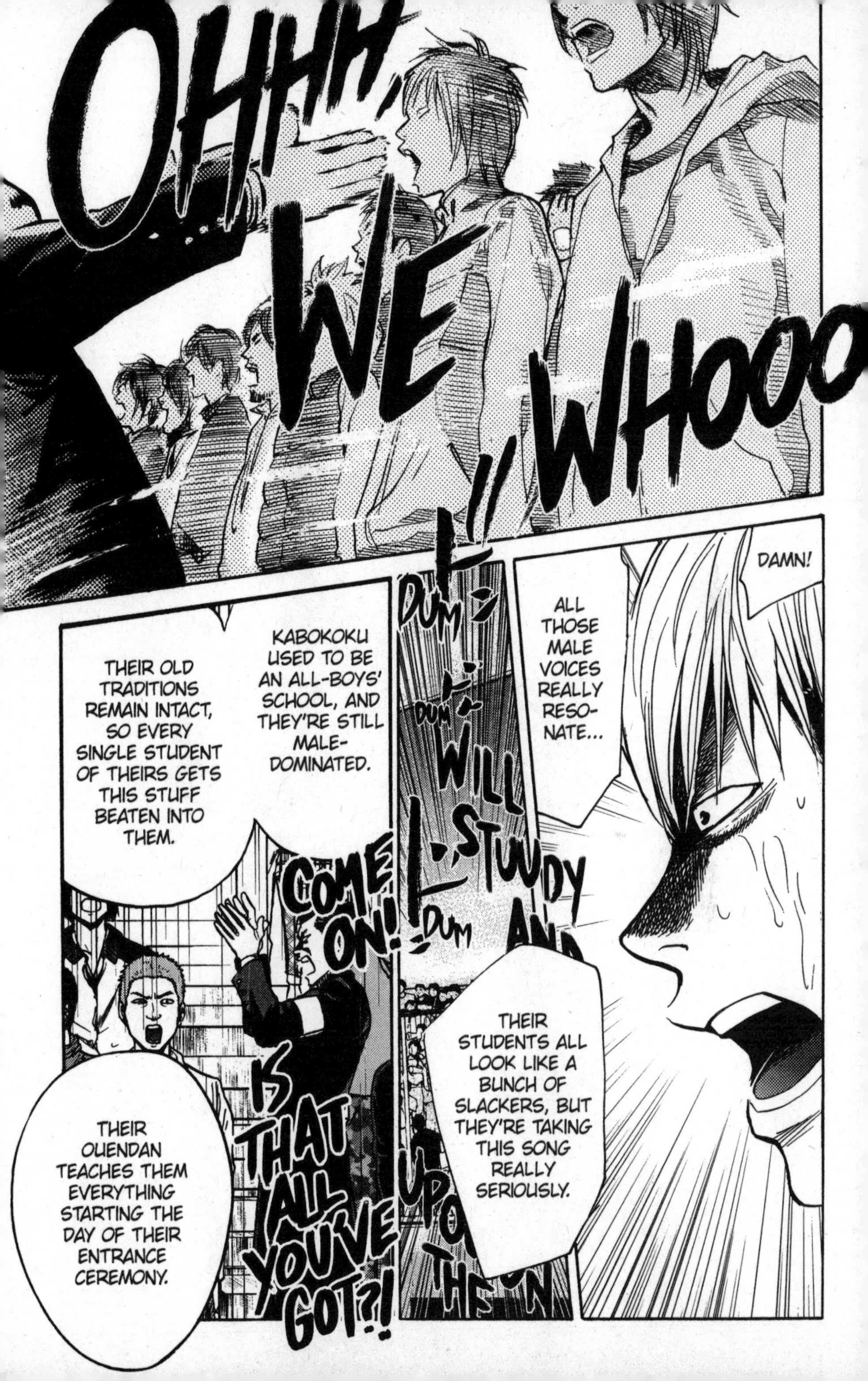
OHHH,
WE
WHOOO
DAMN!
ALL THOSE MALE VOICES REALLY RESO-NATE...
THEIR STUDENTS ALL LOOK LIKE A BUNCH OF SLACKERS, BUT THEY'RE TAKING THIS SONG REALLY SERIOUSLY.
DUM
DUM
WILL STUUDY
DUM
KABOKOKU USED TO BE AN ALL-BOYS' SCHOOL, AND THEY'RE STILL MALE-DOMINATED.
THEIR OLD TRADITIONS REMAIN INTACT, SO EVERY SINGLE STUDENT OF THEIRS GETS THIS STUFF BEATEN INTO THEM.
COME ON!
IS THAT ALL YOU'VE GOT?!
THEIR OUENDAN TEACHES THEM EVERYTHING STARTING THE DAY OF THEIR ENTRANCE CEREMONY.

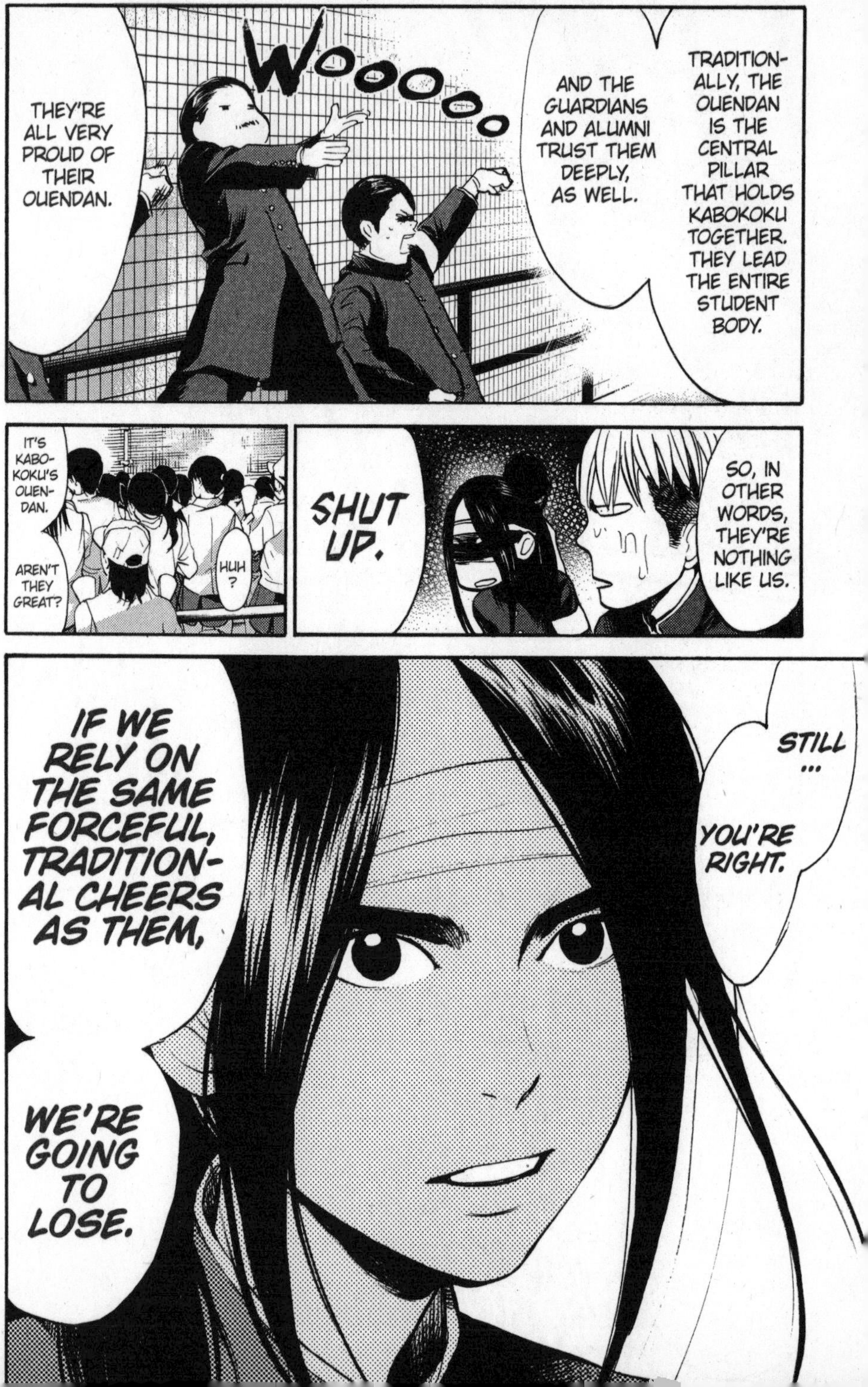
TRADITION-ALLY, THE OUENDAN IS THE CENTRAL PILLAR THAT HOLDS KABOKOKU TOGETHER. THEY LEAD THE ENTIRE STUDENT BODY.
AND THE GUARDIANS AND ALUMNI TRUST THEM DEEPLY, AS WELL.
WOOOOOO
THEY'RE ALL VERY PROUD OF THEIR OUENDAN.
SO, IN OTHER WORDS, THEY'RE NOTHING LIKE US.
SHUT UP.
IT'S KABOKOKU'S OUEN-DAN.
HUH?
AREN'T THEY GREAT?
STILL ...
YOU'RE RIGHT.
IF WE RELY ON THE SAME FORCEFUL, TRADITION-AL CHEERS AS THEM,
WE'RE GOING TO LOSE.

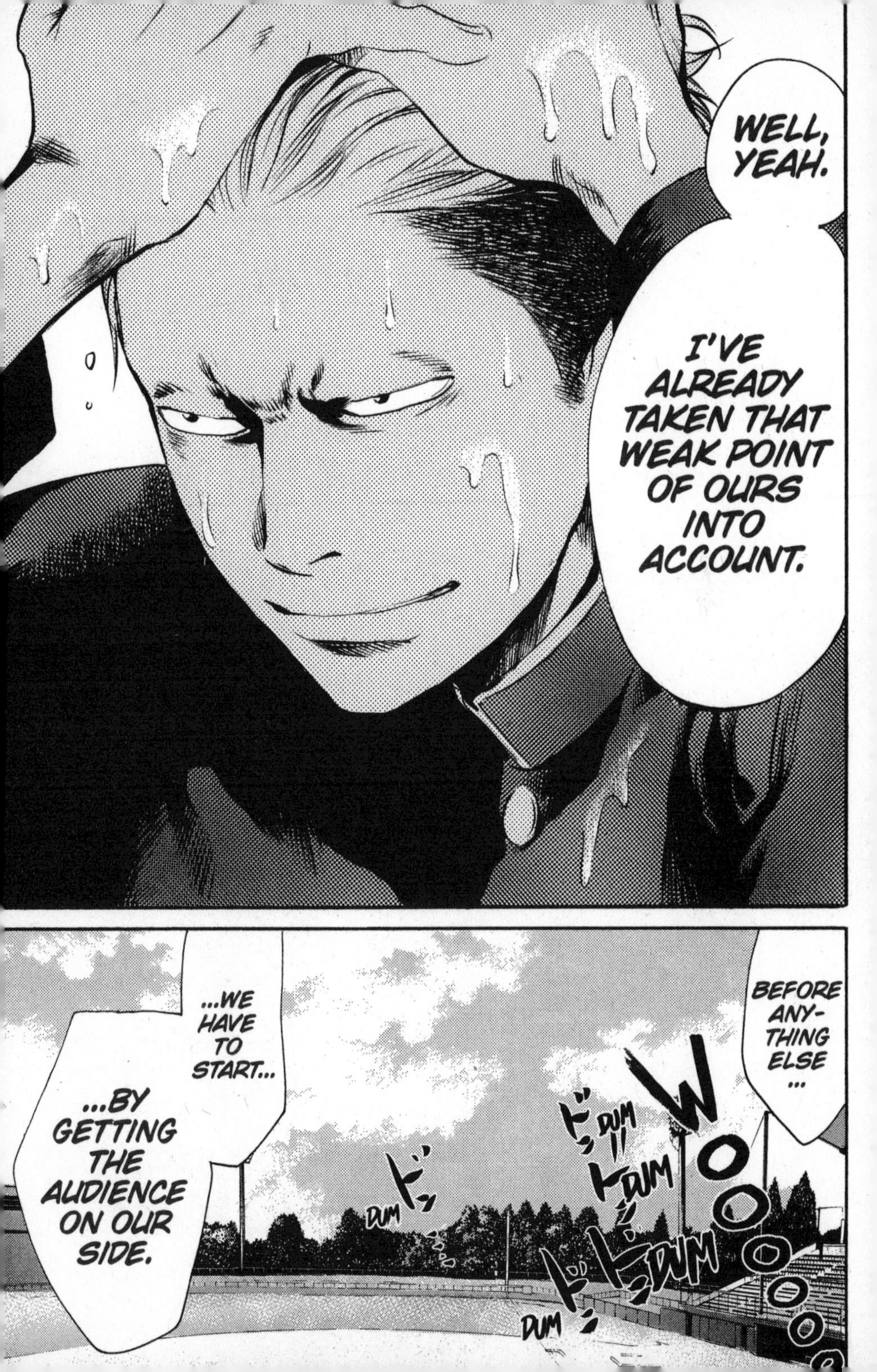
WELL, YEAH.
I'VE ALREADY TAKEN THAT WEAK POINT OF OURS INTO ACCOUNT.
BEFORE ANYTHING ELSE...
...WE HAVE TO START...
...BY GETTING THE AUDIENCE ON OUR SIDE.
WOOOOOOO
DUM DUM DUM DUM DUM

Again!!
アゲイン!!

# 49. WHY I'M HERE

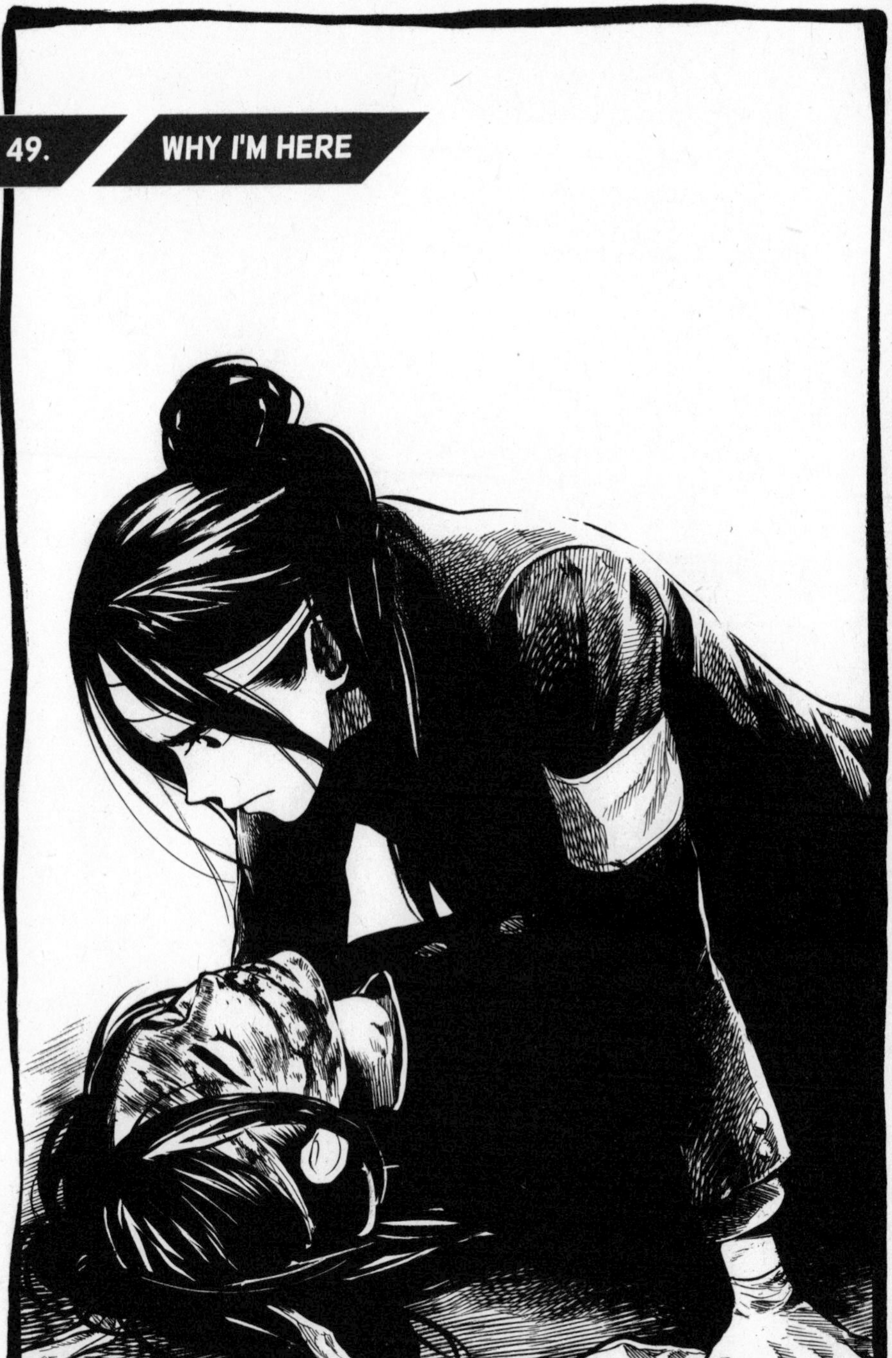

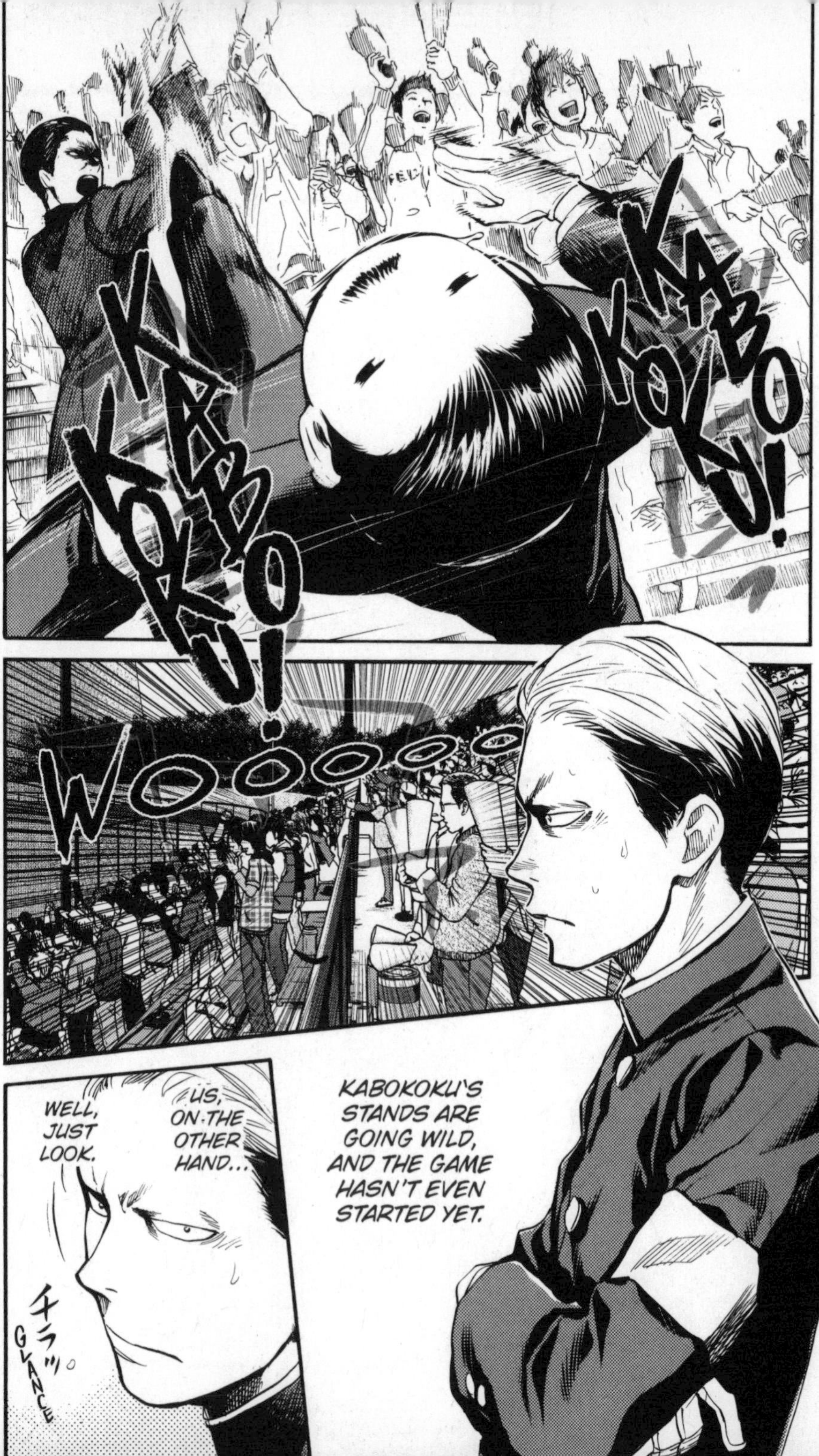
KABOKOKU!
KABOKOKU!
WOOOOOOO
KABOKOKU'S STANDS ARE GOING WILD, AND THE GAME HASN'T EVEN STARTED YET.
US, ON THE OTHER HAND...
WELL, JUST LOOK.
チラッ
GLANCE

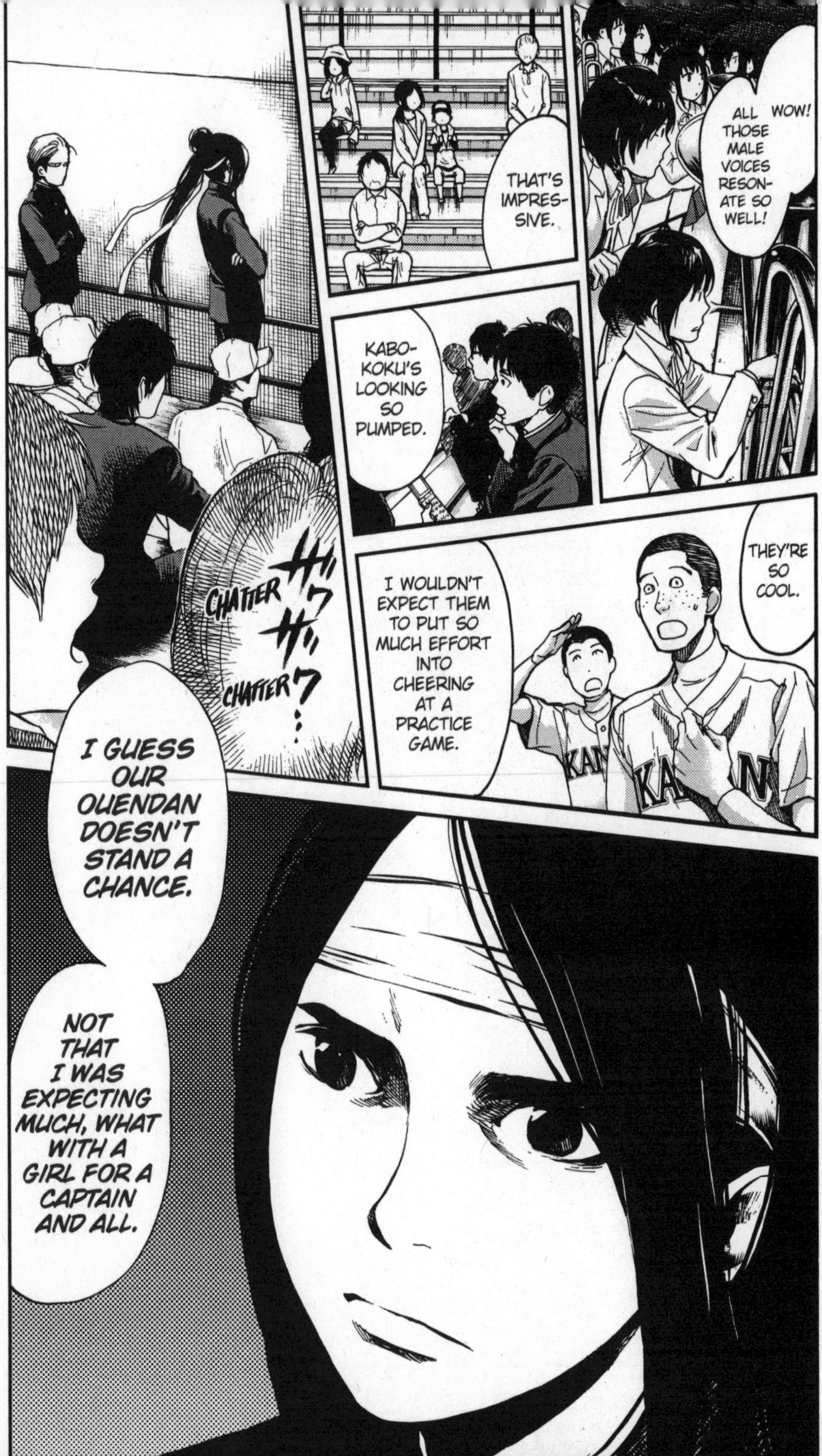
WOW!
ALL THOSE MALE VOICES RESONATE SO WELL!
THAT'S IMPRESSIVE.
KABOKOKU'S LOOKING SO PUMPED.
THEY'RE SO COOL.
I WOULDN'T EXPECT THEM TO PUT SO MUCH EFFORT INTO CHEERING AT A PRACTICE GAME.
CHATTER
CHATTER
I GUESS OUR OUENDAN DOESN'T STAND A CHANCE.
NOT THAT I WAS EXPECTING MUCH, WHAT WITH A GIRL FOR A CAPTAIN AND ALL.

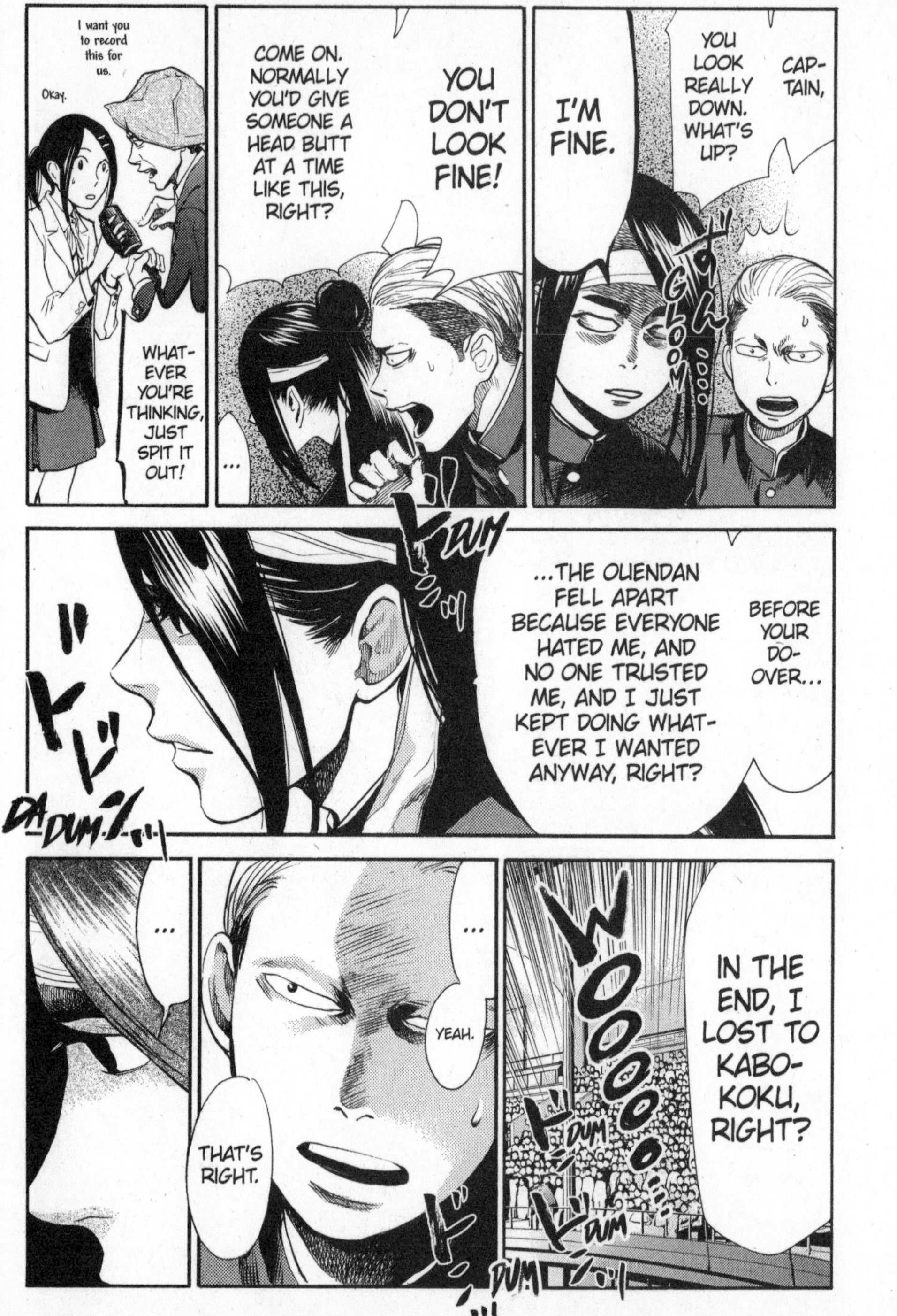
CAP-TAIN,
YOU LOOK REALLY DOWN. WHAT'S UP?
I'M FINE.
GLOOM
YOU DON'T LOOK FINE!
COME ON. NORMALLY YOU'D GIVE SOMEONE A HEAD BUTT AT A TIME LIKE THIS, RIGHT?
...
I want you to record this for us.
Okay.
WHAT-EVER YOU'RE THINKING, JUST SPIT IT OUT!
DUM
BEFORE YOUR DO-OVER...
...THE OUENDAN FELL APART BECAUSE EVERYONE HATED ME, AND NO ONE TRUSTED ME, AND I JUST KEPT DOING WHAT-EVER I WANTED ANYWAY, RIGHT?
DA-DUM
IN THE END, I LOST TO KABO-KOKU, RIGHT?
WOOOOO...
DUM
DUM
DUM
...
YEAH.
THAT'S RIGHT.
...

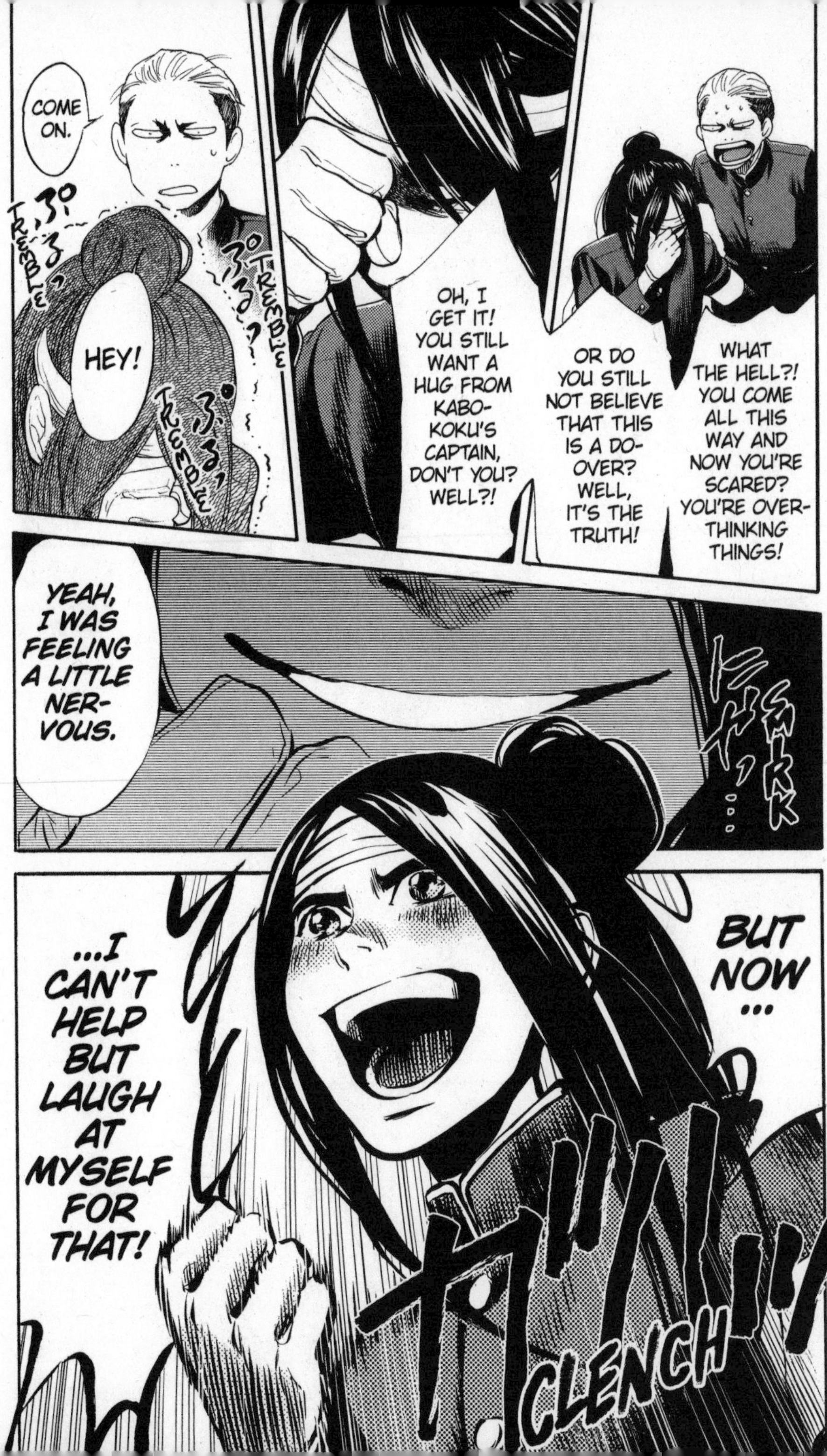
WHAT THE HELL?! YOU COME ALL THIS WAY AND NOW YOU'RE SCARED? YOU'RE OVER-THINKING THINGS!
OR DO YOU STILL NOT BELIEVE THAT THIS IS A DO-OVER? WELL, IT'S THE TRUTH!
OH, I GET IT! YOU STILL WANT A HUG FROM KABO-KOKU'S CAPTAIN, DON'T YOU? WELL?!
COME ON.
TREMBLE
TREMBLE
HEY!
TREMBLE
SMIRK
YEAH, I WAS FEELING A LITTLE NER-VOUS.
BUT NOW...
...I CAN'T HELP BUT LAUGH AT MYSELF FOR THAT!
CLENCH

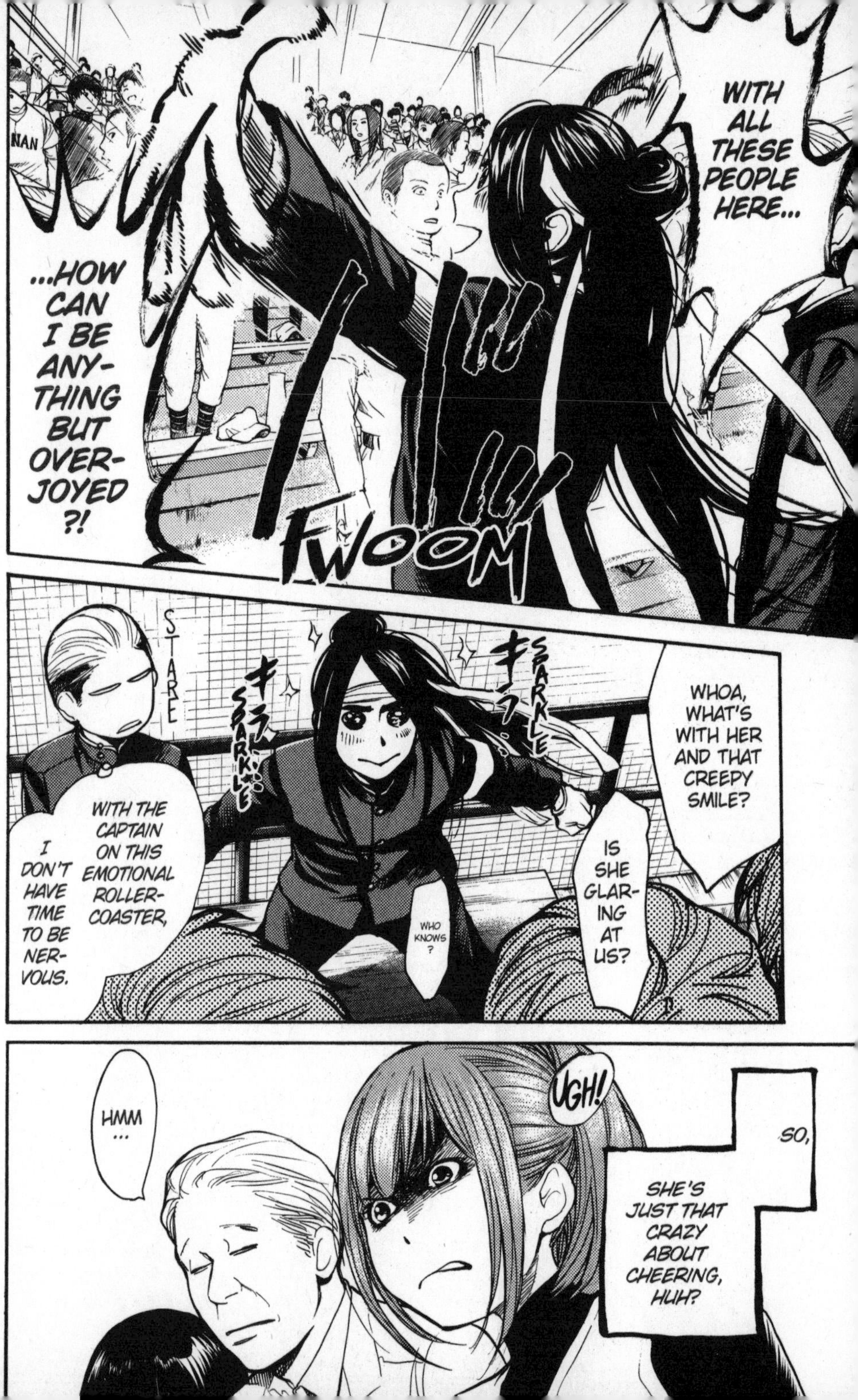
WITH ALL THESE PEOPLE HERE...
...HOW CAN I BE ANY-THING BUT OVER-JOYED?!
FWOOM
WHOA, WHAT'S WITH HER AND THAT CREEPY SMILE?
IS SHE GLAR-ING AT US?
WHO KNOWS?
キラ SPARKLE
キラ SPARKLE
STARE
WITH THE CAPTAIN ON THIS EMOTIONAL ROLLER-COASTER,
I DON'T HAVE TIME TO BE NER-VOUS.
SO,
SHE'S JUST THAT CRAZY ABOUT CHEERING, HUH?
UGH!
HMM ...

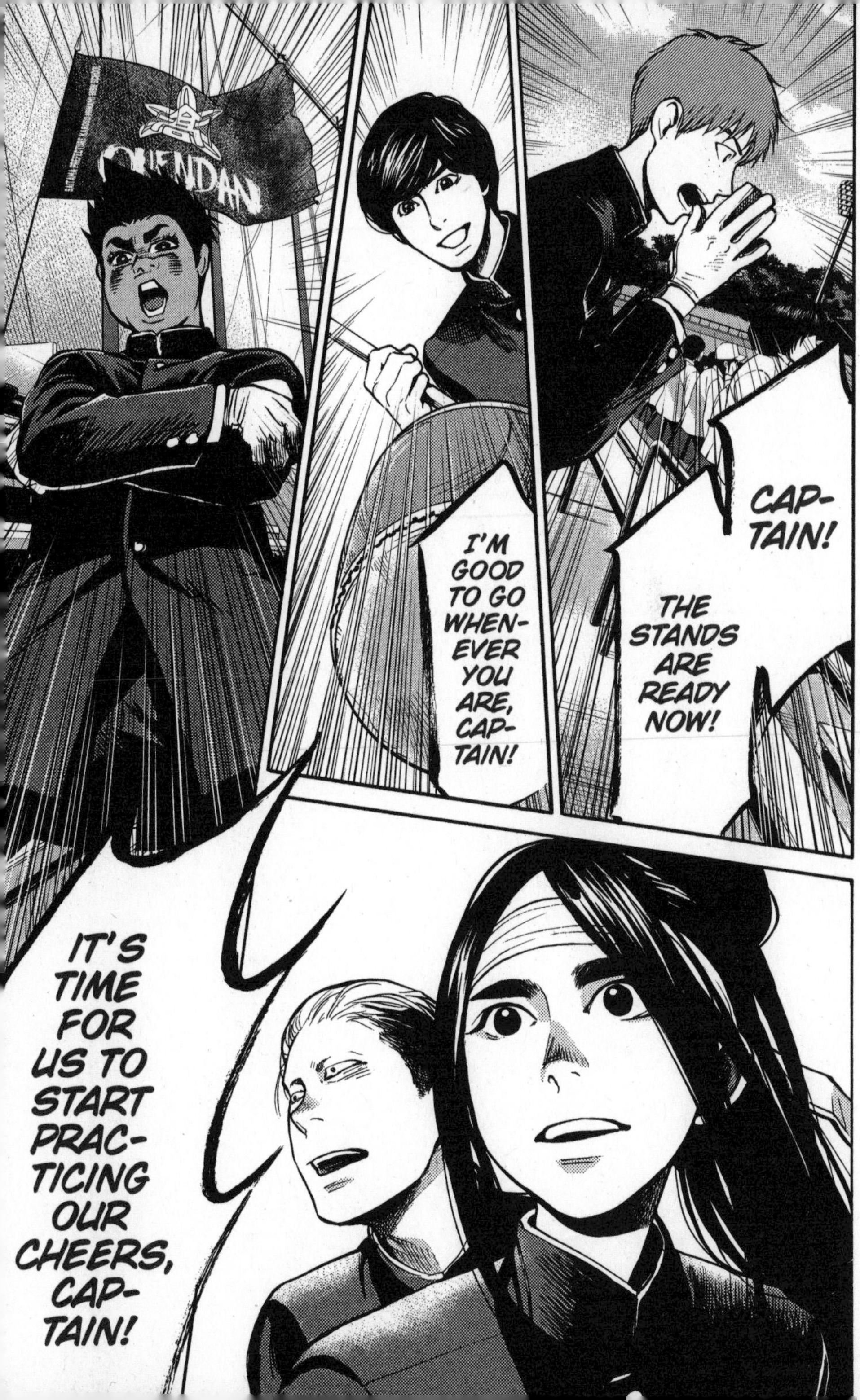
CAP-TAIN!
THE STANDS ARE READY NOW!
I'M GOOD TO GO WHENEVER YOU ARE, CAP-TAIN!
OUENDAN
IT'S TIME FOR US TO START PRAC-TICING OUR CHEERS, CAP-TAIN!

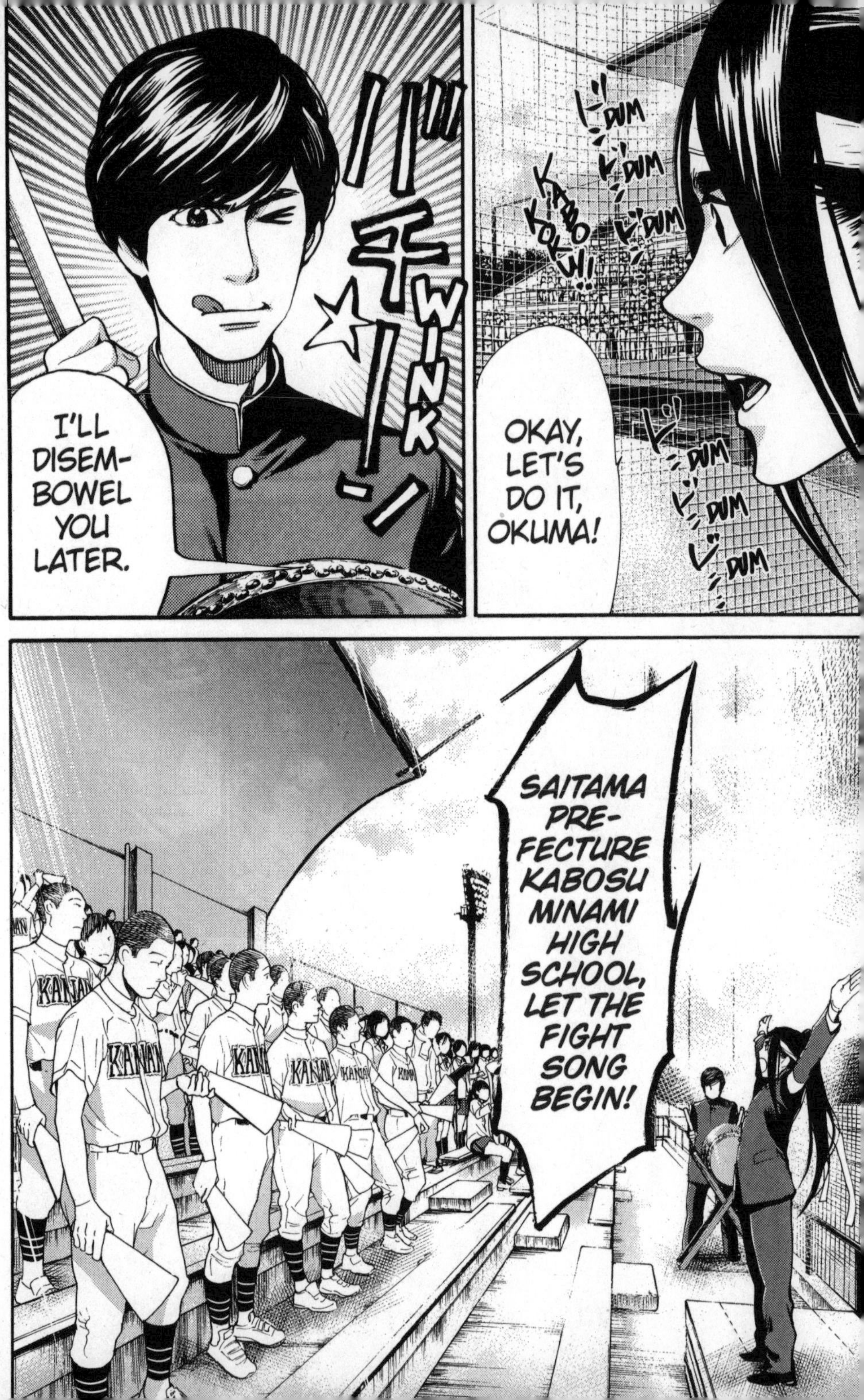
DUM
DUM
DUM
KABOO KOKU!!
OKAY, LET'S DO IT, OKUMA!
DUM
DUM
DUM
WINK
I'LL DISEM-BOWEL YOU LATER.
SAITAMA PRE-FECTURE KABOSU MINAMI HIGH SCHOOL, LET THE FIGHT SONG BEGIN!

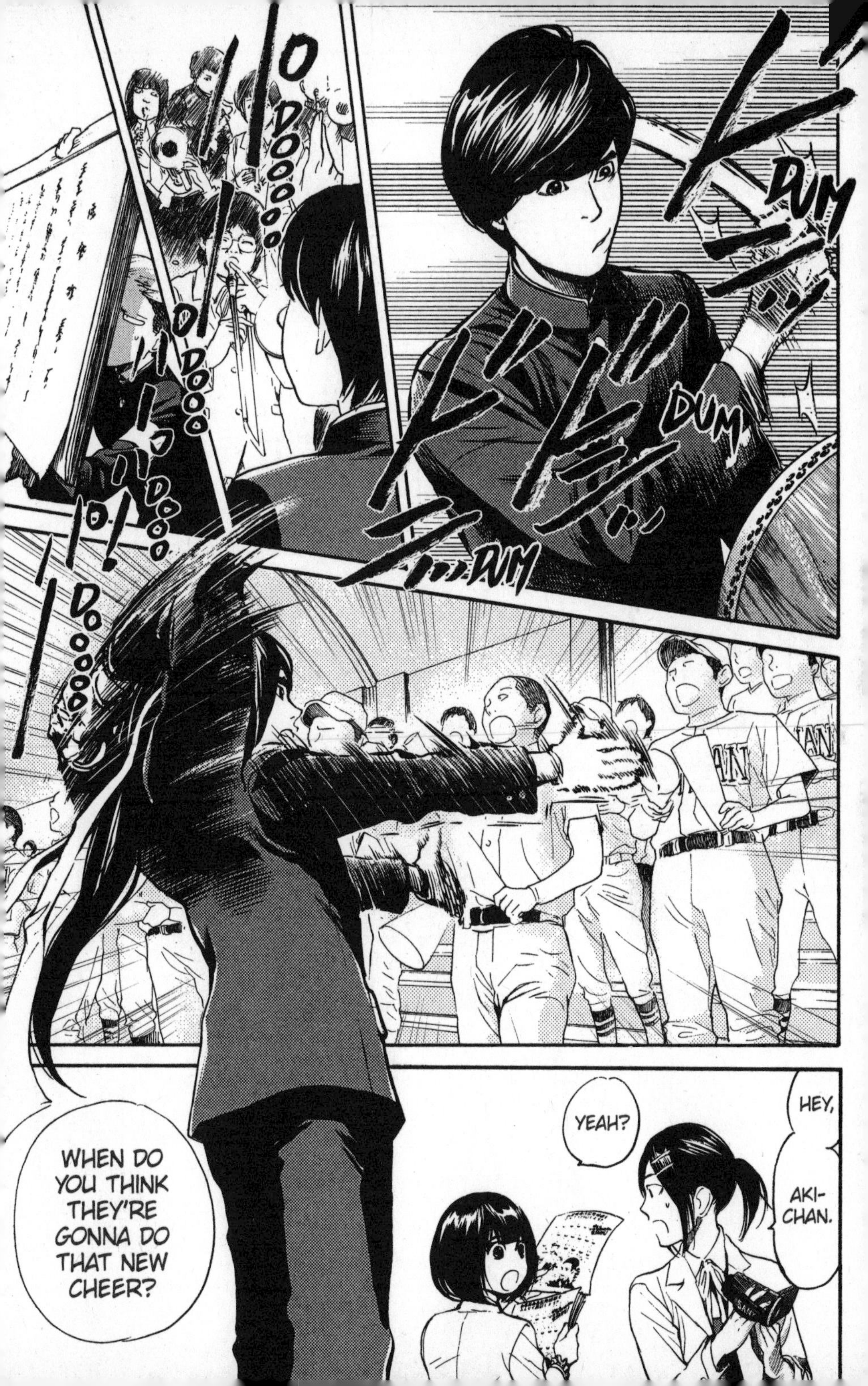
DUM
DUM
DUM
ODOOOOOOOO
DOOOO
DOOOO
DOOOOOO
HEY, AKI-CHAN.
YEAH?
WHEN DO YOU THINK THEY'RE GONNA DO THAT NEW CHEER?

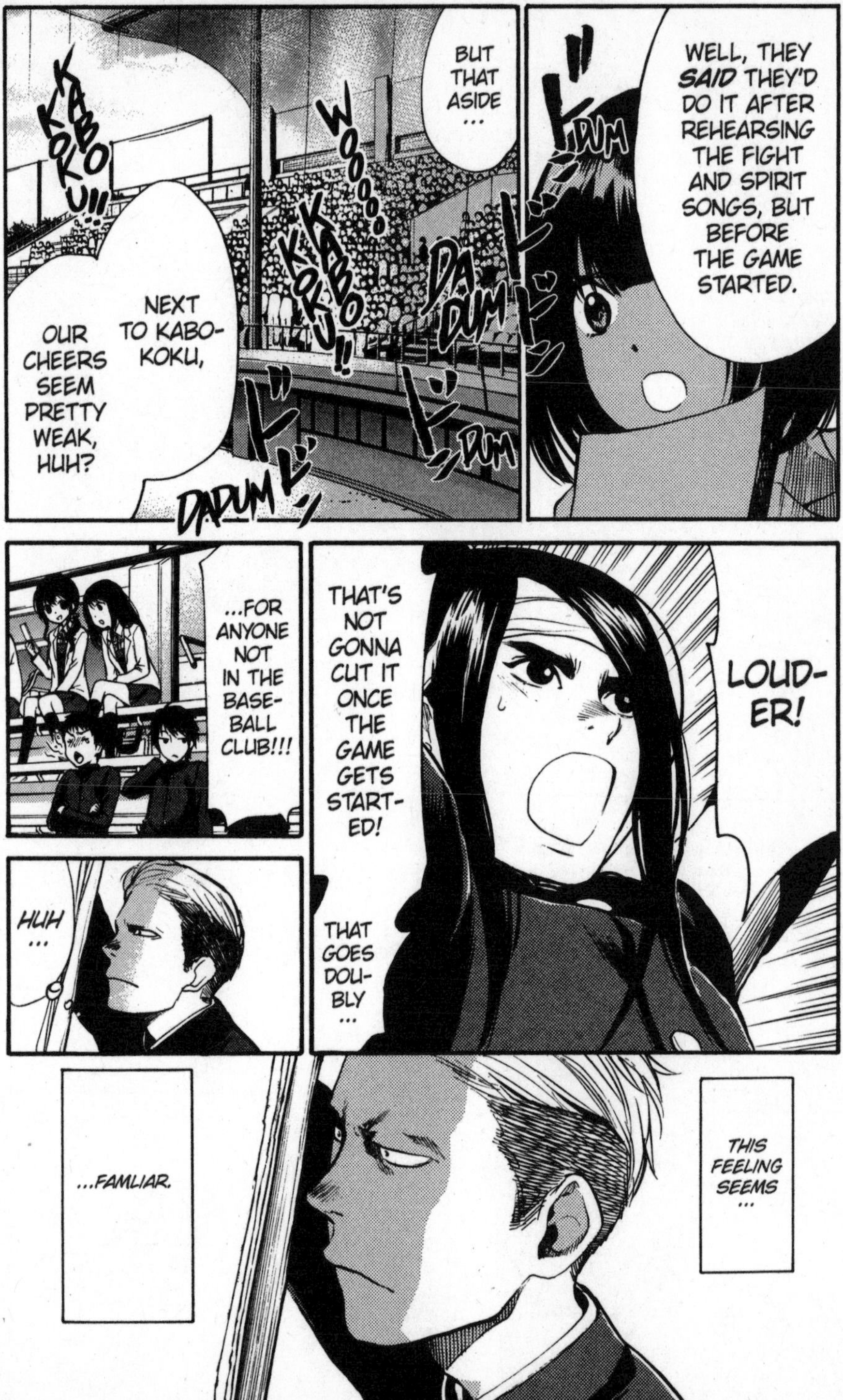
WELL, THEY SAID THEY'D DO IT AFTER REHEARSING THE FIGHT AND SPIRIT SONGS, BUT BEFORE THE GAME STARTED.
DUM
DUM
BUT THAT ASIDE ...
WOOOOO.
KABOKOKU!!
DA DUM
KABOKOKU!!
NEXT TO KABO-KOKU,
OUR CHEERS SEEM PRETTY WEAK, HUH?
DADUM
LOUDER!
THAT'S NOT GONNA CUT IT ONCE THE GAME GETS START-ED!
...FOR ANYONE NOT IN THE BASE-BALL CLUB!!!
THAT GOES DOUBLY ...
HUH ...
THIS FEELING SEEMS ...
...FAMLIAR.

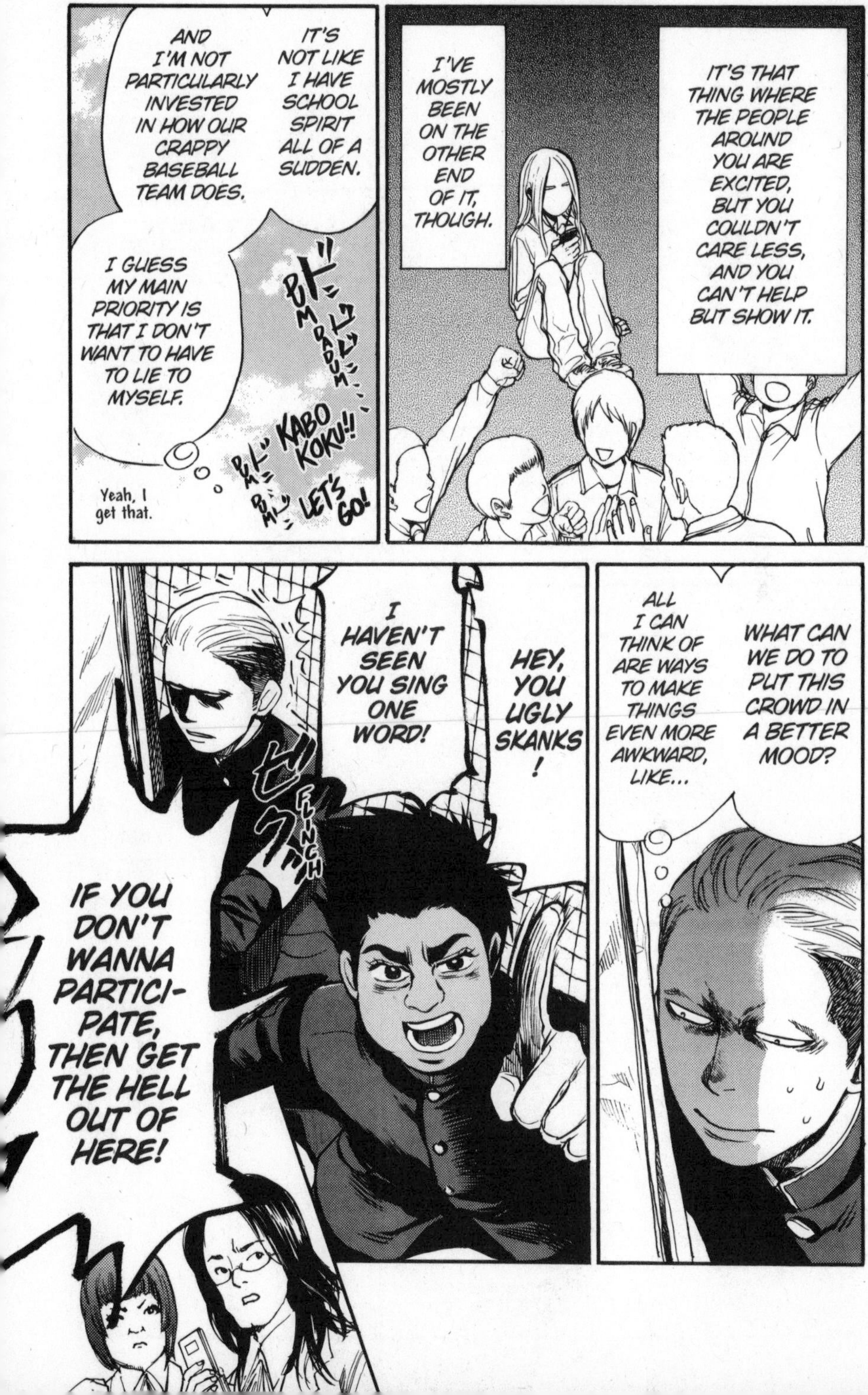

IT'S THAT THING WHERE THE PEOPLE AROUND YOU ARE EXCITED, BUT YOU COULDN'T CARE LESS, AND YOU CAN'T HELP BUT SHOW IT.
I'VE MOSTLY BEEN ON THE OTHER END OF IT, THOUGH.
IT'S NOT LIKE I HAVE SCHOOL SPIRIT ALL OF A SUDDEN.
AND I'M NOT PARTICULARLY INVESTED IN HOW OUR CRAPPY BASEBALL TEAM DOES.
I GUESS MY MAIN PRIORITY IS THAT I DON'T WANT TO HAVE TO LIE TO MYSELF.
BUM BADUM
KABO KOKU!!
BUM BUM
LET'S GO!
Yeah, I get that.
WHAT CAN WE DO TO PUT THIS CROWD IN A BETTER MOOD?
ALL I CAN THINK OF ARE WAYS TO MAKE THINGS EVEN MORE AWKWARD, LIKE...
HEY, YOU UGLY SKANKS!
I HAVEN'T SEEN YOU SING ONE WORD!
FLINCH
IF YOU DON'T WANNA PARTICI-PATE, THEN GET THE HELL OUT OF HERE!

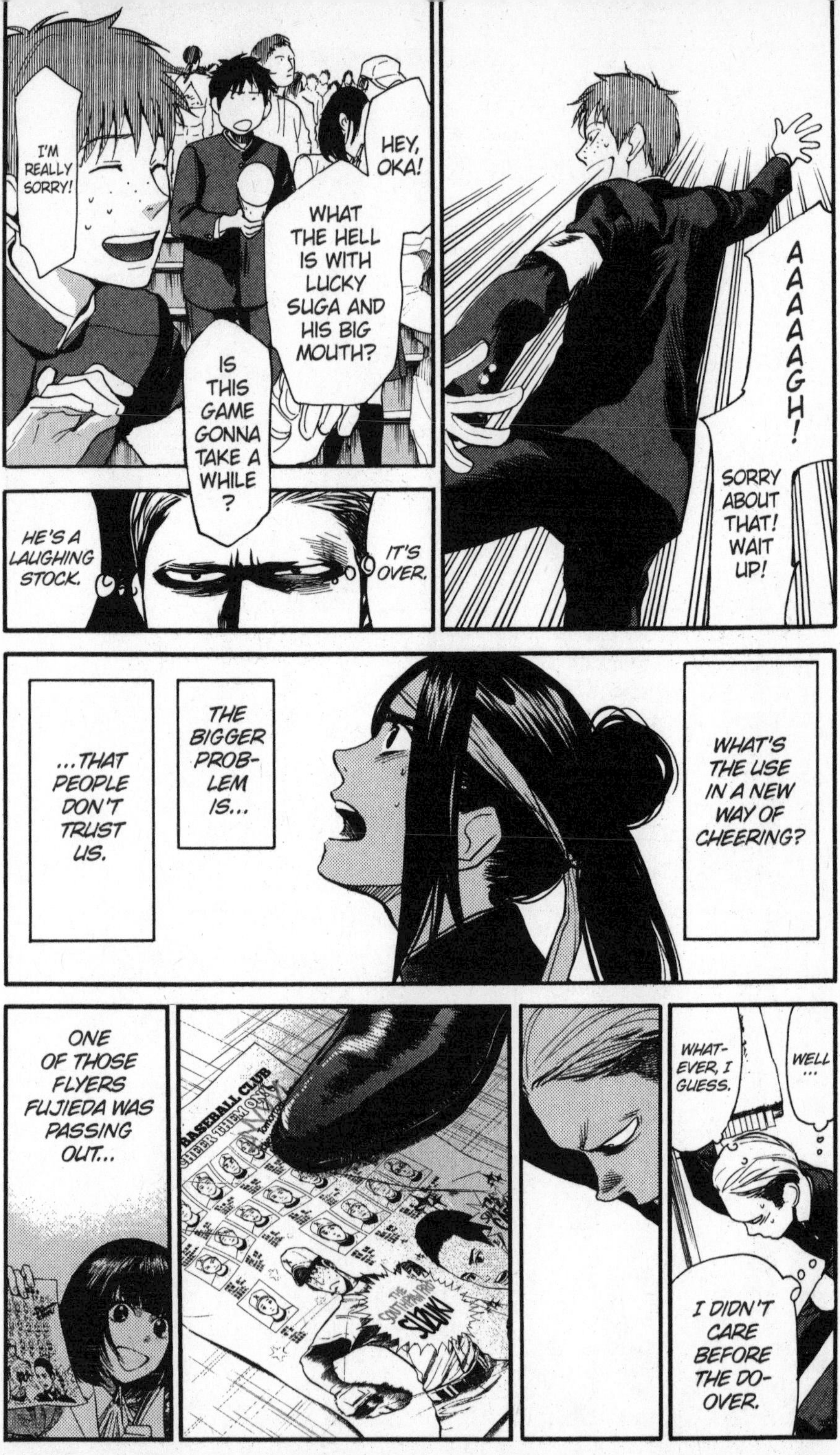
AAAAAAGH!
SORRY ABOUT THAT! WAIT UP!
HEY, OKA!
WHAT THE HELL IS WITH LUCKY SUGA AND HIS BIG MOUTH?
I'M REALLY SORRY!
IS THIS GAME GONNA TAKE A WHILE?
IT'S OVER.
HE'S A LAUGHING STOCK.
WHAT'S THE USE IN A NEW WAY OF CHEERING?
THE BIGGER PROBLEM IS...
...THAT PEOPLE DON'T TRUST US.
WELL...
WHATEVER, I GUESS.
I DIDN'T CARE BEFORE THE DO-OVER.
BASEBALL CLUB
CHEER THEM ON
ONE OF THOSE FLYERS FUJIEDA WAS PASSING OUT...

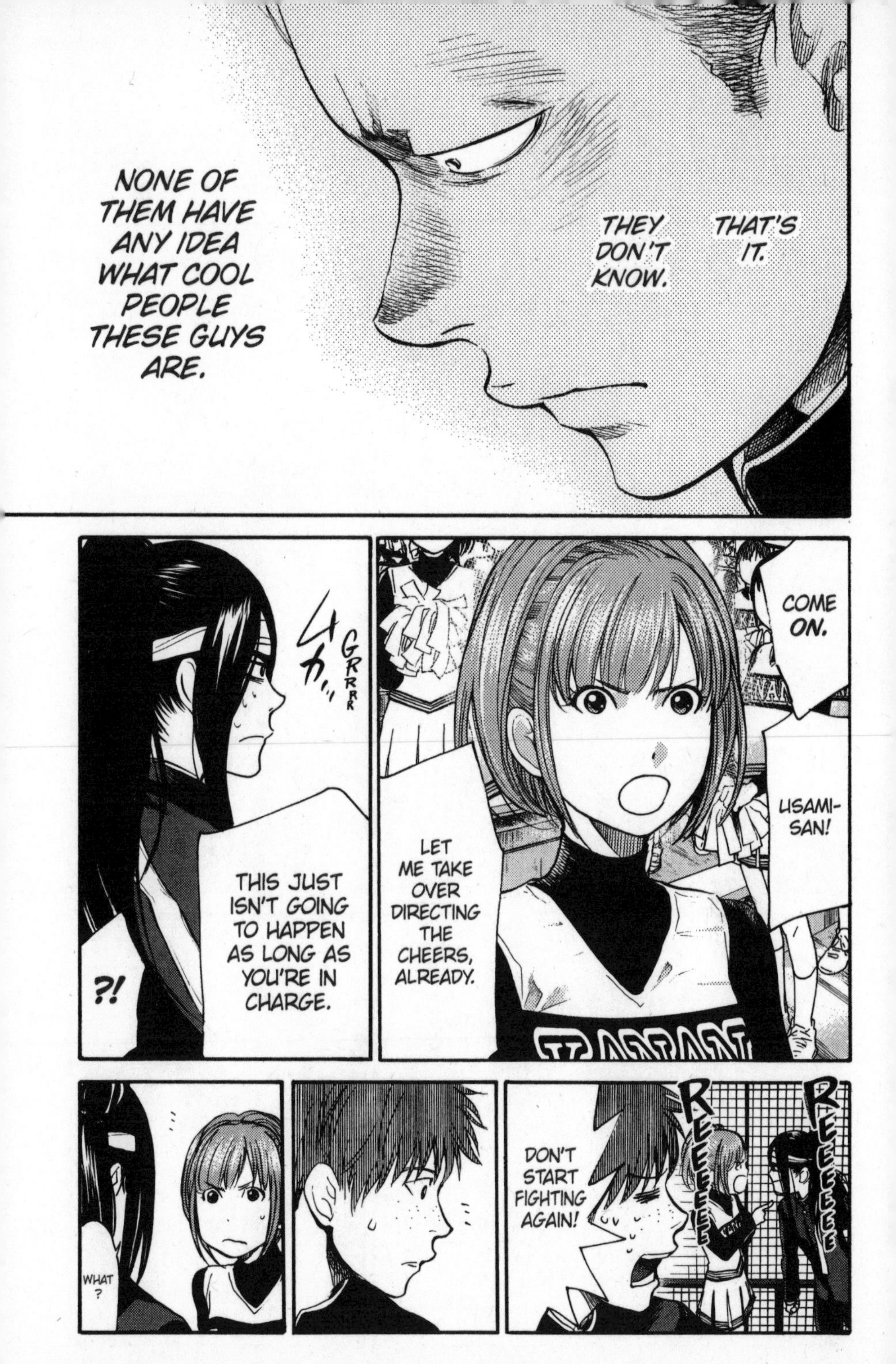
THAT'S IT.
THEY DON'T KNOW.
NONE OF THEM HAVE ANY IDEA WHAT COOL PEOPLE THESE GUYS ARE.
COME ON.
USAMI-SAN!
LET ME TAKE OVER DIRECTING THE CHEERS, ALREADY.
ムカ…
GRRRR
THIS JUST ISN'T GOING TO HAPPEN AS LONG AS YOU'RE IN CHARGE.
?!
REEEEEE
REEEEEE
DON'T START FIGHTING AGAIN!
WHAT?

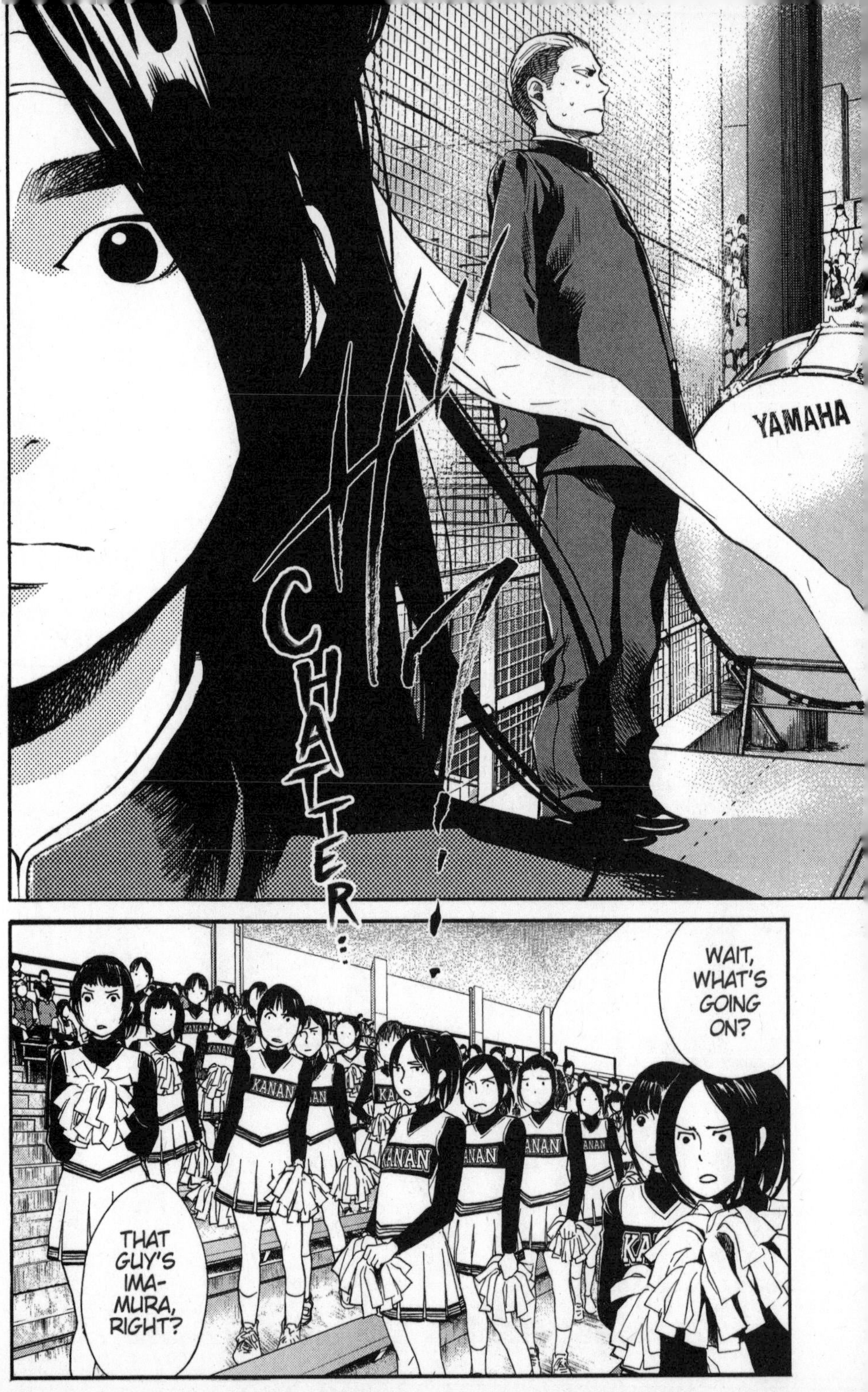
YAMAHA
CHATTER...
WAIT, WHAT'S GOING ON?
THAT GUY'S IMAMURA, RIGHT?
KANAN

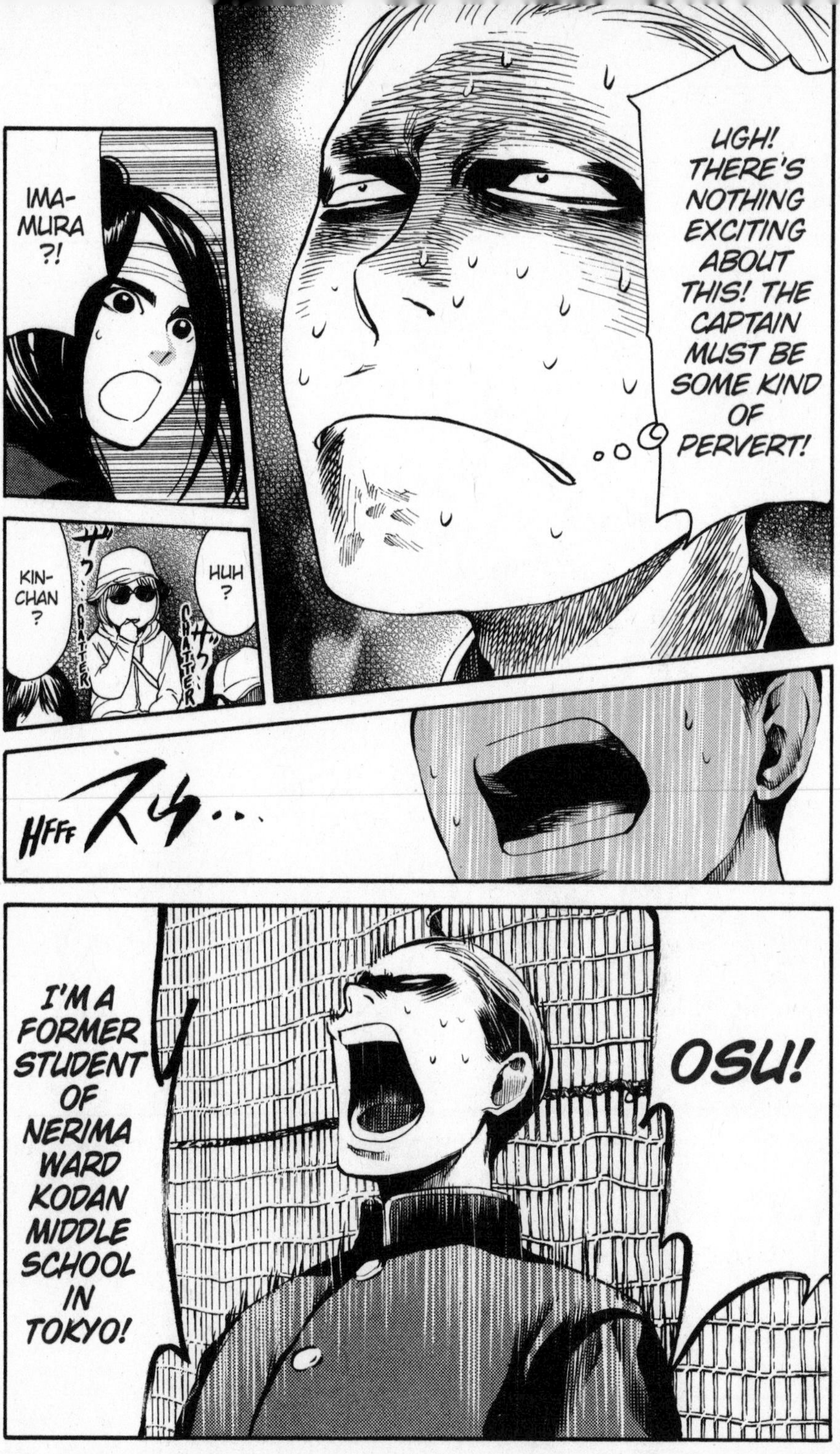
UGH! THERE'S NOTHING EXCITING ABOUT THIS! THE CAPTAIN MUST BE SOME KIND OF PERVERT!
IMA-MURA ?!
HUH ?
CHATTER
CHATTER
KIN-CHAN ?
HFFF
OSU!
I'M A FORMER STUDENT OF NERIMA WARD KODAN MIDDLE SCHOOL IN TOKYO!

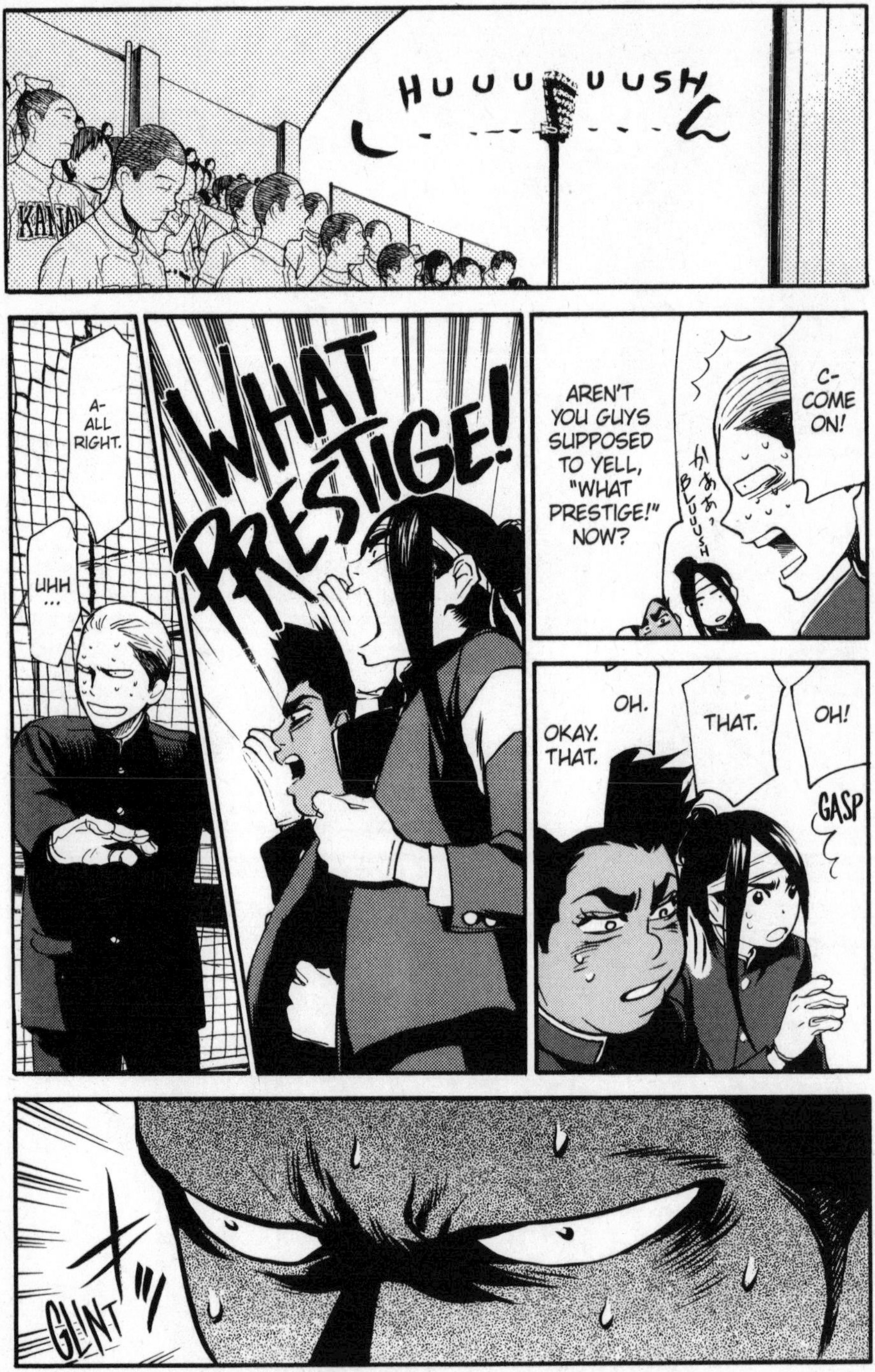
HUUUUUSH
C-COME ON!
AREN'T YOU GUYS SUPPOSED TO YELL, "WHAT PRESTIGE!" NOW?
BLUUUSH
OH!
THAT.
OH.
OKAY. THAT.
GASP
WHAT PRESTIGE!
A-ALL RIGHT.
UHH ...
GLINT

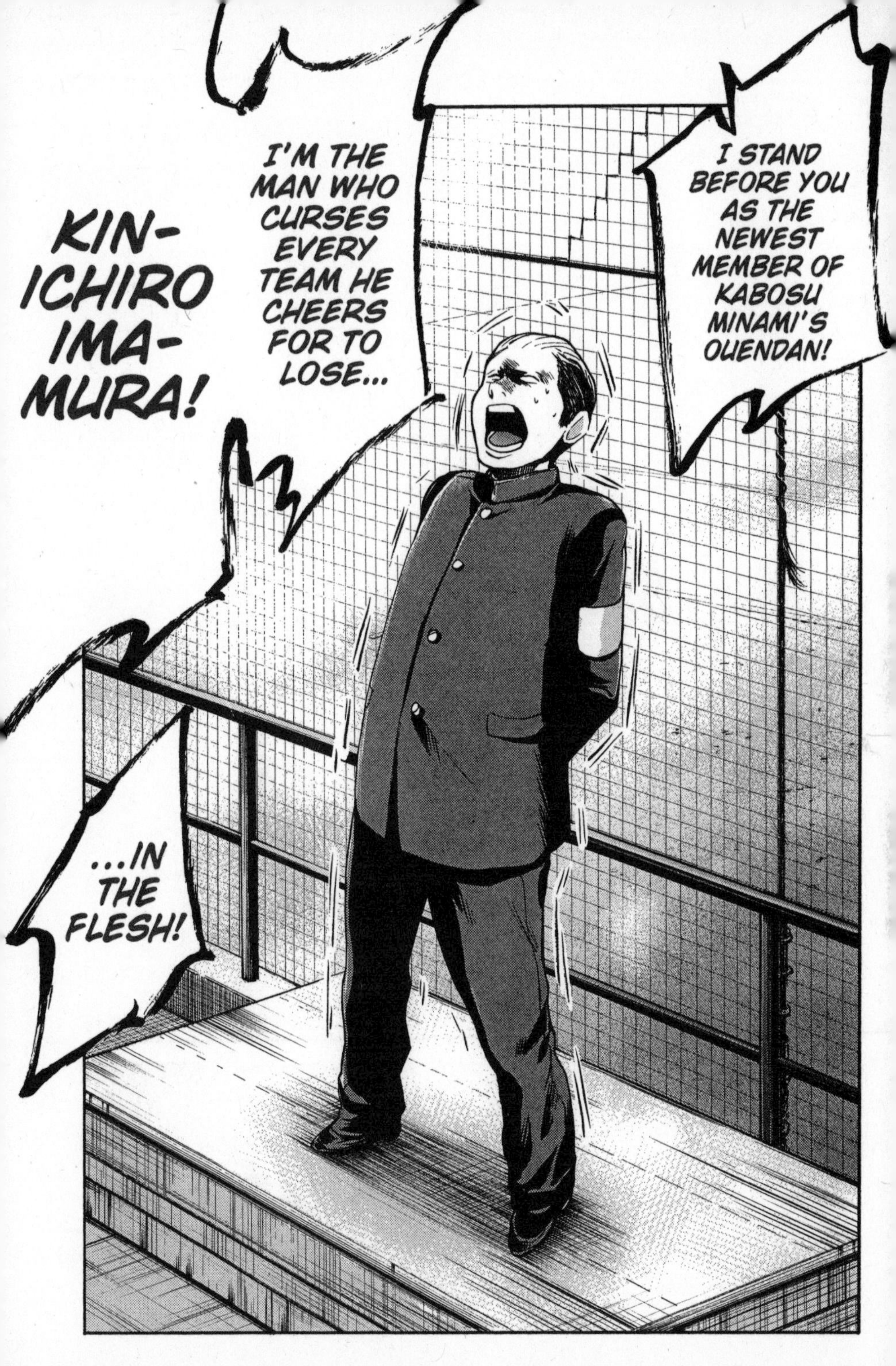
I STAND BEFORE YOU AS THE NEWEST MEMBER OF KABOSU MINAMI'S OUENDAN!
I'M THE MAN WHO CURSES EVERY TEAM HE CHEERS FOR TO LOSE...
KIN-ICHIRO IMA-MURA!
...IN THE FLESH!

Again!!

アゲイン!!

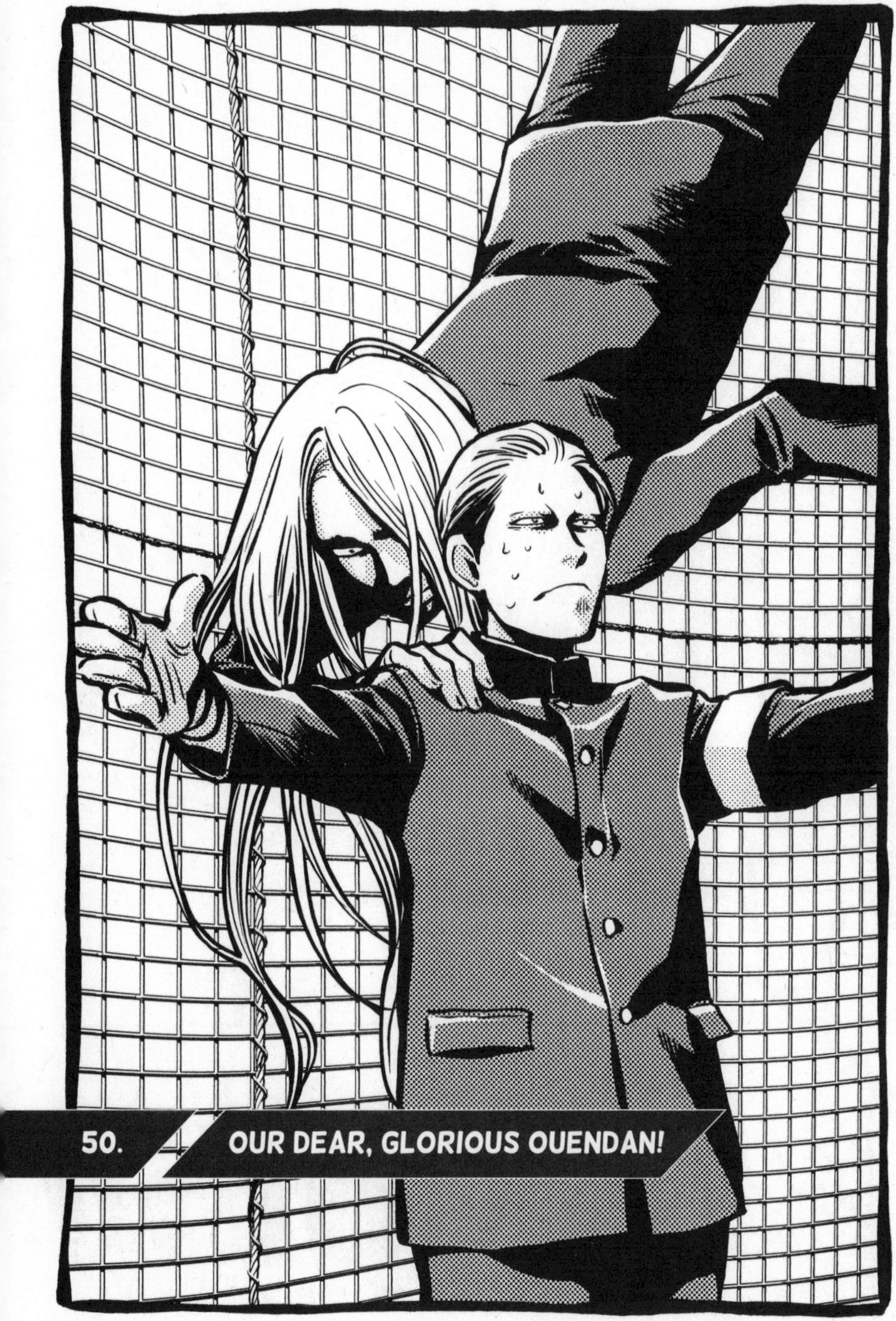

# 50. OUR DEAR, GLORIOUS OUENDAN!

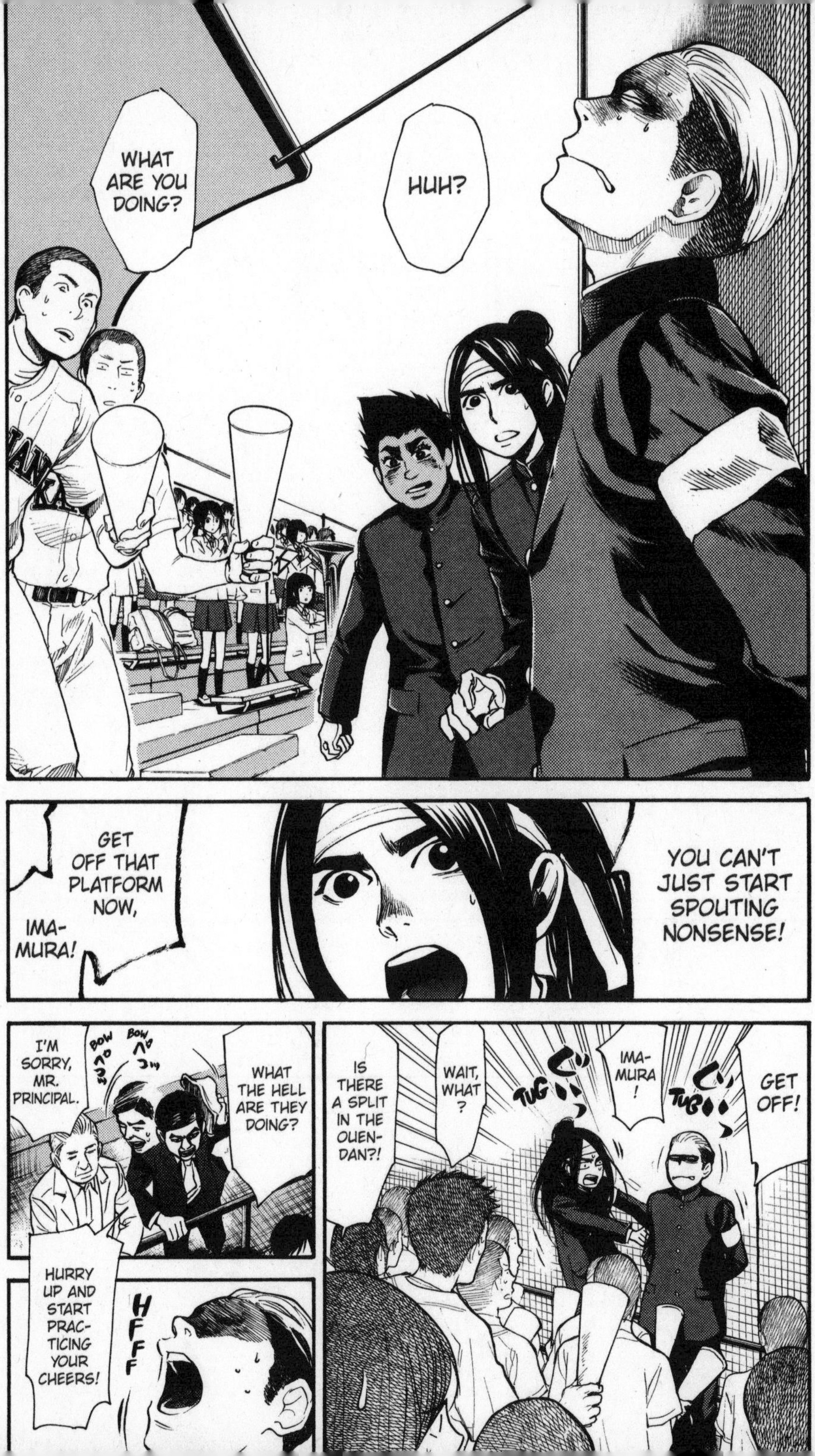
HUH?
WHAT ARE YOU DOING?
YOU CAN'T JUST START SPOUTING NONSENSE!
GET OFF THAT PLATFORM NOW, IMA-MURA!
GET OFF!
TUG
IMA-MURA!
TUG
WAIT, WHAT?
IS THERE A SPLIT IN THE OUEN-DAN?!
WHAT THE HELL ARE THEY DOING?
BOW
BOW
I'M SORRY, MR. PRINCIPAL.
HFFF
HURRY UP AND START PRAC-TICING YOUR CHEERS!

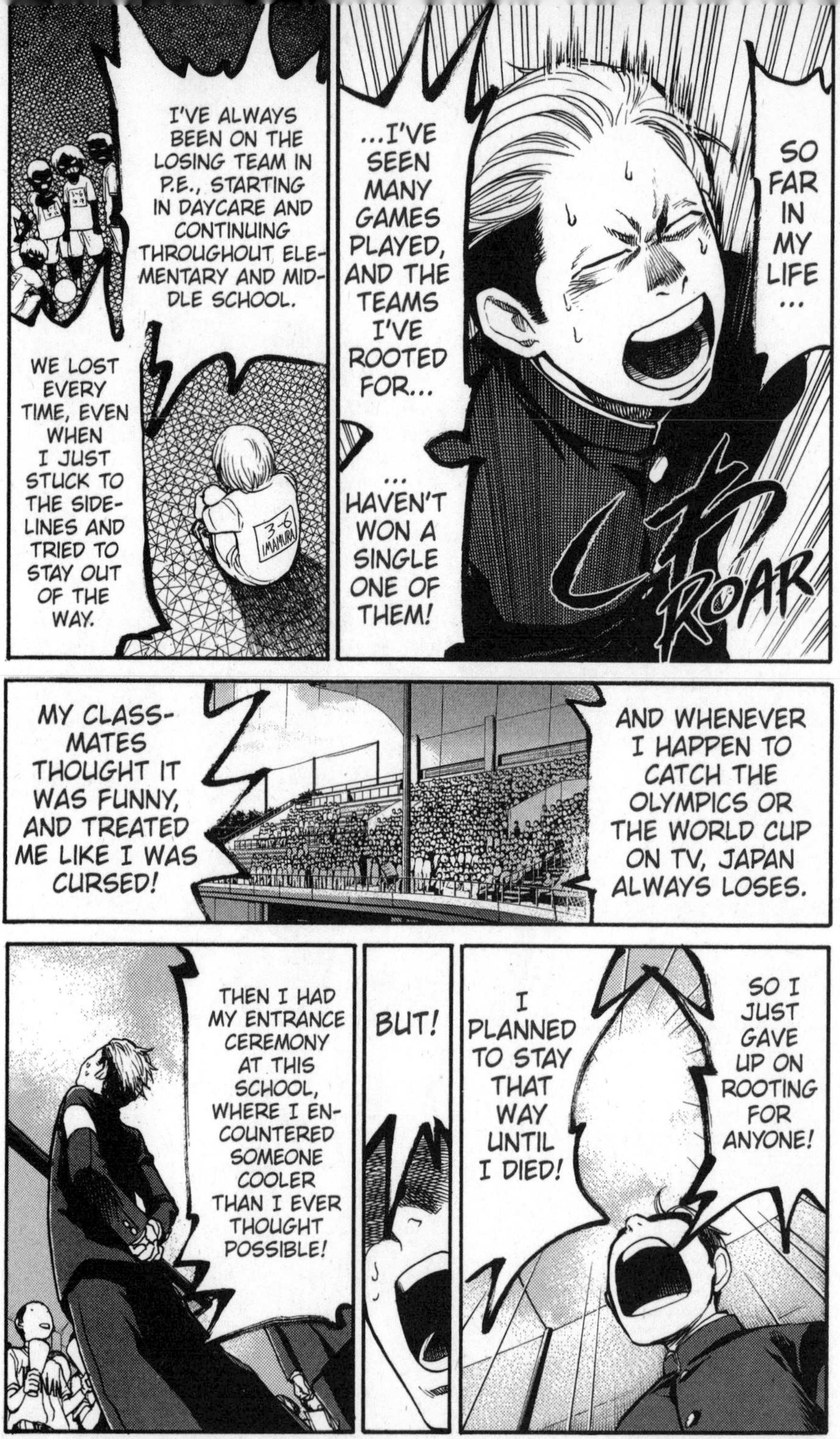
SO FAR IN MY LIFE...
...I'VE SEEN MANY GAMES PLAYED, AND THE TEAMS I'VE ROOTED FOR...
...HAVEN'T WON A SINGLE ONE OF THEM!
ROAR
I'VE ALWAYS BEEN ON THE LOSING TEAM IN P.E., STARTING IN DAYCARE AND CONTINUING THROUGHOUT ELEMENTARY AND MIDDLE SCHOOL.
WE LOST EVERY TIME, EVEN WHEN I JUST STUCK TO THE SIDELINES AND TRIED TO STAY OUT OF THE WAY.
3-6 IMAMURA
AND WHENEVER I HAPPEN TO CATCH THE OLYMPICS OR THE WORLD CUP ON TV, JAPAN ALWAYS LOSES.
MY CLASSMATES THOUGHT IT WAS FUNNY, AND TREATED ME LIKE I WAS CURSED!
SO I JUST GAVE UP ON ROOTING FOR ANYONE!
I PLANNED TO STAY THAT WAY UNTIL I DIED!
BUT!
THEN I HAD MY ENTRANCE CEREMONY AT THIS SCHOOL, WHERE I ENCOUNTERED SOMEONE COOLER THAN I EVER THOUGHT POSSIBLE!

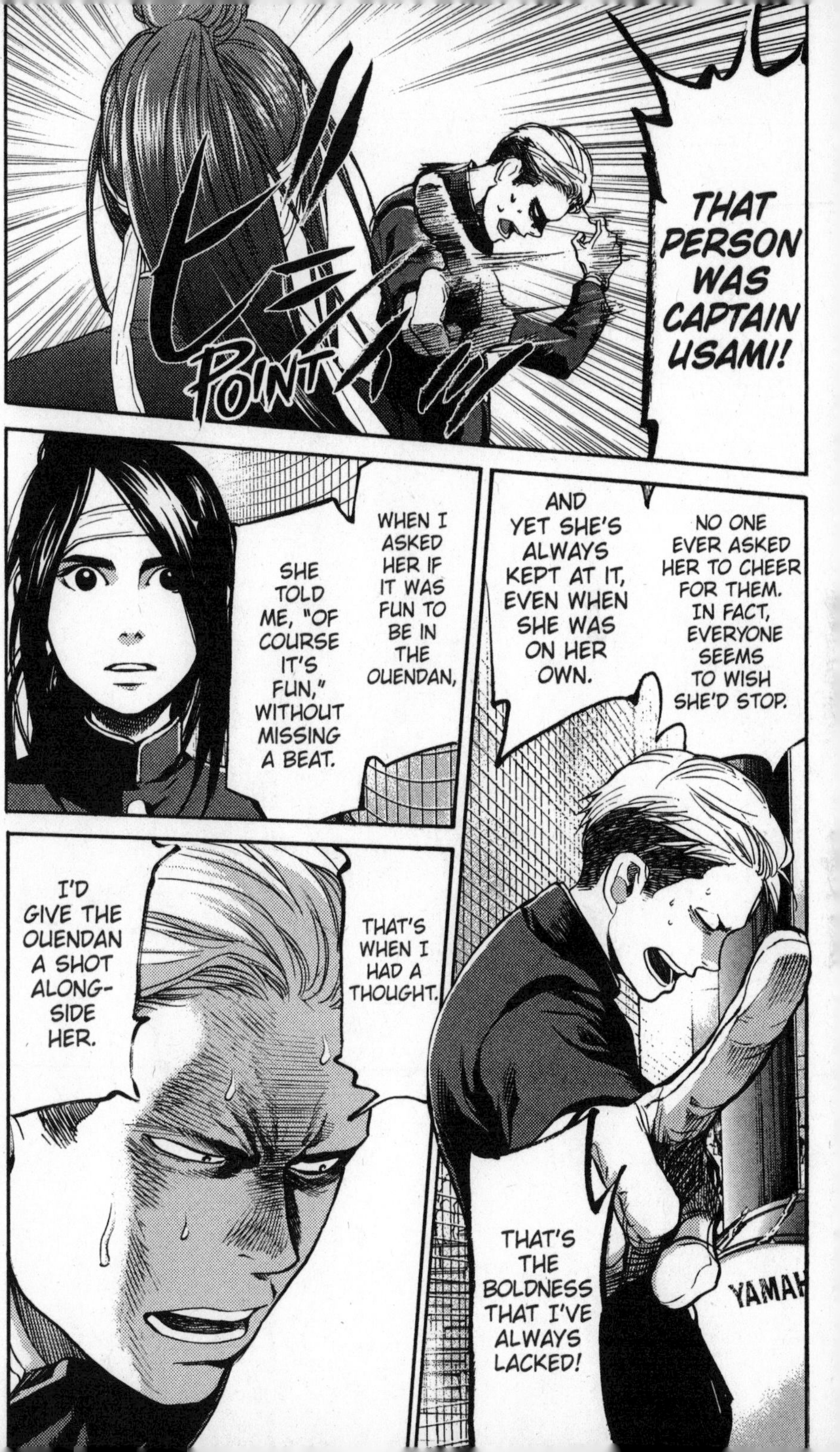
THAT PERSON WAS CAPTAIN USAMI!
POINT
NO ONE EVER ASKED HER TO CHEER FOR THEM. IN FACT, EVERYONE SEEMS TO WISH SHE'D STOP.
AND YET SHE'S ALWAYS KEPT AT IT, EVEN WHEN SHE WAS ON HER OWN.
WHEN I ASKED HER IF IT WAS FUN TO BE IN THE OUENDAN,
SHE TOLD ME, "OF COURSE IT'S FUN," WITHOUT MISSING A BEAT.
THAT'S THE BOLDNESS THAT I'VE ALWAYS LACKED!
YAMAH
THAT'S WHEN I HAD A THOUGHT.
I'D GIVE THE OUENDAN A SHOT ALONG-SIDE HER.

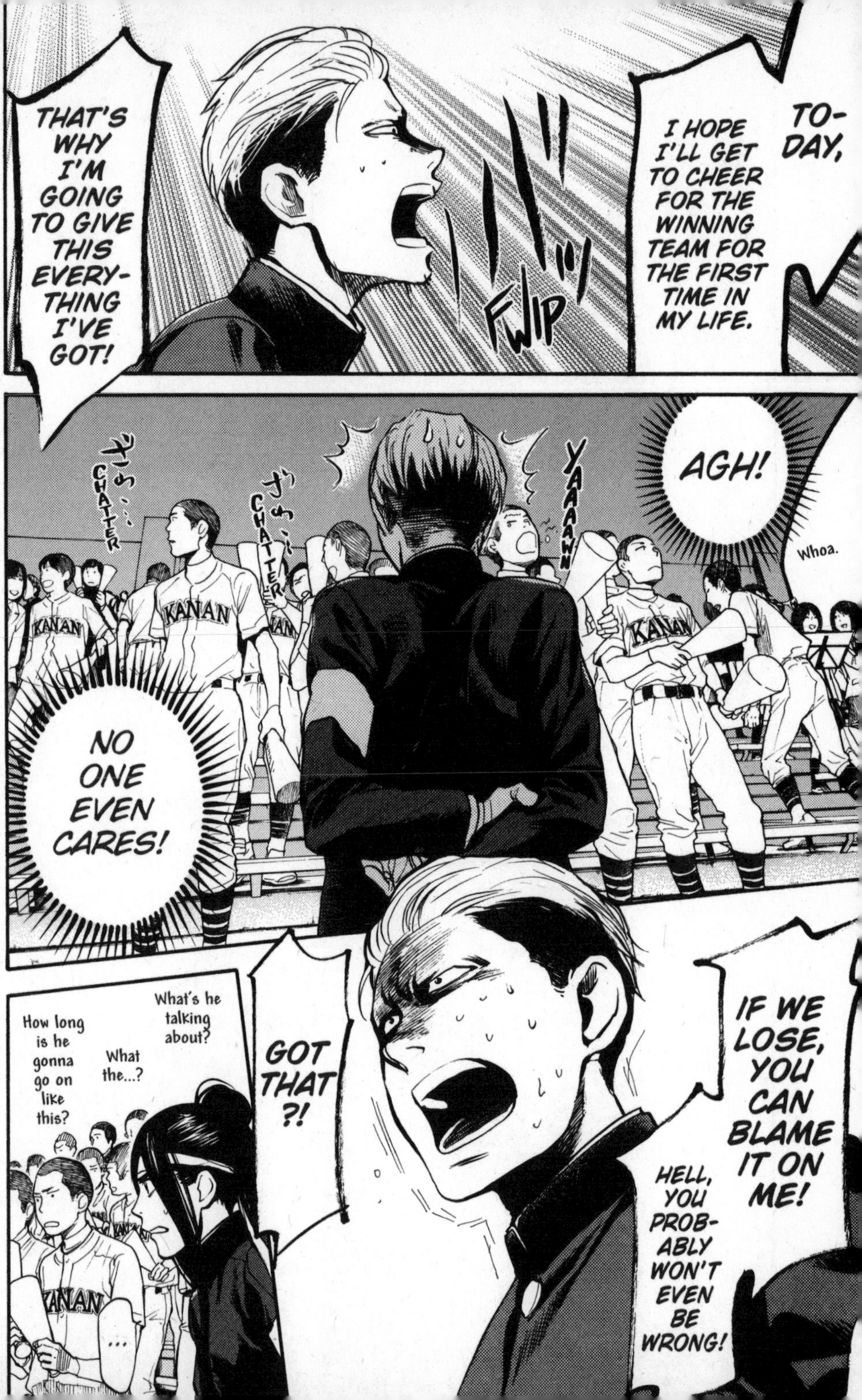
TO-DAY,
I HOPE I'LL GET TO CHEER FOR THE WINNING TEAM FOR THE FIRST TIME IN MY LIFE.
THAT'S WHY I'M GOING TO GIVE THIS EVERY-THING I'VE GOT!
FWIP
AGH!
Whoa.
YAAAAWN
CHATTER
CHATTER
NO ONE EVEN CARES!
IF WE LOSE, YOU CAN BLAME IT ON ME!
HELL, YOU PROB-ABLY WON'T EVEN BE WRONG!
GOT THAT?!
What's he talking about?
What the...?
How long is he gonna go on like this?
...

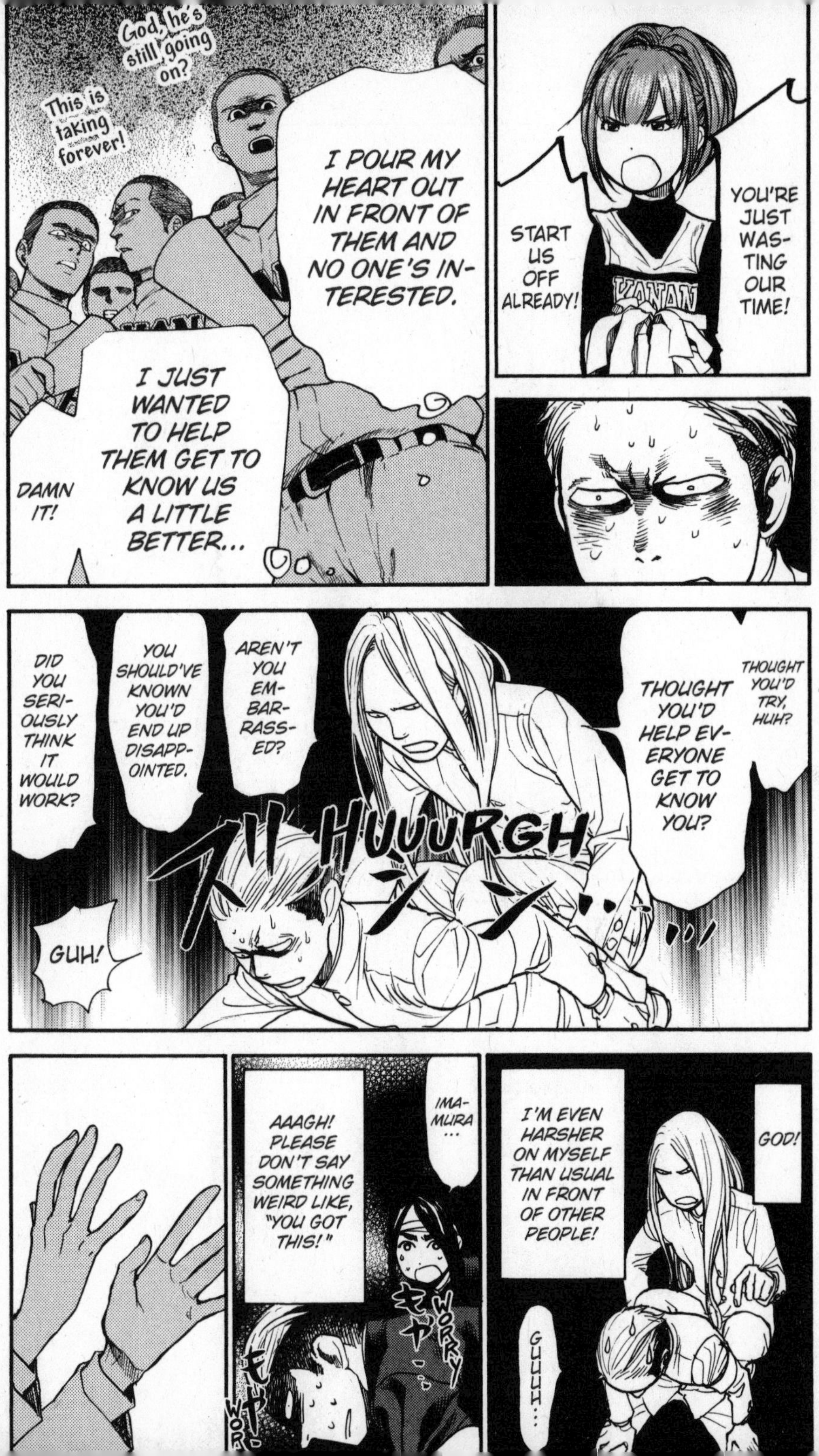
YOU'RE JUST WASTING OUR TIME!
START US OFF ALREADY!
God, he's still going on?
This is taking forever!
I POUR MY HEART OUT IN FRONT OF THEM AND NO ONE'S INTERESTED.
I JUST WANTED TO HELP THEM GET TO KNOW US A LITTLE BETTER...
DAMN IT!
THOUGHT YOU'D TRY, HUH?
THOUGHT YOU'D HELP EVERYONE GET TO KNOW YOU?
HUUURGH
AREN'T YOU EMBARRASSED?
YOU SHOULD'VE KNOWN YOU'D END UP DISAPPOINTED.
DID YOU SERIOUSLY THINK IT WOULD WORK?
GUH!
GOD!
I'M EVEN HARSHER ON MYSELF THAN USUAL IN FRONT OF OTHER PEOPLE!
GUUUH...
IMAMURA...
AAAGH! PLEASE DON'T SAY SOMETHING WEIRD LIKE, "YOU GOT THIS!"
WORRY
WOR

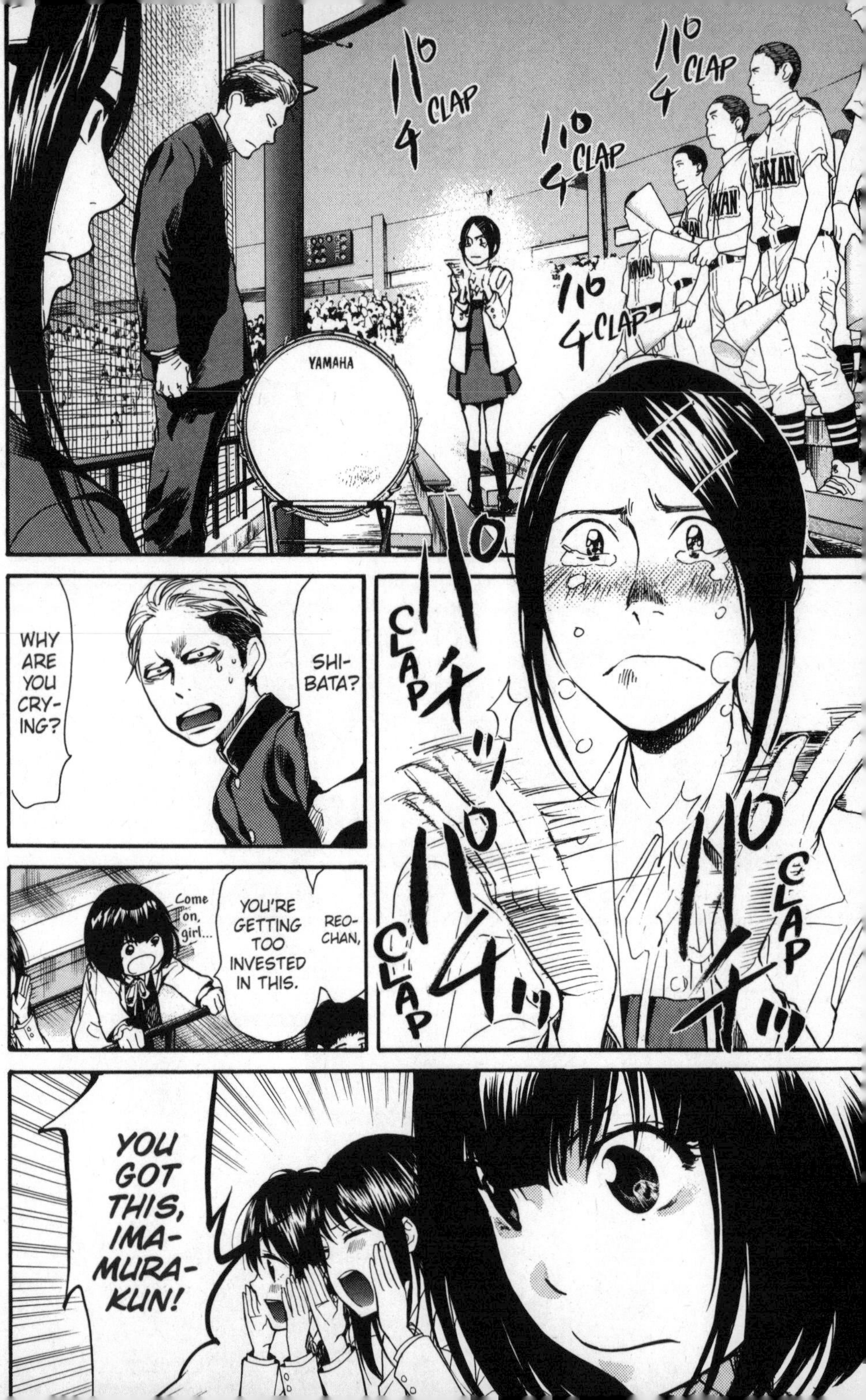
CLAP
CLAP
CLAP
CLAP
YAMAHA
CLAP
CLAP
CLAP
SHI-BATA?
WHY ARE YOU CRY-ING?
REO-CHAN,
YOU'RE GETTING TOO INVESTED IN THIS.
Come on, girl...
YOU GOT THIS, IMAMURA-KUN!

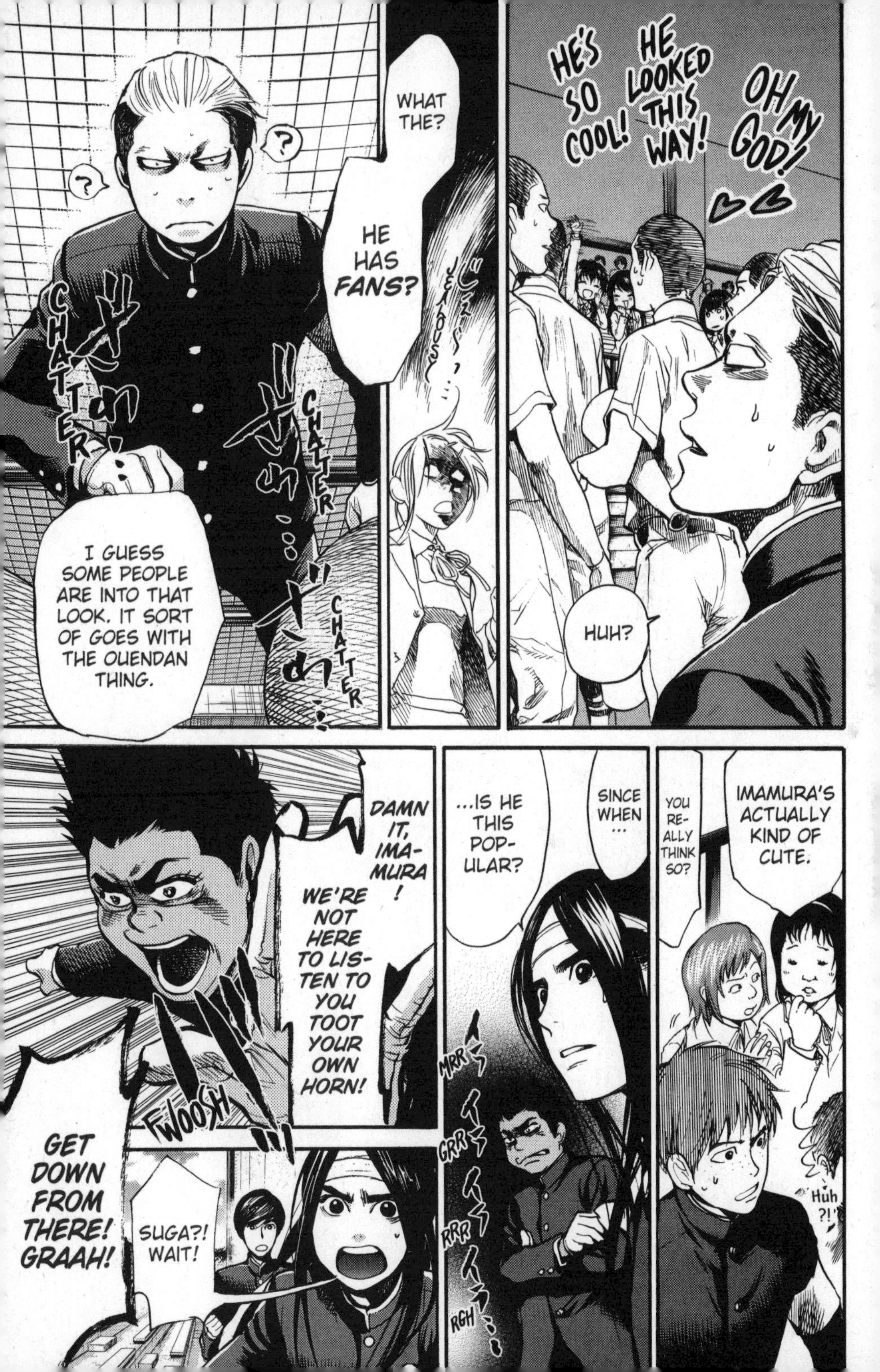

OH MY GOD!
HE LOOKED THIS WAY!
HE'S SO COOL!
HUH?
WHAT THE?
HE HAS FANS?
JEALOUSY...
CHATTER
CHATTER
CHATTER
CHATTER
I GUESS SOME PEOPLE ARE INTO THAT LOOK. IT SORT OF GOES WITH THE OUENDAN THING.
IMAMURA'S ACTUALLY KIND OF CUTE.
YOU REALLY THINK SO?
Huh?!
SINCE WHEN...
...IS HE THIS POPULAR?
MRR
GRR
RRR
RGH
DAMN IT, IMAMURA! WE'RE NOT HERE TO LISTEN TO YOU TOOT YOUR OWN HORN!
FWOOSH
GET DOWN FROM THERE! GRAAH!
SUGA?! WAIT!

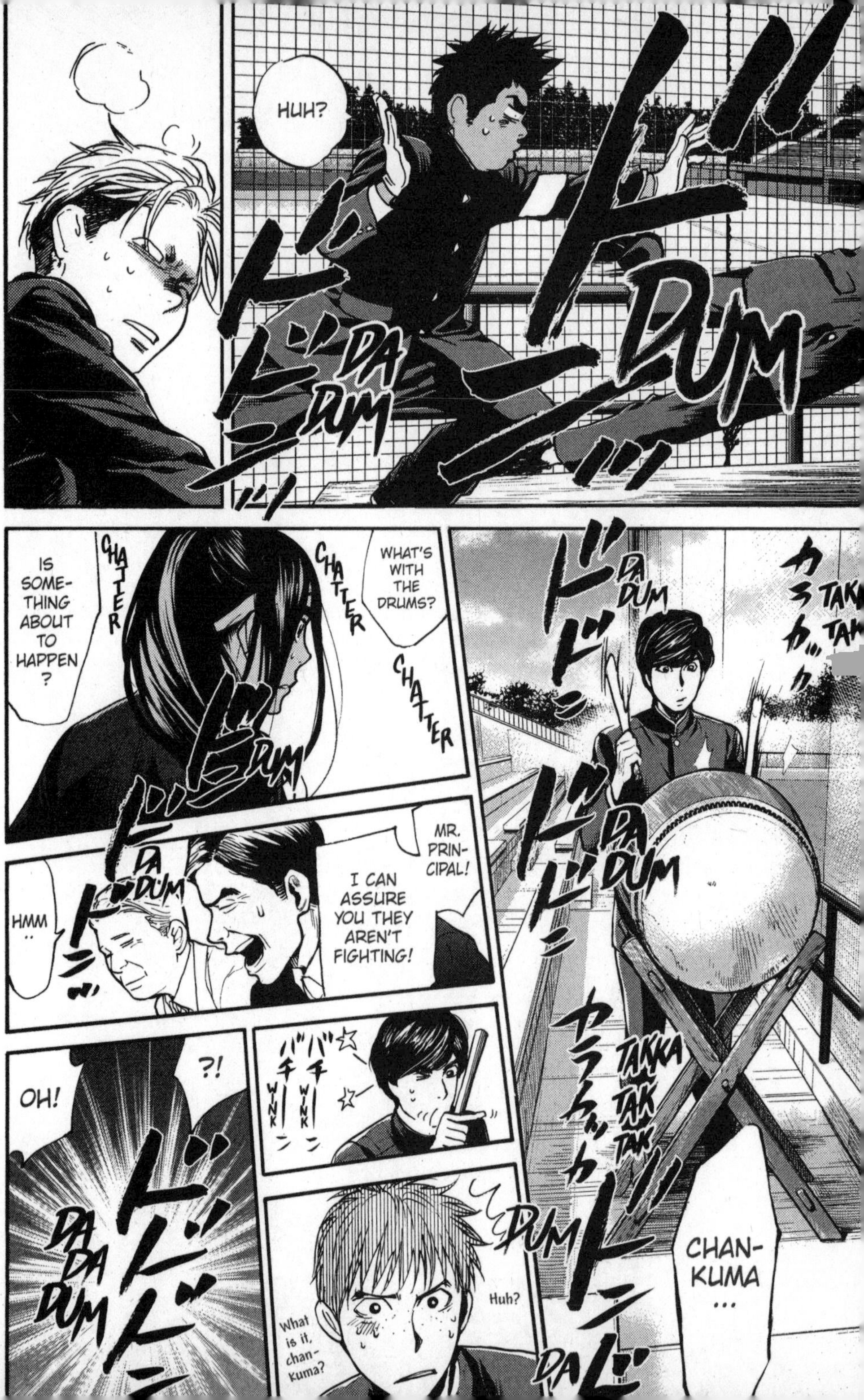
HUH?
DUM
DA DUM
DA DUM
TAKA TAK
DA DUM
TAKKA TAK TAK
DUM
DA
WHAT'S WITH THE DRUMS?
CHATTER
CHATTER
CHATTER
IS SOMETHING ABOUT TO HAPPEN?
DUM
MR. PRINCIPAL!
I CAN ASSURE YOU THEY AREN'T FIGHTING!
DA DUM
HMM ..
WINK
WINK
?!
OH!
DA DA DUM
CHAN-KUMA ...
Huh?
What is it, chan-kuma?

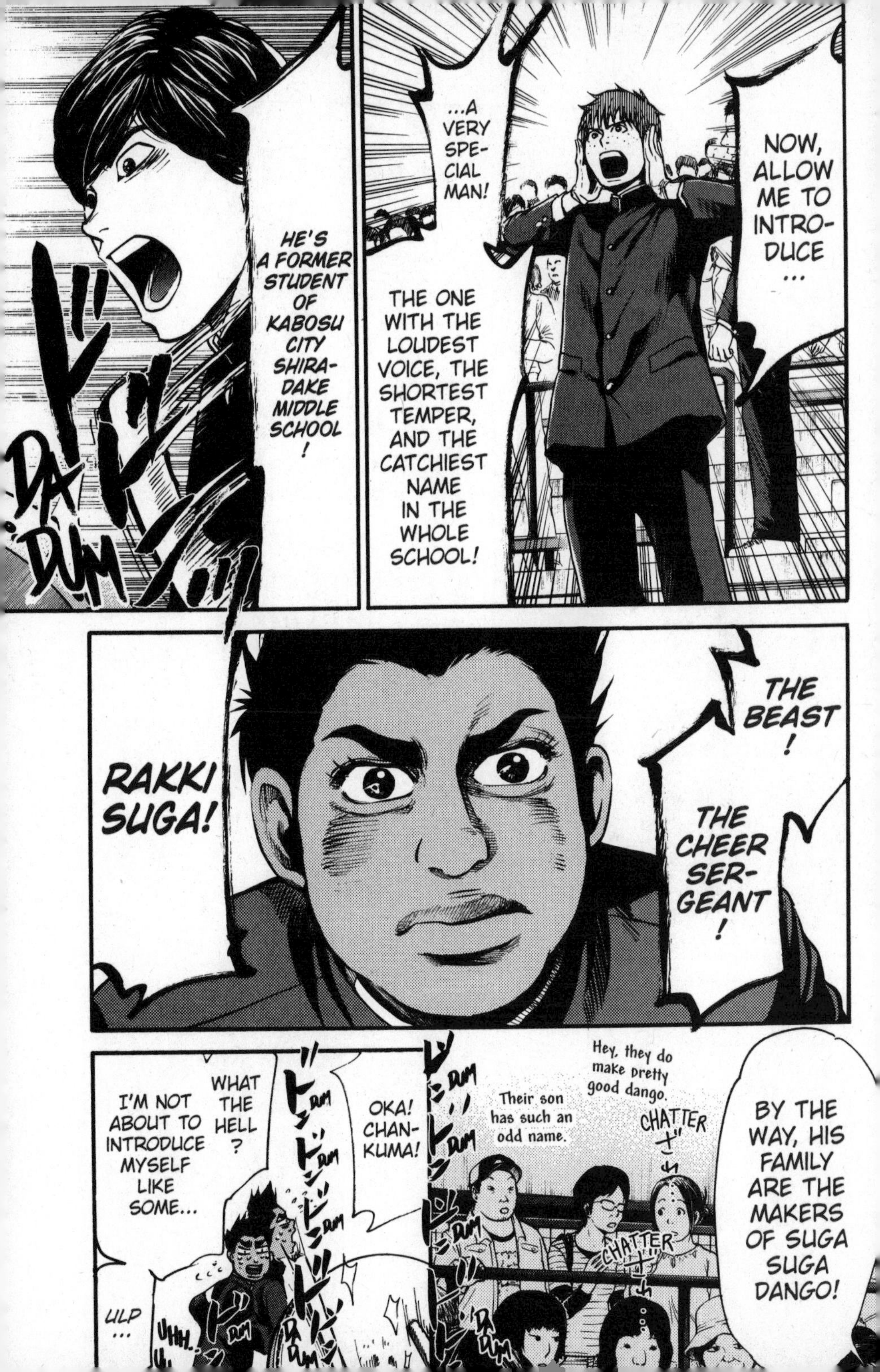
NOW, ALLOW ME TO INTRODUCE...
...A VERY SPECIAL MAN!
THE ONE WITH THE LOUDEST VOICE, THE SHORTEST TEMPER, AND THE CATCHIEST NAME IN THE WHOLE SCHOOL!
HE'S A FORMER STUDENT OF KABOSU CITY SHIRADAKE MIDDLE SCHOOL!
DA DUM
THE BEAST!
THE CHEER SERGEANT!
RAKKI SUGA!
BY THE WAY, HIS FAMILY ARE THE MAKERS OF SUGA SUGA DANGO!
Hey, they do make pretty good dango.
Their son has such an odd name.
CHATTER
CHATTER
DUM DUM DA DUM
OKA! CHANKUMA!
DUM DUM DUM DA DUM
WHAT THE HELL?
I'M NOT ABOUT TO INTRODUCE MYSELF LIKE SOME...
UHH...
ULP...

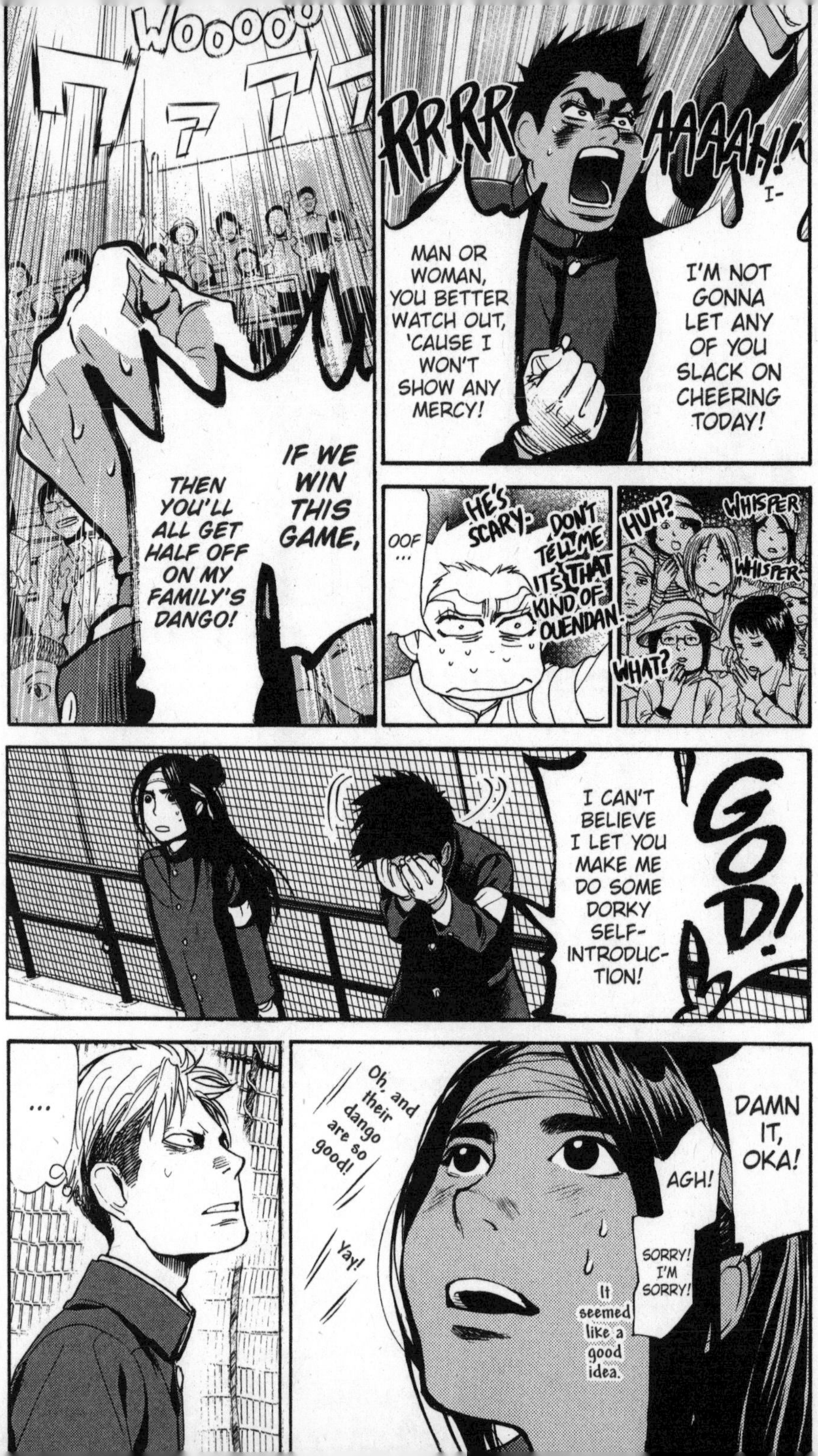
RRRR AAAAH!
I-
I'M NOT GONNA LET ANY OF YOU SLACK ON CHEERING TODAY!
MAN OR WOMAN, YOU BETTER WATCH OUT, 'CAUSE I WON'T SHOW ANY MERCY!
WHISPER
WHISPER
HUH?
WHAT?
DON'T TELL ME IT'S THAT KIND OF OUENDAN.
HE'S SCARY.
OOF ...
WOOOOO
IF WE WIN THIS GAME,
THEN YOU'LL ALL GET HALF OFF ON MY FAMILY'S DANGO!
GOD!
I CAN'T BELIEVE I LET YOU MAKE ME DO SOME DORKY SELF-INTRODUCTION!
DAMN IT, OKA!
AGH!
SORRY! I'M SORRY!
It seemed like a good idea.
Oh, and their dango are so good!
Yay!
...

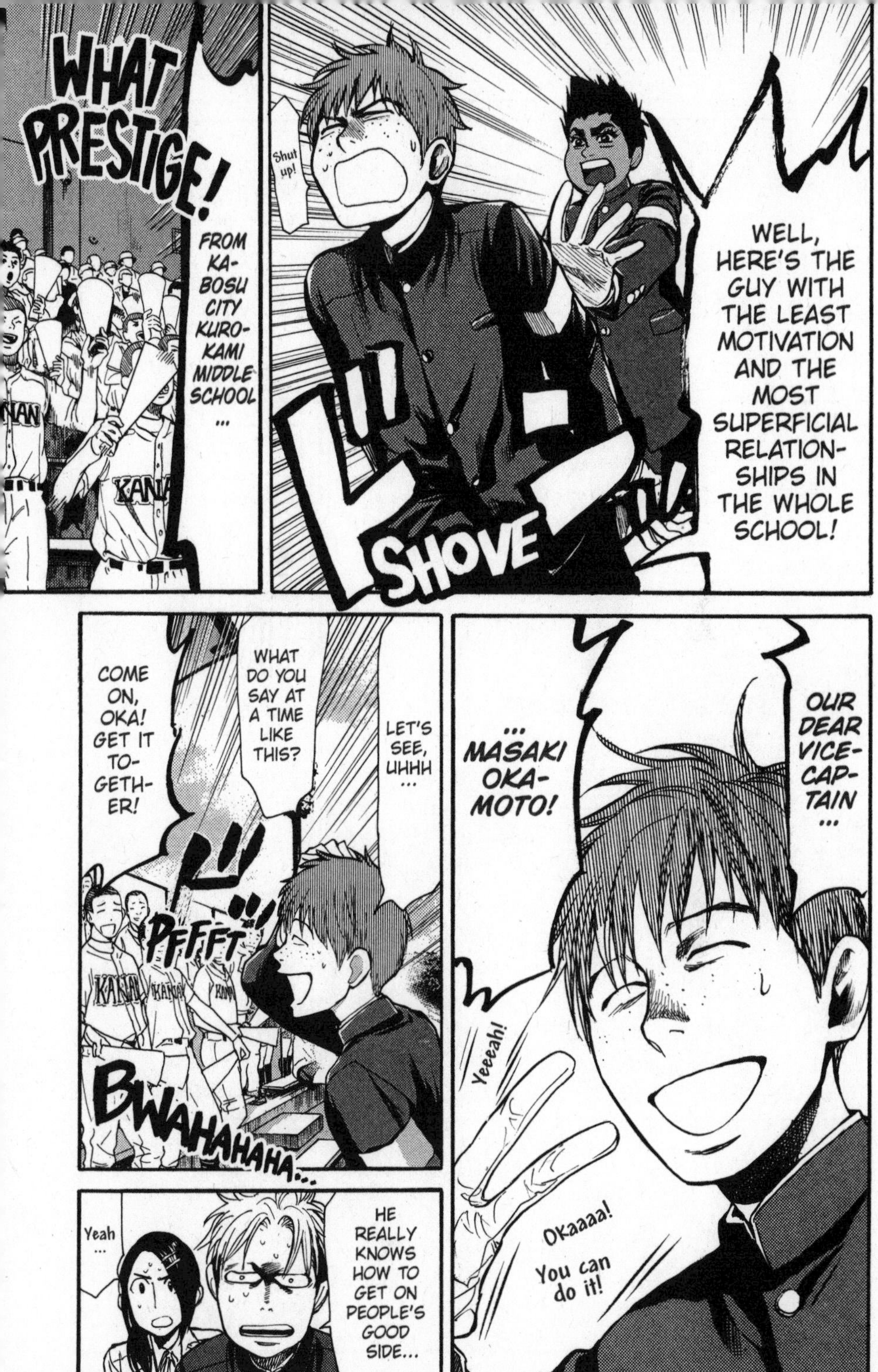
WELL, HERE'S THE GUY WITH THE LEAST MOTIVATION AND THE MOST SUPERFICIAL RELATIONSHIPS IN THE WHOLE SCHOOL!
Shut up!
SHOVE
WHAT PRESTIGE!
FROM KABOSU CITY KUROKAMI MIDDLE SCHOOL...
OUR DEAR VICE-CAPTAIN...
...MASAKI OKAMOTO!
Yeeeah!
Okaaaa!
You can do it!
LET'S SEE, UHHH...
WHAT DO YOU SAY AT A TIME LIKE THIS?
COME ON, OKA! GET IT TOGETHER!
PFFFT
BWAHAHAHAHA...
HE REALLY KNOWS HOW TO GET ON PEOPLE'S GOOD SIDE...
Yeah...

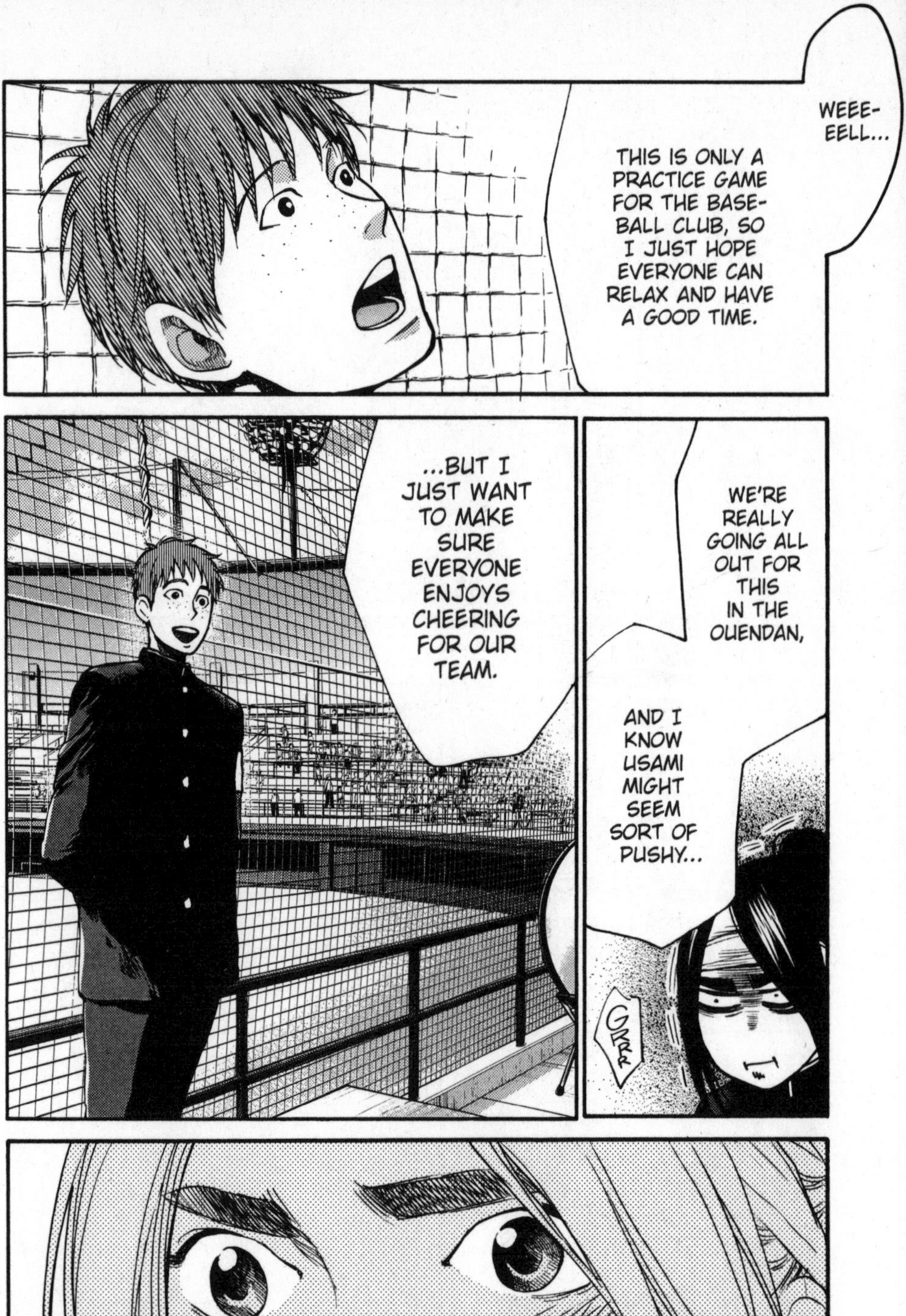
WEEE-EELL...
THIS IS ONLY A PRACTICE GAME FOR THE BASE-BALL CLUB, SO I JUST HOPE EVERYONE CAN RELAX AND HAVE A GOOD TIME.
WE'RE REALLY GOING ALL OUT FOR THIS IN THE OUENDAN,
AND I KNOW USAMI MIGHT SEEM SORT OF PUSHY...
GRRR
...BUT I JUST WANT TO MAKE SURE EVERYONE ENJOYS CHEERING FOR OUR TEAM.

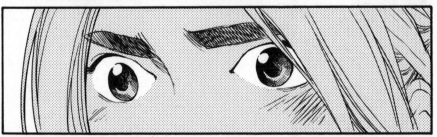

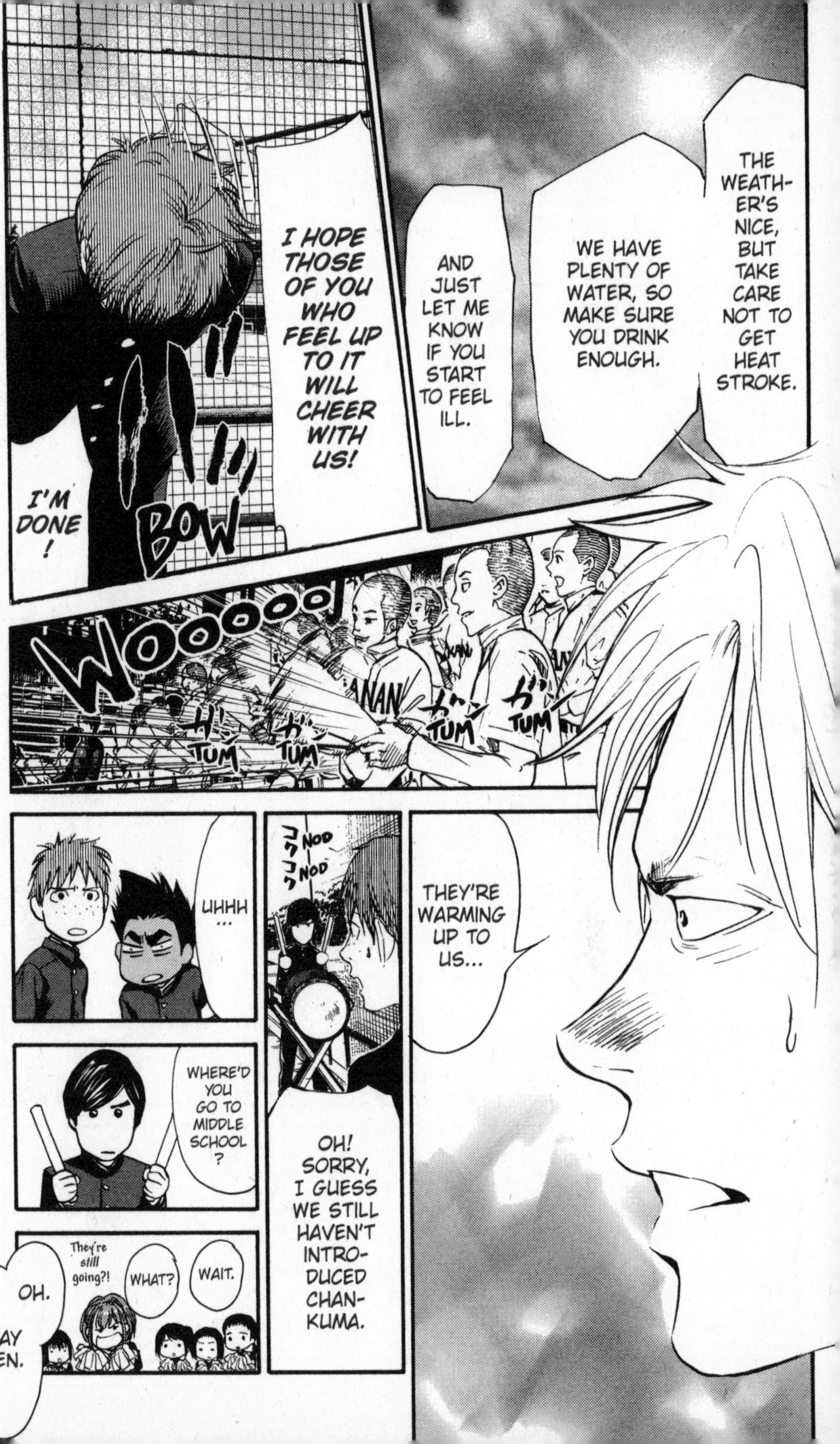
THE WEATHER'S NICE, BUT TAKE CARE NOT TO GET HEAT STROKE.
WE HAVE PLENTY OF WATER, SO MAKE SURE YOU DRINK ENOUGH.
AND JUST LET ME KNOW IF YOU START TO FEEL ILL.
I HOPE THOSE OF YOU WHO FEEL UP TO IT WILL CHEER WITH US!
BOW
I'M DONE!
WOOOOOO
TUM
TUM
TUM
TUM
THEY'RE WARMING UP TO US...
NOD
NOD
OH! SORRY, I GUESS WE STILL HAVEN'T INTRODUCED CHAN-KUMA.
UHHH...
WHERE'D YOU GO TO MIDDLE SCHOOL?
WAIT.
WHAT?
They're still going?!
OH.
OKAY THEN.

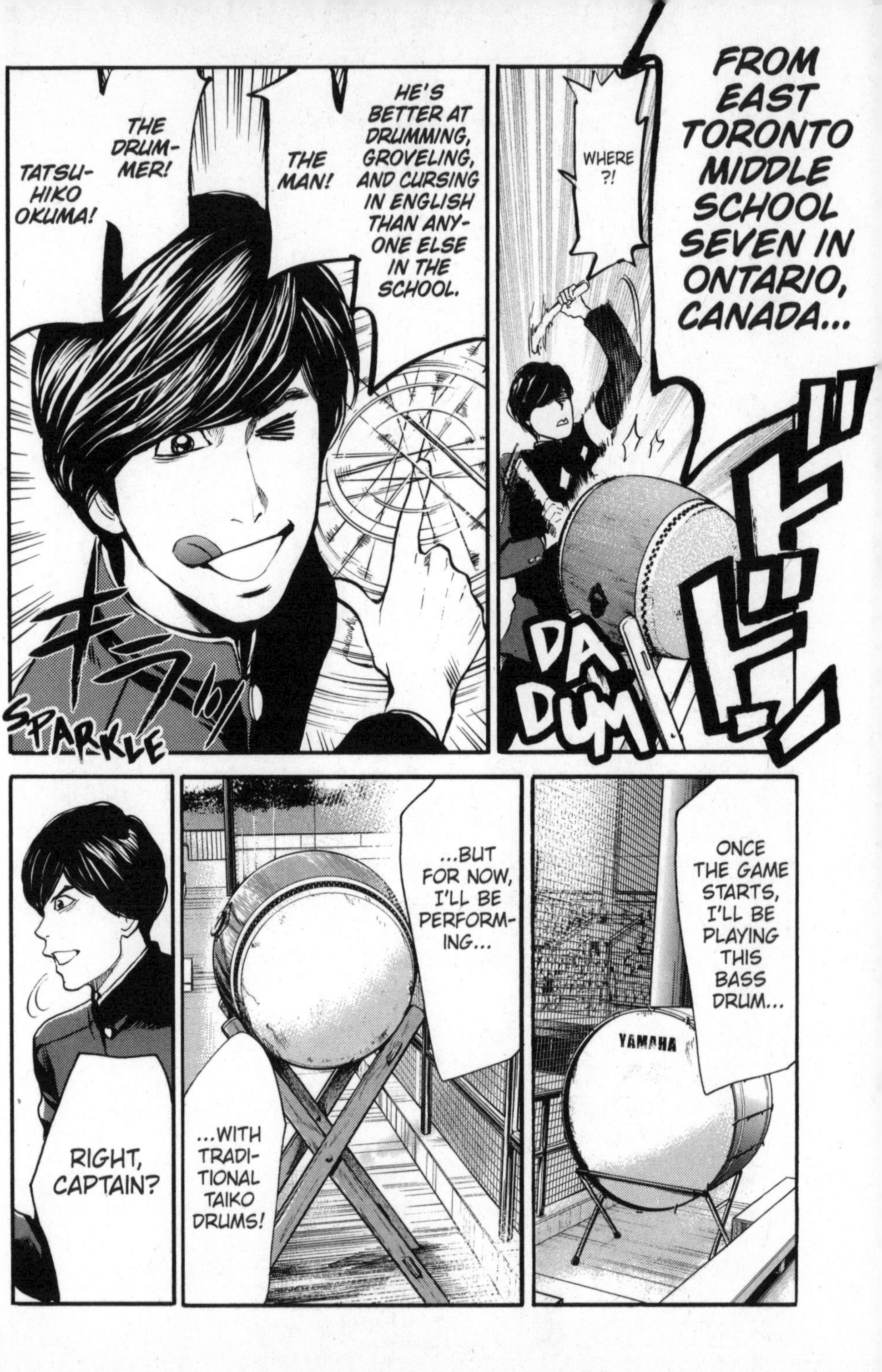
FROM EAST TORONTO MIDDLE SCHOOL SEVEN IN ONTARIO, CANADA...
WHERE ?!
DA DUM
HE'S BETTER AT DRUMMING, GROVELING, AND CURSING IN ENGLISH THAN ANYONE ELSE IN THE SCHOOL.
THE MAN!
THE DRUMMER!
TATSUHIKO OKUMA!
SPARKLE
ONCE THE GAME STARTS, I'LL BE PLAYING THIS BASS DRUM...
YAMAHA
...BUT FOR NOW, I'LL BE PERFORMING...
...WITH TRADITIONAL TAIKO DRUMS!
RIGHT, CAPTAIN?

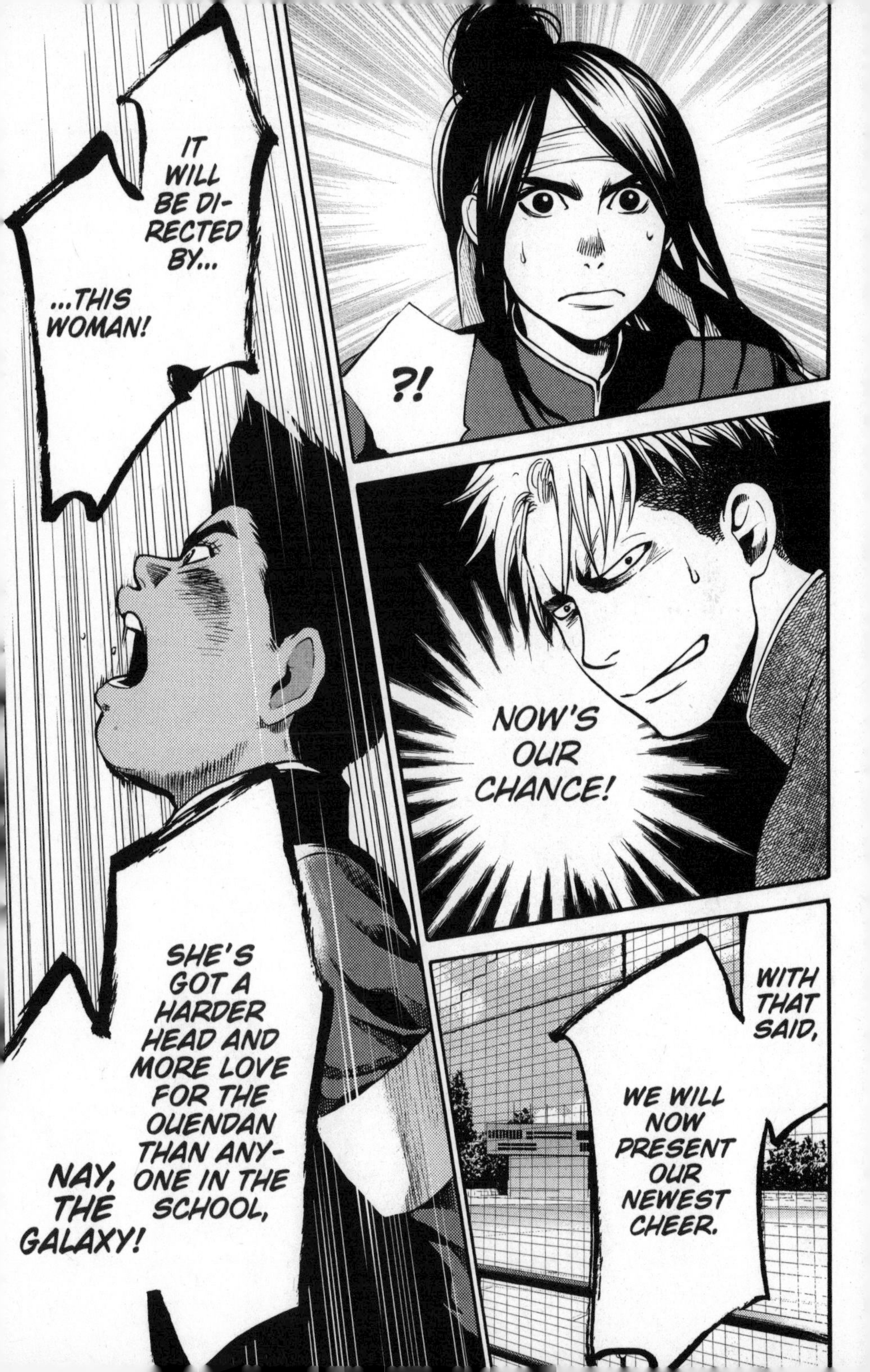
?!
NOW'S OUR CHANCE!
WITH THAT SAID,
WE WILL NOW PRESENT OUR NEWEST CHEER.
IT WILL BE DI-RECTED BY...
...THIS WOMAN!
SHE'S GOT A HARDER HEAD AND MORE LOVE FOR THE OUENDAN THAN ANY-ONE IN THE SCHOOL,
NAY, THE GALAXY!

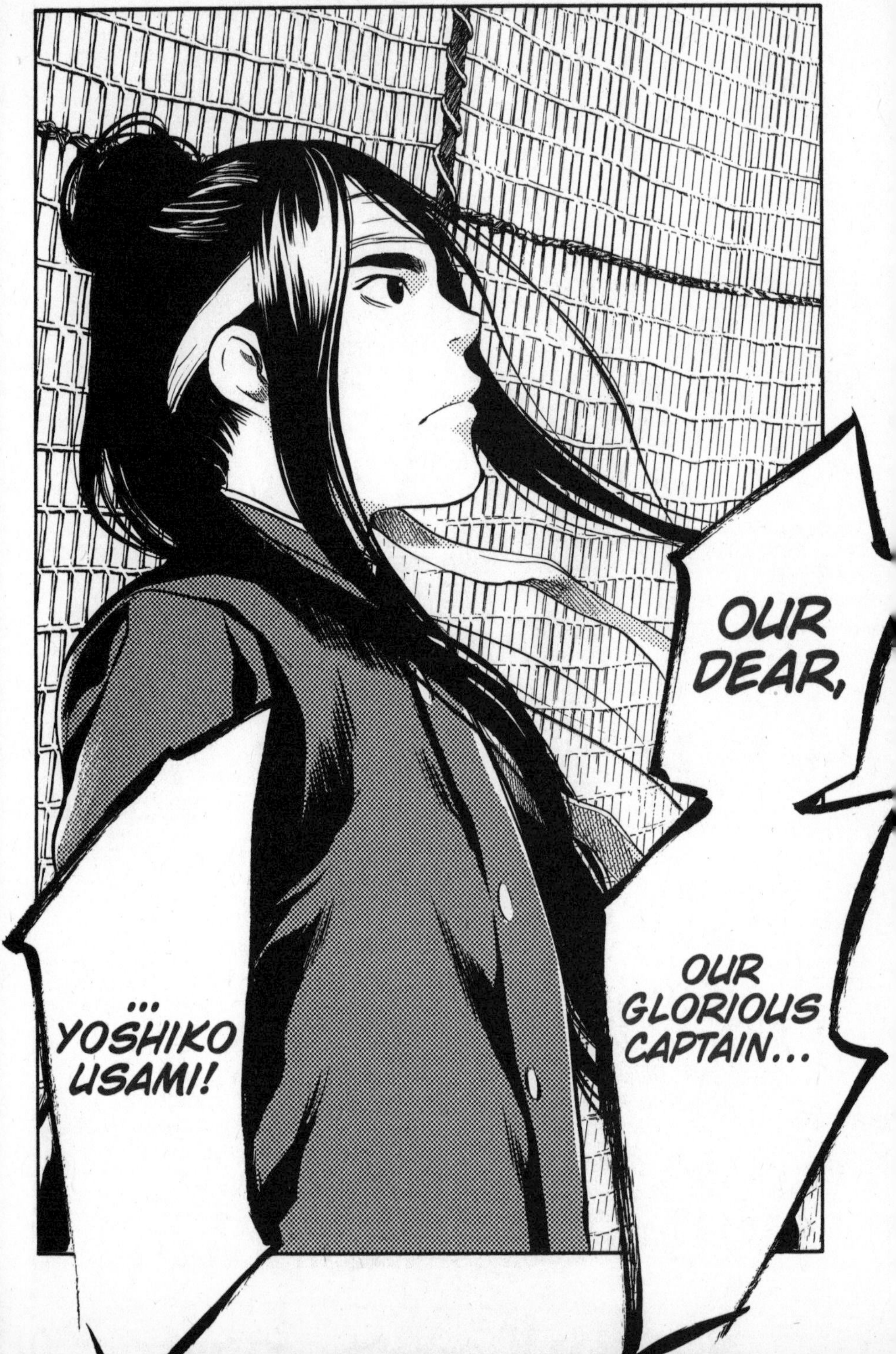
OUR DEAR,
OUR GLORIOUS CAPTAIN...
...YOSHIKO USAMI!

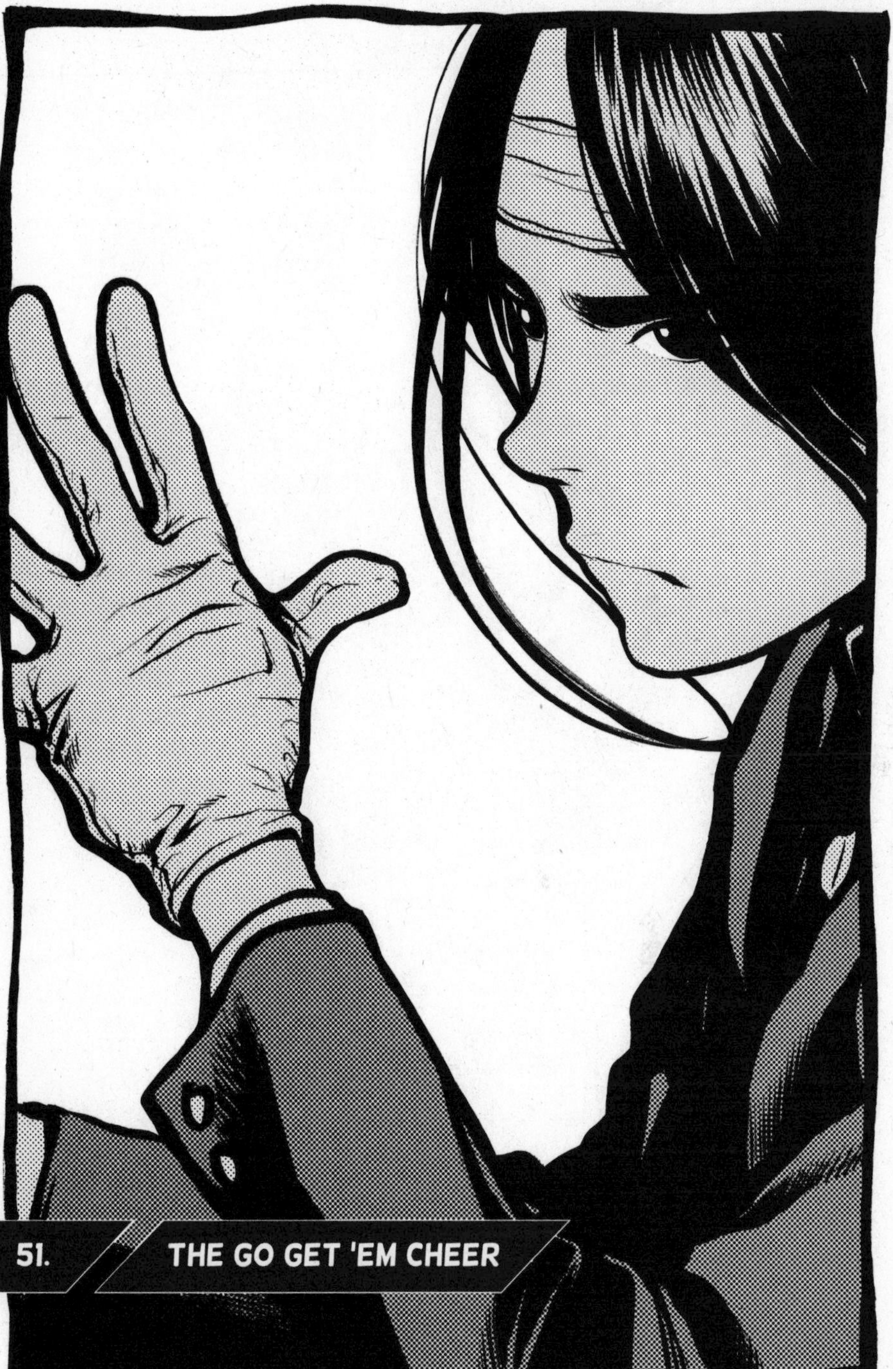

## 51. THE GO GET 'EM CHEER

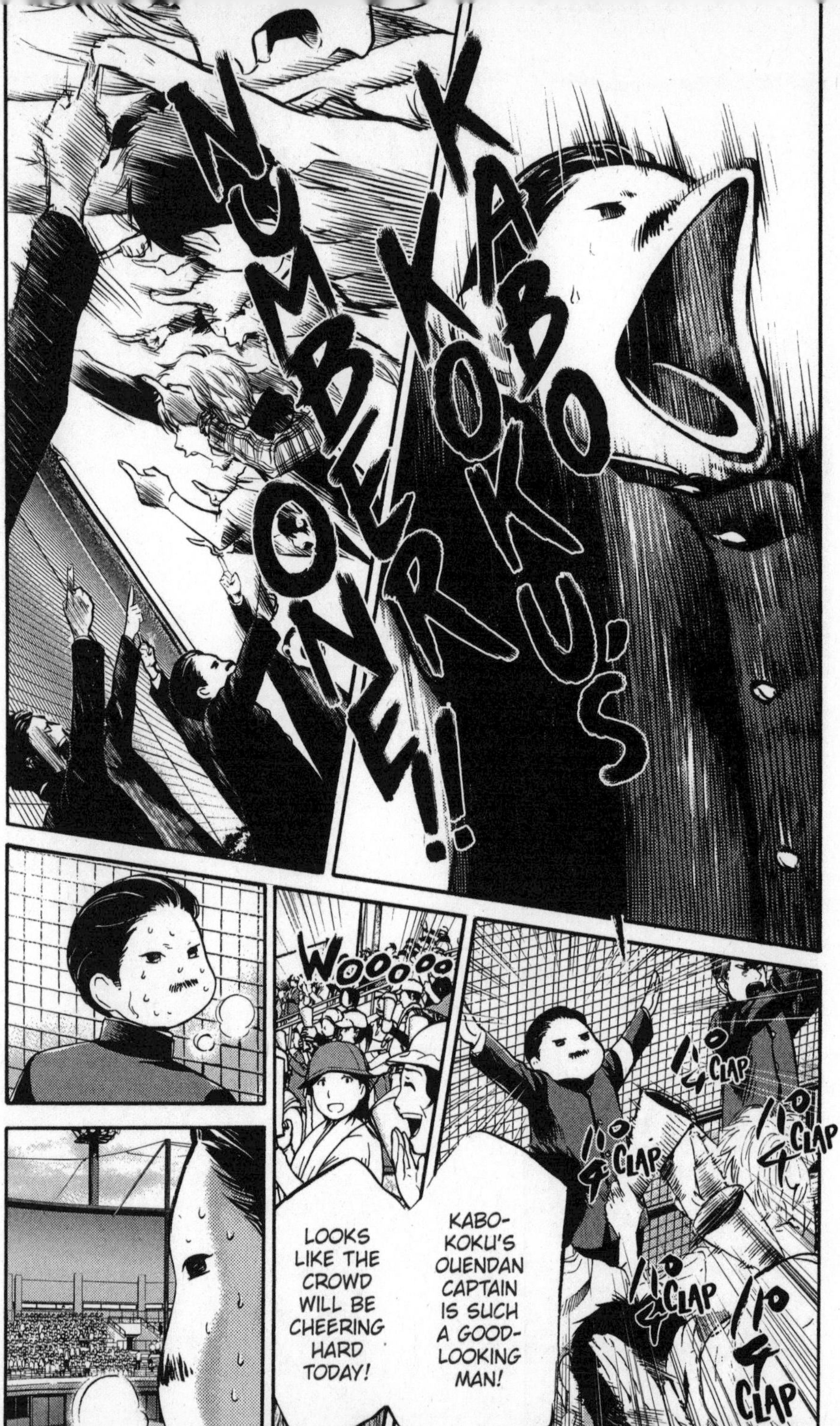
KABOKOKU'S
NUMBER ONE!!
CLAP
CLAP
CLAP
CLAP
CLAP
CLAP
WOOOOOO
KABO-KOKU'S OUENDAN CAPTAIN IS SUCH A GOOD-LOOKING MAN!
LOOKS LIKE THE CROWD WILL BE CHEERING HARD TODAY!

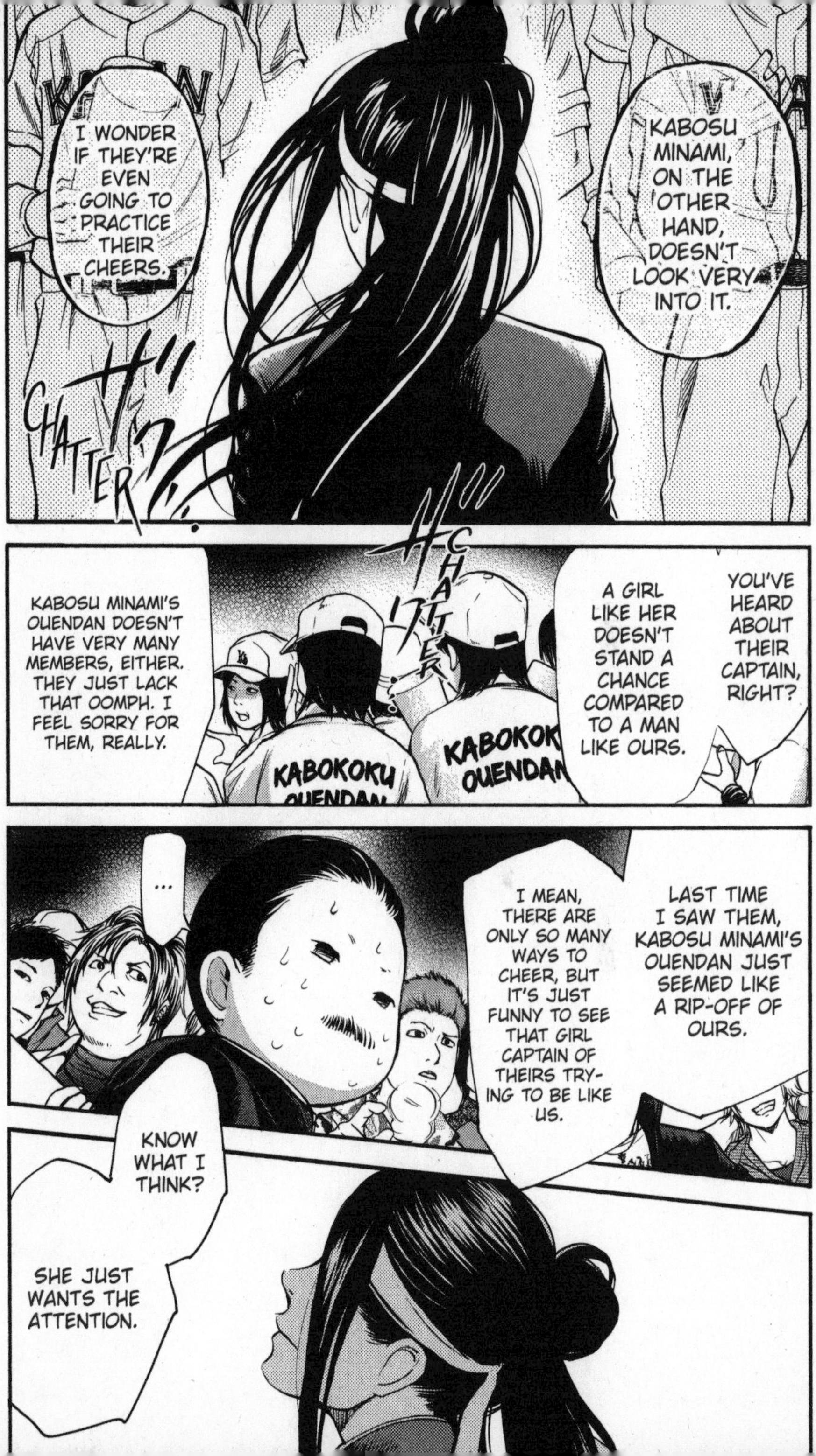
KABOSU MINAMI, ON THE OTHER HAND, DOESN'T LOOK VERY INTO IT.
I WONDER IF THEY'RE EVEN GOING TO PRACTICE THEIR CHEERS.
CHATTER
YOU'VE HEARD ABOUT THEIR CAPTAIN, RIGHT?
A GIRL LIKE HER DOESN'T STAND A CHANCE COMPARED TO A MAN LIKE OURS.
CHATTER
KABOKOKU OUENDAN
KABOKOKU OUENDAN
KABOSU MINAMI'S OUENDAN DOESN'T HAVE VERY MANY MEMBERS, EITHER. THEY JUST LACK THAT OOMPH. I FEEL SORRY FOR THEM, REALLY.
LAST TIME I SAW THEM, KABOSU MINAMI'S OUENDAN JUST SEEMED LIKE A RIP-OFF OF OURS.
I MEAN, THERE ARE ONLY SO MANY WAYS TO CHEER, BUT IT'S JUST FUNNY TO SEE THAT GIRL CAPTAIN OF THEIRS TRYING TO BE LIKE US.
...
KNOW WHAT I THINK?
SHE JUST WANTS THE ATTENTION.

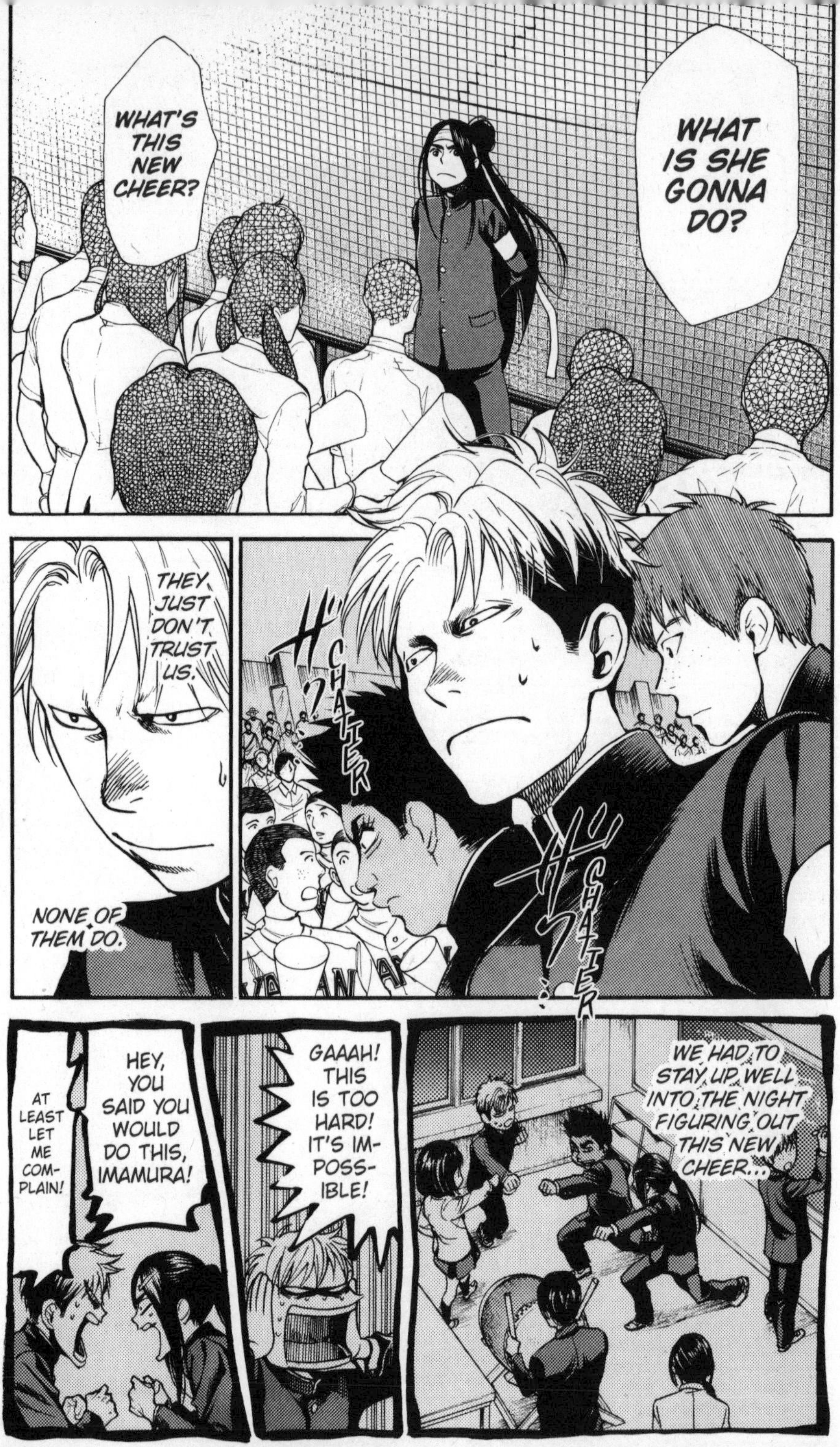

WHAT IS SHE GONNA DO?
WHAT'S THIS NEW CHEER?
CHATTER
CHATTER
THEY JUST DON'T TRUST US.
NONE OF THEM DO.
WE HAD TO STAY UP WELL INTO THE NIGHT FIGURING OUT THIS NEW CHEER...
GAAAH! THIS IS TOO HARD! IT'S IMPOSSIBLE!
HEY, YOU SAID YOU WOULD DO THIS, IMAMURA!
AT LEAST LET ME COMPLAIN!

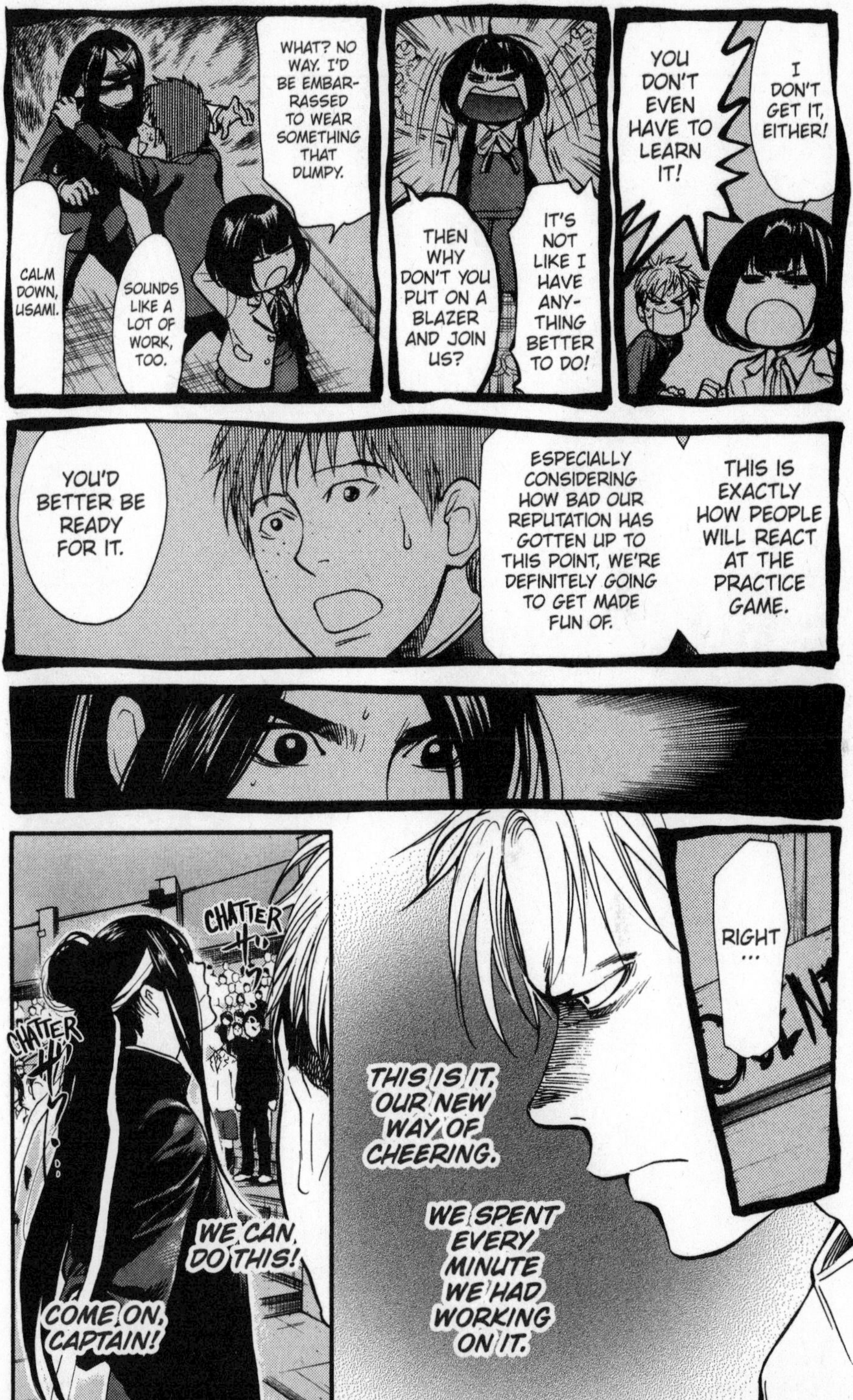
I DON'T GET IT, EITHER!
YOU DON'T EVEN HAVE TO LEARN IT!
IT'S NOT LIKE I HAVE ANYTHING BETTER TO DO!
THEN WHY DON'T YOU PUT ON A BLAZER AND JOIN US?
WHAT? NO WAY. I'D BE EMBARRASSED TO WEAR SOMETHING THAT DUMPY.
SOUNDS LIKE A LOT OF WORK, TOO.
CALM DOWN, USAMI.
THIS IS EXACTLY HOW PEOPLE WILL REACT AT THE PRACTICE GAME.
ESPECIALLY CONSIDERING HOW BAD OUR REPUTATION HAS GOTTEN UP TO THIS POINT, WE'RE DEFINITELY GOING TO GET MADE FUN OF.
YOU'D BETTER BE READY FOR IT.
RIGHT ...
THIS IS IT. OUR NEW WAY OF CHEERING.
WE SPENT EVERY MINUTE WE HAD WORKING ON IT.
CHATTER
CHATTER
WE CAN DO THIS!
COME ON, CAPTAIN!

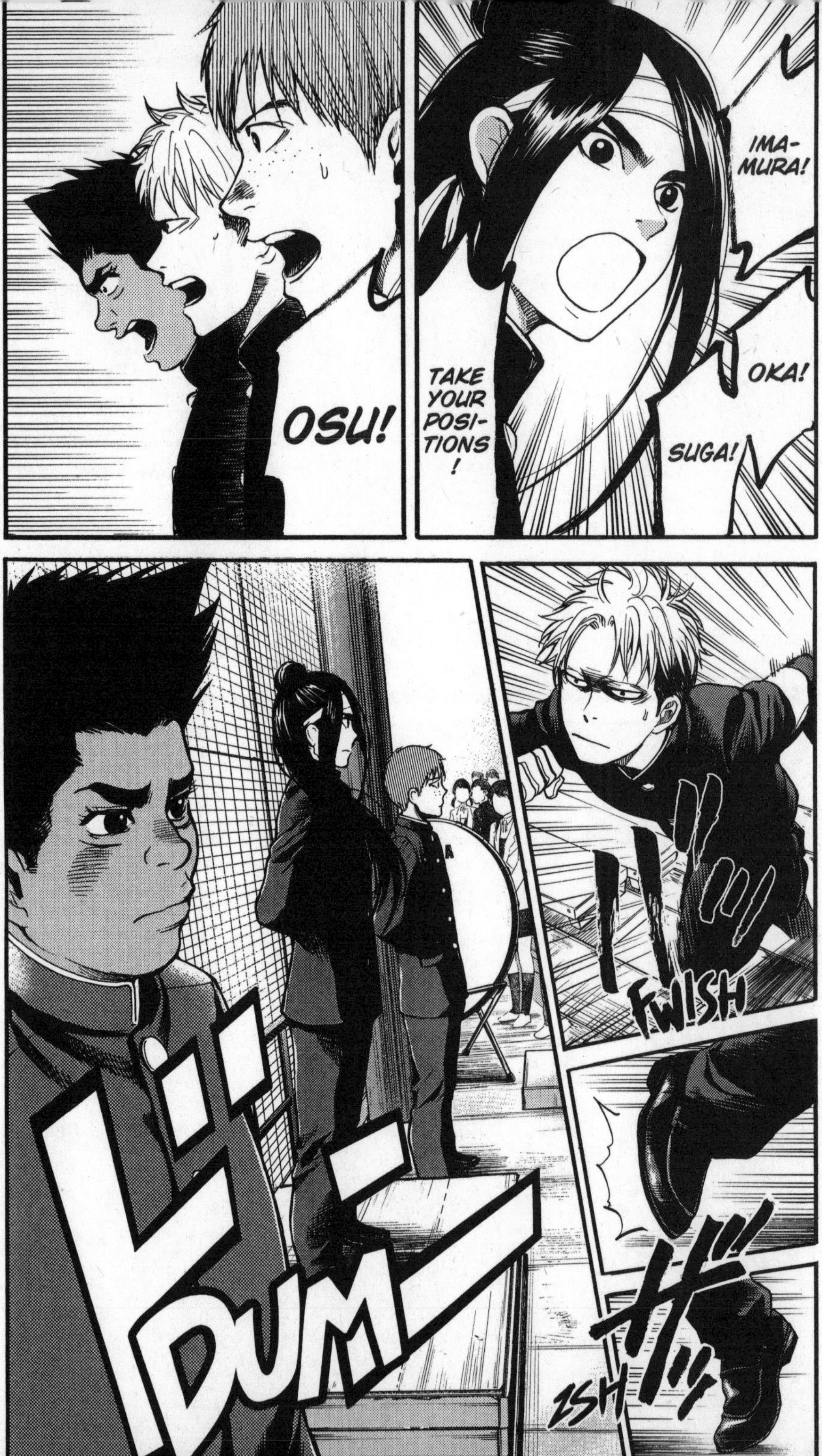
IMA-
MURA!
OKA!
SUGA!
TAKE YOUR POSI-TIONS!
OSU!
FWISH
ZSH
DUM

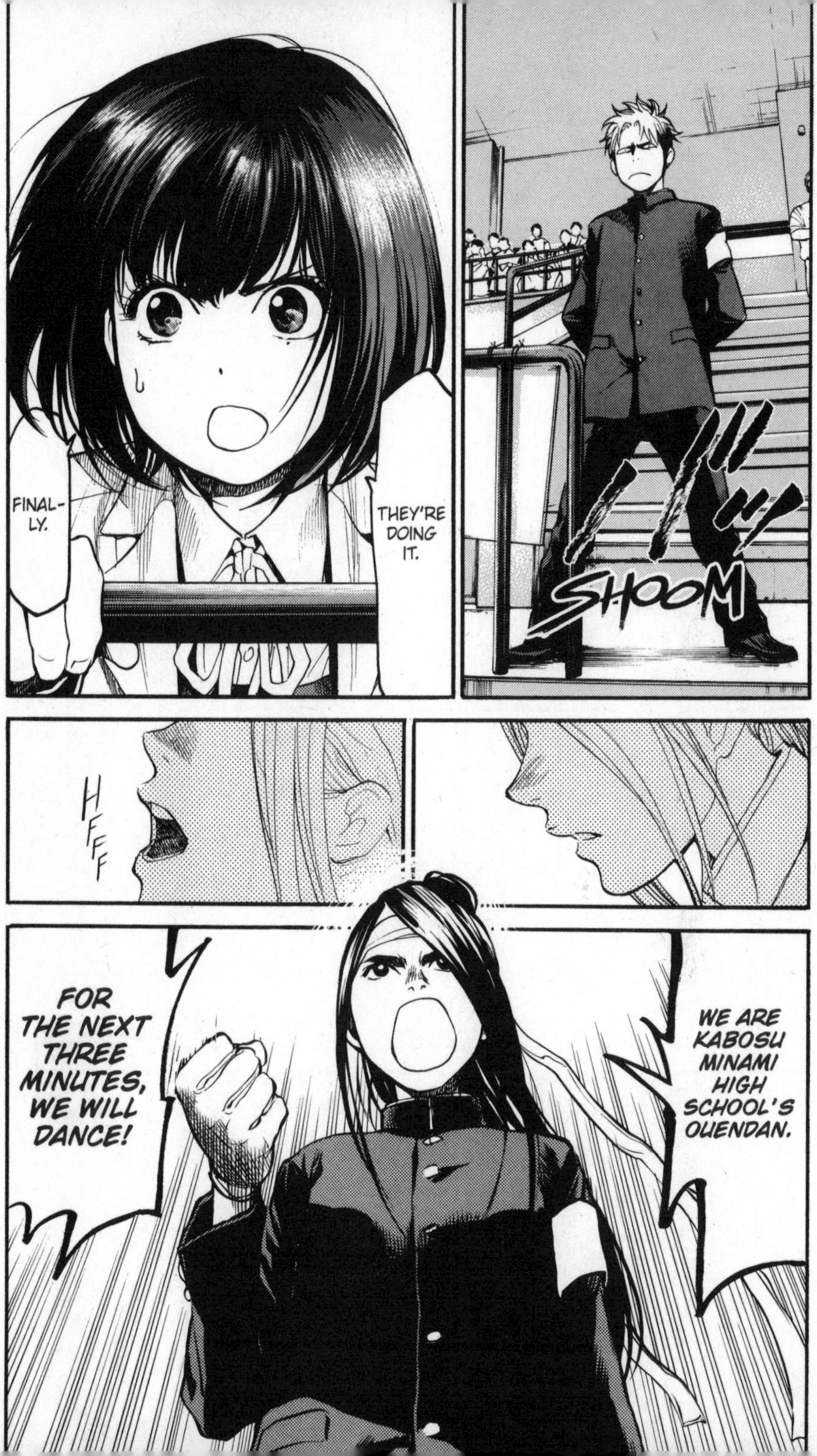
SHOOM
THEY'RE DOING IT.
FINAL-LY.
HFFF
WE ARE KABOSU MINAMI HIGH SCHOOL'S OUENDAN.
FOR THE NEXT THREE MINUTES, WE WILL DANCE!

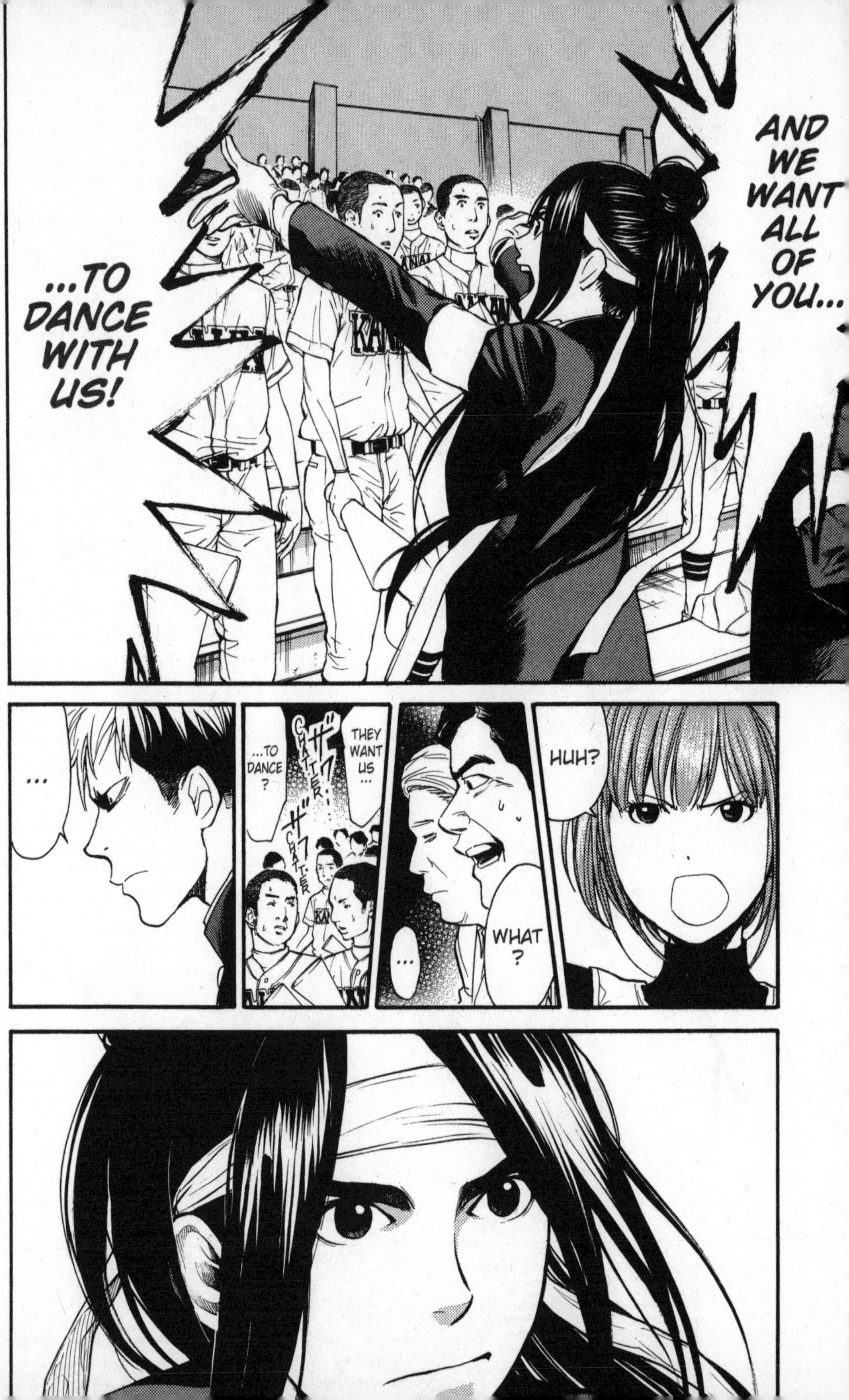
AND WE WANT ALL OF YOU...
...TO DANCE WITH US!
HUH?
WHAT ?
...
THEY WANT US ...
CHATTER
CHATTER
...TO DANCE ?
...

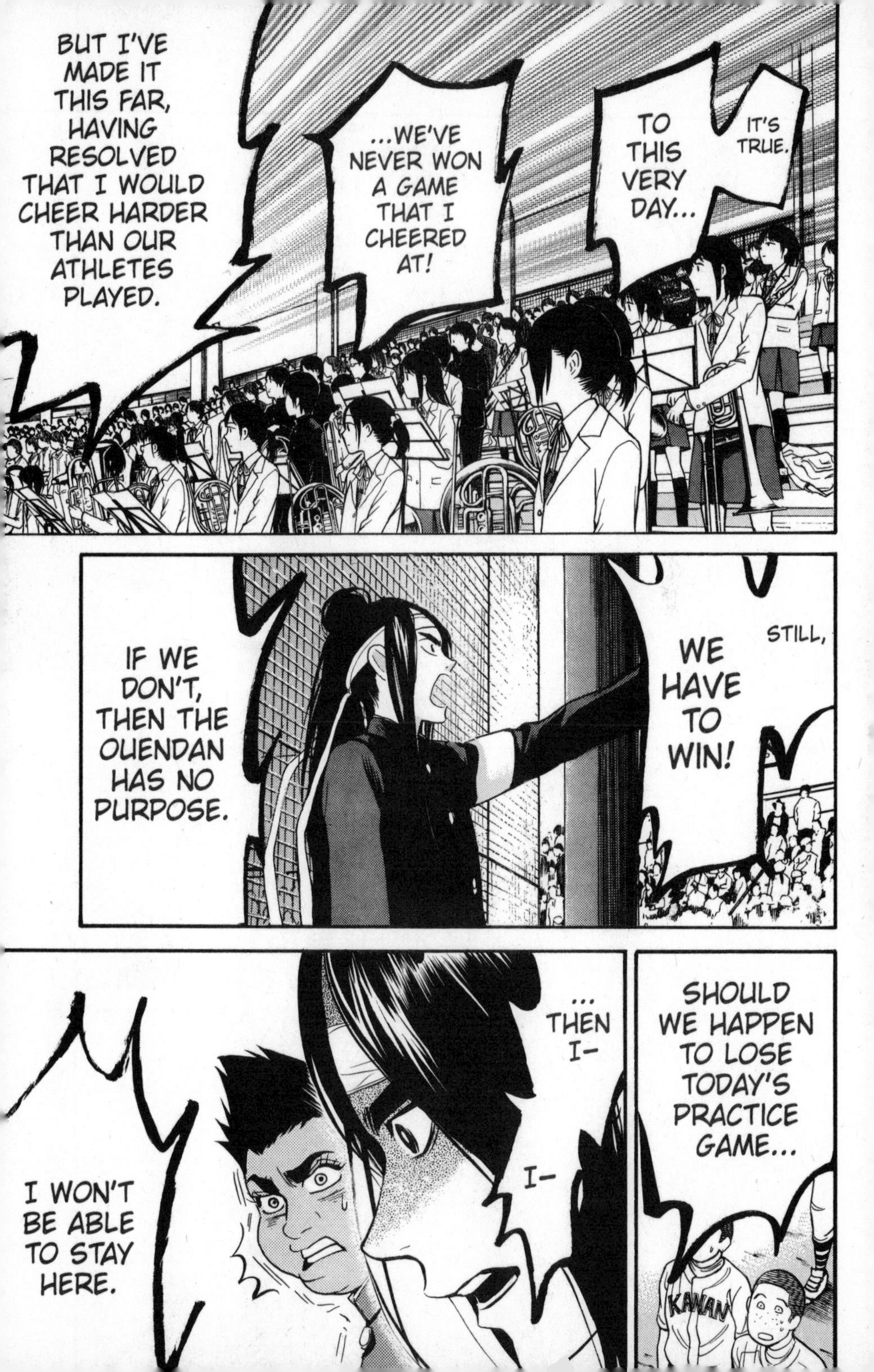
IT'S TRUE.
TO THIS VERY DAY...
...WE'VE NEVER WON A GAME THAT I CHEERED AT!
BUT I'VE MADE IT THIS FAR, HAVING RESOLVED THAT I WOULD CHEER HARDER THAN OUR ATHLETES PLAYED.
STILL,
WE HAVE TO WIN!
IF WE DON'T, THEN THE OUENDAN HAS NO PURPOSE.
SHOULD WE HAPPEN TO LOSE TODAY'S PRACTICE GAME...
KANAN
...THEN I-
I-
I WON'T BE ABLE TO STAY HERE.

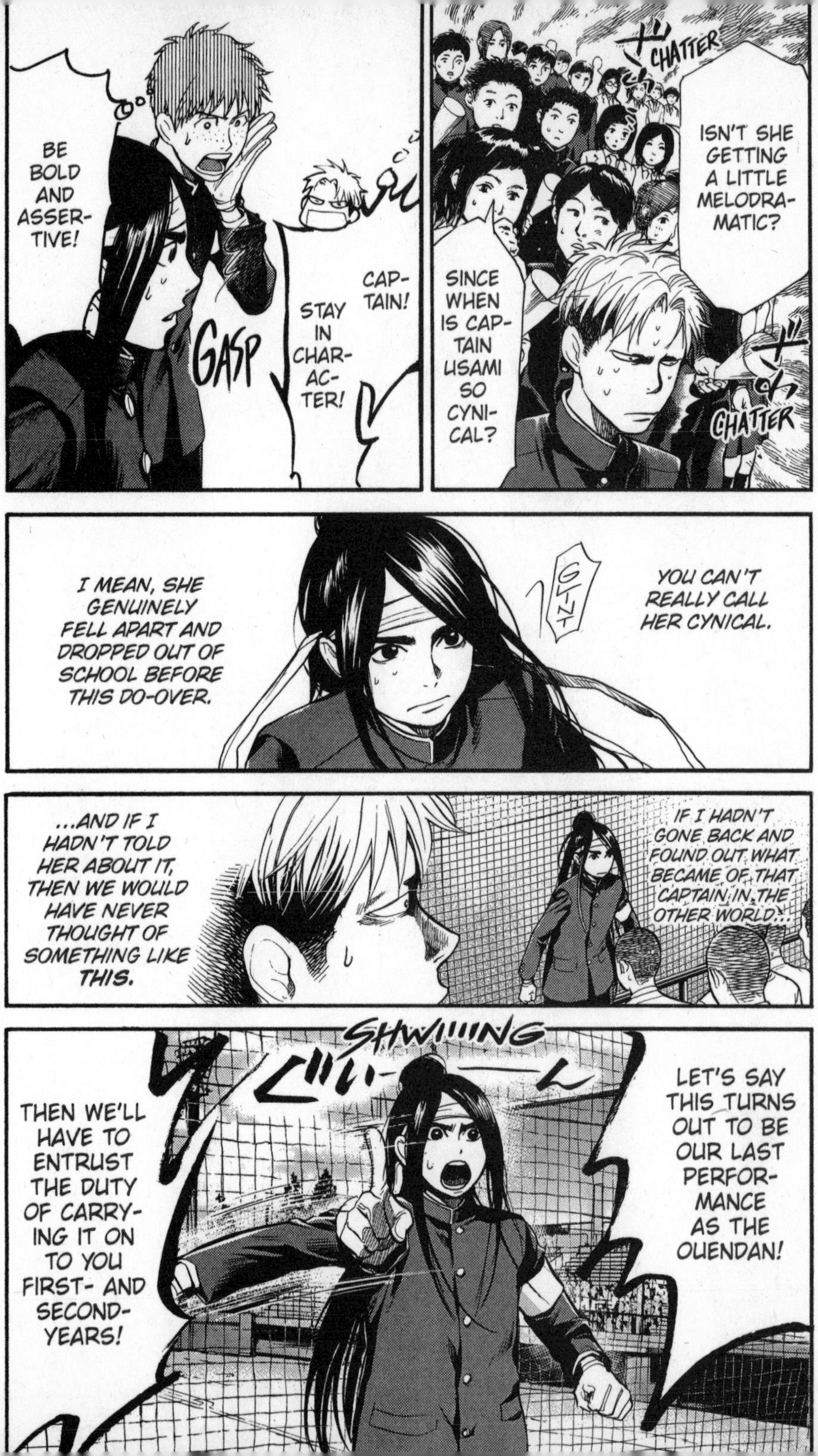
CHATTER
ISN'T SHE GETTING A LITTLE MELODRAMATIC?
SINCE WHEN IS CAPTAIN USAMI SO CYNICAL?
CHATTER
CAPTAIN!
STAY IN CHARACTER!
GASP
BE BOLD AND ASSERTIVE!
YOU CAN'T REALLY CALL HER CYNICAL.
GLINT
I MEAN, SHE GENUINELY FELL APART AND DROPPED OUT OF SCHOOL BEFORE THIS DO-OVER.
IF I HADN'T GONE BACK AND FOUND OUT WHAT BECAME OF THAT CAPTAIN IN THE OTHER WORLD...
...AND IF I HADN'T TOLD HER ABOUT IT, THEN WE WOULD HAVE NEVER THOUGHT OF SOMETHING LIKE THIS.
SHWIIING
LET'S SAY THIS TURNS OUT TO BE OUR LAST PERFORMANCE AS THE OUENDAN!
THEN WE'LL HAVE TO ENTRUST THE DUTY OF CARRYING IT ON TO YOU FIRST- AND SECOND-YEARS!

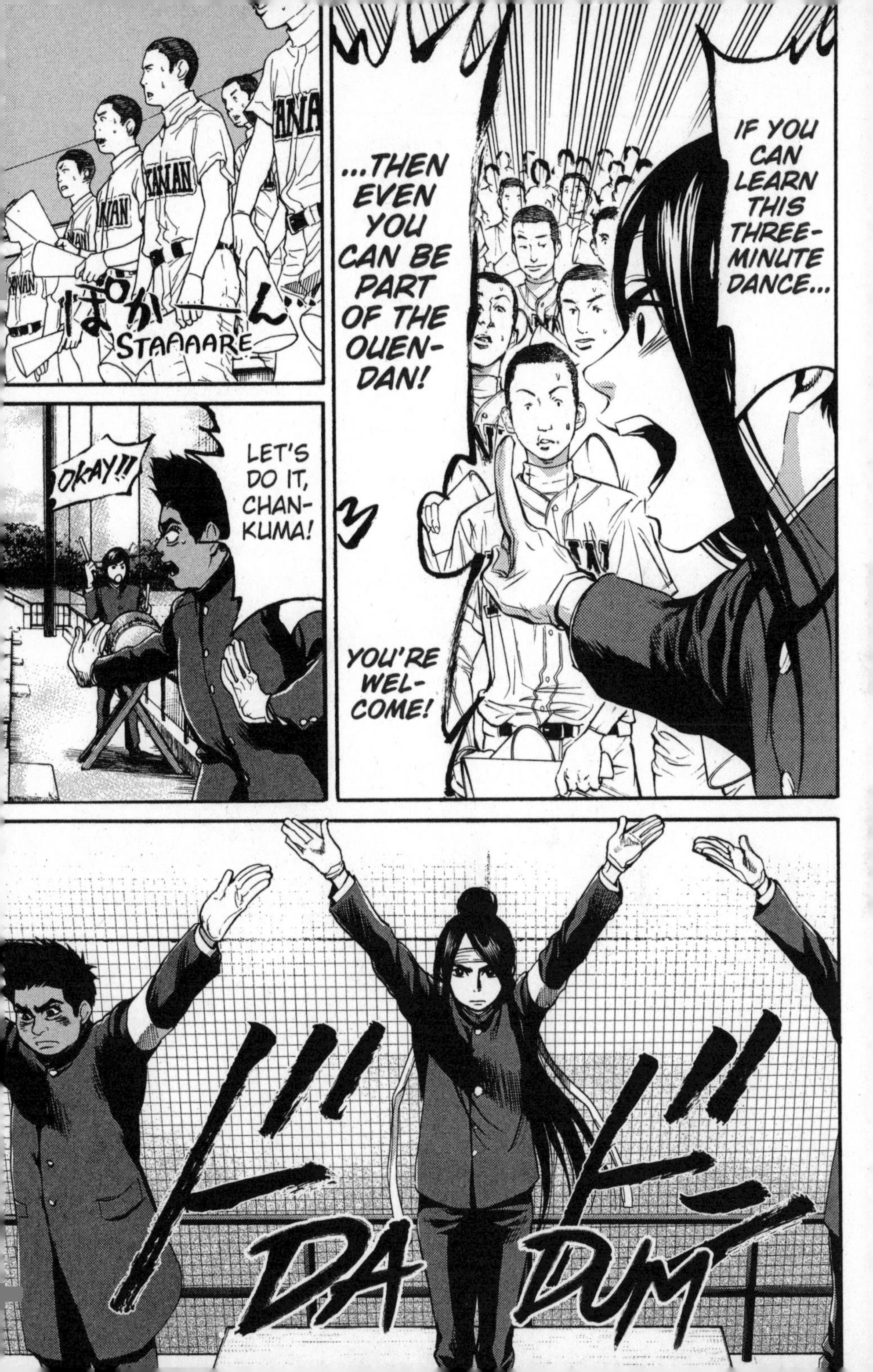
IF YOU CAN LEARN THIS THREE-MINUTE DANCE...
...THEN EVEN YOU CAN BE PART OF THE OUEN-DAN!
YOU'RE WEL-COME!
STAAAARE
LET'S DO IT, CHAN-KUMA!
OKAY!!
DA DUM

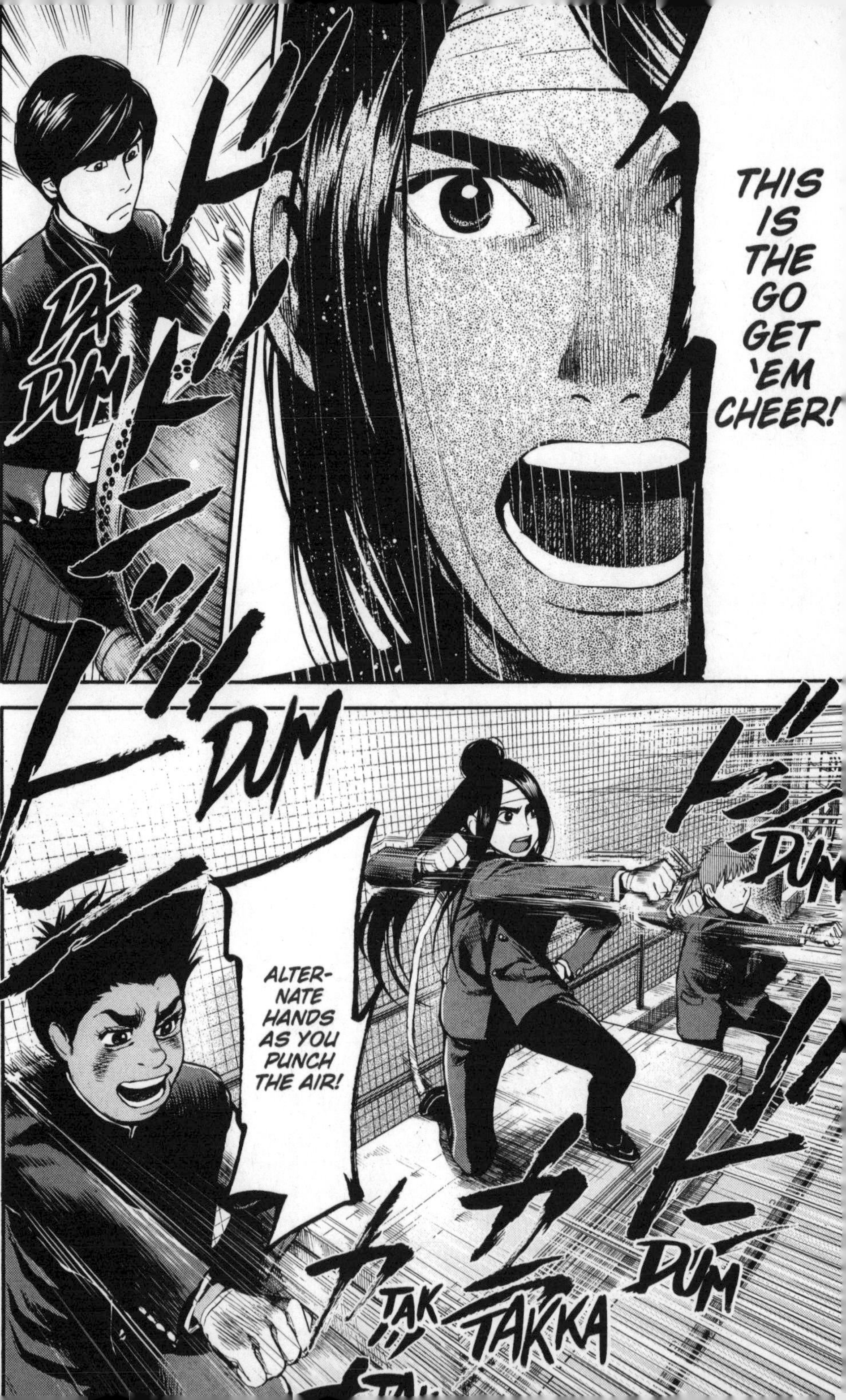
THIS IS THE GO GET 'EM CHEER!
DA DUM
DUM
DUM
ALTER-NATE HANDS AS YOU PUNCH THE AIR!
DUM
TAKKA
TAK

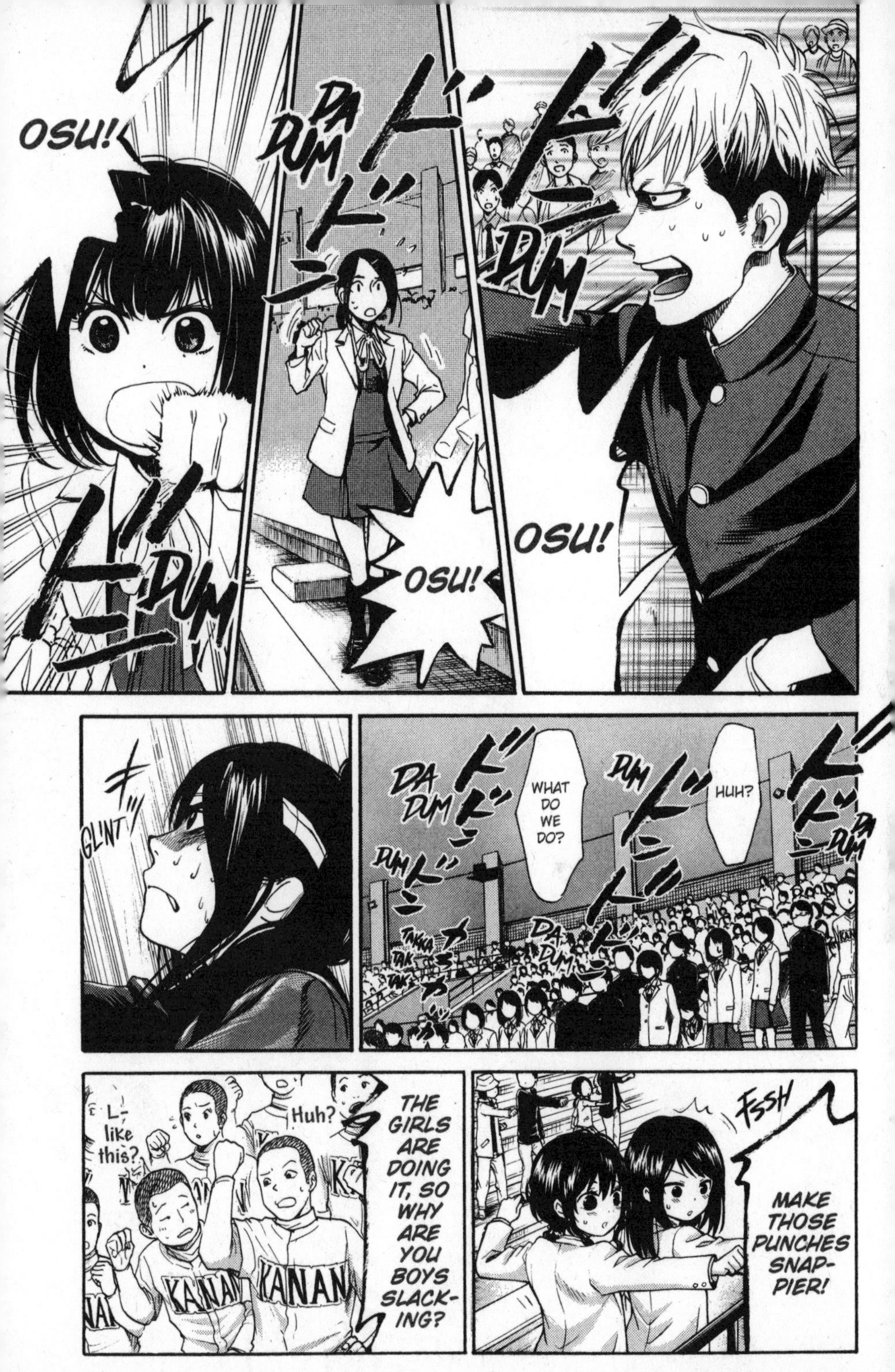
DUM
OSU!
DA DUM
OSU!
OSU!
DUM
DA DUM
HUH?
DUM
WHAT DO WE DO?
DA DUM
DUM
DA DUM
TAKKA TAK TAK TAK
GLINT
FSSH
MAKE THOSE PUNCHES SNAP-PIER!
THE GIRLS ARE DOING IT, SO WHY ARE YOU BOYS SLACK-ING?
Huh?
L-like this?

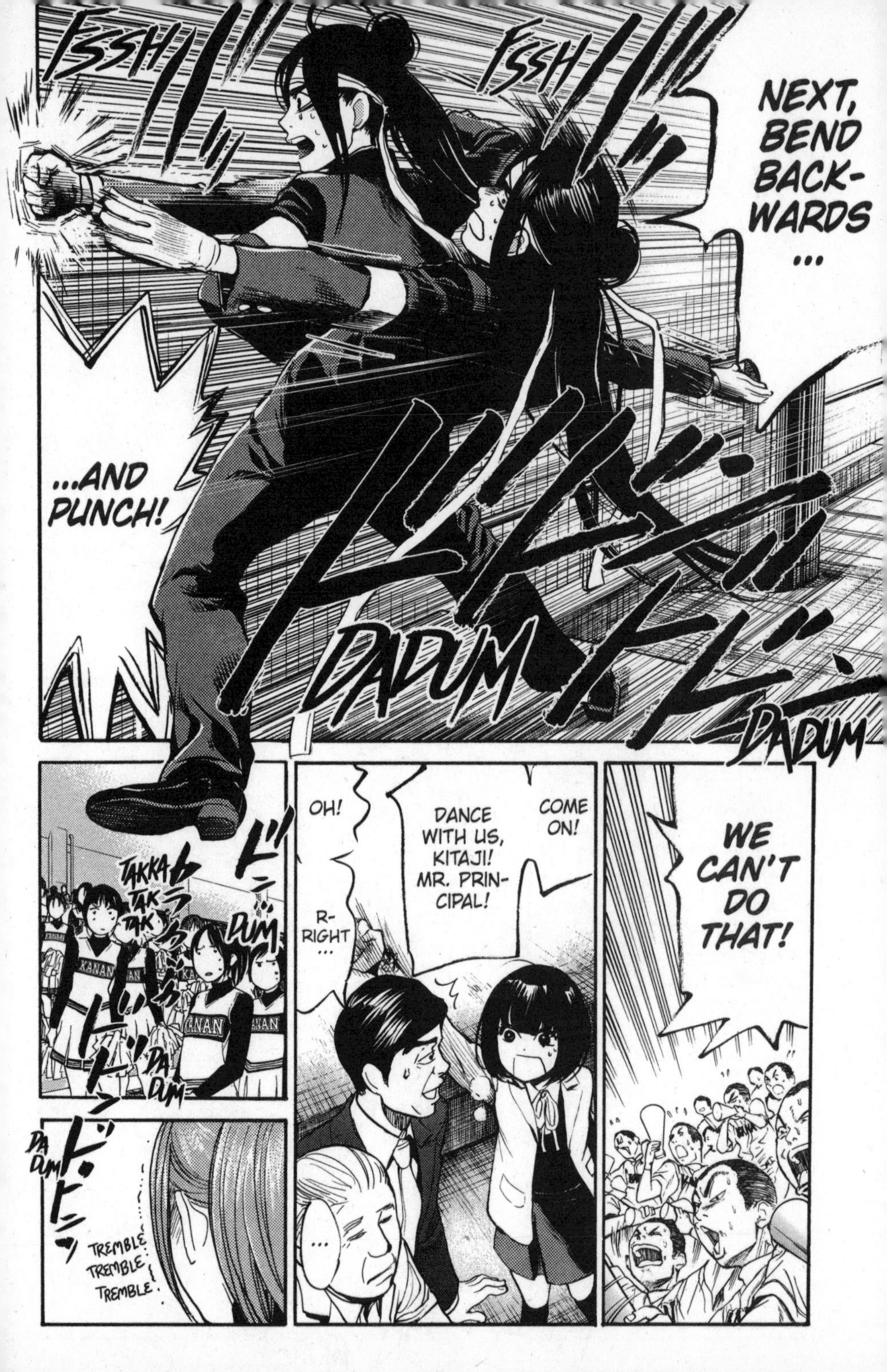
NEXT, BEND BACKWARDS...
FSSH
FSSH
...AND PUNCH!
DADUM
DADUM
WE CAN'T DO THAT!
COME ON!
DANCE WITH US, KITAJI! MR. PRINCIPAL!
OH!
R-RIGHT...
...
TAKKA TAK TAK
DUM
DA DUM
DA DUM
TREMBLE TREMBLE TREMBLE

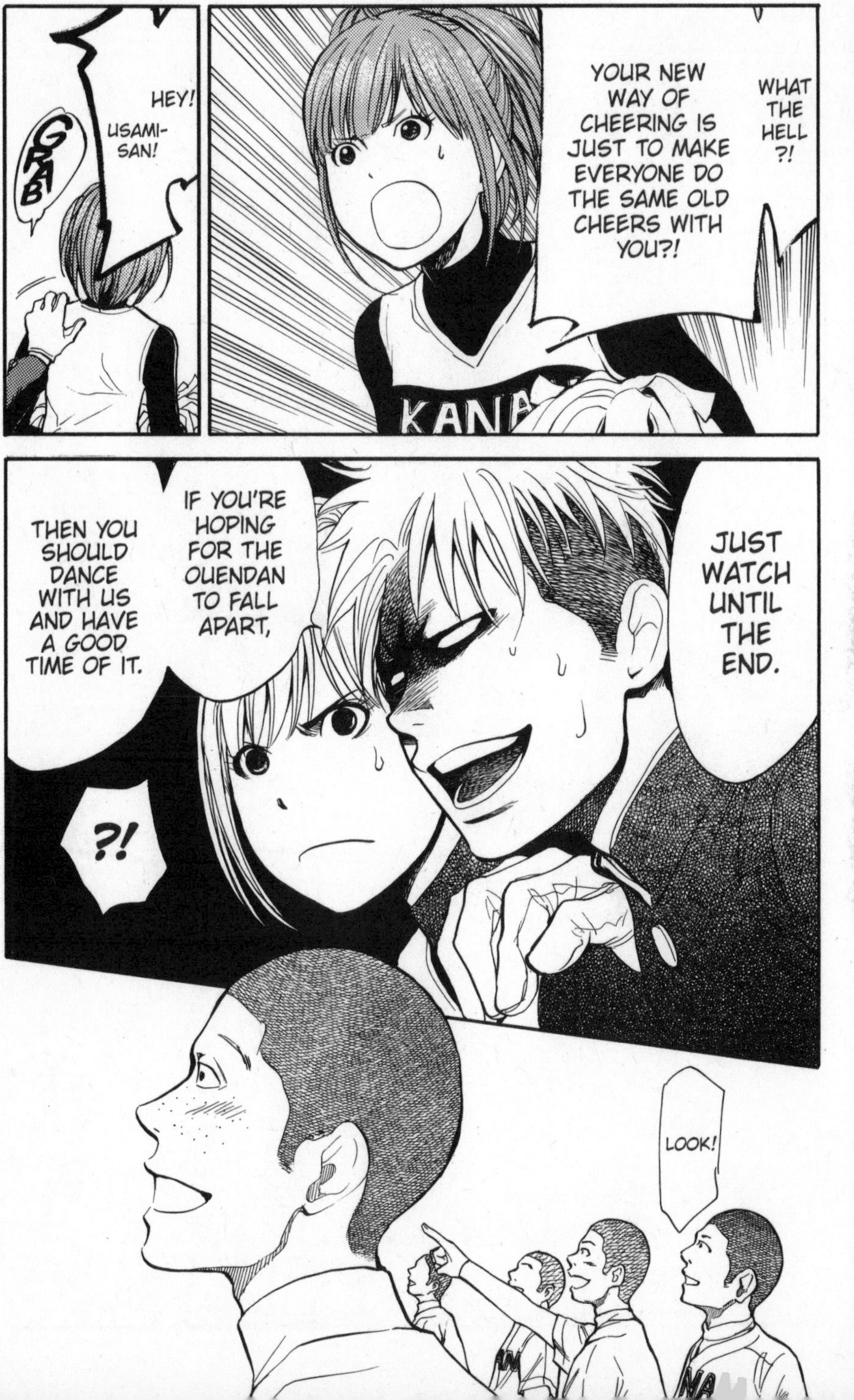
WHAT THE HELL ?!
YOUR NEW WAY OF CHEERING IS JUST TO MAKE EVERYONE DO THE SAME OLD CHEERS WITH YOU?!
HEY!
USAMI-SAN!
GRAB
JUST WATCH UNTIL THE END.
IF YOU'RE HOPING FOR THE OUENDAN TO FALL APART,
THEN YOU SHOULD DANCE WITH US AND HAVE A GOOD TIME OF IT.
?!
LOOK!

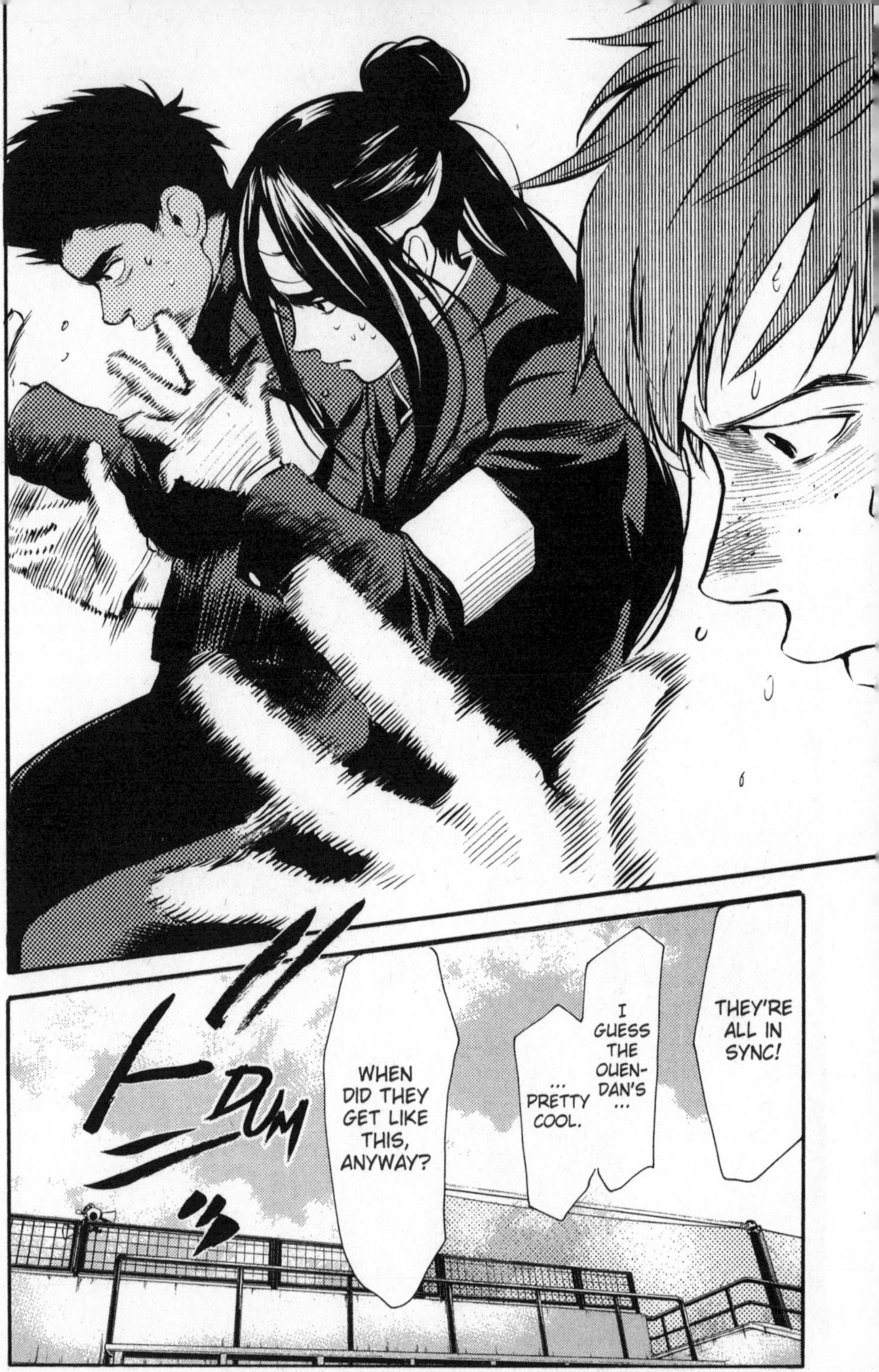
THEY'RE ALL IN SYNC!
I GUESS THE OUEN-DAN'S ...
... PRETTY COOL.
WHEN DID THEY GET LIKE THIS, ANYWAY?
DUM

# 52. VICTORY DANCE!

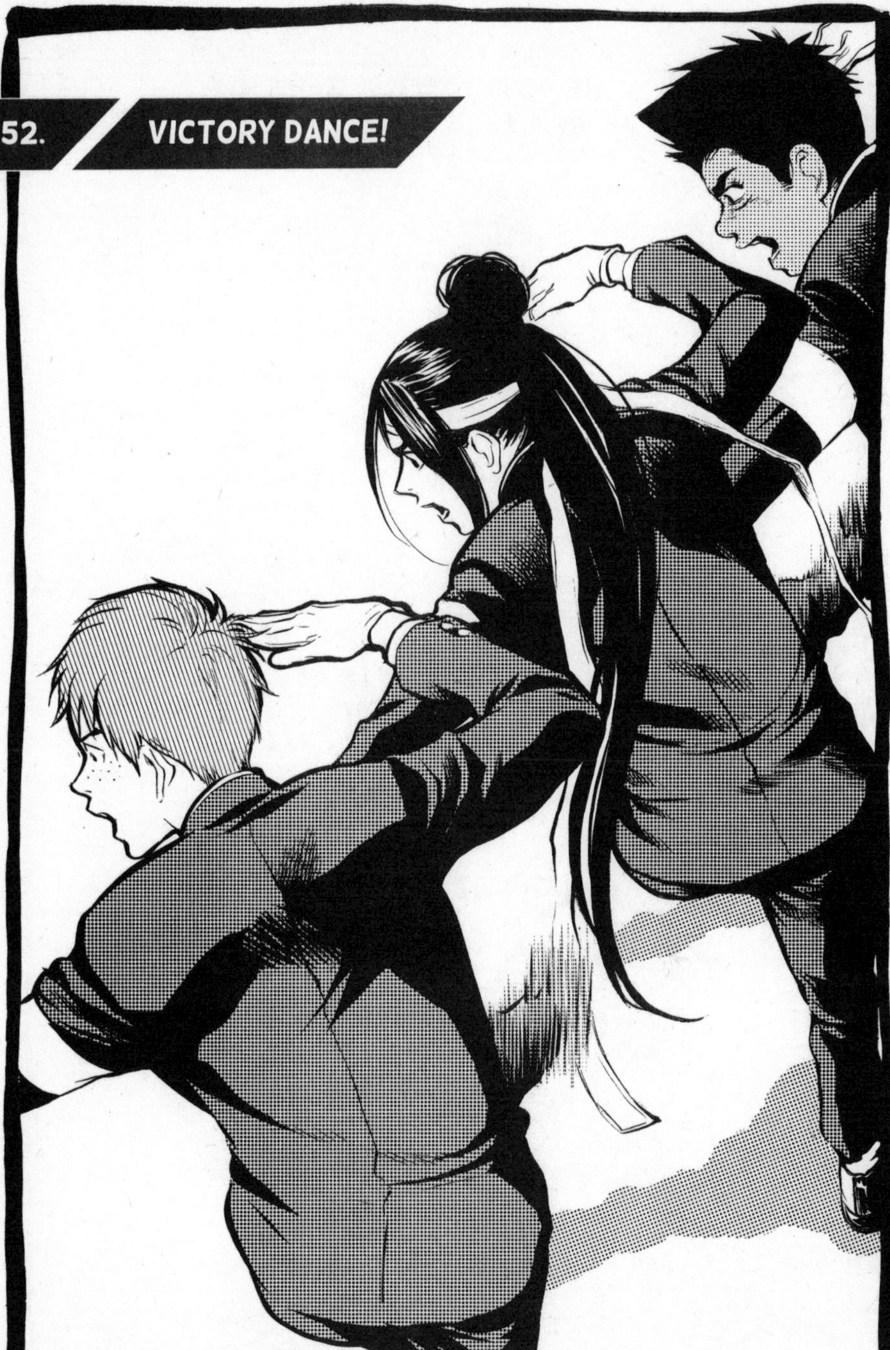

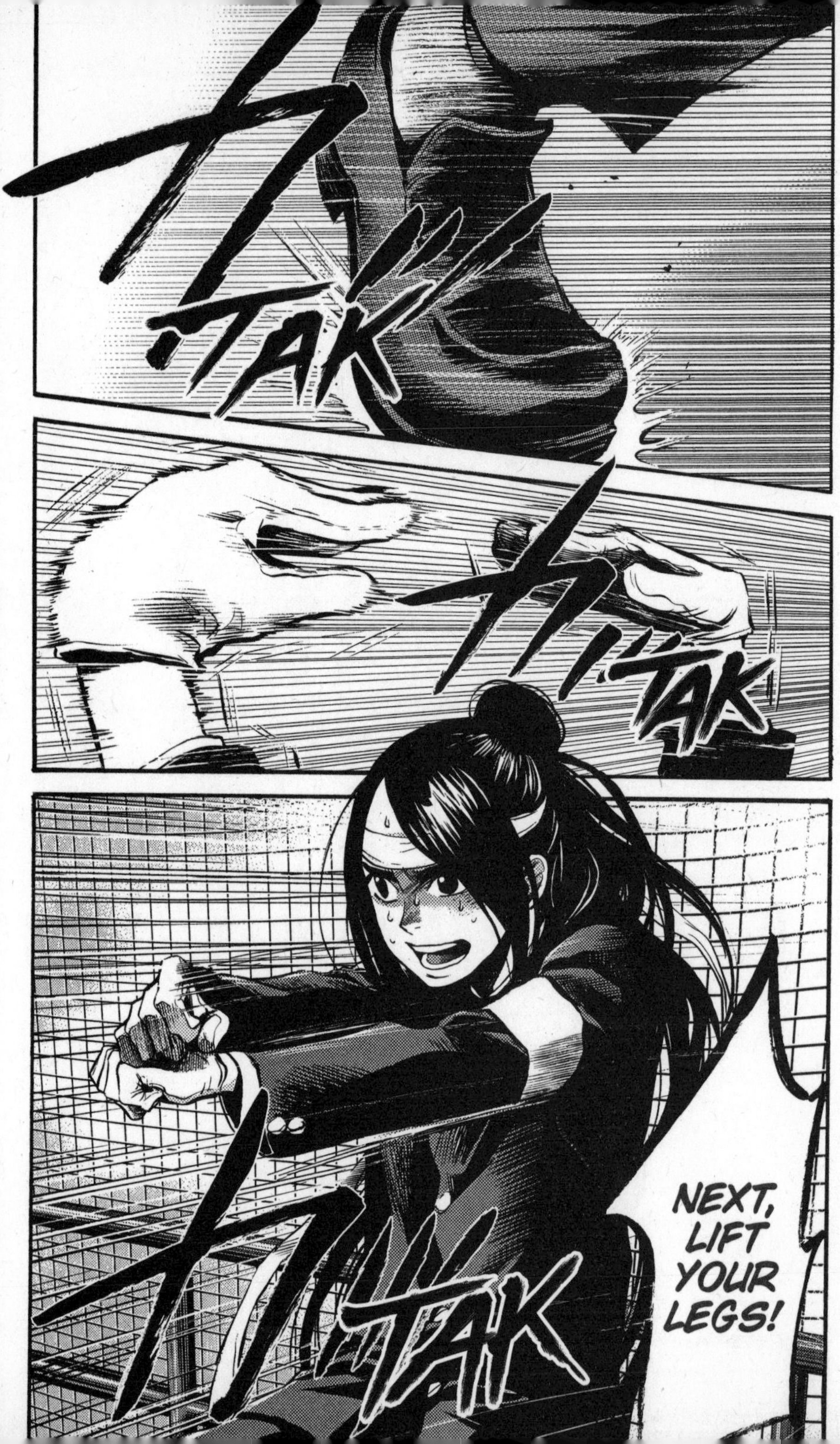
TAK
TAK
NEXT, LIFT YOUR LEGS!
TAK

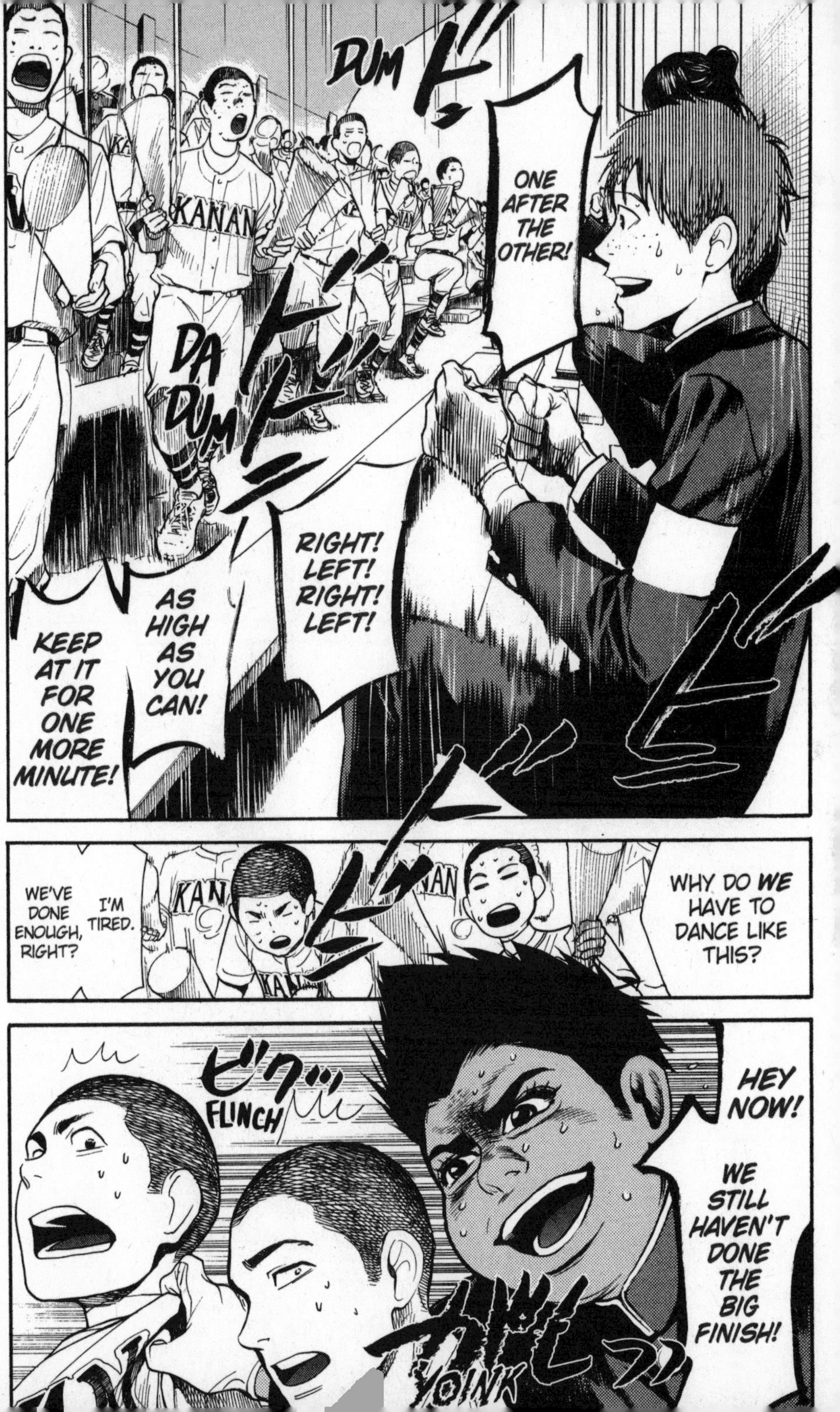
DUM
ONE AFTER THE OTHER!
DA DUM
RIGHT! LEFT! RIGHT! LEFT!
AS HIGH AS YOU CAN!
KEEP AT IT FOR ONE MORE MINUTE!
WHY DO WE HAVE TO DANCE LIKE THIS?
I'M TIRED.
WE'VE DONE ENOUGH, RIGHT?
HEY NOW!
WE STILL HAVEN'T DONE THE BIG FINISH!
YOINK
FLINCH

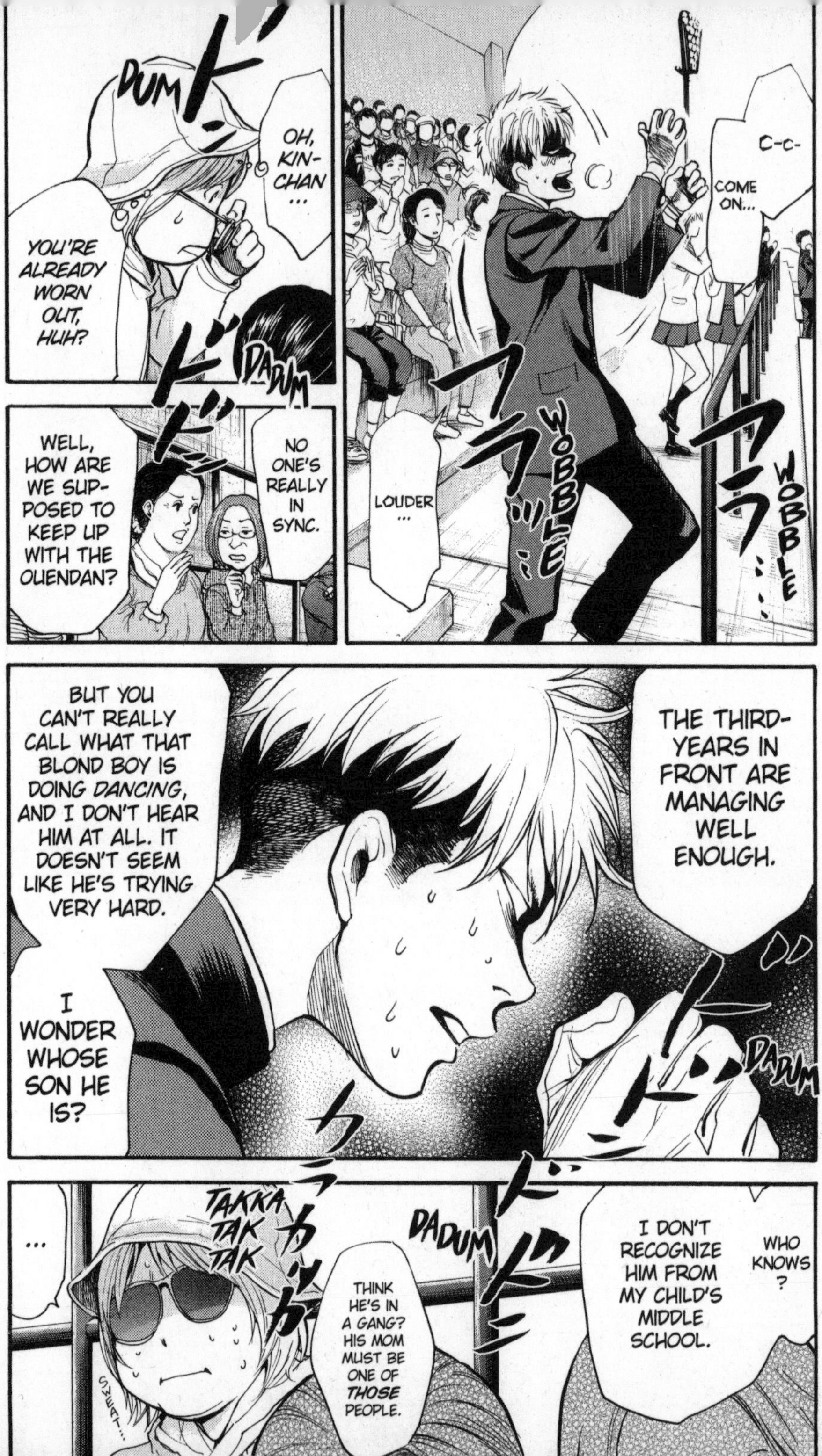
C-C-
COME ON...
LOUDER...
WOBBLE
WOBBLE
OH, KIN-CHAN...
YOU'RE ALREADY WORN OUT, HUH?
DUM
NO ONE'S REALLY IN SYNC.
WELL, HOW ARE WE SUP-POSED TO KEEP UP WITH THE OUENDAN?
DADUM
THE THIRD-YEARS IN FRONT ARE MANAGING WELL ENOUGH.
BUT YOU CAN'T REALLY CALL WHAT THAT BLOND BOY IS DOING *DANCING*, AND I DON'T HEAR HIM AT ALL. IT DOESN'T SEEM LIKE HE'S TRYING VERY HARD.
I WONDER WHOSE SON HE IS?
DADUM
WHO KNOWS?
I DON'T RECOGNIZE HIM FROM MY CHILD'S MIDDLE SCHOOL.
DADUM
THINK HE'S IN A GANG? HIS MOM MUST BE ONE OF **THOSE** PEOPLE.
TAKKA TAK TAK
...
SWEAT...

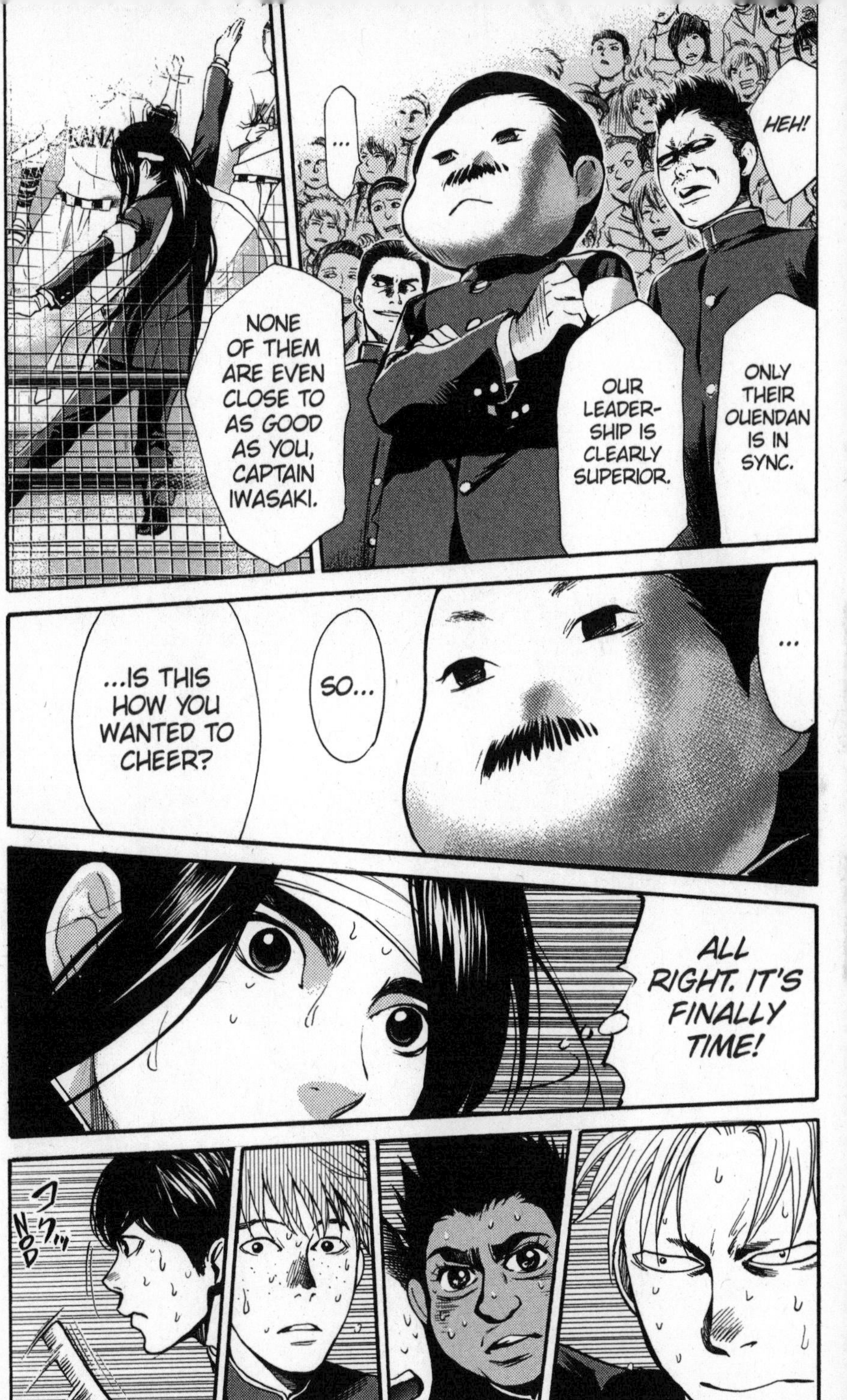
HEH!
...
ONLY THEIR OUENDAN IS IN SYNC.
OUR LEADERSHIP IS CLEARLY SUPERIOR.
NONE OF THEM ARE EVEN CLOSE TO AS GOOD AS YOU, CAPTAIN IWASAKI.
...
SO...
...IS THIS HOW YOU WANTED TO CHEER?
ALL RIGHT. IT'S FINALLY TIME!
NOD

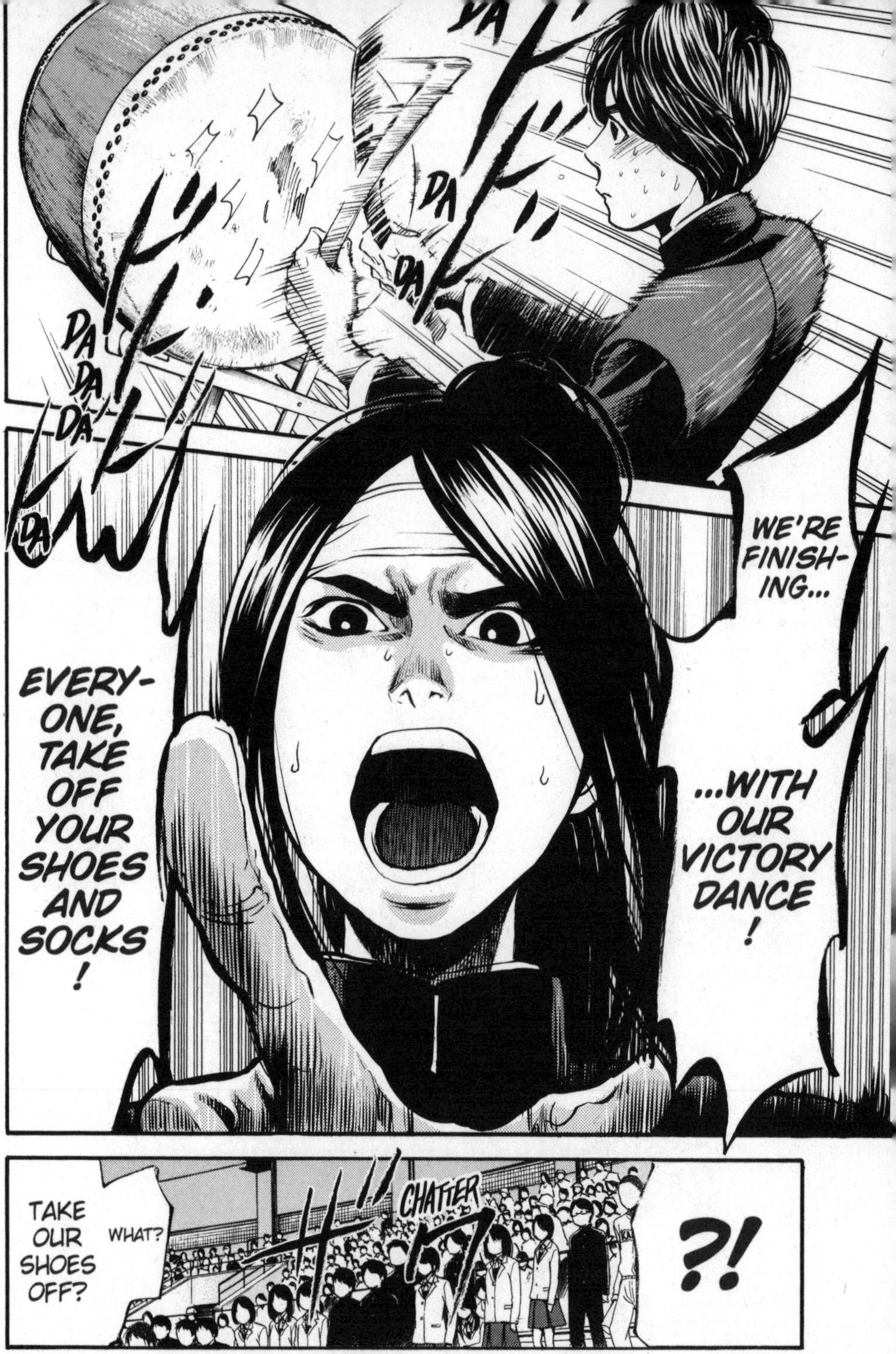
DA
DA
DA
DA DA DA
DA
WE'RE FINISHING...
...WITH OUR VICTORY DANCE!
EVERYONE, TAKE OFF YOUR SHOES AND SOCKS!
?!
CHATTER
WHAT?
TAKE OUR SHOES OFF?

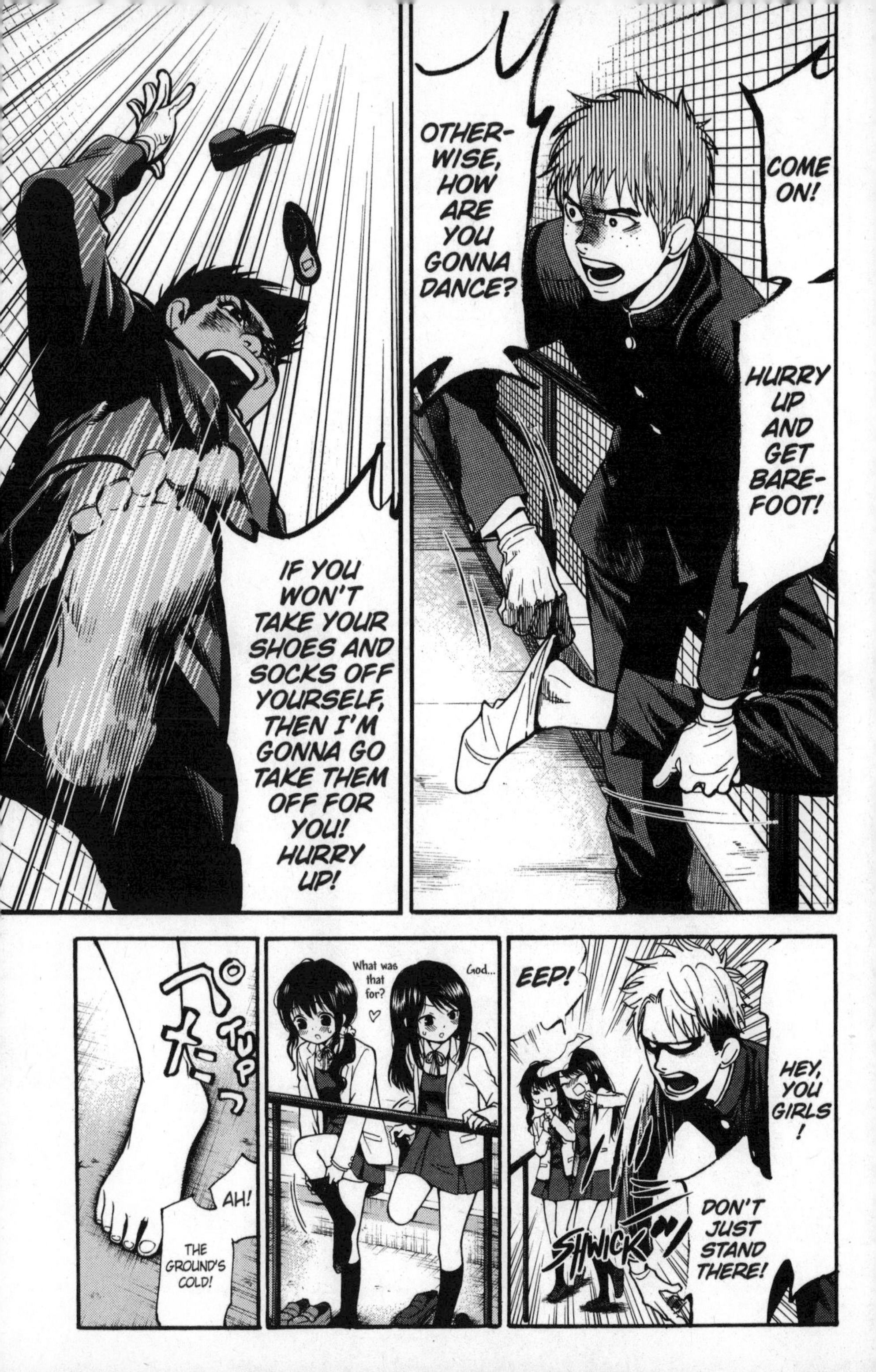

COME ON!
OTHER-WISE, HOW ARE YOU GONNA DANCE?
HURRY UP AND GET BARE-FOOT!
IF YOU WON'T TAKE YOUR SHOES AND SOCKS OFF YOURSELF, THEN I'M GONNA GO TAKE THEM OFF FOR YOU! HURRY UP!
HEY, YOU GIRLS!
EEP!
DON'T JUST STAND THERE!
SHWICK
God...
What was that for? ♥
ペターッ
TUP
AH!
THE GROUND'S COLD!

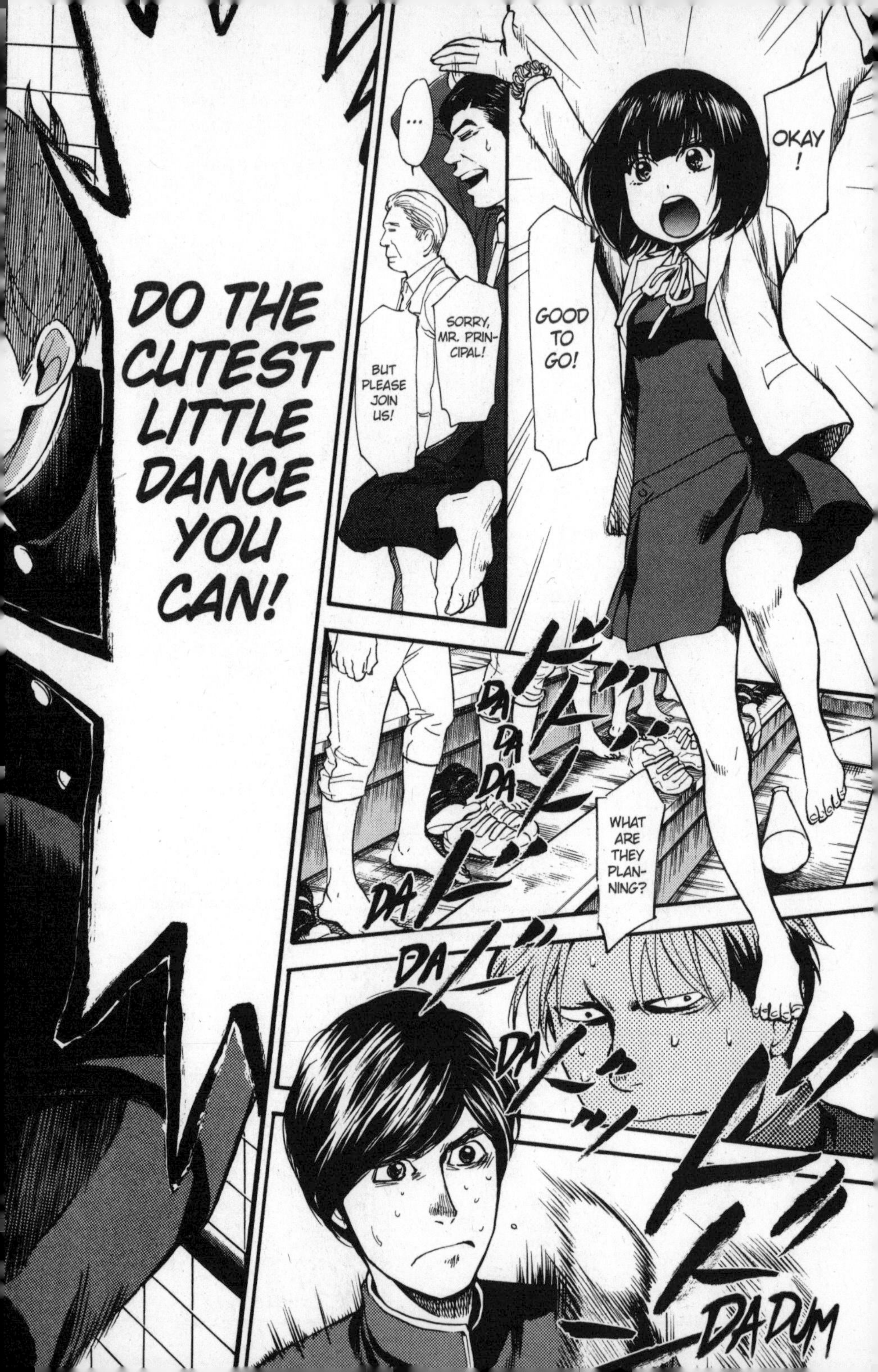
OKAY!
GOOD TO GO!
SORRY, MR. PRIN-CIPAL!
BUT PLEASE JOIN US!
...
DA DA DA
DA
WHAT ARE THEY PLAN-NING?
DA
DA
DADUM
DO THE CUTEST LITTLE DANCE YOU CAN!

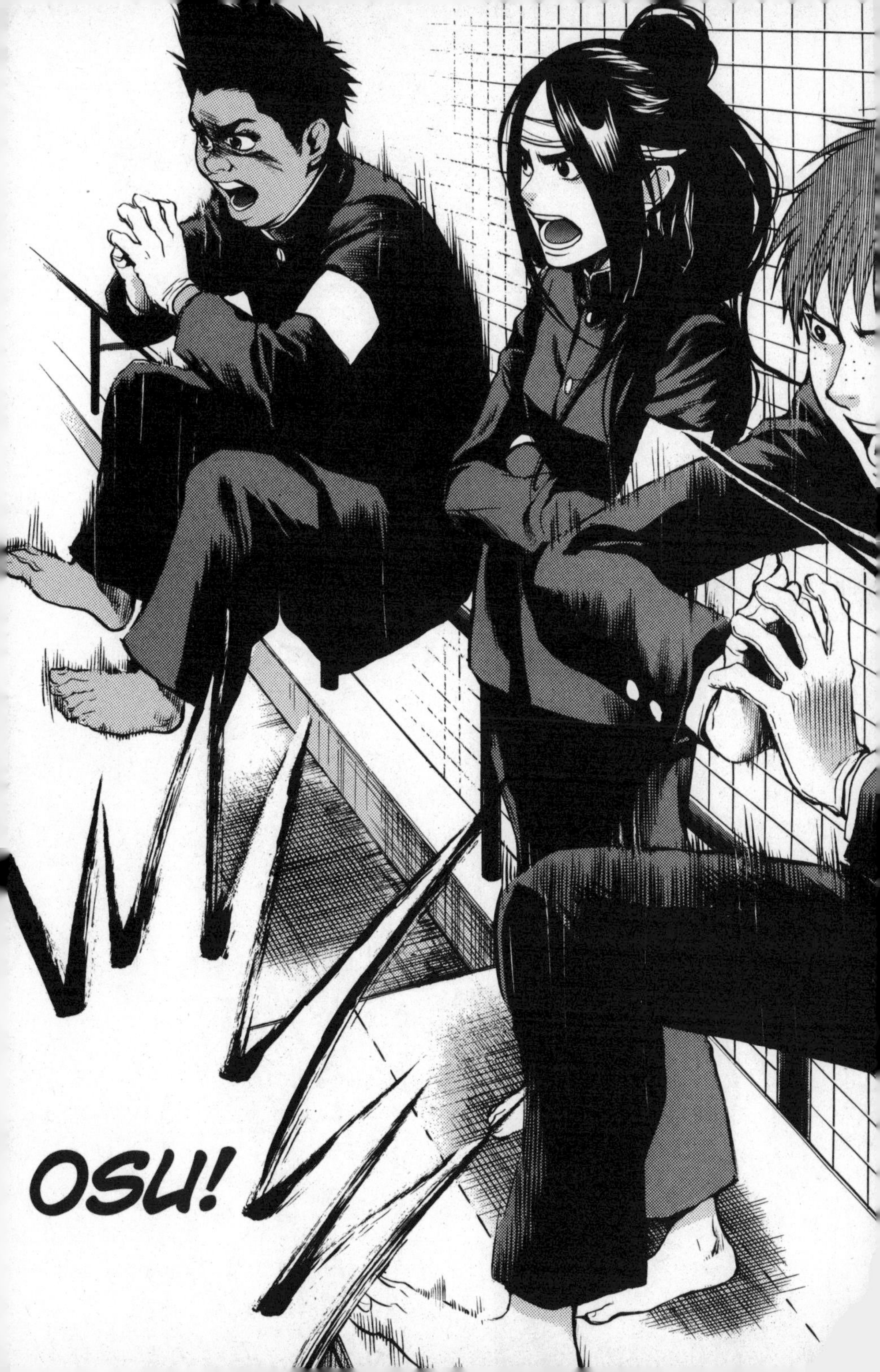
OSU!

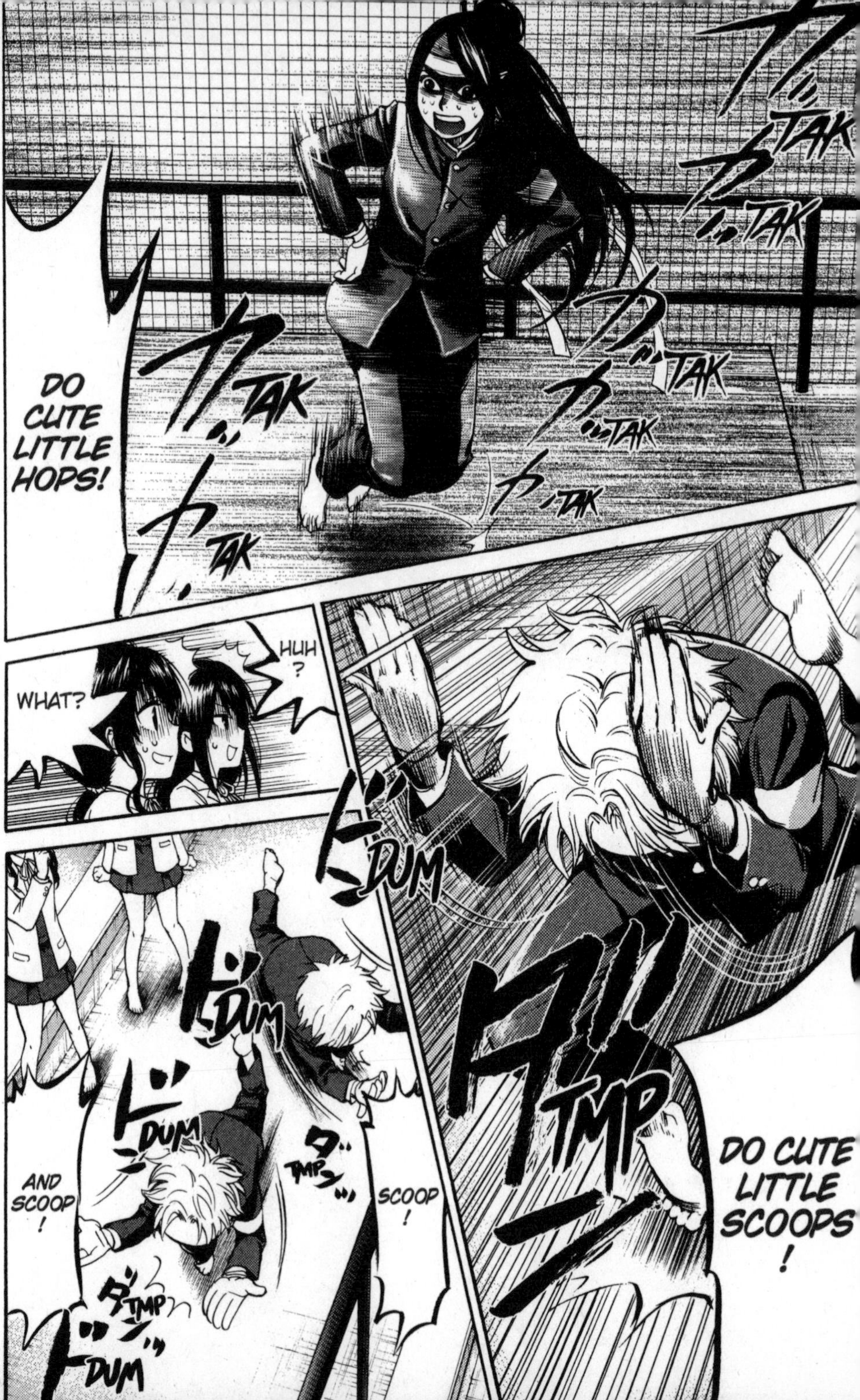
TAK
TAK
TAK
TAK
TAK
TAK
TAK
DO CUTE LITTLE HOPS!
DUM
TMP
DO CUTE LITTLE SCOOPS!
HUH?
WHAT?
DUM
DUM
TMP
SCOOP!
AND SCOOP!
TMP
DUM

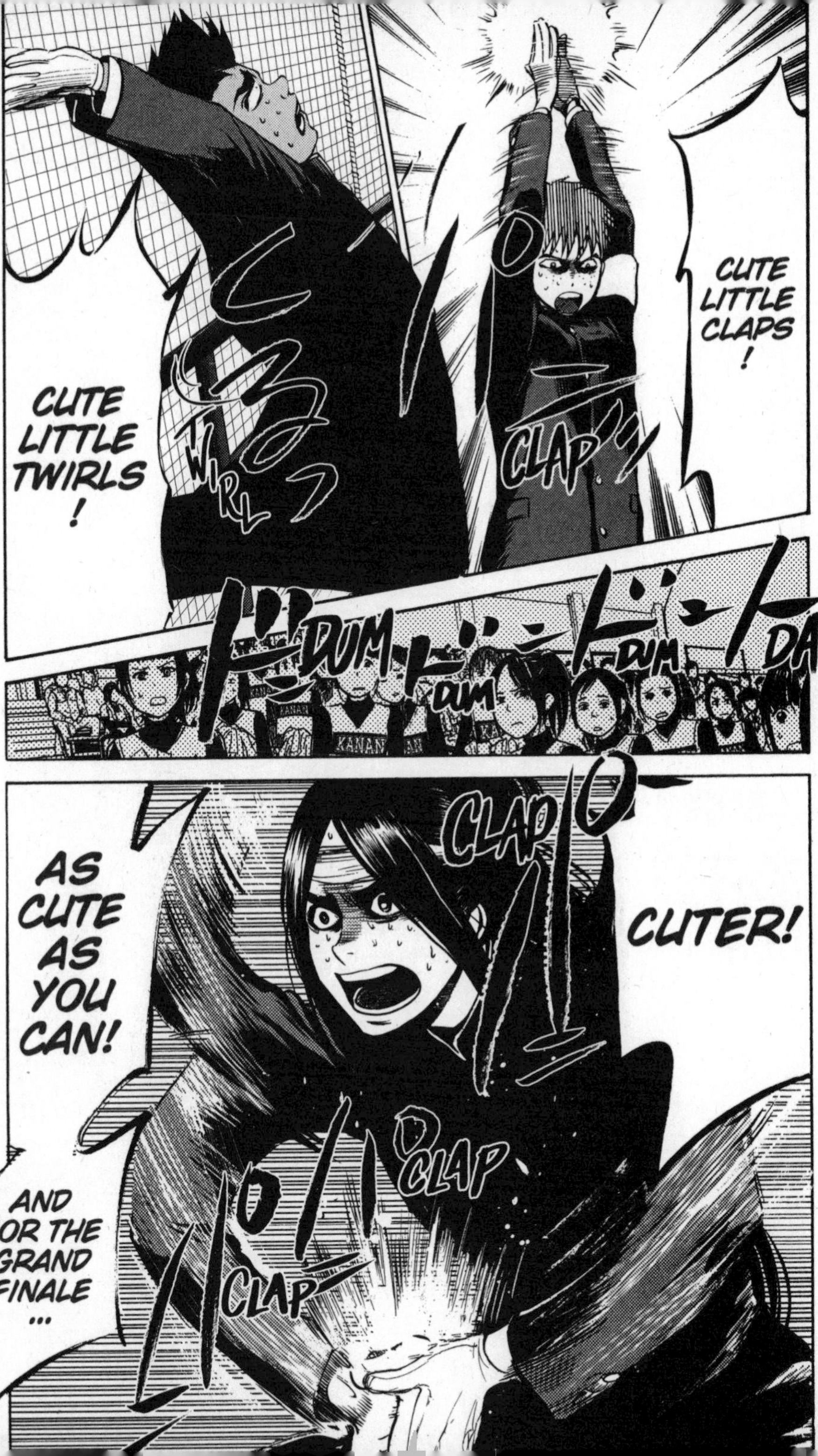
CUTE LITTLE CLAPS!
CLAP
CUTE LITTLE TWIRLS!
WIRL
DA
DUM
DUM
DUM
CLAP
CUTER!
AS CUTE AS YOU CAN!
CLAP
AND FOR THE GRAND FINALE...
CLAP

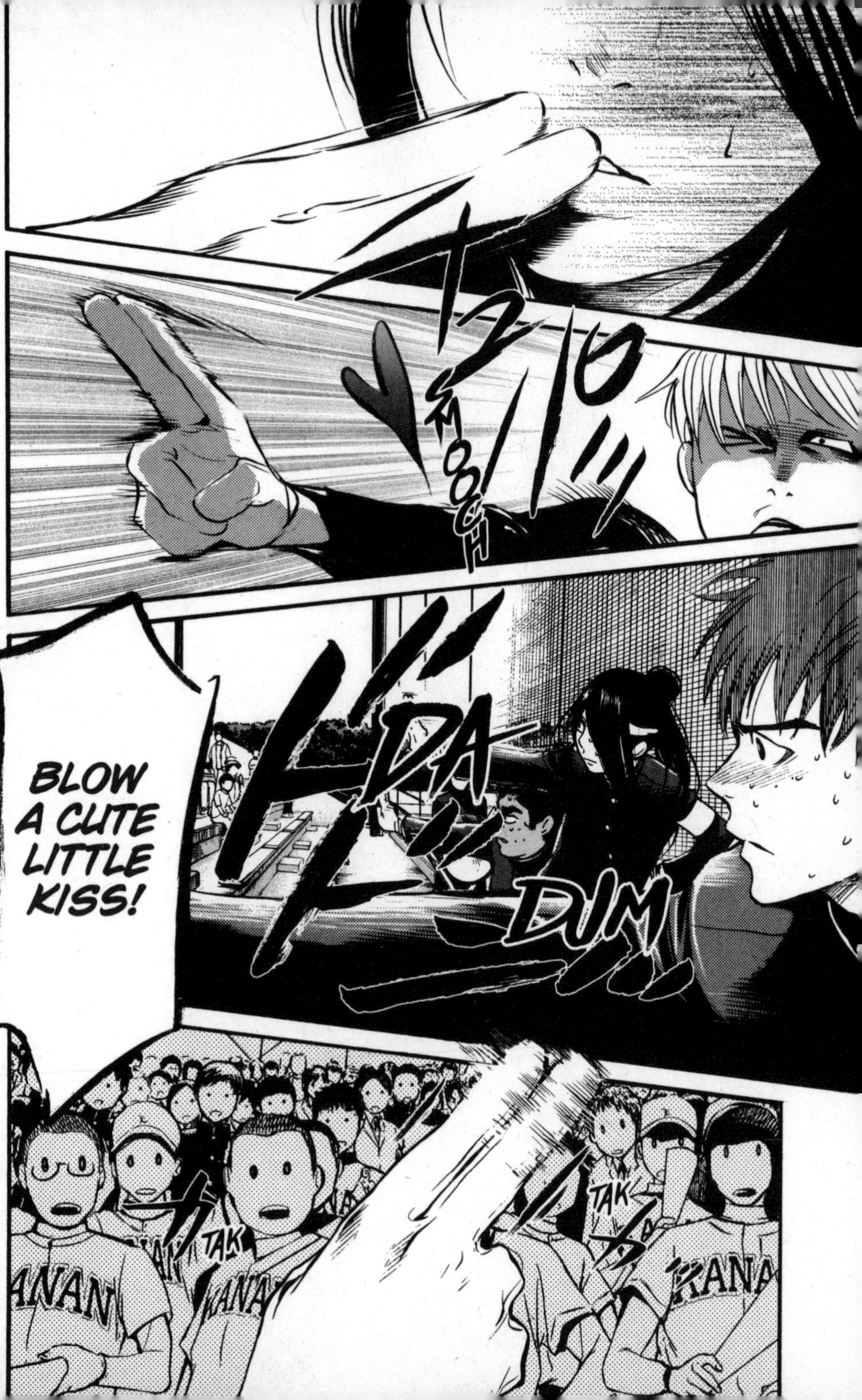
SMOOCH
DA-DUM
BLOW A CUTE LITTLE KISS!
TAK
TAK
TAK

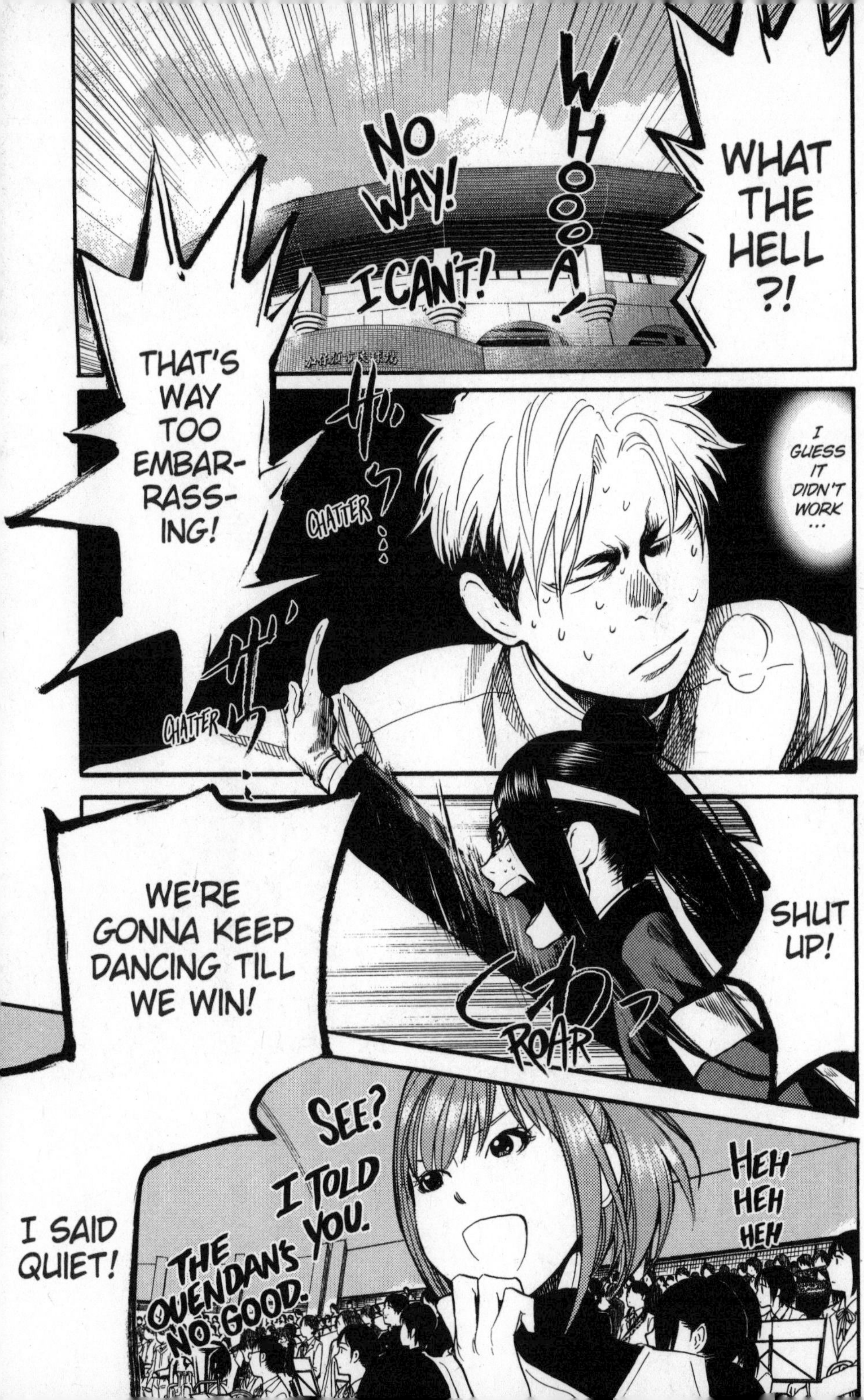
WHAT THE HELL ?!
WHOOOA!
NO WAY!
I CAN'T!
I GUESS IT DIDN'T WORK...
CHATTER
CHATTER
THAT'S WAY TOO EMBARRASSING!
SHUT UP!
ROAR
WE'RE GONNA KEEP DANCING TILL WE WIN!
HEH HEH HEH
SEE? I TOLD YOU.
THE OUENDAN'S NO GOOD.
I SAID QUIET!

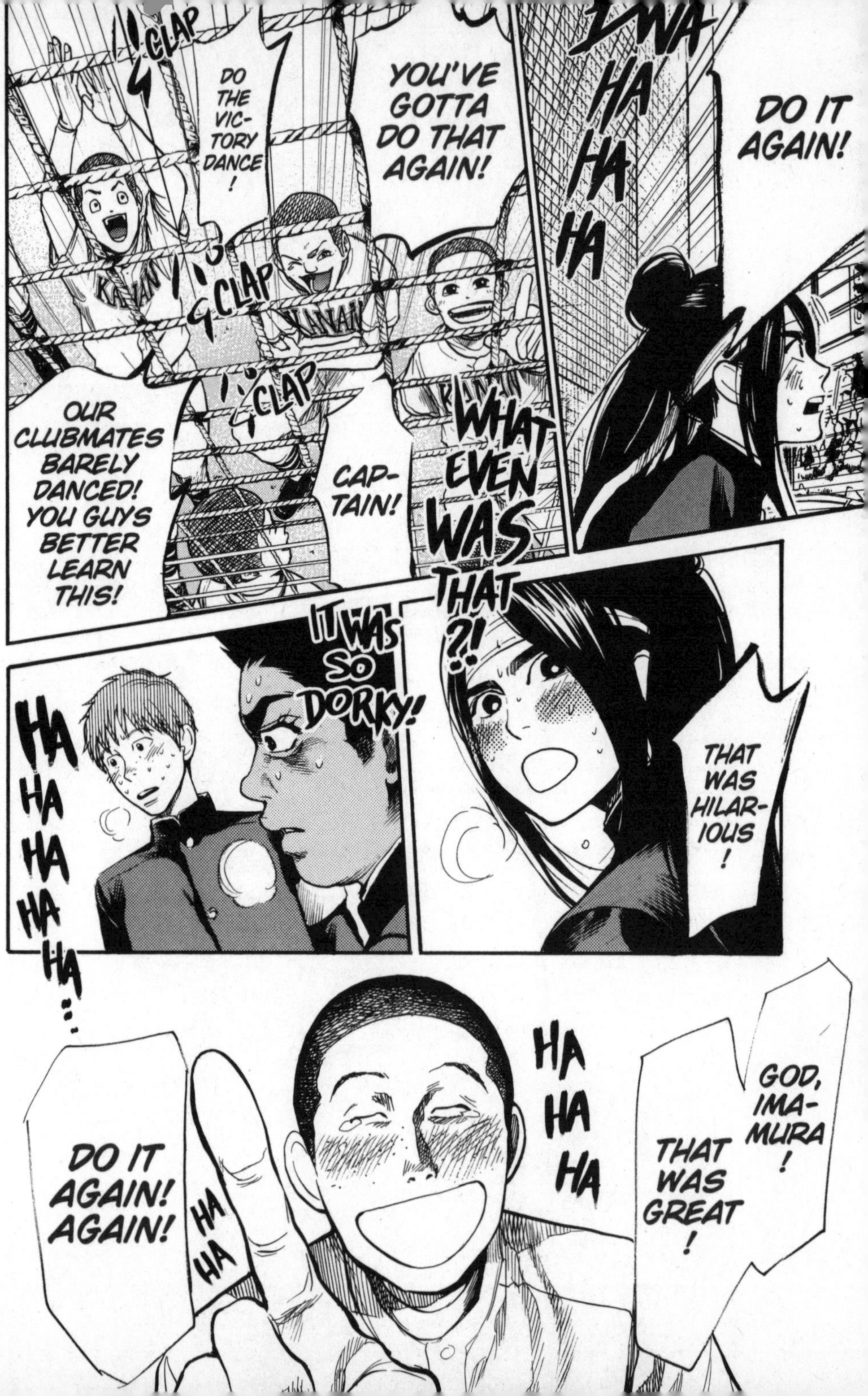
DO IT AGAIN!
WA HA HA HA HA
YOU'VE GOTTA DO THAT AGAIN!
DO THE VIC-TORY DANCE!
CLAP
CLAP
CLAP
CLAP
CAP-TAIN!
OUR CLUBMATES BARELY DANCED! YOU GUYS BETTER LEARN THIS!
WHAT EVEN WAS THAT?!
THAT WAS HILAR-IOUS!
IT WAS SO DORKY!
HA HA HA HA HA...
GOD, IMA-MURA!
THAT WAS GREAT!
HA HA HA HA
HA HA
DO IT AGAIN! AGAIN!

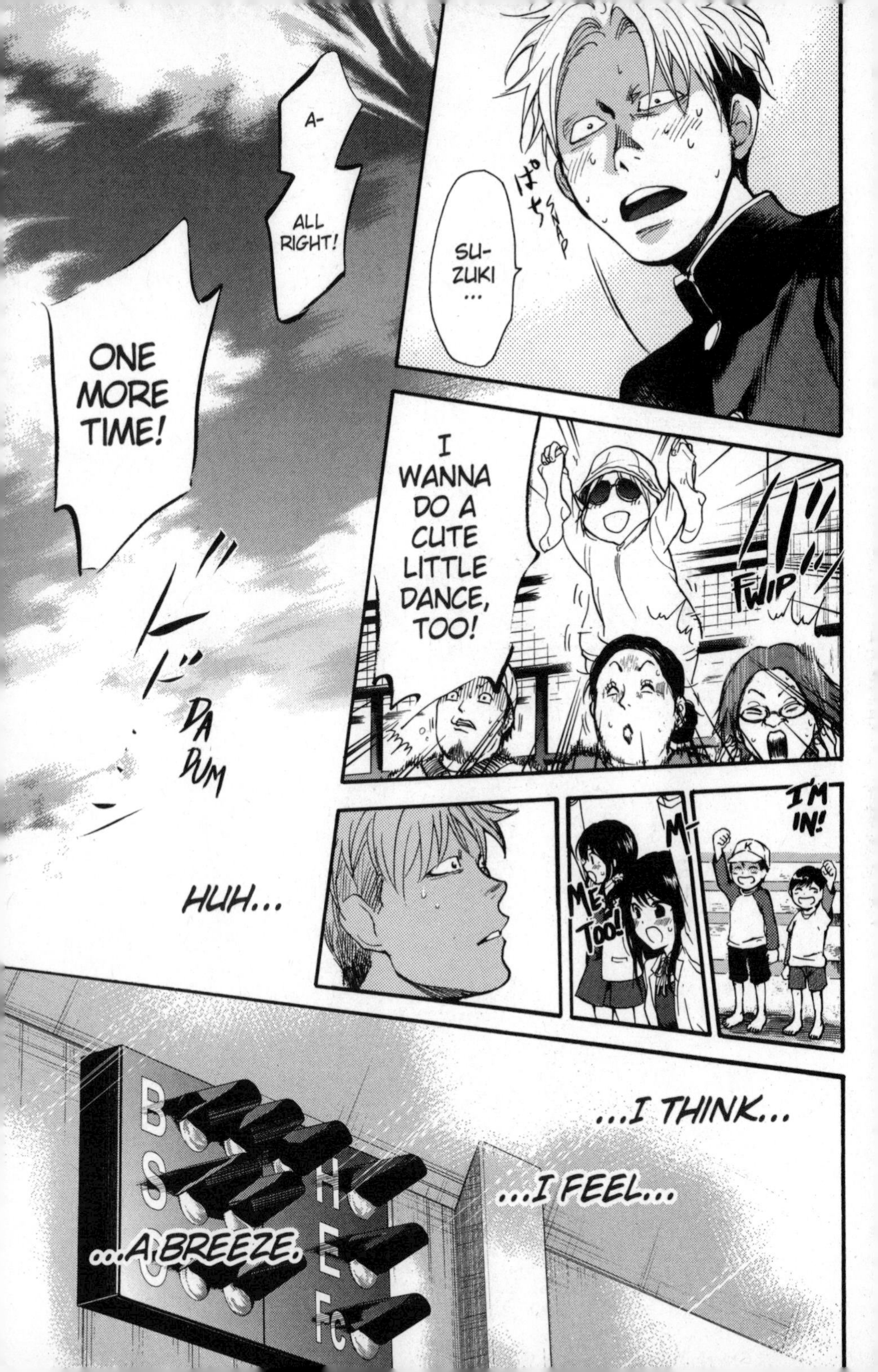
SNAP
SU-ZUKI...
A-
ALL RIGHT!
ONE MORE TIME!
DA DUM
I WANNA DO A CUTE LITTLE DANCE, TOO!
FWIP
I'M IN!
M-
ME TOO!
HUH...
...I THINK...
...I FEEL...
...A BREEZE.

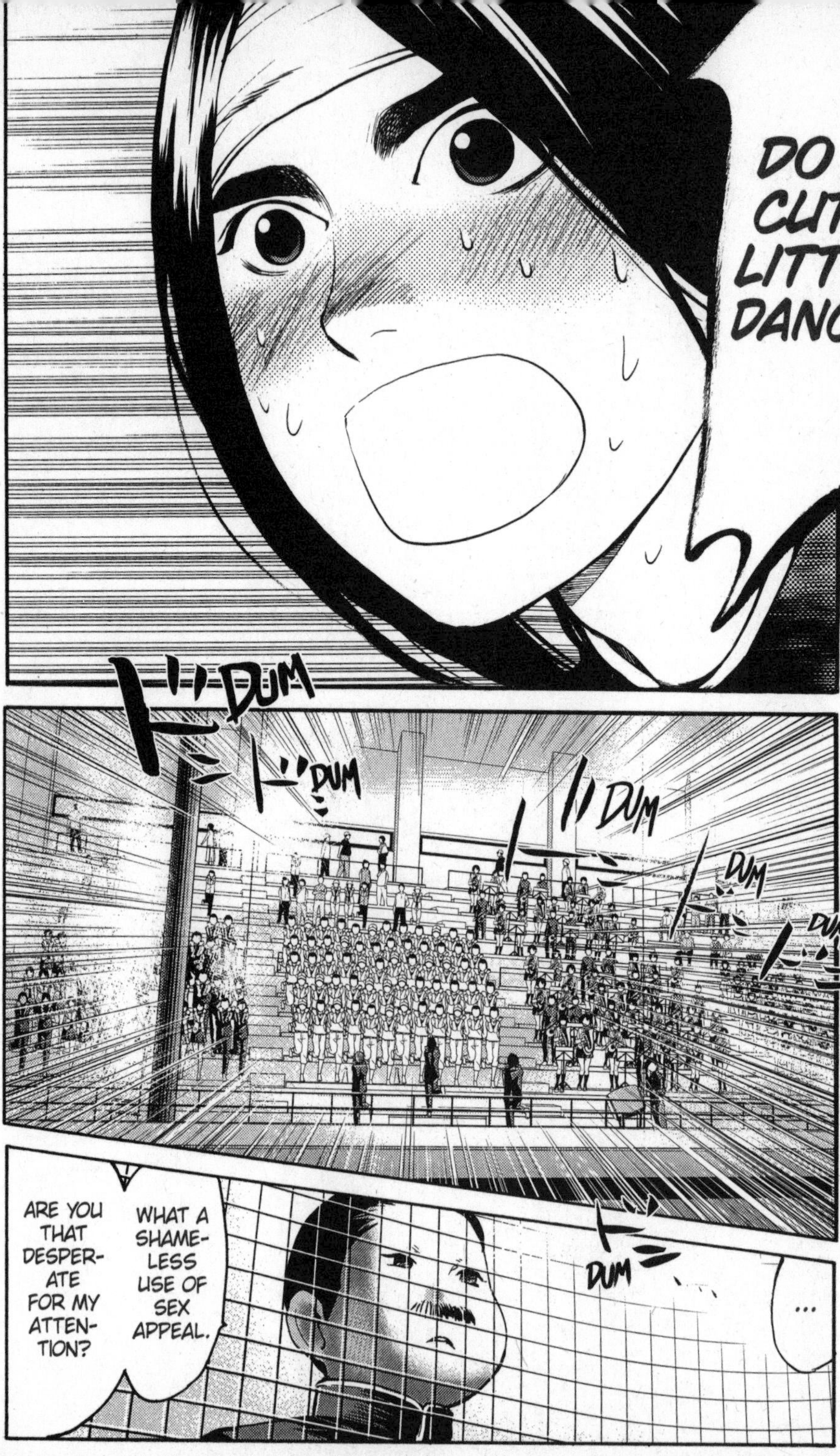
DO A CUTE LITTLE DANCE!
DUM
DUM
DUM
DUM
DUM
DUM
...
WHAT A SHAME-LESS USE OF SEX APPEAL.
ARE YOU THAT DESPER-ATE FOR MY ATTEN-TION?

**TO BE CONTINUED IN VOLUME 6...**

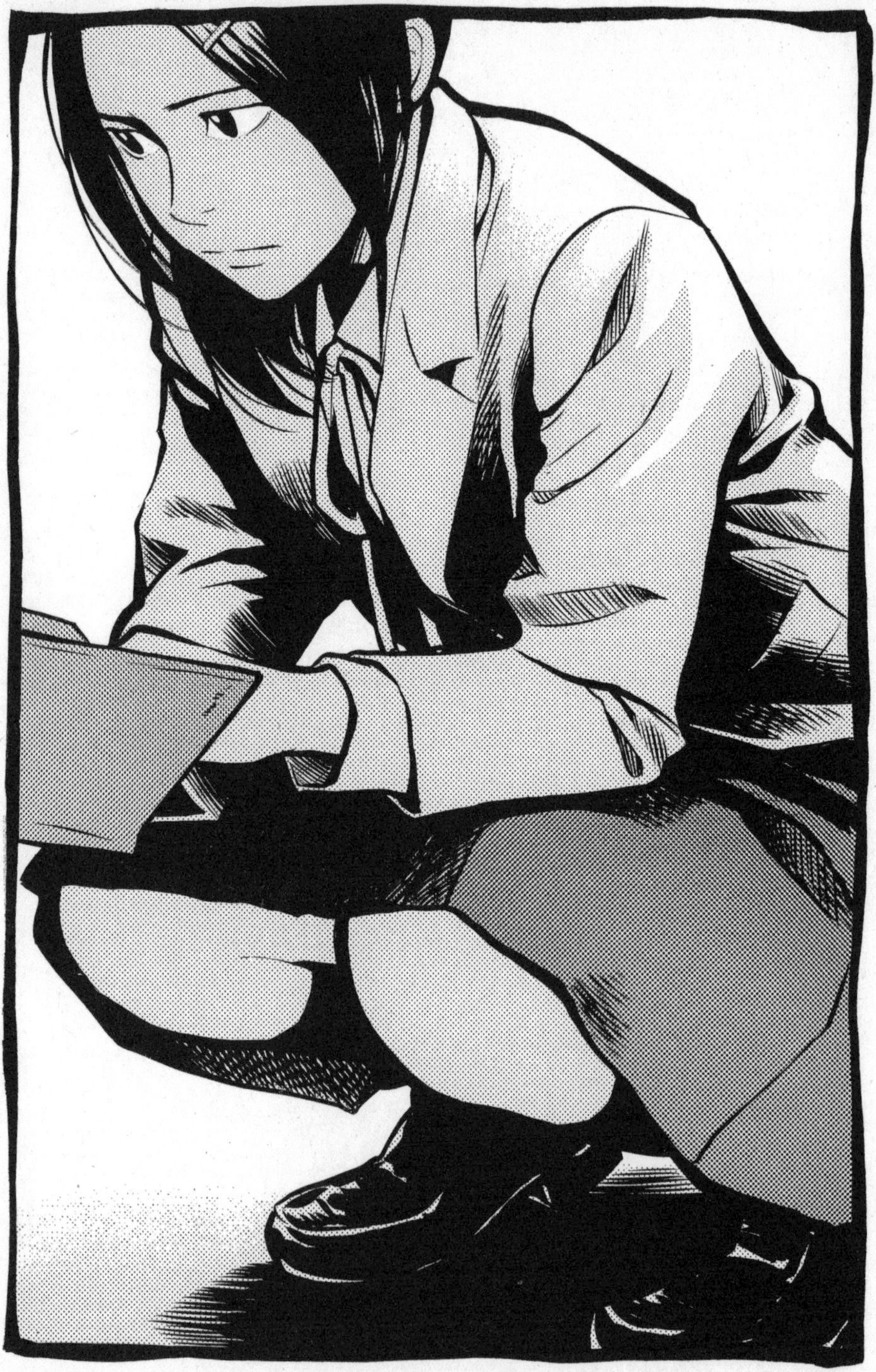

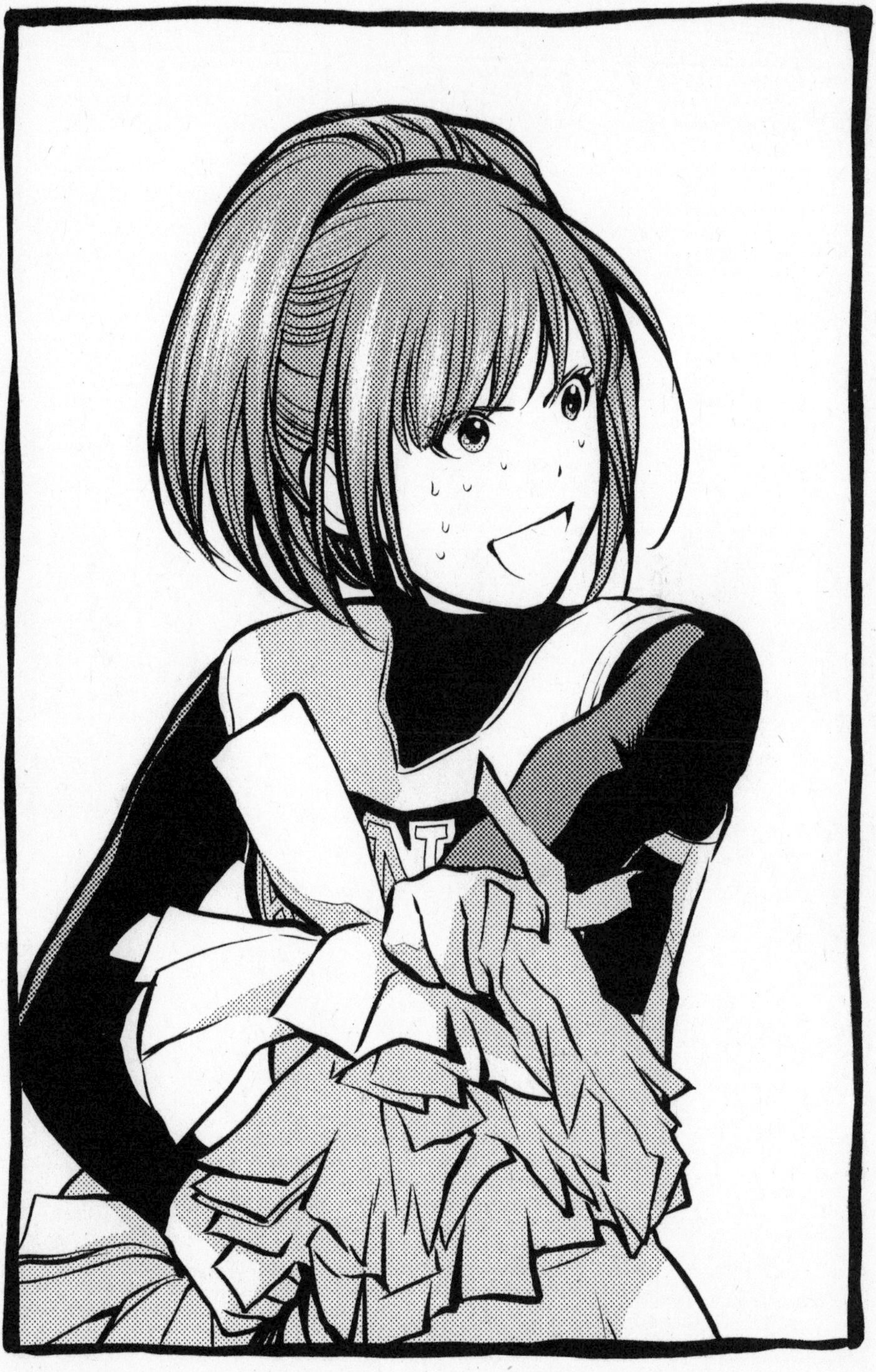

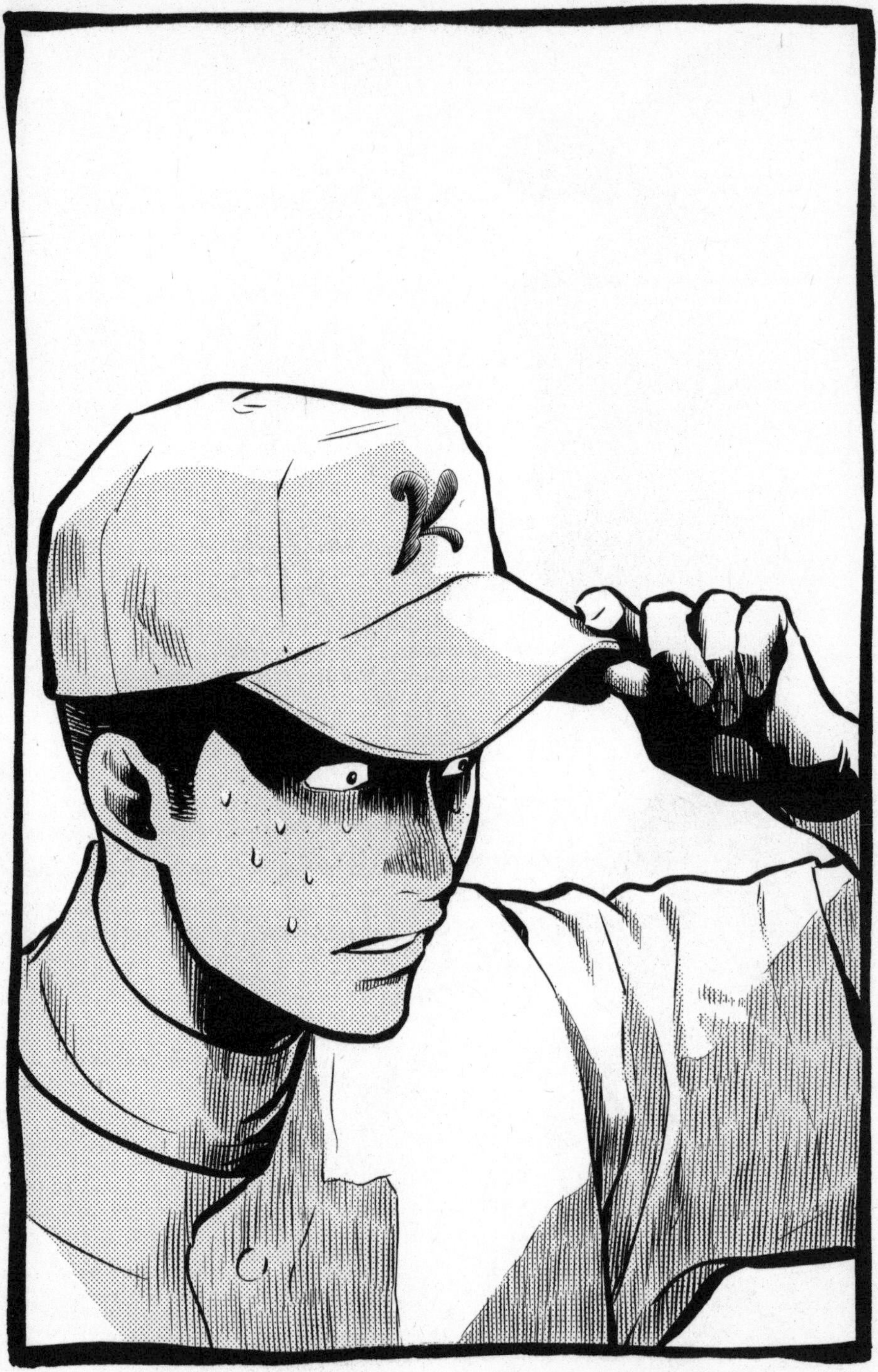

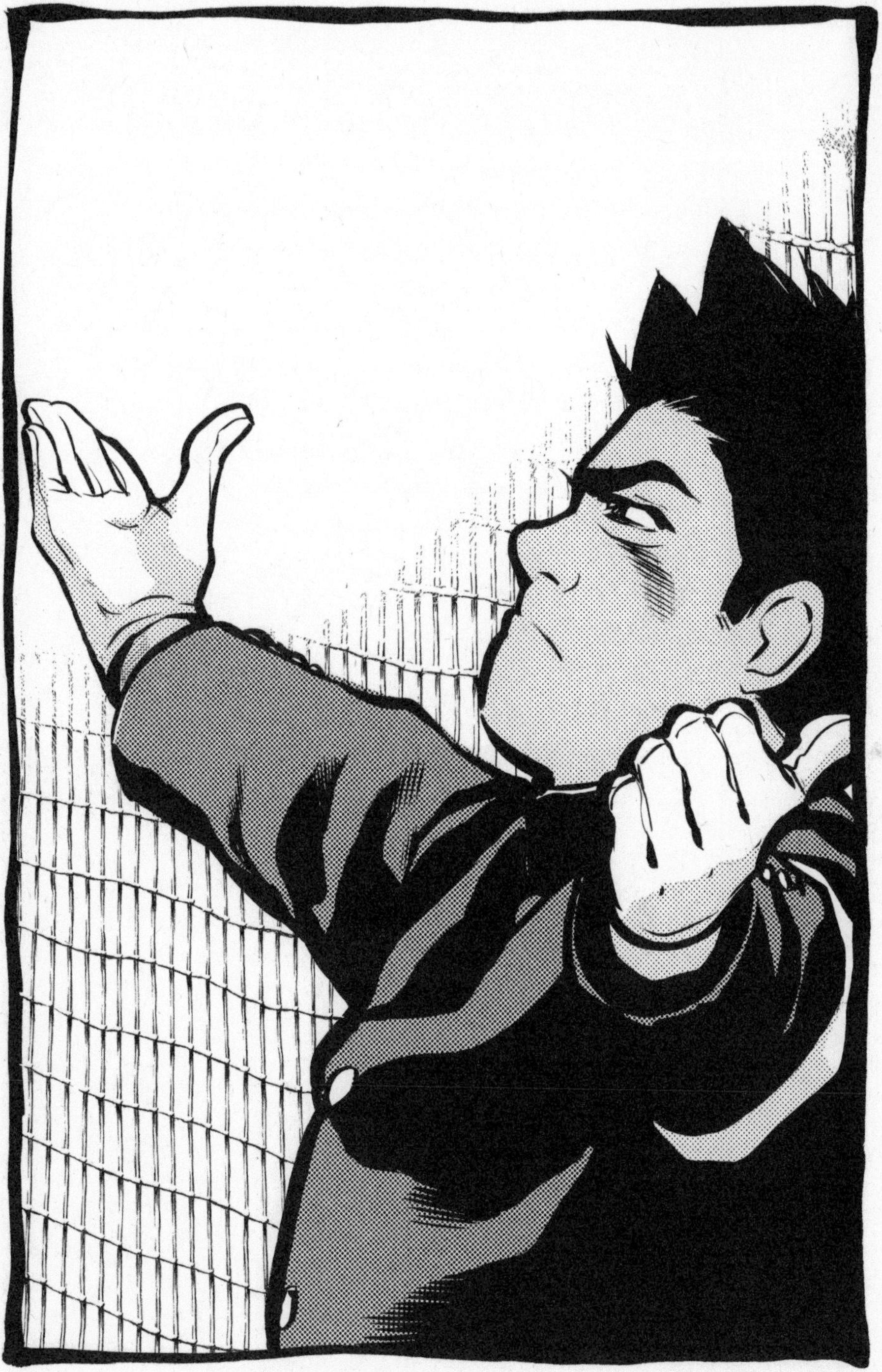

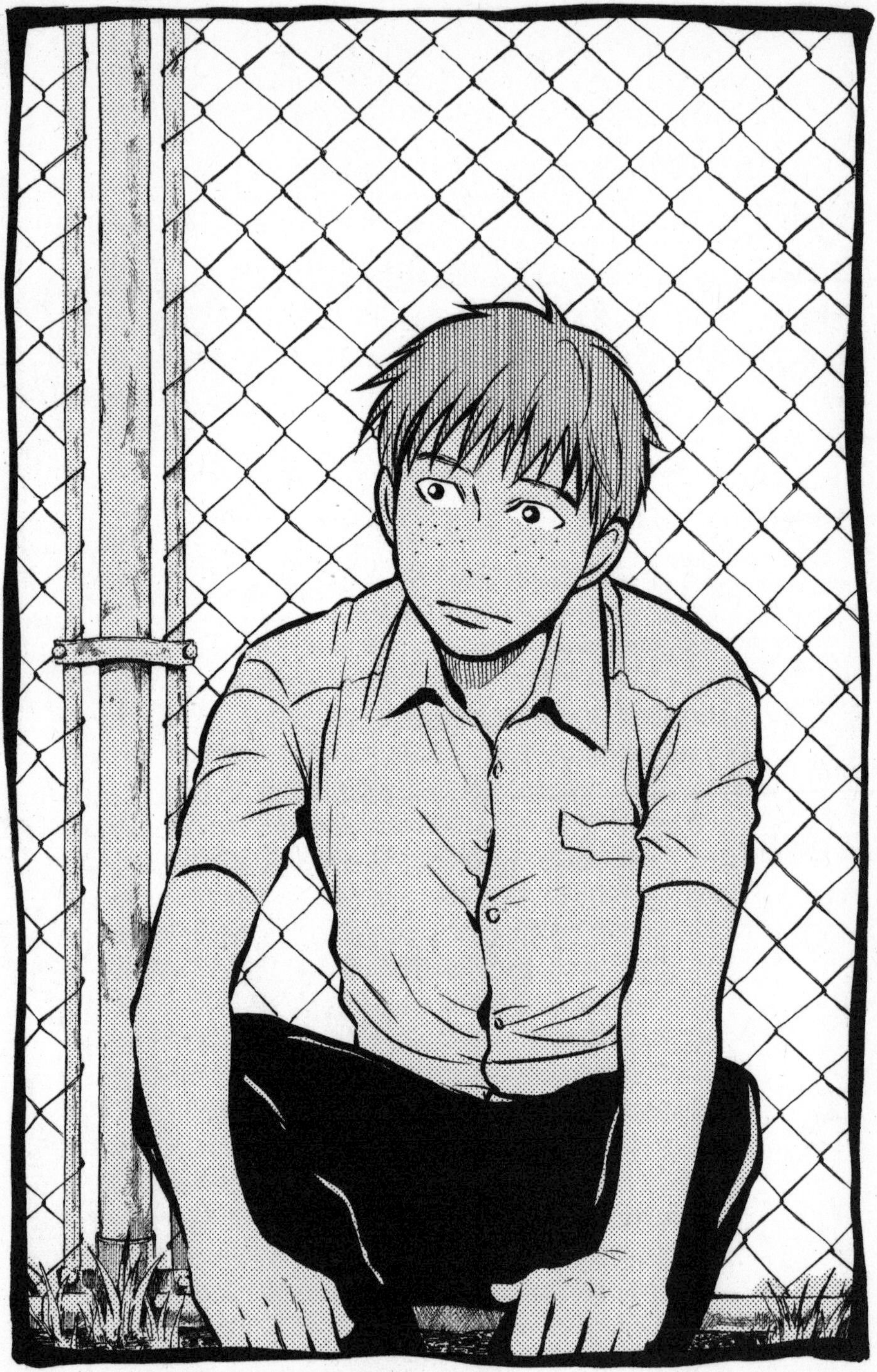

# This is the AFTERWORD!

The Kabosu Minami ouendan that appears ain Again!! is a combination of one from a high school in Kazo City, Saitama, and the one at my old high school in Sasebo City, Nagasaki, so I set the story in the fictional city of Kabosu.

This ouendan isn't necessarily a faithful representation of either of those, though.

Apparently, my alma mater's ouendan only got one new member this year, so no one's sure if they'll be able to keep it alive... I hope they get new members!

2012. 6.

⭐ Mitsurou Kubo, June 2012
My Agent: Hiromi Sakitani

⭐ My Assistants: Shunsuke Ono, Youko Mikuni, Hiromu Kitano, Shiori Mizoguchi, Koushi Tezuka, Rana Satou, Kouhei Mihara...
Eshitaka, Tsunetaka

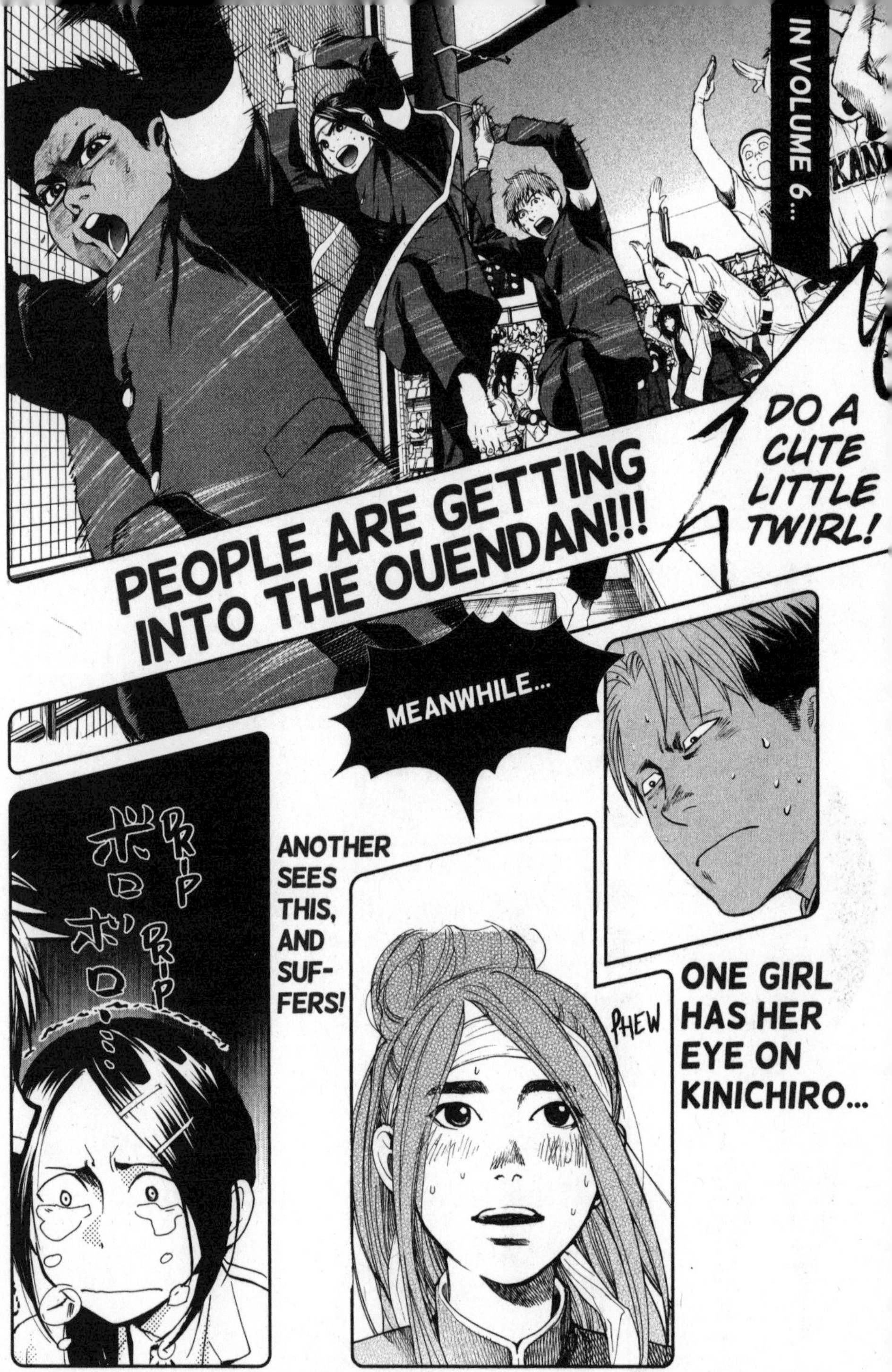
IN VOLUME 6...
DO A CUTE LITTLE TWIRL!
PEOPLE ARE GETTING INTO THE OUENDAN!!!
MEANWHILE...
ONE GIRL HAS HER EYE ON KINICHIRO...
PHEW
ANOTHER SEES THIS, AND SUF-FERS!
ボロボロ
DRIP DRIP

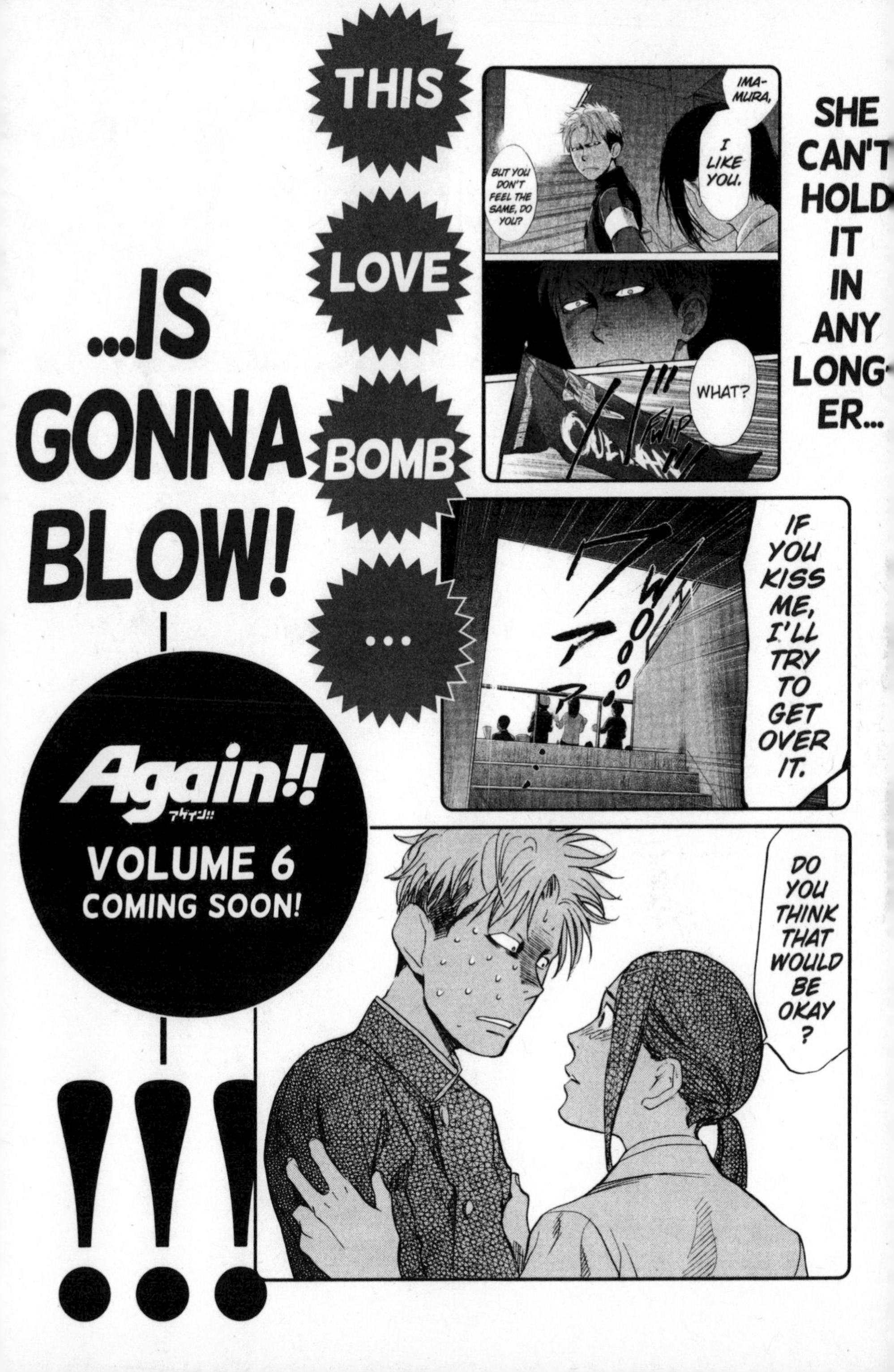
SHE CAN'T HOLD IT IN ANY LONGER...
IMA-MURA,
I LIKE YOU.
BUT YOU DON'T FEEL THE SAME, DO YOU?
WHAT?
FWIP
THIS
LOVE
BOMB
...
...IS GONNA BLOW!
IF YOU KISS ME, I'LL TRY TO GET OVER IT.
DO YOU THINK THAT WOULD BE OKAY?
Again!!
VOLUME 6
COMING SOON!
!!!

# Translation Notes

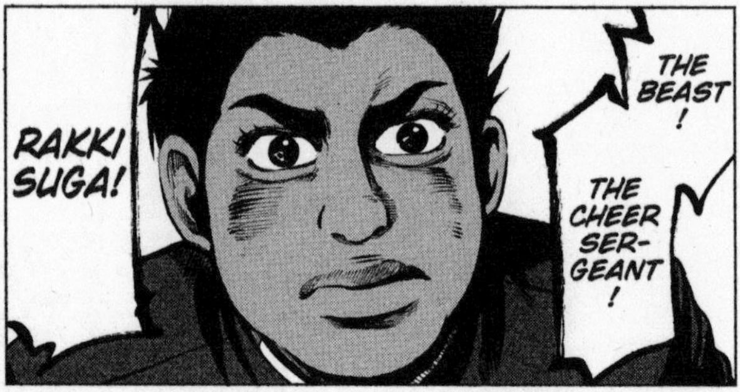
THE BEAST!
THE CHEER SER-GEANT!
RAKKI SUGA!

**Rakki Suga/"Lucky Suga"**
Page 153

Most of the Ouendan's members have a nickname of some kind, and "Lucky Suga" is no exception. His given name is most properly represented with the characters 楽喜, but when his friends address him, they use the homophone ラッキイー, which is the loanword "lucky" spelled out in phonetic katakana characters. This is pronounced identically to the kanji in his name, but the different way of writing it suggests that his friends are referencing the loanword, rather than his actual name. In his big introduction here, though, the kanji are used, so it felt right to give his name as "Rakki."

# Again!!
アゲイン!!

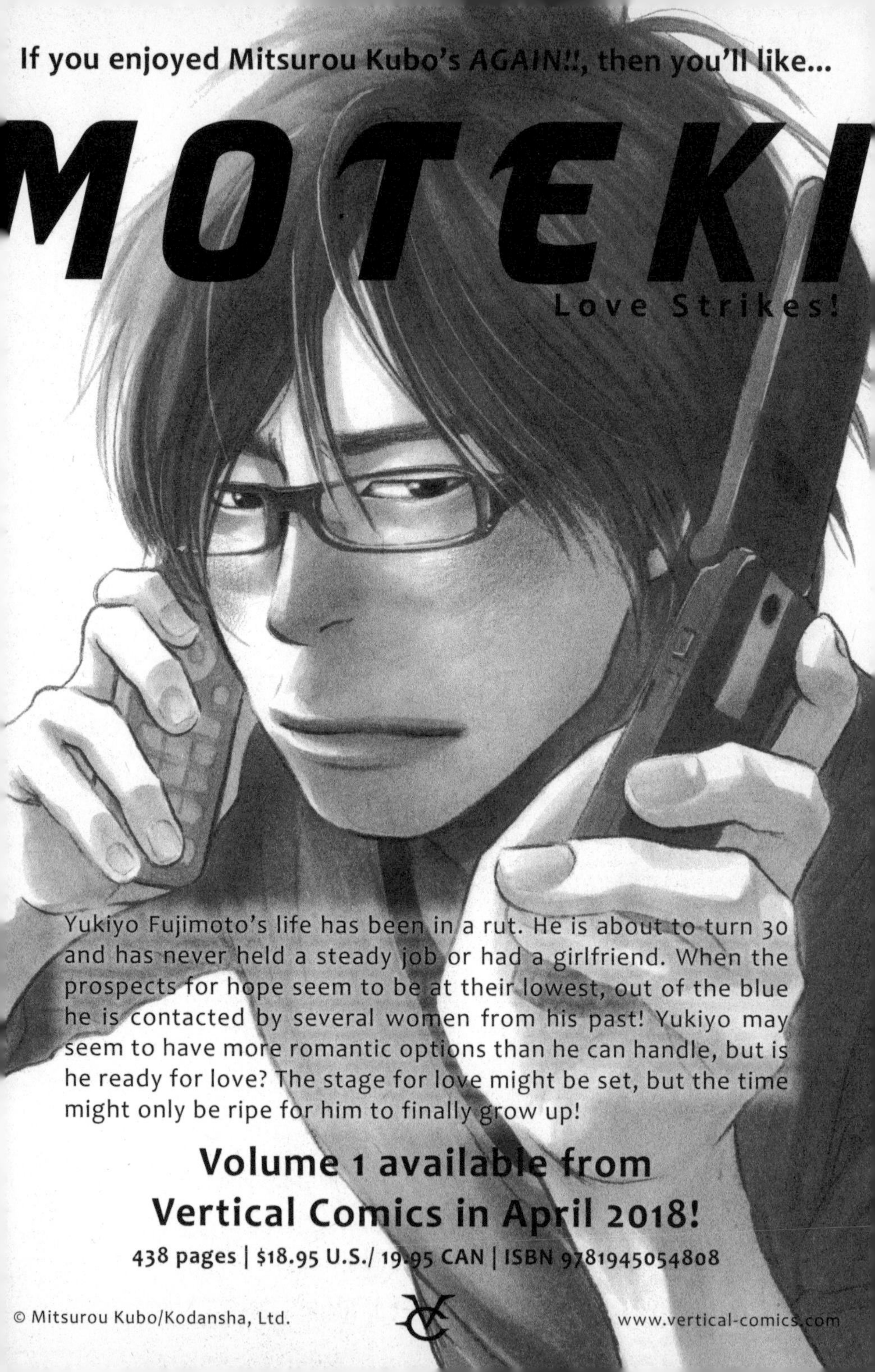
If you enjoyed Mitsurou Kubo's AGAIN!!, then you'll like...
MOTEKI
Love Strikes!
Yukiyo Fujimoto's life has been in a rut. He is about to turn 30 and has never held a steady job or had a girlfriend. When the prospects for hope seem to be at their lowest, out of the blue he is contacted by several women from his past! Yukiyo may seem to have more romantic options than he can handle, but is he ready for love? The stage for love might be set, but the time might only be ripe for him to finally grow up!
Volume 1 available from
Vertical Comics in April 2018!
438 pages | $18.95 U.S./ 19.95 CAN | ISBN 9781945054808
© Mitsurou Kubo/Kodansha, Ltd.
www.vertical-comics.com

KC
KODANSHA
COMICS

# complex age
## yui sakuma

26-year-old Nagisa Kataura has a secret. Transforming into her favorite anime and manga characters is her passion in life, and she's earned great respect amongst her fellow cospayers. But to the rest of society, her hobby is a silly fantasy. As demands from both her office job and cosplaying begin to increase, she may one day have to make a tough choice— what's more important to her, cosplay or being "normal"?

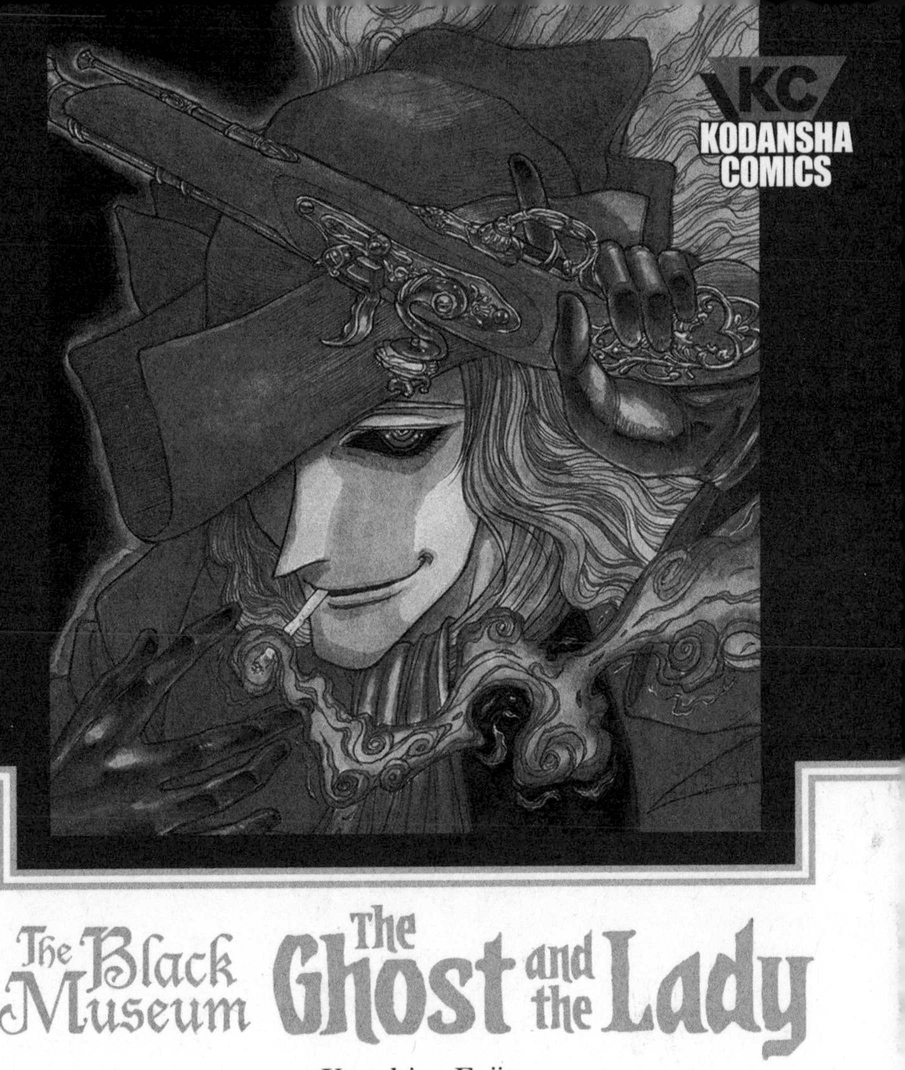
KC
KODANSHA COMICS

# The Black Museum: The Ghost and the Lady

By Kazuhiro Fujita

Deep in Scotland Yard in London sits an evidence room dedicated to the greatest mysteries of British history. In this "Black Museum" sits a misshapen hunk of lead—two bullets fused together—the key to a wartime encounter between Florence Nightingale, the mother of modern nursing, and a supernatural Man in Grey. This story is unknown to most scholars of history, but a special guest of the museum will tell the tale of The Ghost and the Lady...

**Praise for Kazuhiro Fujita's *Ushio and Tora***

"A charming revival that combines a classic look with modern depth and pacing... **Essential viewing both for curmudgeons and new fans alike.**" — Anime News Network

"**GREAT!** The first episode of Ushio and Tora captures the essence of '90s anime." — IGN

*Again!!* volume 5 is a work of fiction. Names, characters, places, and incidents are the products of the author's imagination or are used fictitiously. Any resemblance to actual events, locales, or persons, living or dead, is entirely coincidental.

A Kodansha Comics Trade Paperback Original.

*Again!!* volume 5 copyright © 2012 Mitsurou Kubo
English translation copyright © 2018 Mitsurou Kubo

Published in the United States by Kodansha Comics, an imprint of Kodansha USA Publishing, LLC, New York.

Publication rights for this English edition arranged through Kodansha Ltd., Tokyo.

First published in Japan in 2012 by Kodansha Ltd., Tokyo, as *Agein!!* volume 5.

ISBN 978-1-63236-649-8

Printed in the United States of America.

www.kodanshacomics.com

9 8 7 6 5 4 3 2 1

Translator: Rose Padgett
Lettering: E. K. Weaver
Editing: Paul Starr
Editorial Assistance: Tiff Ferentini
Kodansha Comics edition cover design by Phil Balsman